Argentina

Argentina

Stories for a Nation

Amy K. Kaminsky

University of Minnesota Press
Minneapolis
London

Published by the University of Minnesota Press
111 Third Avenue South, Suite 290
Minneapolis, MN 55401-2520
http://www.upress.umn.edu

Library of Congress Cataloging-in-Publication Data

Kaminsky, Amy K.
   Argentina : stories for a nation / Amy K. Kaminsky.
      p.   cm.
   Includes bibliographical references and index.
   ISBN 978-0-8166-4948-8 (hc : alk. paper) — ISBN 978-0-8166-4949-5 (pb : alk. paper)
      1. Argentina—In literature.   2. Argentina—In motion pictures.
   3. Argentina—Foreign public opinion.   I. Title.
   PN56.3.A74K36   2008
   809'.9335882—dc22   2008011877

Printed in the United States of America on acid-free paper

The University of Minnesota is an equal-opportunity educator and employer.

15 14 13 12 11 10 09 08   10 9 8 7 6 5 4 3 2 1

For Kenny

Contents

Acknowledgments

I am indebted to the American Council of Learned Societies for a research grant that enabled me to write this book. By the same token, the volume would not have been written had it not been for the generous support of the University of Minnesota, which not only granted me the gift of unfettered time in the form of research leaves but also gave me financial support through the McKnight Foundation and its own grant-in-aid funds. Some of that money paid for the invaluable research assistance of Danielle Bouchard, Papori Bora, Elakshi Kumar, and Patricia McGurk.

Many friends and colleagues saw me through the research and writing of *Argentina: Stories for a Nation.* Martha Peach opened her library to me and fed me, body and soul, in the beauty of the Gredos Mountains. Martha and other members of the Gredos Book Club (Nadette De Groot, Martha Handyside, Teresa Dorn, Isabel Cortés, Maria Stella Ceplecha, Lynn Bergunde, and Melinda Jackson) patiently listened as I tried out my ideas, and they gave me encouragement and support from the time I began this project in their company. Pilar Crespo generously provided me with an apartment in Madrid, where I wrote the first half of the manuscript.

The Centro de Arte Moderno in Madrid and Washington University in St. Louis were kind enough to invite me to present my work in progress. Their smart, incisive audiences posed questions and offered comments that helped widen the scope of the book. The anonymous manuscript reviewers for the University of Minnesota Press did the same, and to the extent that I followed their suggestions the manuscript was greatly improved. Richard Morrison, humanities editor at the Press, was unfailingly encouraging and patient.

I am grateful for the generosity of colleagues who were willing to share their research with a stranger. Nico Lorenzutti made me the gift of his knowledge with information on Salgari, and Seth Meisel graciously shared his research in progress on Afro-Argentine soldiers. Adriana Muñoz sent me the book she coedited on paradigm-shattering archeological findings in Argentina. Friends did no less: David Marcowitz teased out faint traces of Hebrew letters; Shaul Bassi and Russell Valentino fed me information on the elusive Carlo Michelstaedter; and Noni Benegas, with all the trust and generosity in the world, plied me with rare books and ephemera from her own precious and lovingly amassed collection. Conversations with her opened up parts of Argentine cultural history that had been closed to me before.

My dear friends and colleagues Naomi Scheman, Elaine Dorough Johnson, and Román Soto gave of their precious time to read and talk to me about drafts of chapters, earning their way into that part of heaven set aside for the wise and open-hearted. As always, Ken Kaminsky was at my side throughout. This book is for him.

Preface

Not long after Virginia Woolf asked her for tales of wild cattle and azure butterflies in the pampas of her native Argentina, Victoria Ocampo sent the British writer a set of mounted and framed blue butterflies. Ocampo's gift and the fanciful Argentina it represented were offered in return for entrée into the world of European modernism. In this interchange, emblematic of the longing of Argentina's social and political elite to be recognized by Europe, and of Europe's pursuit of the exotic but reassuringly familiar other, Woolf and Ocampo were both curiously satisfied. The refined game that the Englishwoman and the Argentinean played suggests that the relationship between periphery and center is not sufficiently explained by accounts of suffocating Eurocentrism or analyses of defiant colonial resistance. At the very least, they fail to capture the complexity of Argentina's relationship to Europe. Instead, as in the exchange between Woolf and Ocampo, Argentina both feeds and feeds off Europe's view of it, and Europe produces and consumes an Argentina that acts as a pivot between the exotic and the familiar.

Argentina's place in the imagination of the Western world has its roots deep in the nineteenth century, when Englishmen, North Americans, and Germans were recruited to build a railroad, an educational system, and a whiter nation for the newly formed republic. It flourished as Baron Maurice de Hirsch imagined a Jewish homeland in the pampas, Angelo de Gubernatis saw Argentina as a solution to overpopulation in rural Italy, and European society was introduced to the children of the Argentine oligarchy, who spent long periods and much money in Europe. By the end of the twentieth century, Argentina's tango and its excellent beef, Eva Perón and the Mothers of the Plaza de Mayo, the Falklands War and the Dirty War, Jorge Luis Borges and Diego Maradona, and economic chaos and a memory of vast Argentine wealth were entrenched in the consciousness of the Western world.

Argentina: Stories for a Nation suggests a theory of national identity via an examination of the place Argentina holds in the European and U.S. imagination. The industrialized North has a stake in this game of national representations, constituting itself in some measure by partaking of Argentina and its myths. The persistence of those myths makes Argentina a kind of Borgesian zahir—something that sticks in the mind, refusing to be shaken. By insisting that it be seen, Argentina allows itself to be a screen onto which others project their anxieties and desires and a mirror in which other nations might see themselves reflected. Literary texts from the United States, Poland, England, France, Germany, Italy, Spain, and Argentina itself, as well as internationally produced feature films, advertisements, jokes, and newspaper features, all recirculate ideas about Argentina and work to create the country's meaning. "Argentina" crystallizes in the representations made of it, representations it invites but that are not always to its liking.

I began doing research for *Argentina: Stories for a Nation* simply because I was intrigued by the fascination that Argentina holds for people who have never stepped foot there, but I have since come to believe that my examination of this phenomenon can help us get beyond the current impasse in thinking about colonialism and representation. I am proposing that what we call national identity is a production of both internal and external readings of the nation and of the relationship between them, and that, like Borges's zahir, it is both very serious and vaguely absurd. The formulations currently in circulation that describe once-colonized nations as either trapped in the web of exoticizing dominant representations or heroically claiming their own identity seem oversimplified to me. Even theories that make room for meaning established through the relationship between the colonizer and the formerly colonized tend to cast the latter in a perpetually subaltern position. Yet historically, the Argentine cultural elite actively invited the gaze of its others. Moreover, a nation's identity, like a person's, is neither totally fixed nor hopelessly scattered but is, rather, produced, reproduced, and contested in an ongoing, interactive process.

Because I am shaped by my training in the humanities, I resist reducing a living entity, Argentina, to a marker for "nation" in general. Yet insofar as "Argentina" consists of multiple meanings across borders, it may provide a way to think about globalization in relation to nation. These days, scholars and businesspeople alike pronounce that the future is in the global as it interacts with the local. Nevertheless, it is worthwhile to pay attention to the tenacious claims of nation. Not only does the nation-state endeavor to continue inserting itself between the global and the local, it acts as a refracting lens between the global and the local that allows us to see the complex relations among all three.

This book explores what makes Argentina, at the bottom of the world from the point of view of European cartographers, such a fertile and appealing place. Its genesis was my startled reaction to Judith Katz's second novel, *The Escape Artist*. Katz's previous novel had been a semi-autobiographical fantastic narrative whose rebellious lesbian protagonist is firmly rooted in the familiar landscape of the late twentieth-century United States and the impossible desire of some of its dissident daughters for a utopian lesbian feminist culture. *Running Fiercely toward a High Thin Sound* is also a deeply Jewish-American novel, part of a literary tradition also solidly embedded in the United States. I knew this second novel was coming, that Katz was thinking about turn-of-the-century Argentina, about the international traffic in women, about Jewish gangsters in Buenos Aires. I even knew she was planning a trip to Argentina, to see the streets she would write about and to do research in the archives of the Asociación Mutual Israelita Argentina that would, less than two years later, be blown to bits by a bomb that was set to kill hundreds of Jews and managed to kill dozens. Still, when I read the novel, I was taken aback. How was it that Argentina had made its way into the imagination of Judith Katz? What was it about Argentina that drew her? Certainly that an important piece of Jewish history was to be found there, and that this history was deeply tied to women's sexuality. But Argentina was cropping up all over. Eva Perón was resurrected in London and on Broadway; the tango was enjoying an international resurgence of popularity; the Mothers of the Plaza de Mayo had created a new kind of political practice, stimulating other mothers' movements not only in other Latin American countries but all over the world. The Dirty War and the Malvinas/Falklands fiasco had grabbed the attention of writers and filmmakers.

This was not the first time Argentina had seized hold of the imagination of other parts of the world. Moreover, Argentina takes on different meanings in different historical periods. At the beginning of the twentieth century Argentina was a land of opportunity, luring European immigrants with promises of work and social advancement. In the last quarter of that century it became notorious for its state violence, political repression, and the permutation of the word "disappear," making it a transitive verb.

My own trajectory as a scholar has put me in the way of Argentina, beginning with my choice of a dissertation director. Martin Stabb is a specialist in the Argentinean essay, and I was perfectly happy to benefit from his expertise by setting my work in the country he knew best, especially since he seemed willing to entertain my doing a feminist analysis at a time when few established scholars in the field would countenance such an idea. (It is not incidental that Stabb's major work on the subject of the Latin American essay is entitled *In Quest of Identity*.) Thus did Argentina begin to wear its way deeper into my consciousness than the other Latin American countries whose recent literature also so entranced me. As I read Argentine political history to contextualize the novels and short stories I was reading, the news from Argentina in the papers drew me as reporting from other parts of the world did not. Little by little the place grew real to me. My writing on Argentine literature introduced me to a number of Argentinean scholars working on similar subjects in the United States, and Argentina became more real to me still. My own firsthand knowledge of the place is minimal—two months, one separated from the other by twenty-five years and the violence of a brutal dictatorship, enough to see a place, see the changes made there, be an outsider looking in, looking at, looking through my own eyes, very like many of the writers I discuss here. It is thus that I stand in a relationship to Argentina remarkably similar to that of the non-Argentine writers and filmmakers I look at in this book, though I am probably more familiar with the Argentine literary canon than most of them. I, like them, approach Argentina from the outside, faced with a set of prefabricated ideas assumed to inhere in or cohere around this place called Argentina.

Even so, I have been less than faithful to Argentina than might have been expected of me. Literary studies have historically been parsed by nation and period, but my work as a feminist literary critic in an interdisciplinary department, with colleagues who did not know that I was breaking a cardinal rule of my discipline of origin, gave me leave to make my primary category of analysis gender, not nation or time period or literary movement. I wandered across Latin America, even spent time in pre-twentieth-century Spain, before I came back to the Southern Cone of Latin America, to Chile and Uruguay as well as to Argentina, only to write about those places in terms of the exiles they generated as part of a system of state violence in the 1970s and 1980s. The Argentina I looked at in *After Exile* was one version of that nation seen from a distance. *Argentina: Stories for a Nation* engages quite another.

This book, which looks at how Argentina is perceived by and represented in other parts of the world, is necessarily also a contemplation of what perceptions of nation and citizenship mean for Argentina. This is not merely a study of the image of Argentina in fiction and film from abroad, but an exploration of why someone from one place would want to write, or make a movie, about another place. It examines what a nation might offer as shorthand for an idea, how a nationality can become a metaphor, and the effects of that condensation and simplification of meaning.

In the chapters that follow, I rely heavily on literary texts written in the United States, England, Spain, and France, and to a lesser extent on internationally produced feature films, as my primary way of understanding the presence and meaning of Argentina in the global imaginary.[1] Although literature and film might seem to be just another occasion of cultural discourse, the place of these narrative art forms within culture remains central. In the early days of independence, making national art in Latin America was a means of staking claim on national identity because literature's universal aesthetic merit was understood to confer value and to give the nation standing with other nations. By the end of the twentieth century, art, representation, and literature have been unmasked as self-interested, not universal, and attached to the values of the global market. Néstor García Canclini, considering the place of literary studies in the project of cultural studies, notes that the historical shift that included the transfer of power from Europe to the United States coincides with a rethinking of the value of art:

> One of the changes that occurred in the shift from European to American predominance in culture was that we began this century testing, with the avant garde, how to link art with life, and we end it asking ourselves how to differentiate it from the market. (2000, 34)

This new awareness of the base underpinnings of artistic creation resonates with José Enrique Rodó's complaint about the shift from culture to commerce as a measure of value. In 1922 Rodó posited a Latin American Ariel, the spirit of creativity and art, caught in a losing battle against the United States' Caliban, dedicated to amassing wealth.[2] U.S. dominance is, in this theory, nothing but material and commercial. It should not surprise us that art should have lost its spiritual valence during the current historical moment, dominated as it is by the antispiritual, when all value is economic value. Yet we persist in returning to the naive pleasures of the text.

Argentina: Stories for a Nation follows both a loose chronology and a thematic order. Chapters 1 through 3 examine the transnationality of Argentina, a product of European colonialism that nevertheless troubles the postcolonial paradigm and is an object of fascination for Europe. Chapters 4 through 8 explore these themes with reference to the otherness of sex, race, and ethnicity. Chapters 9 and 10 focus on the international literary and film response to the period of dictatorship, the so-called "Process of National Reorganization" and what became known as the Dirty War, and, like chapter 7, suggest the importance of a counterhegemonic discourse in a time of repression, whether it comes from within the nation, from the nation in exile, or from foreigners. Chapter 11 returns to the persistence of formulaic constructs in foreign representations of Argentina, years after they cease to correspond to reality.

In looking at the way Europeans and North Americans have imagined and represented Argentina I make a distinction between artists, filmmakers, creative writers, and casual observers on the one hand and contemporary scholars on the other. I do this in part out of a recognition that I need a location from which to speak, and that such a location is not an uninhabited island. I rely on the work of other scholars of Argentina in particular and of Latin America in general. I do not propose to deconstruct the work of my colleagues, to find the places where we are all part of the cultures that produce us and complicit with the objectives of the societies in which we live. We all know by now that the field of Latin American studies (like other area studies) was heavily financed by the United States as part of a program to create (or as we said then, gather) knowledge for use during the cold war. When I was an undergraduate, the U.S. government lent me five hundred dollars under the noneuphemistically named National Defense Education Act to go to Spain to learn

enough Spanish to teach it. After Sputnik, education in "foreign" languages was part of the nation's defense plan. Nevertheless, the generation
of scholars who grew up in that era, which after all was the sixties, includes a large cadre of politically engaged researchers and teachers whose
work is characterized by a critical consciousness of their own position
and project. These are people who looked the government's gift horse
straight in the mouth, and I am happy to situate myself in their scholarly conversation.

This is not to say that my work and that of others is free of preexisting
assumptions, traces of unexamined Eurocentrism, and even the arrogance of the specialist. But there is no spot outside the system of representation from which to observe it, no box seat where we can munch on
our hot dogs and sip our Cokes while we watch the players on the field.
We are all implicated in this game; and I believe that we must play it,
because to abandon it to those who pretend disinterestedness is to give
up hope of creating change.

My position is, in the end, hopeful. I believe that the "other" can never
be totally different, otherwise representation would be impossible; and
I also write out of the conviction that neither alienation nor subalternity
is ever so extreme as to preclude self-representation. Perhaps I remain
optimistic about the possibilities of representation and communication
because the anomie produced by the belief that whatever is outside
oneself is forever foreign and unknowable, available only in a relation of
domination and subordination, is too bleak for me to imagine.

CHAPTER ONE

Bartered Butterflies

Let us begin with the story of two women. Victoria Ocampo, the Argentine creator of *Sur*, one of her country's longest-lived literary and cultural journals, recalls in a memoir how Virginia Woolf asked her to describe the blue butterflies of the pampas, butterflies that Ocampo had never seen and that probably had never lighted on any pampas flowers. To please Woolf, whom she idolized, Ocampo made the British writer a gift of a set of mounted and framed butterflies, feeding the fantasy that would give her entry into Woolf's company. She would trade butterflies and the fanciful Argentina they represented for access to the Europe of her own desires:

> I had the luck to have Aldous Huxley introduce me to Virginia Woolf at
> an exhibit of Man Ray photos. What was even luckier, she saw something
> "exotic" in me that awoke her curiosity. Although I felt like an imposter
> exploiting that first impression, since I did not believe I deserved it, I
> took advantage of it and went to talk with Virginia Woolf a number
> of times. It was 1934. She was not an easy person to get access to. My
> coming from a foreign country abundant with butterflies (that is how
> she saw Argentina, a detail I suspect she found in a travel book by
> Darwin) turned out to be very useful to me. I reinforced her curiosity
> by sending a collection of butterflies in a glass case to her house in
> Tavistock Square. The majority were Brazilian and I did not deceive her
> about their origin. But South America is a solid block for Europeans,
> even for people from the British Isles. . . . And like someone standing in
> front of a child whose eyes are fixed on a rattle or a spinning top, to
> keep her interest I waved before her a world of insects, pumas, parrots,

enormous flowers, "señoritas" (my great-grandmothers) wrapped in mantillas of the finest lace (as Darwin saw them), swift ostriches, Indians chewing coca leaves, gauchos drinking maté, all resplendent in local color; all in all, I surrounded her with the human, animal, and vegetal whirlwind of Latin America. That is how I paid for the filet of sole I ate with the Woolfs and entered their intimate circle, crowned with the flora and fauna of an entire continent. (Ocampo 1975b, 212–14)[1]

Victoria Ocampo, dressed by Chanel, well-traveled, fluent in three languages, friend (as she is not loathe to remind her readers) of writers and artists, does not conceal her calculating manipulation of Woolf's naively colonialist view of Latin America. Hardly a rustic denizen of the Argentine plains, she encourages Woolf to enjoy imagining her in that way. When she recalls Woolf's version of the gift of the butterflies, Ocampo delights in pointing out just how much of a fantasy the Englishwoman's notion of Argentina is:

> The people sent to bring the large package to Tavistock Square were a cousin of mine and an English governess. Neither one looks mysterious or strange. But with Virginia it was hard to foresee what kind of person she would invest with a mystery that flowed from her, or what her antennae captured.
>
> On this occasion she writes to me: "*Two veiled ladies* (I underline because I have never seen my cousin or Miss May wearing veils), two mysterious women arrived in the hall of my house . . . these ladies handed me a large package and after murmuring some unintelligible musical words they disappeared." (Here I will make a note. My cousin speaks English. Miss May was as English as Virginia. Unintelligible? Let us follow, after this parenthesis, the author of *Orlando;* her imagination is more seductive than our overly matter-of-fact vision.) It took me— she continues—ten minutes to realize that it was a gift, and that this gift was a box filled with butterflies under glass. Nothing could have been more fantastically unreal. (Nothing but you yourself, Virginia, I thought.) (1975a, 43–44)[2]

Surely the kind of othering and self-exoticizing that occurs between Virginia Woolf and Victoria Ocampo is less toxic than the stentorian, self-congratulatory writing on the part of European writers and their Argentine followers, whose public disdain for Argentina in particular, and Latin America in general, has been so damaging to Argentina's self-image and to its place in the European political imaginary. The gift of the butterflies, which is a gift of Woolf's own imagination made concrete, becomes a trope that unifies the correspondence of these two culturally influential women. In her letters to Ocampo, Woolf more than once speaks of the butterflies of South America, refers to orchids that Ocampo sent her as "butterflies," and reminds Ocampo of the mysterious ladies who brought her the gift of mounted butterflies. Nevertheless, a textual disconnect gainsays a perfect correspondence between the two. Woolf looks at the butterflies hanging over her doorway and sees them as a purple disruptive enough to inspire the disapproval of the puritan ancestor whose portrait hangs alongside them. Ocampo remembers them as a more prosaic blue.

By delivering to Woolf the Englishwoman's fantasy of Argentina, Ocampo deliberately disrupts the fantasy that Argentina's intellectual elite so carefully crafted of and for itself.[3] That fantasy, in contrast to Woolf's, is not of a savage land rife with multicolored butterflies and wild cattle (another of Woolf's notions) but, on the contrary, of a country of European sensibility, white and civilized.[4] In a 1977 speech that she made on the occasion of her inauguration into the Argentine Academy of Letters, Ocampo—often disdained by her countrymen for her attachment to and promotion of European literature, music, art, and thought—deliberately provoked the Argentine academy by evoking her own indigenous past. Furthermore, she proclaimed that it was being descended from Agueda, her indigenous great grandmother, that made her, as an Argentinean, as truly American as anyone on the continent. Far from claiming that Agueda was an Indian princess who could inject a dose of exotic royalty into her European family, Ocampo depicted her as the hidden ancestor exploited by the patriarchal conqueror. In writing and speaking of Agueda, Ocampo reveals the shameful secret of an oligarchic family: that their putatively heroic ancestor, the soldier of conquest whom the family had always so proudly vaunted, had maintained a sexual liaison with a young indigenous woman. Ocampo was hardly a revolutionary, but she insisted on attending to the hidden side of culture, to the wives and servants who enabled the heroes to win Argentina's independence, and in this case to the victims of that struggle.[5] Ocampo was fully aware of the explosive potential of invoking an Indian woman in the Argentine Literary Academy, an institution carefully protective of its civilized nature and civilizing program. As the first woman named to the Academy, Ocampo opened the door not only to gender disruption, but to racial disorder as well.

Ocampo's gesture of bringing Agueda into the sightlines of the Argentine academicians responds, in an oblique way, to the designers of the Argentine pavilion at the 1889 Paris Exhibition, who were determined to hide whatever was indigenous about their nation. The concerted effort on the part of the nineteenth-century Argentine elite, bent on claiming a place in the modern world and setting the tone for a resolutely European Argentina, still holds sway. The Paris exposition allowed the Argentine planners to create a particular Argentina in the European imaginary, and in large part it succeeded. It conveyed an image of wealth and innocence, of a new country unsure of what to do with its riches other than to flaunt them. Argentina wanted to be seen as modern and sophisticated; succeeding partially, it portended the future, like a gawky but promising adolescent.

The Argentine pavilion, designed by French architects and decorated by French artists and artisans, erased as well as it could any traces of the indigenous presence in Argentina.[6] The exposition planners had politely refused regional offers of Indian crafts and "curiosities" as exemplars of Argentine culture. The cities were presented as alive with commerce; the country's interior, implied the pavilion's designers, was empty of people but rich with natural resources, ready for development with the help of European capital. One Frenchwoman who asked about the savages was told that there were none—they had all gone to the city and been educated (Fey 2000, 76–77). But the ceremonial guards who had been imported to flank the exhibition's doors offset the desired effect. The pavilion, carefully policed by its designers to exclude signs of "savagery," was literally policed by mixed-race soldiers from the interior. The uniforms, bearing, and other accoutrements of soldiery may have been proof that savagery had been restrained—and retrained—to serve the European elite, but the physical presence of the guards undermined the pavilion's designers' desire to erase all reminders that there ever had been an indigenous presence in Argentina.

The government of Argentina dressed its soldiers in uniforms copied from the French and sent them to France to guard its pavilion as part of its attempt to sell Argentina to France. However, the Argentine desire to cover over the indigenous or mixed-race body meant a refusal to show Europe what that continent most desired: an other against which to measure itself. Nevertheless, this repression is barely restrained, as suggested by the anecdote of the disappointed Frenchwoman. The frisson she hoped to experience of uncivilized America, safely contained in the architecture of modern Europe, was readily available to the European imagination. The Argentinean elite would have much preferred that the world it was trying to woo and endeavored so to emulate had ignored Argentine signs of savagery, as you might ignore rude sounds or gestures, unbecoming bodily effects, in polite company.

Both the pavilion in 1889 and the Academy in 1977 publicly represent Argentina's sense of its cultural worth. Whether or not an indigenous woman will be visible in that culture is the question Ocampo answers differently from the pavilion's makers. I am deeply aware that the Argentina I am looking at is the product of an elite project. So successful has the metropolitan white elite's hold on literary culture been that there is virtually no internationally visible representation of Argentina as a national culture produced from, or even that much takes into account, the considerable indigenous presence in the country, or the history of Afro-Argentineans. These histories are beginning to emerge thanks to anthropological and historical studies, but even a recent book on literary blackness in Argentina focuses almost entirely on representations of Afro-Argentines by white writers.[7] Internal differences in the country are typically drawn along class lines, although lately gender has come to be seen as another important internal divide thanks largely to the recent emergence of gender studies programs at Argentine universities, as well as the work of feminist scholars outside Argentina.[8]

The liberal Argentine elite of the nineteenth century exerted a mighty effort to manufacture a national self that would extinguish the barbarism it found so distressing. *Barbarie,* perhaps better translated as savagery than as its cognate, barbarism, is at the heart of liberal Argentina's notion of itself, the repressed that insists on returning. For Europe, the wilds of Patagonia, the Indians of Tierra del Fuego, and the vast pampas, that is to say Argentina in its "wild" and "natural" state, all suggest a fearsome and rather seductive savagery. But the *barbarie* that Argentinean liberals opposed, that is, the *barbarie* named by Domingo Faustino Sarmiento in his germinal text, *Facundo,* had, on the surface, little to do with Argentina in a state of nature. It was, rather, the state of illegitimacy and political immaturity they associated with the rough-and-ready rural social and political economy that distressed the liberal proponents of a strong central government based in Buenos Aires. The locally based regional leaders, the *caudillos* who challenged the political hegemony of a Europeanized capital, and the gaucho, symbol of miscegenation (metaphorically, at least, the son of an Indian mother and Spanish father), represented a symbolic danger of their own vulnerability to the partially conquered frontier in a way that pure nature, utterly "other," did not.[9] The *barbarie* that was Sarmiento's despair, and the even deeper savagery of the Argentine wilderness that underlies it, is, ironically but not surprisingly, part of what attracts Europe to Argentina.

For much of the world, and certainly for Europe and the United States, Argentina is made up of a lively interplay of representations. Such representations can be dangerous, even crippling, as Edward Said has been perhaps the most eloquent of many to argue. Diana Taylor puts her finger on exactly this kind of noxious representation, in which Argentina is the "other" of the United States and Europe:

> The "othering" mechanism situates Argentina as the transgression
> and the "body" of deviance. It serves as a cautionary message: that
> way disorder, dissolution, and danger lie. Moreover, it invisibly posits
> the watching "us" at the stable center. This unreciprocal seeing is
> part of the colonialist and militarist gesture of appropriation and
> internalization of the other to reinforce the defining self. (1997,
> 260–61)

Yet national imaginaries are produced from within nations as well, and that production can be for good or ill. Benedict Anderson (1983) theorizes the nation as a community imagined by those within its geographic boundaries, and Yossi Shain (1989) discusses how national subjects located outside the nation's boundaries also construct the nation. Rey Chow (1993), Winifred Woodhull (1993), Mary Louise Pratt (1992), and Uma Narayan (1997), among others, have studied the relation between gender and nation as ideological constructs. Within the context of writing on Argentina specifically, Nicolas Shumway demonstrates amply how that nation's own guiding fictions of national illness and "endemic incurability" (1991, 166) have functioned to disable the nation; and Graciela Scheines argues that Argentinean intellectuals' embrace of Europe's debilitating interpretation of their nation has done terrible damage to the country. The editors of a recent collection of essays on Argentine myths, memory, identity, and culture have their tongue only partly in their cheek when they call their book "Delusions of Grandeur" (Pons and Soria

2005). For their part, Francine Masiello (1992) and Donna Guy (1992) have produced major studies relating to sex and gender in Argentina in the early twentieth century that go far to illuminate the nation's self-concept. Thus, although this book owes an enormous debt to the critiques of colonialist discourse of Said, Rabasa, Bhabha, Spivak, and others, I am also interested in how the interaction between internally and externally generated fictions of the nation enable each other. Argentina is a relatively young country, in which it is possible to witness the emergence of a discourse of nation that depends on colonial and, more importantly, neocolonial verification of its existence as a separate entity. As such it is distinguishable from other countries and possessed of a character that adheres to the idea of Argentina, not only differentiating it from other places but establishing it on its own.

Argentina has created a small national industry dedicated to its own identity. Much outstanding scholarship has been dedicated both to perpetuating this practice and to coming to an understanding of it, and I will not try to improve upon that scholarship here. One of the salient elements of Argentine national identity is its tortured relationship with Europe: how it incorporates and disseminates European ideas, how it understands itself in terms of European political philosophy, to what extent it desires to create itself on the basis of European immigration. Argentina—and here I refer to the intellectual, political, and economic elite—has struggled to see itself through European eyes, to measure itself by European notions of progress. This has meant material interchange between Argentina and Europe in the form of trade relations, armed conflict (most recently the war with Britain over the Islas Malvinas/Falkland Islands), immigration, the importing of books, and the travel of artists, writers, and politicians. It is inevitable, then, that Argentina has left its own impression on Europe and the United States, as well as on the rest of Latin America and, more recently, in a time of increasing globalization, on Asia as well. The points from which Argentina is perceived, from inside and from without, do not merely rest inertly side by side, but rather interact with each other in the creation of the multiple, conflicting, interdependent yet mutually destabilizing notions of Argentina as a place and a culture.

When Victoria Ocampo writes of her first meeting with Virginia Woolf she narrates the uneven, but still mutual, relations of representation between Argentina and England that the two women exemplify:

In the light and warmth of a living room, with panels painted by a woman, another two women talk about women. They examine each other, they ask each other questions. One, curious; the other, delighted. . . . These two women look at each other. Their gazes are different. The first seems to say, "Here I have a book of exotic pictures to thumb through." The other, "On what page of this magical story will I find the description of the place where the key to the treasure is hidden?" But of these two women, born in different realms and climes, one Anglo-Saxon, the other Latin and from America, one attached to a formidable tradition, the other attached to the void . . . it is the richer woman who will leave enriched by the encounter. The richer one will have immediately gathered her harvest of images. The poorer woman will not have found the key to the treasure. (1935, 6)[10]

Ocampo is not abject before Woolf; on one level she recognizes that Woolf's quick bounty of exotic images is superficial. Despite not finding the key to the treasure that is Woolf's mind, she gains more from their meeting than does the British writer. She recognizes Woolf's own role in creating a narrative of their encounter; but for all her talk of poverty, she recognizes that she is in a better position to understand what is not available to her than is Woolf. Ocampo's use of the trope of poverty is a grand gesture: she was a very wealthy woman, a woman who could afford to travel regularly between continents, bearing exotic gifts to writers who needed to support themselves though commercial ventures. (Unlike Editorial Sur, the publishing company she established to foster intellectual and artistic exchange between Europe and Argentina, which lost money for Ocampo, Hogarth Press was an important source of income for Leonard and Virginia Woolf.) Ocampo greatly admired Woolf, but she hardly came to her in deferent supplication. Each of them found in the other a story she wanted to tell. Moreover, Ocampo had a stake in being recognized by Woolf as an equal, a woman with whom she could speak of other women and who could authorize her as a writer.

Their encounter, as Ocampo tells it, begins with the equilibrium of the two women looking at each other. That balance is soon disturbed by the difference in their gazes and the distinctions of poverty and wealth between them. Yet these distinctions are, in the end, deceptive. Woolf's rich tradition and her harvest of exotic pictures are oddly trumped by Ocampo's overstated lack of tradition and her deeper, needier questions (to which she gets no answer). Woolf comes away with a book of exotic pictures, but Ocampo has come face to face with a mystery whose solution is nothing less than a treasure. The very speed with which Woolf reaps her quick harvest of images ultimately cheapens them. Ocampo knows that the images are ephemeral, even false.

Ocampo and Woolf's friendship was a relation of unequals. Woolf was intrigued, amused, bewildered, and sometimes angered by Ocampo, who in turn desired recognition but could also be demanding and imperious.[11] This complex, cross-cultural relationship was also marked by the fact that here were two remarkable women who could enjoy each other's company and each come away from their encounter somehow enriched. And although friendship is too strong a word to describe their interactions, acquaintanceship is too weak. Woolf and Ocampo were not intimate friends. Woolf wrote to her true intimates about the somewhat odd, even intrusive Ocampo, who remained a mystery to her. Ocampo wanted that intimacy, and what Woolf experienced as her somewhat brash manner was no doubt a result of the oligarchic sense of entitlement mixed with the insecurity born of being a woman in a male-dominated culture that marks Ocampo's life and work. The friendship between these two women is, I think, emblematic of the complex relationship between Argentina and the metropole. Both Woolf and Ocampo, loosely representative of Europe and Argentina, enter into a relationship as fully participating subjects, each desirous of the interchange, each for her own reason, each a bit disdainful of the other.

Seen in terms of the exchanges between Victoria Ocampo and Virginia Woolf, neither the smothering Eurocentrism that Rabasa identifies nor the dance of othering and resistance traced by Said captures the complexity of Argentina's relationship to Europe. Nor does Homi Bhabha's notion of mimicry, in which the colonial other is induced to perform a lesser version of the colonizing subject. Instead, as in the odd, and oddly satisfying, friendship between Woolf and Ocampo, Argentina consumes Europe's view of it, not only in a self-defeating desire to be seen by the metropole and to be its "other," but also to establish a visible, viable self in the world. In Argentina Eurocentrism is not separable from, because worse than, the purer identity of the colonized or the precolonial. Europe and the United States, the most significant others of Argentina, in turn constitute themselves in some measure by partaking of Argentina and its myths in a reciprocal gesture. Other countries also reflect Argentina back to itself as they identify in contrast or connection to it as a same-but-different Latin American nation.

My aim in this book is, primarily, to reflect upon Argentina in the international imaginary, without losing sight of Argentina's stake in its being present in the mind of the rest of the world. Argentina's desire to be represented, to be seen, brings with it the danger of its being seen other than it would wish, not in accordance with its own deliberate self-representation, but in ways that it cannot control and may not like at all. Offering itself up to the gaze of the more powerful other (in Argentina's case, first Europe and to a lesser extent the United States) means relinquishing control, trusting that the desired other will view it with charity and good will. Moreover, with the very gesture of asserting its place in Europe's field of vision, Argentina betrays its awareness of the inequality between itself and that continent, even though Argentina is hard-pressed to acknowledge that inequality.

Emblematic of this conundrum is the French reception of the Argentine nouveaux riches of the late nineteenth and early twentieth centuries. The French elite called these newly wealthy Argentineans *rastaquouères,* from the Spanish *rastacueros*—the menial Argentine laborers who cut the hides off cattle. The name, if nasty, was apt, since Europe's desire for leather was what made Argentina (and some few Argentines) rich; the European hunger for Argentine beef would come later.[12] The figure of the *rastaquouère* was a recognizable stereotype. Not only did this group of wealthy Argentines merit their own derogatory appellation, but they were represented in visual media, not least by a young Pablo Picasso. Picasso's sketch of a *rastaquouère* couple, just a bit too smartly dressed, the woman's hair just a touch too elaborately coifed, can still be seen in the Picasso Museum in Barcelona. Ridicule mixed with a touch of envy was the formula; thus did the French elite establish their superiority (or reveal their need to feel superior) to the fabulously wealthy Argentineans whose money was made off the skins of dead cows. The Argentine pavilion in the Paris Exhibition of 1900, overexpensive and overwrought, erected at the foot of the Eiffel Tower, in the shadow of French modernity, as Ingrid Fey points out, can be seen as the apt expression of the *rastaquouère* culture.[13]

The discourse around the *rastaquouères* provides a measure to gauge the divergence between elite Argentina's projected self-image (the ways it wants to be seen) and the ways it is perceived. This divergence constitutes a space of exchange in which the nation's identity can be produced. Any theory of national identity that attaches not to the individual but to the nation as a whole necessarily relies on both internal and external "readings" of the nation. I am inclined to believe that national identity, like individual identity, is neither totally fixed nor hopelessly scattered, but is, rather, produced, reproduced, and contested in a constant process that ends only when the subject dies—and perhaps not even then.[14] At the same time, it is crucial to resist the idea of the reducibility of a living entity (here, "Argentina") to a marker for "nation" in general. Argentina has its own specific history, and a major part of this project is to elucidate precisely what it is about Argentina that makes this particular site, at the bottom of the world from the point of view of European cartographers, such a fertile and appealing place.

I have written elsewhere that the quest to understand the meaning of national identity as it attaches to nation is a close to impossible task that involves chasing down the abstraction, "identity," of an abstraction, "nation."[15] Yet since nationalism and the claims of nation are so compelling as to refuse, tenaciously, to disappear even when scholars and businesspeople alike pronounce that the future is in the global as it interacts with the local, apparently bypassing the national, it seems to me that it is worthwhile to pay attention to the claims of nation and the identity of the nation. These exist as a refracting lens between the global and the local that allows us to see the complex relations among all three scales. Moreover, the nation is itself constructed and held in place by the global and local forces upon it. Nevertheless, any notion of identity suggests consciousness and agency, attributes of people and not the nations they comprise, burdening discussions of national identity with a confusing personification. Moreover, competing claims to national identity and the persistence of power that resides in some groups and not others trouble claims to a nation that speaks with a single voice, even if we understand that speech and voice to be figurative. When I personify Argentina in this study, either as subject or object, I mean for it to be shorthand for the political and intellectual elites who have had the platform to make their version of Argentina heard both nationally and internationally.

Because such an Argentina has emerged so visibly in the tension between the gesture toward Europe and the locally produced ideas of nation, I believe that it is a particularly apt object of study in a time when the global is ascendant. That the national vision itself has been divided historically, most notably between the liberal *Unitarios*' ironically provincial desire for a unified Argentina, in which all provinces are one and that one is Buenos Aires, and the Federalist dream of a nation made up of a loose confederation of provinces, each under strong local control, keeps us constantly aware of the complexity of the process of nation making. Moreover, the local conflict highlights the fact that this multifaceted process depends not only on abstract notions of identity, but, importantly, on contests over the form of the state and the struggle for political and economic power.

Globalization is not a neutral process; it does not begin from some point outside the world and spread evenly around and over all nations and all people, like warm honey poured from on high. On the contrary, globalization signifies the spread of cultural and economic norms that originate in the already powerful centers of Europe, Asia, and North America and reactions to those norms by differently situated groups and individuals in the receiving sectors, which in turn wash up on the shores of the originating nations. Because the already powerful centers are powerful in relation to other parts of the globe, those norms are already contaminated by the (formerly) colonized, the economically uncertain, the national other. It is a process in which all are implicated, but in which differently placed nations influence others and are in turn acted upon differentially.

Specifically, Argentina has meaning for the powerful centers of cultural production that help Argentina understand itself, that make the centers legible to themselves, and that are in conversation with Argentina's own considerable cultural production. Argentina is imagined elsewhere, and that imagining is consumed by Argentina, nourished by its own reprocessed images. But the center would not bother with this imagining if it stood to gain nothing by doing so. Argentina, then, is a screen on which Europe and the United States project what might seem to be an unusual form of otherness, an otherness that encompasses the same. The "other" is not simply the nonself, not only the projection of elsewhere, but a complex kit that includes the screen on which a version of the self can be played out and the projection machine itself.

One object of this study is to look at cultural otherness through the lens, and at the level, of nation, and more specifically as the idea of a particular nation crystallizes in the representations made of and around it. Representation takes various forms, and we will look at several of them, including film and advertising. The bulk of the discussion, however, will take up narrative fiction. I believe that the novel continues to be a rich vein to tap, since it is sustained and detailed and so unabashedly *about* representation. Moreover, novels (but also films) are meant to occupy the whole of our consciousness during the time we experience them. This distinguishes them from cultural forms like advertising, which interrupts our attention briefly but acutely, or television, which in its coolness is notoriously permeable.

Argentina in relation to its representations can function as a model of the way the idea of a nation can be conscripted to make meaning elsewhere. But it is critical to keep in mind that the constellation of meanings that Argentina holds is historically specific, unique to that place and its interactions with the rest of the world, and not generalizable. The fact, and the way, that Argentina makes meaning, or others make meaning of it, might serve more as a case study than as a model, to the extent that the content of that meaning is crucial to and constitutive of the form it takes and is not reproducible. Other Latin American nations, Mexico and Brazil most notably among them, have also caught the attention of outsiders, but in those cases the presumed exoticism of these places is less tempered, and less complicated, by the overt links to Europe sought by Argentina.

Each writer or filmmaker produces the Argentina that is most meaningful to him- or herself, but not all the foreign representations of Argentina make their way back there. Maria Luisa Magagnoli's *Un caffe molto dolce,* the story of the search for traces of an Italo-Argentine anarchist, was quickly translated into Spanish and published in Argentina; but Judith Katz's *The Escape Artist,* a novel about the Jewish underworld in Buenos Aires, has, at this writing, still not been translated. How, then, do I make the claim that this is about reciprocal identity construction? How is rhetorical or discursive power distributed here? This may be the crux of the matter. I do not wish to bespeak an abject Argentina; but in insisting that the country be seen, Argentina's intellectual, political, and cultural elite opens the nation to outside interpretation and allows it to be a screen onto which others project their concerns. On one level, Argentina's determination to take control of its self-presentation implies a claiming of power.[16] However, to be seen—as Argentina certainly is—to be naming its reliance on the way others see it is a sign of dependency. Argentina's determination to be known on its own terms, then, both guards against abjection and is a sign of abjection. Furthermore (from the point of view of Argentina's others) the fact that Argentina cannot ever fully control its representation is essential to its participating in a reciprocal relationship.

Insofar as writers, like the ones dealing with Jewish, British, or Italian themes, play out their own concerns on Argentine soil, there is a temptation to think that the Argentine setting is incidental. It is not, however, because Argentina's own history precipitates this interest and these representations, suggesting a complex web of colonial, postcolonial, neocolonial, and national representation woven by a range of stakeholders. All are deeply invested in these representations: Argentina needs the reflection back of its reality, and the outsiders need Argentina to name the self that is also other.[17] Underlying all of this study is the play between Argentinean desire to be known and outsiders' desire for a particular Argentina to know. But questions arise. Must things always go awry? Are these needs necessarily at odds with each other, or is there the possibility of some true reciprocity in this interaction?

In one chapter's title I have referred to Argentina as Europe's "uncanny other." The reference to Freud is fully intended. Because Argentina acts out processes of identity formation that are usually buried (either in the past or because it is unseemly to take notice of them in public), it is justifiable to look at Argentina using some of the insights of psychoanalysis. Using the tools of psychoanalysis it may be possible to think of Argentine identity not simply as a matter of that nation's either fitting hegemonic definitions or wholly other to the hegemonic, but concretely as the process itself, the explicit telling of a story that is usually buried. Certainly, there is a poetic sweetness to using the psychoanalytic mechanism of calling attention to the latent and making it manifest in the case of Argentina, since of all the nations in the world, Argentina is the one most captivated by psychoanalysis.[18] It is not by chance that Freud is a useful guide to understanding the relationship between Europe and Argentina, given that Argentina has one of the most relentlessly psychoanalyzed populations on earth.

Freud defines the uncanny as "the class of the frightening which leads back to what is known and familiar" (1919, 220).[19] For Freud the uncanny is predominantly concerned with the double: "The subject identifies himself with someone else, so that he is in doubt as to which his self is, or substitutes the extraneous self for his own" (234). In the case of Argentina and Europe, the identification with the double goes both ways.

Argentina quite consciously names Europe as its double, its model. It begins and ends with what is known, familiar, and desirable about Europe, short-circuiting any possibility of fearfulness. When Europe or the United States takes note of Argentina, however, the uncanny comes into play. People writing from these places project onto Argentina the savagery, the stagnation, and the penury that the West fears in and for itself, and that it worries may be insufficiently covered over or compensated by the civilization, the progress, and the promise of wealth that Argentina also represents. Argentina is both familiar and not familiar to the West; strangely familiar, or familiarly strange, it elicits a particular fascination in the global imaginary.

Writing about the relationships between Latin America, Europe, and the United States, Néstor García Canclini stresses the changes that have taken place in those relationships due, among other things, to the vastly increased ease of mobility of both people and production, and to the ease of transnational communication (2000, 34–35). He also warns against facile oversimplification, noting class differences among those who do and do not have easy access to transnational circuits and differences "between the generations for which Latin America was 'invented' by Europe, and the young people, or not-so-young people who find their horizon in the United States" (35).

García Canclini's syntax, the shift from the passive to the active voice within a single sentence, encodes the unstated assumptions that there is some connection, as well as a disconnect, between one generation's passive experience of being invented (by Europe) and a subsequent generation's active pursuit of a foreign model (in the United States). It is this interaction (Latin America participated in its own invention, and the foreign model continues to invent its Latin American other) that I am trying to make manifest here. The shift in focus from Europe to the United States from the point of view of Latin America was accompanied and likely encouraged by the United States' growing interest in Latin America during the twentieth century, although its primary focus was not on Argentina but rather on the much closer Spanish Caribbean and Mexico. (This lag was perhaps reciprocal, for although Sarmiento had brought U.S. teachers to Argentina to further his educational program, most cultural reflection on foreign teachers came from the upper classes, who still imported British and French governesses for children.) Politically, Latin America began to signify for the United States around the turn of the century, but Argentina was not much of a presence in the U.S. imagination, as opposed to Europe's, until after the Second World War.

The Europeanization of Argentina, and the resulting sense in Europe and North America that Argentina was like "us," made the repressive period of the 1970s and 1980s more vivid and more threatening personally to many Europeans and North Americans than brutally tyrannical governments in Asia and Africa, where a much more assiduously manufactured sense of distinction between "them" and "us" had been carefully maintained. Argentina is far away but close to home.

Argentina is even closer to home to the other nations of Latin America, where Argentina's pretensions to being a European nation elicit a very different response. Once, at a lecture-presentation of her work in Minneapolis, Minnesota, the Cuban-American performance artist Coco Fusco remarked that Cubans and Argentines were known to be the most arrogant of Latin Americans—and of the two, Argentines were worse. The comment drew knowing laughs, as it was intended to. The rivalry between unassuming Chile and self-important Argentina is a familiar trope in Latin American discourse and is the subject of numerous humorous anecdotes. Less funny was the resentment of Mexicans who, in the 1970s and 1980s, admitted numerous Argentinean political refugees into their country, only to be treated to what they experienced as Argentinean presumptions of superiority. The Argentinean's ironic stance, and its corollary, his untrustworthiness, is a familiar trope, and it finds its way into representations of Argentineans in the work of novelists from other parts of Latin America.

Although both Argentineans like Graciela Scheines and foreigners like Evert Taube conflate Argentina with the rest of Latin America, the rest of Latin America most often sets itself apart from Argentina. Argentina's distinctiveness is not unique to Latin America: within the continent each nation is recognized in its individuality. At the same time, the old Bolivarian notion of a single continent, of a region that has meaning as a single entity as well as a conglomerate of sometimes contentious states, makes its way into representations of Argentineity as well. In the early part of the twentieth century Argentineans and non-Argentineans alike dreamt of "Greater Argentina," which still includes the assumption of a certain Argentine superiority.[20]

The projection of itself as whiter, more educated, more sophisticated, and more cultured than other Latin American nations has made Argentina seem arrogant and self-important. This perception can be seen not only in literary texts, but also in off-hand comments and jokes, the vast majority of which center on the presumed arrogance and egotism of Argentineans:

- How does an Argentine commit suicide?
  He jumps off his ego, but he doesn't die from the fall. He dies of hunger on the way down.

- How do you make a lot of money quickly?
  You buy an Argentine for what he's worth, and you sell him for what he thinks he's worth.

Naturally, this arrogance makes Argentines seem insufferable; hence the following:

> God was busy creating the world and he realized that in one place he had put the best land, the most beautiful mountains, the loveliest and most abundant coastline, the most interesting islands, a great range of different climates, in sum, the best of the best. "But this is not fair," God said to himself. "Every other country has some defect; no place else has such an abundance of riches and beauty. I know—I'll put the Argentineans there."

In contrast to the Argentine characters who appear in European novels, who are characterized by their wealth or their desire for it, their arriviste tendencies, and their Latin American otherness, Argentine characters in novels from other parts of Latin America are often characterized by another sort of otherness: their pretensions to European culture and whiteness, their ironic view of life, and their overbearing personalities.[21] These characterizations intersect precisely at the place where Argentina meets both Europe and Latin America, however. The Argentine who would be as elite, rich, and cultured as his European counterpart is viewed as just as pretentious and untrustworthy on either side of the Atlantic. Neither accepts Argentina as fully European. Latin America sees it as arrogant and pompous in a way that Europe, with a right to its claims, does not; Europe sees Argentina as exotic and primitive, as well as familiarly European. Europe's Argentina, then, is not only a screen onto which it projects its desires and fears. It is also a mirror that, like the one Virginia Woolf describes in *A Room of One's Own*, reflects Europe back to itself at twice its size, and a zahir, a twenty-cent coin passed from hand to hand whose image, once seen, just won't go away.

CHAPTER TWO

Identity Narratives; or, It Takes Two to Tango

Imperialism, colonialism, Eurocentrism, and Orientalism are keywords in a discourse of resistance to practices of othering, exploitation, and incorporation. The imperial quest for power and the colonial exploitation of people and resources are historical facts rationalized and justified by the worldview of Orientalizers and Eurocentrists, and the negative charge of the words describing these exercises is unmistakable.[1] Globalization may be added to this list of keywords, with the caveat that it is not only descriptive of a process of distribution of power but also an interpretive stance about that process that makes it seem benign. The language of globalization, perhaps with the help of Foucauldian notions of the ubiquitousness of power and its odd democracy (i.e., everyone participates in the structures of power), barely conceals the reality of a global system in which we all partake of power differentially. Nevertheless, to suggest that there is a simple dichotomy in which the West, Europe, and the globalizers line up neatly against the East, what-is-not-European, and the globalized is far too facile. Its simplicity, moreover, is no guard against its conscription by those who would justify and prolong existing global power relations.

The simplicity of binary analysis has not fared well since structuralism was challenged; and, when we get down to individual cases, the reduction of the complexity of the world to a model that divides it neatly, if not evenly, in two seems simply bizarre. It is critical that we attend to the nuances of the processes of othering. Not to do so leaves us in the untenable situation of an othering process so complete that there can be no stirring or speech from the place of abjection, for even the slightest freedom of movement reconstitutes the other as subject.[2] But even on the level of the definition and sturdiness of its terms, the binary will not hold. Moreover, Empire has produced a litter of unexpected offspring. Recently, in a somehow nostalgic gesture that seems both inclusive and imperialistic, France, the nation of Rousseau, has offered French citizenship to those born in any of its former colonies, including, for example, Louisiana. A newly prosperous Spain is hotly debating the rights of immigration of people from its former colonies and beyond: South and Central Americans, Africans, Asians, and Eastern Europeans. In Great Britain, "We are here because you were there" is the defiant motto of South Asians and Caribbeans. The descendants of those born in former British colonies are demanding their rights in England proper. As any number of theorists of postcolonialism have noted, former colonies are a repressed that are ever returning.

Eurocentrism is the enactment of the power of Europe to define its implicitly inferior others.[3] In Argentina the force of Eurocentrism has been so compelling that, among the elites, it has long elicited a claim of European identity.[4] But Europe is not monolithic, and therefore itself manifests internally determined relations of power. Europe is, for one thing, a masculine construction. Its political, religious, and economic power structures have, historically, been in the hands of men. This commonplace, obvious-on-the-face-of-it observation is, for that reason, no less significant. The strong gender bias in favor of men is not only a condition that makes Europe different for men and women, but it frees femininity and all things associated with "woman" for use as a metaphor for further otherings. As feminist theorists as unlike each other as Mary Daly, Simone de Beauvoir, and Sherry Ortner have shown, "woman" is the other onto whom the masculine subject displaces the elements of his own being he wants to deny in himself, among them physicality, irrationality, and immanence.

Argentine historian Hugo Biagini notes that the stereotypical view held by Europe of America is gendered, with Latin America playing the feminine role to Europe's masculinity. Biagini, following a by now familiar feminist analysis, argues that the essentializing of Latin America that takes place by means of the gendering of Europe and Latin America makes it possible to ignore economic and sociopolitical factors in favor of notions of "blood, destiny, and land."[5] Yet feminist theory also pays heed to the problematic differentiation of characteristics along the axis of gender in order to account for the incomplete and contradictory othering that is encountered not only in the gender-inflected relationship between Argentina and the United States or Europe, but within Argentina itself.[6]

For the use of gender as a metaphor in differentiating between the subject and its other takes places within Argentina as well, of course. The undisputed masculinity of the Argentine gaucho, for instance—his rejection of enclosed spaces, his willingness to resort to violence, his masculine loyalty to both his "natural" superiors and to his friends, his preference for the company of other men—is set against the apparent contradiction of the displacement of the feminine onto both the elite city dwellers and the indigenous denizens of the wilderness. The gaucho is necessarily a masculine figure, not only because he is defined by his work at a time when the gendered division of labor is pronounced and unquestioned, but because he is enlisted for symbolic use, by some at least, as representative of the nation. His virility is called upon to illuminate both the effeminacy of the ineffectual Europeanized elite and the essential femininity of the Indians—close to nature, dangerously irrational, and in need of domination.

Feminist theorists like Marilyn Frye have shown how the idea of femininity as masculinity's "other" is ascribed to both these poles. Elite, urban society tamed into a kind of domesticity by an effete civilizing code, and the untamed, irrational Indian, close to and mysteriously knowledgeable of nature are both feminized extremes against which rational, purposeful, competent masculinity is measured.[7]

Not only gender, but class differences create distinctions in the way different Europeans, even from the same country, are perceived in the Europeanization of a place like Argentina. Europe's prima facie cultural superiority to America opened the doors of Argentina wide to poor as well as rich Europeans. The terms civilization and barbarism, the former denoting European liberalism and its influence, particularly in Buenos Aires, and the second originally referring to the conservative political culture of the interior, at first made all Europeans welcome. But the influx of impoverished immigrants, most from southern and eastern Europe, precipitated a reassignment of the terms "civilization" and "barbarism." The already Europeanized, cultured, industrializing Argentina was in a position to civilize the newly arrived Europeans.[8]

Moreover, this class difference went hand in hand with regional difference as Europe and its internal others were now contemplated by Argentina's self-defined European elite. The most desirable Europeans were northern and western, German and British. People from eastern and southern Europe were thought not to be quite as beneficial to the growing nation. It was only in the 1880s that Argentina extended its invitation to Europeans to include Jews, for example. Religious and ethnic difference collapsed into each other by a new system of categorization. So many Jews came to Argentina from Russia and eastern Europe that they were often simply known as *rusos* ("Russians"), and *ruso* came to mean "Jew."

Furthermore, Spain, as the former colonial power, held a different meaning for Argentina than did the rest of Europe. After achieving their independence from Spain, Argentineans looked at it as the antimodel whose example was to be avoided. France was culturally more alluring; and England, Spain's ancient enemy, was, in the nineteenth century, both a source of capital for developing industries and infrastructure and a cultural exemplar. Moreover, for France, Germany, and England, Spain was never quite European (Africa starts at the Pyrenees, they said, pointing both to geography and to the long sojourn of Jews and Muslims in Spain). Spain long struggled to be part of Christian Europe, first during the seven hundred years of what used to be called the Reconquest and more recently through Spain's enthusiastic membership in the European Union. The Reconquest, which began in 722 when the Christian warrior Pelayo won the battle of Covadonga and ended in 1492 with the defeat of Granada, the last Muslim kingdom in Iberia, and the expulsion of the Jews from Spain, has now been renarrativized in some quarters as a time when the three cultures peacefully coincided.[9] As the Jews of Spain dispersed, many joined the rest of Europe's Jews as the continent's internal other. Four hundred years later, in Argentina, the descendents of these Jews were received as Europeans. The reception was belated, it is true, but ultimately the Jews were Europeans like, or as unlike, any others, with all the differences among them, including the differences that nourish intercultural suspicion and feed anti-Semitism.

However internally riven Europe might be, Eurocentrism is nevertheless deeply implicated in determining the East/West binary. If on the one hand we can say that the binary cannot hold because of the pressure on it of its multiple meanings, on the other we might do well to recognize that it is such a powerful signifier that it retains its ability to confer meaning even under that pressure, always encapsulating a power relationship encoded as cultural difference. In the British colonialist version of the East–West division, the West is Europe and the East is south and east Asia as well as the Maghreb. In the Orientalist version that Edward Said examined, Europe invents its other in that Arab world: the "Middle" East. And in the cold war version, the West is Europe and the United States (but also Japan), and the East is the Soviet Bloc, but also China. In all these formulations, the West stays fairly stable, but its other in the East is in motion. One provocative reading of the East/West divide emerges from the Argentinean theorist Enrique Dussel's thoughts on development. Dussel observes how development is narrativized as a progression from undeveloped to developed, from childhood to adulthood, from East to West (Dussel 1995; Spanos 2000, 42–43). He thus cloaks development theory in psychoanalytic terms. For Dussel, Africa and Latin America do not even enter into the framework of this kind of thinking about development. Nevertheless, following Dussel's psychoanalytic language, which suggests the oedipal struggle between father and son lurking under the surface of development stories, we might imagine psychoanalytically savvy Argentina as the adolescent who embraces this structure, claiming grown-up status from a place of subordination. Argentina makes its claim, demanding the attention of the European "father," thus eliciting a reaction from him. Furthermore, on this model, we can think of the shift in focus from Europe to the United States as a shift in focus from Europe as the parental figure to the United States as sibling rival. Oversimplifying history for the sake of this metaphor, we might imagine Argentina facing this other powerful child of Europe as the postcolonial moment in nineteenth-century Argentina elides into the neocolonial, with economic power at the end of the nineteenth century in the hands of England—Argentina's stepparent, and the father in the United States' successfully resolved oedipal drama.[10] After the Monroe doctrine, but especially after World War II and the anti-Soviet panic in the United States occasioned by the cold war, economic and political hegemony shift to the United States.

It is not incidental, therefore, that Rob Wilson finds in Marta Savigliano and Jorge Luis Borges Argentinean examples to disturb the facile "West and the rest" formulation. To his criticism of what we might characterize as a form of Eurocentrism that condenses and homogenizes all that is not Europe and produces it as the not-West, Wilson adds this parenthetical remark:

> Marta Savigliano may be surprised to learn that Latin America is not part of "the West," —try telling that to the learned postmodernist, Jorge Luis Borges, who argued in his classic essay from *Labyrinths,* "The Argentine Writer and Tradition," "I believe our tradition (in Argentina) is all of Western culture." (2000, 595)

Savigliano is an Argentine scholar whose criticism of anthropological readings of the tango is lodged in a broader critique of the tendency among Europeans and North Americans to exoticize Argentina.[11] She is particularly annoyed by those who enlist in that project even the cosmopolitan Jorge Luis Borges, the other Argentine to whom Wilson refers in his parenthetical aside. For Wilson, Borges is a "learned postmodernist," presumably two things no one from "the rest" of the world can be. Moreover, Borges stakes a claim to all of Western tradition, and not just for himself.

Borges in the European imagination often seems to rise sui generis from the Río de la Plata, like Venus on her scallop shell; but, as he is quick to remind both Europe and Argentina, his is a nation born of the West. This is not an untroubled stance. Within Argentina, Borges has been criticized for an overly developed attachment to things European. Still, as an unreconstructed Anglophile, Borges would claim all Western heritage for Argentina's own—and with more right than any single European country, since, he argues, all Europe converges in Argentina.

In its own liberal, elite narrative, a narrative that Borges retells, Argentina is Western and modern. At the same time, as Nicolas Shumway has shown, Argentina has long nurtured a conflicting master narrative of its distinctiveness from Europe. The cleft in Argentina's self-image (the modern, liberal, Western cultured subject and his contrary, the unspoiled natural Argentinean of the pampas) creates an unsettled state that is never resolved. This indeterminacy is part of Argentina's energy and attraction, but it is also an internal gash that bleeds the nation. Moreover, it helps make Argentina a nodal point in contesting the "West and the rest" model. Quintessentially West and not-West, oscillating between the two, Argentina can function as a lever that pries this formulation apart.

Implicit in this discussion is the idea that the region (Europe, but also Latin America) is a coherent but insufficient unit of analysis. The nations that make up a region need to be understood in all their distinctiveness and in terms of their internal difference as well. In this discussion of Argentina, it is important not to lose sight of the way Argentina intersects with the rest of Latin America. Hugo Achugar (2000) argues that the tendency among European writers to collapse Argentina into Latin America diminished as the twentieth century progressed and Argentina stopped being easily assimilated into "South America." Nevertheless, this slippage is still to be found among Argentine thinkers. For them Argentina is not only very much part of South America, it is the most important part. Graciela Scheines's book-length essay, *Las metáforas del fracaso* (The metaphors of failure), all but collapses America into Argentina; and even when she is speaking of America as a whole, her point of reference remains Argentina. Arguing that Latin America is Europe's other, an other that is a projection, Scheines uses the thoroughly Argentine vocabulary of civilization and barbarism:

> From another perspective as well, one we could call sociocultural, *barbarous America* is an appetizing product for Europeans. If the North has turned into a world without differences in the last decades, homogenized by comfort, technology, and mass communications, then it vitally needs *a space uncontaminated by civilization,* apart from progress, a space of the marvelous and the monstrous *in barbaric form; savage,* elemental heaven and hell; for curious travelers anxious to see and touch the original, primeval past, before they were touched by history and the sophistication of the spirit. (1991, 76, emphasis added)[12]

The hint Scheines leaves here of Argentina as America in her use of the contrast between barbarism and civilization, so inextricably bound to Argentina's discussions of its own identity, soon becomes explicit. Her discussion of the prophetic myth that projects a European version of America is, by the end of the passage, an America that can be thoroughly contained in Argentina:

> I said that *the myth of America* is older than Columbus, that there is a whole "prophetic" literature of the discovery of America that is popularized and generates, during the Middle Ages, a legend of an Edenic, virgin continent waiting to be discovered beyond the Western sea. The entire conquest is guided by the illusion and the search for that paradise, and a dark obstinacy irrationally propelled those adventurers to force reality

until it fit into the mold of the legend. *What else but illusion could have inspired the names Argentina and Río de la Plata in a land without mines, like ours?* (23, emphasis added)[13]

Although Scheines begins by evoking America as a whole, she ultimately tips her hand in the apposition "America—Argentina" of the following sentence, and the myth of America becomes the myth of Argentina:

> The belief that *South America—Argentina—*was an empty space waiting to be turned into utopia made us so proud that we believed we were chosen, held in reserve for a nonexistent country, citizens of Utopia without the utopian context. (78, emphasis added)[14]

Scheines's countryman Hugo E. Biagini has no trouble assuming that the America about which Scheines is writing is equivalent to Argentina. Whereas she elides America and Argentina, he cites her essay to talk about Argentina alone. For Scheines and Biagini, whose location as Argentines makes that country the logical point of reference, Argentina and America still overlap in meaning, even when they do not fully coincide.[15] Similarly, César Fernández Moreno, writing in the context of Argentine poetry, states:

> Argentina is, then, America pure and simple, at best a crossing of the culture of Europe with the landscape of America, a crossing that does not allow for unification as easily as those attempts at synthesis suppose, and that is the root of our search for a nonexistent nationality. (Fernández Moreno and Becco 1968, 32)[16]

In contrast to Fernández Moreno, who concentrates here on the troubled and resistant melding of America and Europe in Argentina, Scheines argues that Argentina's preoccupation with its national identity is linked to its dependence on European interpretations of (Latin) America in general. Her concern with what she sees as Argentina's overdependence on the acknowledgement and analyses of outsiders in developing its own sense of identity may find an example in Hugo Achugar's focus on the meaning of the Río de la Plata for Europeans and North Americans. Scheines is particularly critical not only of European intellectuals who define Argentina, or all America through Argentina, but more importantly of Argentinean thinkers who embrace their ideas:

> Keyserling was one of those foreign intellectuals (also Ortega y Gasset, Jacinto Benavente, Jiménez de Asúa, Le Corbusier, Levy-Bruhl) who

assiduously visited Argentina in the 1920s to propound about South American idiosyncrasy or the Argentine being, and that the criollo "intelligentsia" fawned over and listened to unctuously, proud that learned Europe was interested in us. It was Keyserling who reaffirmed and rounded out the idea of barbarism, South American geographic fatalism, with dire consequences for our countries. And Ezequiel Martínez Estrada (1895–1964) takes it from the count and diffuses and enriches it with his talent. (1991, 51)[17]

Scheines is angered at the progression of European thought that imagines America in general and Argentina in particular first as paradise, then as utopia, and finally as barbaric wilderness; and she observes, sadly, that Argentina has internalized this view of itself. She points out that all these conceptions of empty space turn America/Argentina into a nonplace, a nontime, a time of waiting and of nonsignificance, for Argentine as well as European thinkers:

More than ever, America is an insignificant space, a no-place, but instead of sheltering a future made of dreams and hopes, it is the exile where there is room only for the longing for the absent country and the parricidical hatred of the Europe that expelled us from our childhood home. But it is also an empty, insignificant time, because it is the time of waiting. (70)[18]

Scheines maintains that if America/Argentina is to achieve ideological liberation, it must break free of the European-created paradigms that constrain it. This deep dependence on the other's view of the nation is characteristic of Argentine thinkers, but so is the critique of intellectual dependency.

Until we free ourselves of the spatial or geographic images of America (paradise, empty space, or barbarism) of European origin, from which the terrible theories of the Fatum, the Unformed, the Facundic [from Sarmiento's *Facundo*], and the telluric that fix and immobilize us like the pin immobilizes the butterfly, and that make America an uninhabitable dimension, distant from all human measure, we will not escape the circular movement, the forward march and about face, the infinite returns to the place we started to start over once again and never get more than half way. (79)[19]

Writing to answer the familiar question "What is an Argentine?" Biagini agrees with Scheines, that the problem with Argentina is that it has allowed itself to be defined by Europe and, with his reference to the North Atlantic, by the United States and Canada as well:

Over the years, a discourse has been built up, deriving from multiple sources and orientations. It is a discourse that insists on the lack of order that predominates among us, a disorderliness that comes from our impulsive and infantile nature, in contrast to North Atlantic prudence and equilibrium. These are strictly dichotomous and reductionist sketches of a culture and a nationality, of the men and women of our lands, characterizations that, denying intelligence, morality, and fundamental humanity to our people, have contributed to the toppling of majority governments and the founding of dictatorships. (Biagini 2000, 118–19)[20]

Biagini's research into documents of the last fifty years interrogates not only the 1976 document of dictatorship, *Defensa de la Argentinidad* (Defense of Argentineity), that promotes God, country, and army in an isolationist view, but also the writing of early twentieth-century European observers, whose view of Argentina was no less oppressive than that of the writer of the *Defensa*. Like Scheines, he singles out the impact of Hermann Keyserling, invited to Argentina by Victoria Ocampo, who writes of Argentina as a land of capricious beings (Biagini 2000, 114).[21] Biagini traces Keyserling's pernicious influence on Martínez Estrada, who quotes him directly, and on other influential national writers such as H. A. Murena and Julio Mafud. Biagini also cites Hegel's vision of America as chaotic, repeated by later authors who wish to justify colonization and the authoritarianism of military governments (118). Apparently these Germans, the countrymen of those immigrants who were to civilize Argentina, found it to be utterly beyond redemption.[22]

Scheines's and Biagini's analysis of Argentina's dependence on outside ratification is echoed on the individual level by Julie Taylor, who writes about Argentines' preoccupation with how others think of them, and of their worry that they will seem foolish or provincial. This ambivalent attitude, happy to be seen by others, distressed at the way they are seen, contrasts with the way the interchange of perceptions between inside and outside is received in Brazil. Ana Reynaud shows that, like Argentina, Brazil is dependent upon what the world thinks of it in creating its own sense of identity. Reynaud, however, contends that Brazil is untroubled by its othering in the eye of Europe and the North, and that in fact Brazil serves as its own other, creating and re-creating its own exoticism for consumption at home as well as abroad. In her discussion of the 1990 video *What Do You Think People Think Brazil Is?*

Reynaud argues that Brazil becomes its own other, self-exoticizing for the purpose of creating a space for itself in the global cultural economy:

> I suggest that in the case of Brazil, identity can actually be found in its refractions, and propose that, because representation plays such a fundamental role in the country's cultural constitution, Brazil's "other" is Brazil itself. (2000, 72)

She goes on to say that

> *What Do You Think People Think Brazil Is?* is a reflection upon the power of representation, first in colonialism and now in a postcolonial, global world. Otherness and identity are inextricably bound up together in this video: one is not possible without the other. It may be that in its historical lack of fixed and stable cultural boundaries with regard to its "identity," Brazil has nonetheless produced, and keeps on producing, a fluid but reiterative sense of identity. Doreen Massey reminds us that the identity of a place does not derive from some internalised history, but from the specificity of its interactions with "the outside," and this is very much the case here. What "people" think Brazil is—including foreign, "exterior" expectations that may be strongly internalised by the "natives"— in fact largely constitutes what it is. This fluid identity . . . consists ultimately of so many projections, in turn projecting itself back. We could call this a case of "reverse cultural influence," in which the process of "cultural" influence works in two directions because the "place" that is projected upon also projects back. A cultural artifact or expression can go from being considered as "original" and then as "appropriated," and finally as "coming back" to its site of origin with new features incorporated into it. (87)

In Reynaud's account, Brazil seems content to reincorporate itself as Europe's exotic other, becoming exotic to itself.

Seconding Reynaud's reading of Brazil, but also echoing Scheines and Biagini, Marta Savigliano writes that "exoticism and auto-exoticism are interrelated outcomes in the colonial encounter" (cited in Wilson 2000, 601). Argentina insistently refuses exoticization even as it desires to be noticed by a Europe whose primary way of seeing the Argentine other is precisely as exotic. Argentina thus projects itself as Europe's "same," but Europe receives this projection as Argentine difference. Similarly, Argentina seems to want to distinguish itself from other Latin American nations (as the leader in rising up for independence, for one thing, but also as a model for nationhood more generally) but also to claim its centrality in and as America.

Scheines and Biagini focus on the damage done by Argentina's reliance on others' representations, but Argentina represents a confluence of colonization and globalization, both acted upon and acting, nourishing itself on ideas about it from elsewhere, and also planting the seeds of those ideas quite deliberately. (One of those ideas, which we will look at more closely later on, is the idea of racial purity.)

Argentina has stayed alive in the metropole's imaginary because it has pushed its way onto the global stage and demanded a part in the metropolitan show. But Argentina did not get a leading role; instead it was cast as a foil for the lead players. Its very audacity, and its easy dismissal of its racial and cultural similarity to the rest of Latin America, earned it the reputation of self-importance and pride in the rest of the continent. Argentina's fascination with its own identity and its concomitant self-involvement, perhaps its most salient national characteristic, may be invisible to most in the West, but it is apparent to any Latin American, and to alert European or U.S. observers.[23] Consider these jokes: from Chilean literary theorist Román Soto, "What is pride? Pride is the little Argentinean we all carry around inside us"; and from Umberto Eco, "What is an Argentine? An Argentine is someone sitting in a bar asking himself what it means to be Argentine" (cited in Scheines 1991, 110). Luisa Valenzuela, an Argentinean writer, first makes a joke of her own, in recognition of how little most Mexicans appreciated the presence of Argentinean exiles in their country, saying that if there was anything Argentineans gave Mexico it was the chance to make great jokes about Argentina. Then she recirculates a joke told in Mexico: "Why don't Argentineans bathe in hot water? Because they don't want the mirror to get fogged up." Valenzuela's reading of the Mexican joke is revealing, as she goes on to say that the mirror—that is to say, the mirror of Argentine history—is already misted over. In other words, what the joke presents as the neurosis of the individual Argentine, Valenzuela renarrativizes as a question of national identity. Furthermore, she goes on to say that the blurriness of the mirror itself tells an important story.[24]

Valenzuela here performs in small an act that is common among Argentinean thinkers. She takes what others say about Argentina and then reworks that observation and incorporates it into her own reading of the nation. Argentina, as we can begin to see from this modest example, is not simply a passive victim of Orientalist, Eurocentric accounts, but rather the author of a narrative that gets reworked outside its borders and then recirculated within. Note Valenzuela's pleasure in retelling these somewhat antagonistic little jokes.

This kind of storytelling across borders has also been done on an official, state-sanctioned level. One of the first to engage in it for clearly instrumental ends was Domingo Faustino Sarmiento, who strove to stimulate European immigration to his country in the nineteenth century. However it is also a tactic that has been used recently by opposition groups, such as the Mothers of the Plaza de Mayo who, during the dictatorship that effectively silenced all other dissent, took advantage of the presence of the world press at the World Cup soccer tournament to call international attention to the disappearance of their children by the state. They used, and continue to use, public spectacle in their weekly demonstrations, and their recirculated importance has been inscribed on the pavements: The Plaza de Mayo is decorated with images of their white scarves in the pavement, in a circle around the obelisk, the circle that the mothers walk every Thursday. Similarly, Argentines demanding that former torturers be brought to justice in the face of hurriedly passed laws of impunity that effectively pardon the perpetrators have resorted to a kind of street theater in the form of *escraches*. These are a form of public humiliation in which groups of demonstrators converge on or near the homes of known torturers and call attention to their behavior during the Dirty War.[25]

Argentina, then, is not simply a projection of the West, but rather is a full-fledged construction in which it is a partner, a product of invasion, colonization, immigration, and self-assertion. For Argentina is also an invention of its settlers, contested and relying on the authority of Europe as well as on a claim to autochthonous character.

In *Inventing America*, José Rabasa argues that America did not preexist the encounter or invasion of the Europeans, but rather that it has been made by colonialist discourse. Graciela Scheines holds that America did indeed exist before Columbus came ashore, but that it existed as a European myth. For all their differences, both Rabasa and Scheines tell of an America derived exclusively from Europe's stories of it.[26] By adopting and reworking European stories, the colonial in much of America eventually constructs itself as the postcolonial hybrid. The criollo elite in Argentina, however, denies racial or cultural hybridity in favor of a theory of metamorphosis: the new geography and history of America create their own new subject out of European matter. Neither the hybrid nor the metamorphosed Latin American postcolonial entirely sheds the ambivalence of an elusive subjectivity that seems to reiterate, or to mime, colonial authority. In the end, this new postcolonial subject, whether hybrid or metamorphosed, does violence to the indigenous people, whom he considers a nuisance to be gotten rid of, by either incorporation or extermination.

Spivak has defined the quandary of most postcolonials, who "are still interested either in proving that they are ethnic subjects and therefore true marginals or that they are as good as the colonials" (1989, 290). The postcolonial in Argentina is certainly out to prove he is as good as the colonials. However, in the nineteenth century, when Argentina gained its independence from Spain, there was little currency in proclaiming one's "ethnic subjectivity." Argentina's independence came at a time of positivist belief in order and progress (in fact Brazil's national slogan). The idea that there might be a European-style state governed by indigenous peoples was beyond the imagination of the European-descended settlers of southern Latin America.

As we have already noted, the elite's largely urban version of a Europeanized Argentineity is disputed by a story of Argentineity that claims deeper ties to the land, largely through the figure of the gaucho.[27] The gaucho is assimilated into national myth as the quintessential Argentinean, more because of his connection to the pampas and the grounding myth of his fierce loyalty, his honorability, and his simplicity of life than because of any ethnic or racial mixing. Gauchos were supposed to be the children of Spanish fathers and indigenous mothers, or descended from those who were. Yet the founding myth of *mestizaje*, as in Mexico, or Vasconcelos's notion of the *raza cósmica* that vaunted this racial mixing as a Darwinian path to the improvement of the human race, or as the basis for a new kind of culture, did not gain purchase in Argentina. The gaucho remains more a tragically romantic figure whose natural terrain, the pampa, is slowly eaten up by privatization and who was slowly brutalized by forced conscription and the disappearance of the cattle economy than as the progenitor of a new people. The two key literary works of the gauchesque, José Hernández's foundational text, *Martín Fierro*, and its swan song, Ricardo Güiraldes's *Don Segundo Sombra*, both chronicle the demise of a way of life. Racial and cultural hybridity are masked or secondary to begin with, and then the figure of the gaucho himself is, at least in these literary representations, always already in the process of extinction. (I am tempted to point out that the world of the gaucho is so relentlessly masculine that it is not surprising that the gaucho finds difficulty in reproducing himself, but in fact what happens to the women in these stories is worse than simple absence. They may be there long enough to produce the gaucho's sons, as in *Martín Fierro,* but then they disappear from the page, often tragically kidnapped, raped, and/or murdered by rapacious soldiers or Indians.)

Whereas the gaucho is always in danger of disappearing, the immigrant as avatar of the quintessential Argentina refuses to submerge his identity as such into perfect Argentineity. Marked by the incomplete absorption of an immigrant population, Argentina is at best a melting pot with lumps. Immigration was supposed to improve Argentina's racial stock: overwhelming indigenous America with infusions of Europeans, not hybridity, was Argentina's goal. Nevertheless, at the height of immigration, the immigrant was considered inferior to the native Argentinean, and the goal became the absorption and assimilation of the foreigner, the civilizing of the rough immigrant.

Argentina incorporated European values of civilization, but in doing so it refigured those values. The already fractured Europe that sent both its engineers and its unskilled laborers to Argentina could not simply be transplanted wholesale, nor could it be swallowed whole by its other. In the perpetual motion machine of Argentina and Europe, each playing off against the other, but unequally, Argentina has more at stake. For Europe Argentina is just one of its many mirrors, one of the many places to invest its money for a quick return or to send its poor and, more recently, from which to accept political and economic refugees. For Argentina, its very meaning has depended on its reflection in the eyes of its others.

This desire to be seen by the global North has become such a commonplace about Argentina that it is sometimes found even where it is not hiding. In her study of Victoria Ocampo's autobiographical writings, María Cristina Arambel-Güiñazú creatively misreads Carlos Fuentes, who notes the Porteño need to come to self-consciousness via language. Fuentes writes:

> Buenos Aires needs to name itself to know that it exists, to invent itself a past, to imagine a future for itself: unlike Mexico City or Lima, a simple visual reference to the signs of historic prestige is not enough for it....

> Could there be anything more Argentine than this necessity to verbally
> fill these empty spaces, to take recourse in all the world's libraries to fill
> the blank book of Argentina?[28]

For Fuentes, this is primarily a function of self-definition, but Arambel-
Güiñazú disregards Fuentes's insistent reflexives of self-naming, self-
invention, and imagining one's own future. The Mexican writer's reference to the universalizing stories that the (very Borgesian) world's
libraries have in their stores, and that set the standards for Argentine
selfhood, becomes, in Arambel-Güiñazú's reading, a reflection of Argentina in the world's eyes.[29] But her chronology is wrong: Argentina is
not (yet) present in the books housed in Fuentes's European libraries.
In Arambel-Güiñazú's formulation, *Buenos Aires's* need to *speak itself*
via European standards doubly metamorphoses into *Argentina's* longing to *be seen by others*—a desire for the very visual proof that Fuentes
argues Argentina abjures, presumably for lack of Aztecs and Incas that
would bestow upon it any "historic prestige." It is certainly true, as
Arambel-Güiñazú asserts, that the Porteño elite (and, by somewhat
problematic extension, Argentina in general) relies on the gaze of its
European others. What is interesting is that this reliance has become so
much a part of the myth of Argentine self-obsession that proof of it is
perceived even where it does not exist.

Jorge Luis Borges invents at least one symbol of this obsession. His
aleph is the site where all time and place converge, and it is one metaphor,
certainly hyperbolic, for Argentina. Its presence under the basement
stairs in a Buenos Aires house drives home the Porteño connection. However, it is another of Borges's amazing objects that might best figure
Argentina as obsession, the "notorious, visible" zahir, which in different
times and places takes different forms: a tiger, a blind man, a compass, an
astrolabe, a vein running through a slab of marble, the bottom of a well.
"Zahir," Borges tells us, is a term "used in Moslem lands ... 'to designate
beings or things which possess the terrible virtue of being unforgettable, and whose image finally drives people mad'" (1967c, 134). Despite
its exotic provenance, Borges's zahir is narratively linked to a pretentious
and beloved Argentina, once rich and fashionable—if derivative—and
now a caricature of itself, in the figure of Teodelina Villar. Borges, who is
both author and character, "still, however partially, Borges" (128), mocks
Teodelina's slavish devotion to the models offered by Hollywood and
Paris, but he also remembers her tenderly and is saddened by her decline

into relative poverty and death. Returning from her wake he comes into possession of the zahir. In Buenos Aires the shapeshifting zahir is a coin, a token of exchange, virtually worthless but still unforgettable.

As a nation, however, Argentina is akin to the tiger-zahir, an image of an infinite tiger that "a Moslem fakir had designed. . . . This Tiger was made up of many tigers and fused in the most vertiginous manner: this Tiger was traversed by tigers, striped with tigers, and encompasses seas and armies and Himalayas resembling tigers" (Borges 1967c, 135). Like Argentina in this book, the infinite tiger painted in a prison cell by Borges's Moslem fakir is an image, taken from and brought back to the many of its kind. The zahir is a hyperbolic, parodic version of Argentina, invented for Borges's readers, as Argentine and cosmopolitan as Borges himself. It is a common twenty-centavo coin with a mystic aspect that connects it, primarily, to the Jewish, Muslim, and Hindu worlds. Like the aleph, the zahir is associated with the death of a charming Porteña; Borges (the character) is grounded in Buenos Aires geography and its local, society-page history. The zahir as Argentina, like Borges's coin of little value, does not fascinate completely. It does not encompass everything, but it has the capacity to insert itself between those who view it and their vision of the world. This zahir, troubling and trivial object that it is, insignificant and deeply important, resonates with the figure of Argentina in the global imaginary, and it is best comprehended through Borges's own complex mix of tenderness, loss, and irony.

CHAPTER THREE

Imperial Anxieties

Trying to map the relations of global dominance on an East–West axis ends in frustration. Such a crude compass is insufficient to name the complex relationships among the nations and the regions of the world. Enrique Dussel, for example, contends that Africa and Latin America are left out of the East-West construct altogether, but it is just as reasonable to maintain that they are fitfully, multiply, and contradictorily integrated into it. Africa is in part simply "dark" and unknowable in the familiar racist construction, but it is also "East" insofar as Arabian and Persian North Africa comprise the Middle East—the very locus of the Oriental in the European imaginary, as Said has so richly argued. For its part, as a European settler colony, Latin America is arguably "Western"; Argentina in particular has an immigration history similar to that of the United States. On the other hand, Latin America is also arguably "Eastern" because of its largely Spanish, and therefore Arab, heritage.[1] Strictly speaking, of course, Latin America is physically located in what we call the western hemisphere.

East and West are not the only superficially geographic designations naming complex historical relations. Perhaps because they constitute so troublesome a binary, the North/South divide has also emerged to sketch the unequal distribution of wealth and the legacy of colonialism. As a geographical metaphor for a historical phenomenon, however, the North/South distinction is similarly insufficient. Australia and New Zealand, for example, do not conform to the pattern. Geographically "south," though politically "North," they are the inverse of India, another notoriously bad fit for the model. If we jiggle the map and set the beginning of the South at 30 degrees north of the Equator, to include India and South East Asia, as well as Mexico and Central America and the good chunk of Africa that lies north of degree zero, we also have to include a sizeable piece of Texas and most of Florida. Moreover, to the European imagination, "South" is equivalent to "tropical," conjuring images of steamy, disease-ridden, insect-infested, impenetrable jungles filled with exotic plants and creatures.[2] In the end, the definitions of North and South, like those of East and West are only marginally geographical, so it is no surprise to discover that a nation like Argentina eludes precise localization in what is a hopelessly vague taxonomy to begin with. Inserting the grounded, historical situation of Argentina into the generalization of the binary is one way to reveal the inadequacy of the latter's simplistic formulation.

As South-traversed-by-North and East-within-West, Argentina functions as a pivot between the exotic and the known. For a Venetian character written by a U.S. mystery writer, Buenos Aires is the intermediate place, neither totally familiar nor thoroughly exotic:

> Why didn't he say farewell to all care and just walk away from the library? Why didn't he abandon his unhappy little daughter and his impossible mother-in-law and fly off to Monte Carlo, or Madrid, or Buenos Aires or the South Pole? Or perhaps the North Pole? (Langton 1999, 116)

After imagining an irresponsible escape to familiar European sites: Monte Carlo and Madrid, the character ends by fantasizing the utterly outlandish, and therefore impossible, destinations of the North and South Poles. The middle point in this sequence is Buenos Aires, linguistically connected to Europe via Madrid, but just one step from the literal ends—the poles—of the earth. The mental process that begins with Monte Carlo and ends at the North Pole passes through Buenos Aires.

At the other end of the climactic scale is the narrative that shoehorns Argentina uncomfortably into a tropical vision of South America.[3] If the "West" seems to presuppose "North," Argentina, as far south as it is, has too temperate a climate to make it so entirely other. Argentina's undecidability for Europeans and North Americans—now West like "us," now South like "them"—makes it an ideal site for projection. Moreover, Europe's power to turn its fantasies of the South into reality has had material consequences affecting the built environment. Miranda France comments on one Buenos Aires structure:

> the magnificent Waterworks, every stone of which had been imported from Britain and France. Flanked by a cordon of palm trees, the Waterworks was a Victorian vision of colonial life in the tropics, and therefore fantastically out of place in Buenos Aires. (1998, 8)

Whether construed via longitude or latitude, the geographical binary is code for modern/not modern. The West/North constructs itself as modern against the underdeveloped Orient/South, upon which it built its modernity. It was, after all, the spoils of colonialism that financed Europe's lunge into modernity and provided the wealth for creating capital, as so many have argued so convincingly. Argentina's wealth, however, was late in being exploited, and as an independent nation it was eager to participate as a protagonist in the project of modernity. As Nicolas Shumway points out, Argentina did not have the more obvious treasure of gold and silver, a disappointment to those who named it under the illusion that it was the beginning of the route to such riches. Argentina's wealth, not of silver but of rich grazing and farmland, was developed in the modernizing state, the independent republic, not in the colony. At the beginning of the twentieth century, on the heels of the Spanish-American War, Latin America *tout court* was conscripted by Spain to be part of a greater Hispanic commonwealth, connected by bonds of spirit and history. By the time Spain lost the last of its American colonies to the United States in 1898, Argentina had already been an independent nation for eighty-two years. It was, nevertheless, largely to Argentina that Spanish intellectuals turned when they substituted a notion of pan-Hispanism for the material reality of a colonial empire in staking a claim for Spanish greatness. Spain's claim to modernity would be through the Argentine example; Spanish history would provide a glorious past for Argentina, and Argentine modernity would be the future and continuation of Spain.

For other Europeans, and especially for the British, who participated in the increasing industrialization of Europe by engaging in trade relations with Argentina and by investing in the development of its infrastructure, Argentina was an opportunity for exploitation. British state policy in the nineteenth century was explicit about avoiding political entanglements in Argentina in favor of economic intervention there. It was a policy designed to enrich England as a nation and to make wealthy men of individual investors, and it often did. From the Argentine elite's point of view, English participation in their country's development was a welcome prospect. The representation of this symbiotic relationship in British narratives, however, often shows the Englishmen either as unproblematic heroes of benign development of the country or as innocent victims of crafty Latins and corrupt officials. In *The Mysterious Mr. Quin,* for example, Agatha Christie tops off her list of questionable groups who have degraded British society with the Argentines:

> "You're rather a big bug socially, aren't you?" he asked. . . . "I mean you know all the Duchesses and Earls and Countesses and things."
>
> "A good many of them," said Mr. Satterthwaite. "And also the Jews and the Portuguese and the Greeks and the Argentines."
>
> "Eh?" said Mr. Rudge.
>
> "I was just explaining," said Mr. Satterthwaite, "that I move in English society." (1943, 94–95)[4]

By the 1930s, when Great Britain withdrew as Argentina's primary customer for its wheat and beef, Argentina had become, in British fiction, the place where English rubes went to buy the Latin American equivalent of the Brooklyn Bridge. In these narratives, speculation and greed get out of hand, and unscrupulous con men take advantage of ordinary Englishmen who merely want to get rich quick. This plot line is reserved for men. An analogous story line for women surfaces in the narratives in which they trust that promises of marriage, the feminine equivalent of speculation, will give them security and respectability. As we shall see in later discussions of *Scum, The Escape Artist,* and *Naked Tango,* the women are duped as well.

In Agatha Christie's *Lord Edgware Dies,* published first in 1933 and many years later incorporated into the popular Poirot television series by the BBC, poor Captain Hastings, Hercule Poirot's plodding, literal-minded, but always honorable sidekick, ever the innocent, is taken in by an Argentine confidence scheme. Argentina remains in the background of this mystery novel. As the tale begins, Hastings is recently returned from Buenos Aires, where he has left his Argentine wife to sort out their sorry financial situation. Ignorant of Argentina's terrain, Hastings has been swindled out of his fortune in a plan to build a railroad across a massive mountain range. Such fictional fraudulent get-rich-quick schemes typically involve taming some natural wilderness, and in the case of Hastings, his absolute ignorance of the existence of a mountain range that Christie herself imagines for Argentina makes him an easy target. A chastened Hastings comments that the Pampas de Fernández Consolidated railway is in fact not consolidated, given the huge mountain range between the two places it was supposed to connect.

A subsequent Poirot story with an Argentine connection, "The Yellow Iris," has had multiple lives. After producing it as a radio drama in 1937 and publishing it as a short story in 1939, Christie modified and expanded it into a novel, *Sparkling Cyanide*. It was later developed for BBC television under its original title. In both the radio version and the novel the Argentine references are almost entirely absent. However, in 1993, less than a decade after the Falklands/Malvinas War, the short story, complete with its original Argentine content, was adapted for the BBC Poirot series. The television version in particular is quite detailed in its representation of a perfidious Argentina. In a flashback narrating his own visit there, Poirot recalls that he had gone to visit Hastings, who had acquired not only an Argentine wife but an Argentine ranch as well. Because he was detained by the police, Poirot never got to see his friend. The story includes a struggle between the British characters involved in a fraudulent scheme involving the rights to oil production and other Englishmen opposed to such machinations. In this version of the Latin American political corruption narrative, the British evildoers are in league with an officer who has helped plot the coup to overthrow Argentine president Irigoyen. Thus is Argentinean history called into play and fictionalized for the purposes of the British mystery story. The political intrigue is merely a part of the background, and it is purely Argentine and purely evil—hence the British character who consorts with the Argentine military turns out to be the murderer. English interest in Argentina's natural resources again surfaces in this story: the British have invested in Argentine oil, and the crash of the fictional Sovereign Oil Company is imminent. Poirot, too close to uncovering the dirty dealings of corrupt officials, is arrested by the military government and thrown out of the country by the general and his Englishman henchman.

The cultural milieu of "The Yellow Iris" is decidedly cosmopolitan: much of the action takes place in a French-owned restaurant and nightclub that is later reconstituted whole in London. The nightclub scene involves an African American blues singer, musicians in rumba-style

Cuban ruffled-sleeved shirts, and a character named Lola Valdez who, described as a "South American dancer" in the 1937 radio drama, protests in the television version that she is not from Argentina but rather Peru. In the radio drama the first death takes place in a nightclub in New York, but after the Falklands War, it once again occurs in Buenos Aires. The return of the narrative to its Argentine setting links the Buenos Aires of 1934, darkly lit, politically unstable, and dangerous, to recent British history, never abandoning the stylized modernist pleasure the Poirot television series offers.

The clash between high-minded and corrupt British characters, in which the evil and unprincipled ally themselves with unscrupulous Argentines to the detriment of other Englishmen, also appears in Oscar Wilde. In *An Ideal Husband,* the ruthless Mrs. Cheveley tries to blackmail the upstanding Sir Robert Chiltern into supporting a scheme to build a canal through Argentina. Mrs. Cheveley links this scheme to another colonial adventure, the building of the Suez Canal, during which Sir Robert used inside information to make his patron's fortune and his own. In the terms of the play, the Suez Canal, as a route to India, a sanctioned British colony, is understood to have been a proper undertaking (albeit marred by Sir Robert's behavior), but the Argentine canal scheme is simply a fraud—unnecessary and dangerous.

Historically, Britain chose to keep its intervention in Argentina purely economic and not political in order to avoid the unpleasantness of overt colonization. The canal scheme in Wilde's drama underscores the danger of foreign entanglements, no matter how "cleanly" economic they are. By including a parliamentary debate on this nineteenth-century boondoggle, the playwright lays open the tangled connection between the overt colonialism of military and political domination and the version that purports not to be colonization at all, but merely economic investment.

Wilde and Christie give us a good indication of the anxieties of economic imperialism. Their work, as social satire and escapist mystery-writing respectively, is not overtly concerned with ponderous political issues. Yet it is in these texts that the symptoms of anxiety about Great Britain's relations with Argentina bubble to the surface. Not long after the time the British were in Argentina building railroads and other parts of the nation's infrastructure, not out of pure good will, but rather in order to support their export businesses, the idea of investment in

Argentina is redolent of risk, scandal, and fraud, ready to be used as the background unease of light fiction or drawing-room comedy. It is recycled in the wake of the Falklands War, when anxiety about Argentina has once again surfaced. A film version of *An Ideal Husband* was released in 1999 and did very respectably at the box office in both Britain and the United States.

It is perhaps in the context of this trope in early twentieth-century British writing that we may understand the apparently irrelevant reference to Argentina's wealth in the last pages of Alan Hollinghurst's 2004 Man Booker Prize–winning novel, *The Line of Beauty*. Nick, a young gay man from the provincial middle class who has insinuated himself into an upper-class family headed by a Tory MP, is made a scapegoat to deflect criticism from a potential scandal involving the MP's insider trading. Just when heterosexual normativity and class privilege are coming together to close ranks against Nick, the narrator inserts a reference to an old classmate of his, newly returned from Argentina with a very rich bride. There is no overt narrative link between the MP's illegal financial maneuverings and the easy availability of Argentine riches to straight, aristocratic Englishmen. Nevertheless, the insertion of this extraneous anecdote, in the midst of Nick's fall and the MP's escape from opprobrium, makes sense in the context of texts like those by Wilde and Christie that associate Argentina's fabled riches with financial shenanigans. A Wildean archness, nothing like the novel's predominant realist tone, makes its way into Hollinghurst's text here: the new bride's four-month pregnancy and her previous husband's death in a polo accident are related briskly, with no sentimentality and some irony.

In the late nineteenth and early twentieth centuries, the theme in British texts of the risks of economic adventure in Argentina may well have been a response to the transition from the perception of Argentina, land of opportunity, to Argentina, an autonomous and, from the British point of view, somewhat chaotic nation. England was, after all, an empire used to making the rules in its colonial outposts. What was it to make of this unlikely independent republic with its own agenda? The trope may also be read as a narrative sleight of hand, conjuring a European victim at the hands of the unscrupulous Argentine in the face of a history of British exploitation, or to be more precise, a joint venture in exploitation involving British investors and the Argentine elite.[5] One Argentine novel of the period also rehearses this scenario. Julián Martel's *La bolsa*

(1891) concerns a young, second-generation Argentinean of English background who loses his money in get-rich-quick schemes. Martel's work
has an anti-Semitic twist—the character who comes up with the schemes
that ruin the upstanding, but naive, British-descended youth is a "sinister...Jewish financier" (Delaney 1998, 451). In sympathy with the unfortunate investors, but reluctant to cast the blame for their plight on
mainstream Argentine society, into which the protagonist and his family have been integrating, the author writes the swindler as a Jew.

Joseph Conrad's *Nostromo*, which presents a somewhat more fleshed-
out version of the folly of British commercial ventures in Latin America, also invokes the cliché of the Jewish merchant. Like Martel, Conrad
resorts to anti-Semitic stereotypes in his depiction of the Jew, Hirsch.
Nevertheless, Hirsch is, as Elaine Jordan (1980, 98) points out, the only
character in the novel to defy oppression: he spits in the face of his torturer, who responds by shooting him dead.

Nostromo takes place not in Argentina, but rather in a patently invented country, Costaguana, that is a mélange of Latin American nations. Although the narrative contains a smattering of Southern Cone
geography and custom, as well as ample reference to the sort of British
influence and interest that existed in Argentina, Argentina is not directly
invoked in the novel. In a way, Costaguana can be understood as the
inverse of Argentina: with a name evocative of bird droppings, it holds
wealth in the form of silver. Argentina, named for its nonexistent access
to silver, derived its considerable wealth in natural resources in the less
romantic form of fertile farmland. Coded references aside, Conrad evokes
an imagined Latin America that is tethered at its edges to historical
sources and his own experience on the continent. In its actualization of
the tension between action and historical record (in Said's reading),
myth and history (according to Erdinast-Vulcan), or politics and psyche
(as Jameson sees it), *Nostromo* exemplifies the metropole's invention of
its Latin American, and sometimes specifically Argentine, other. Elaine
Jordan, who discusses the textual, historical, and biographical sources
of the novel that link the narrative to Colombia, Venezuela, Central
America, and Paraguay, ultimately dismisses Conrad's gun running in
Venezuela and failed gold-mining venture in a Latin American country
she does not name as critical sources for a novel whose importance lies
in its symbolic function of the production of meaning and identity.

Both Said and Jameson warn readers away from a political reading of the novel, but by this I think they refer to the futility of taking seriously Conrad's cartoonish, not to say racist, depiction of a Latin American revolution. A deeper political reading, perhaps no longer grounded in the dependency theory that informs Jean Franco's still apt 1975 analysis, and which Said and Jameson themselves perform in the spirit of post-colonial critique, is still in order.

It can be argued that there is no protagonist in the novel, nor is one necessary. The title character is a shadowy immigrant figure whose mythic stature is created and maintained at the expense of a lived reality; Conrad appears to have modeled him on a colorful Corsican sailor whom he met on one of his journeys. The sobriquet "Nostromo" is simultaneously evocative and trivially descriptive. It looks like it means something like "our man," but "nostromo" can also be read simply as a corruption of "nostramo," in Spanish the generic name given by sailors to a boatswain.[6] Perhaps the lack of a clear central figure in the novel is a result of Conrad's own investment in a range of characters. The introspective intellectual, Decoud, has often been understood as the figure who most closely represents Conrad's point of view, and Charles Gould shares Conrad's history of a failed and costly mining venture. Any one of them could have taken center stage; as it is they jostle each other, each refusing the other's preeminence. Of the three characters, Gould is the one whose story best illuminates the relationship between the imagined other and the dominant subject.

Charles Gould's family is one of the oldest in Costaguana, but Charles, like his father, always maintains his sense of self as an Englishman. Conrad goes to some lengths in describing Gould's indelible British stamp. His thin features and ruddy complexion are the visible, embodied signs of his nationality and "breeding," and the narrator affirms his unmistakably British way of being in the world, despite his fluency in Spanish and indigenous languages, his brilliant riding skills, and all the other learned characteristics that would mark Gould as a local rustic oligarch. Conrad's narrator takes pains to describe how well loved is Gould's wife, Emily, and how well respected is Gould himself by all the inhabitants of Sulaco, the region of Costaguana dominated by his mine.

The silver mine that affords Gould his political power as well as his wealth has a history that makes its successful development by an Englishman virtually inevitable. Discovered by the Spanish invaders, it was mined halfheartedly, with the forced labor of Indian slaves. The exploitation of these people is ascribed solely to the Spaniards, recalling the famous and not ill-deserved *leyenda negra,* and skirting the participation of the British in its own slave trade and the use of slaves in its colonies.[7] The mine is abandoned: mismanagement makes it unprofitable even with an unpaid labor force. Years later, a British company buys the rights to the mine, discovers a rich vein, and successfully extracts the ore, but an uprising among the workers, coinciding with a revolution, whips the miners into a fervor and they kill all the British owners. Conrad provides a synopsis of this history as remembered by Emily Gould, the very British angel in the house who both benefits economically from the exploitation of the mine and suffers emotionally because of the dehumanizing effect it has on her husband:

> Mrs. Gould knew the history of the San Tome mine. Worked in the early days mostly by means of lashes on the backs of slaves, its yield had been paid for in its own weight of human bones. Whole tribes of Indians had perished in the exploitation; and then the mine was abandoned, since with this primitive method it had ceased to make a profitable return, no matter how many corpses were thrown into its maw. Then it became forgotten. It was rediscovered after the War of Independence. An English company obtained the right to work it, and found so rich a vein that neither the exactions of successive governments, nor the periodical raids of recruiting officers upon the population of paid miners they had created, could discourage their perseverance. But in the end, during the long turmoil of *pronunciamientos* that followed the death of the famous [dictator] Guzmán Bento, the native miners, incited to revolt by the emissaries sent out from the capital, had risen upon their English chiefs and murdered them to a man. The decree of confiscation which appeared immediately afterwards in the *Diario Oficial,* published in Santa Marta, began with the words: "Justly incensed at the grinding oppression of foreigners, actuated by sordid motives of gain rather than by love for a country where they came impoverished to seek their fortunes, the mining population of San Tome, etc. . . ." and ended with the declaration: "The chief of the State has resolved to exercise to the full his power of clemency. The mine, which by every law, international, human, and divine, reverts now to the Government as national property, shall remain closed till the sword drawn for the sacred defense of liberal principles has accomplished its mission of securing the happiness of our beloved country."
> And for many years this was the last of the San Tome mine. (1904, 76)

The mine again falls into disuse and after a few years it no longer exists; reclaimed first by wild marauders, it has been swallowed up by a wild landscape:

> The buildings had been burnt down, the mining plant had been destroyed, the mining population had disappeared from the neighborhood years and years ago; the very road had vanished under a flood of tropical vegetation as effectually as if swallowed by the sea, and the main gallery had fallen in within a hundred yards from the entrance. It was no longer an abandoned mine; it was a wild, inaccessible and rocky gorge of the sierra, where vestiges of charred timber, some heaps of smashed bricks, and a few shapeless pieces of rusty iron could have been found under the matted mass of thorny creepers covering the ground. (77)

In this state it is deeded over by the corrupt government to Charles Gould's father, who finds himself unable to refuse it as payment for the debts that the government has incurred with him. He is then dunned by that same corrupt government when he does not pay royalties on the nonfunctioning mine. In other words, the indigenous people are ignorant of the wealth of their own land; the Spanish conquerors and their descendants are incapable of making proper use of it once they find it; and in the end the very ownership of the mineral wealth by Englishmen (who are the only ones to make a success of it) is represented as a form of Latin American exploitation of the British.

Charles Gould reopens the mine with the financial backing of an Andrew Carnegie–like magnate in the United States, and the silver is mined and shipped out of Costaguana. The mine's exploitation by the British makes it the basis for a relatively stable and wealthy nation. When the revolution comes, the narrator is sympathetic to neither side, but he reserves his greatest contempt for the corrupt revolutionaries who claim the right to the country's resources. The presumption is that they, like their ancestors, would be unsuitable stewards of their nation's treasure. As Said points out in his discussion of *Heart of Darkness* in *Culture and Imperialism* (1993), Conrad is critical of colonization, but he is unable to see the "natives"—here the criollo descendants of Spanish settlers, as well as mestizos and Indians—as ever being capable of running their own affairs.

The description of Gould's reopening of the mine, and his making a success of it once again, is a paean to British entrepreneurial skill. Overall, the British, encapsulated in the Gould family, behave as great patriots whose reward for fighting in the cause of freedom is death (Charles's uncle was a Federalist governor who was killed by the evil Unitarian dictator), victims of the crafty, corrupt mixed-race Latin Americans who entangle them in disastrous economic schemes, and brilliant engineers, miners, and builders who are responsible for the progress that is made in the Argentina-like nation. Conrad is, of course, hardly sanguine about all his British characters. They can be self-satisfied, petty, arrogant, and dull; but Charles and, even more, his wife Emily remain substantially sympathetic throughout.

Conrad's Charles Gould is no dupe of the Costaguaneros, but his plodding British competence is under threat by what the narrator calls the "political immaturity" of the "natives" who surround him. Although Conrad is ultimately critical of British and American exploitation of South American mineral wealth, he is less disturbed by its colonialist injustice than by the moral damage it does to the colonizers. Conrad ridicules the politicians and revolutionaries who cry for nationalization of the mine, and when they do have control of the mine it falls into ruin. He is sympathetic to the Europeans whose lives are destroyed by it. In the end, the silver that was to save Gould and Sulaco serves to destroy the domestic intimacy between Gould and his wife Emily. It is implicated in the suicide of the intellectual author of Sulaco's independence, Decoud, who weighs himself down with silver ingots so that he will sink into the sea; and it corrupts the heretofore incorruptible title character and precipitates his death.

What is perhaps most striking in Conrad's representation of Costaguana is how closely it follows Sarmiento's civilization/barbarism dichotomy, even though the terms are inverted in Conrad. Sulaco's oligarchic and ultimately separatist Europeans and European-identified "Blancos" are civilized Federalists, fighting the barbarous liberal Unitarians; and the plan to save the region and Gould's mine by secession resonates with Uruguayan history.[8] The racial subtext of "civilization and barbarism" remains intact, however. Textual examples are numerous; one should suffice to give a sense of them. Sulaco's Black and mestizo revolutionaries are described as slovenly, unintelligent, and cruel:

> And first came straggling in through the land gate the armed mob of all colours, complexions, types, and states of raggedness, calling themselves the Sulaco National Guard. . . . Through the middle of the street streamed,

like a torrent of rubbish, a mass of straw hats, ponchos, gun barrels, with an enormous green and yellow flag flapping in their midst, in a cloud of dust, to the furious beating of drums. (Conrad 1904, 276)

The leader of this ragtag army, Pedro Montero, like his brother the general, is described with utter contempt, the justification for which seems to be "the presence of some negro blood" (277).[9] What in another man would be considered accomplishments—refined manners and the ability to speak several languages—are ascribed to an animal-like capacity for simple mimicry, and he is overtly characterized as irrational:

> Pedro was smaller than the general, more delicate altogether, with an ape-like faculty for imitating all the outward signs of refinement and distinction, and with a parrot-like talent for languages. . . . His ability to read did nothing for him but fill his head with absurd visions. His actions were usually determined by motives so improbable in themselves as to escape the penetration of a rational person. (277)

Upon seeing the wreckage his men have made out of the grand government building he has occupied, Pedro announces, "We are not barbarians" (280). The narrator reports this utterance with an irony that makes it clear that the word barbarian describes them quite accurately. The mestizo leader of another political faction is similarly characterized as stupid and savage. The discourse of civilization and barbarism that fuels the narrative resonates with Argentina's national discourse, even though the topography of Costaguana might argue that it is more Chilean than Argentinean, and while Garibaldino's presence in the novel may argue for Uruguay as the prototype for Conrad's imaginary nation.[10]

Virginia Woolf, interested primarily in the emotional lives of her characters, writes a Latin America in *The Voyage Out* that is much more generic than Conrad's. To fulfill the needs of her narrative, the setting need only be faraway, a little tropical, and lax to the point of danger. Unlike Conrad, for whom the problems of imperialism and colonialism drive the narrative, Woolf appears to care little about the imperial project that makes such a place available to Rachel Vinrace, her Aunt Helen, and the other British characters who make the trip with them.[11] Like the adventuresome aunt in India of *A Room of One's Own* who may be imagined to fall off a horse and leave an Englishwoman with the five hundred pounds a year that will afford her the independence she needs to become a writer, the fortuitous existence of a Spanish-speaking British colony in South America may be a simple narrative device. This inno-cent assumption of entitlement is hardly innocent at all, of course, and in fact Woolf herself injects considerable irony into her colonial asides. A close reading of Woolf's *Three Guineas* reveals the writer's deep distrust not only of British patriotic nationalism, but also of the imperialist imperative that is its outgrowth. The conveniently dead aunt in *A Room of One's Own* refracts Woolf's comment on the essentially masculine nature of colonialism in the same essay when the writer claims that "one of the great advantages of being a woman is that one can pass even a very fine negress without wishing to make an Englishwoman of her" (1957, 52). This deeply ironic, but also patently false, assertion does, how-ever, illuminate Woolf's own hands-off treatment of indigenous and mestizo figures in the novel, whose consciousness remains unrepresented, though implied.[12] Woolf writes the colonial other from the outside, narrating only the effect they have on the British characters.

Perhaps as a result, few South Americans inhabit Woolf's South Amer-ica. They are there in the background, visible preparing meals and as the object of a promised journey upriver. The very silence of the Indian women she encounters makes Rachel uneasy, and the Spanish American figures who hover below the level of the plot serve to disturb her. The distressing vision of a cook chopping off a chicken's head returns as part of Rachel's dream of an old woman beheading a man. In another episode, Rachel is angered by the high-handed Englishmen who humil-iate a local prostitute, ejecting her from their hotel.[13] A fantasy of primi-tive and dangerous sexual desire is one of the undercurrents of the novel, making Woolf's South America the site of racialized sexual danger. Celia Marshik (1999) points out that anxiety about forced prostitution pervades *The Voyage Out*, and what was called the "white slave trade," associated with Argentina in the popular imagination, if not overtly in Woolf's novel, was purported to provide light-skinned women to satisfy the voracious sexual appetites of dark-skinned men.[14] We have seen how, even two decades later, Woolf's South America as it emerges in her correspondence with Victoria Ocampo is a collage assembled of previ-ous representations and the writer's own fancy. Mark Wollaeger (2001) presents convincing evidence that when Woolf was writing *The Voyage Out*, her perception of European colonies in Africa and South America was shaped largely by picture postcards.

Conrad, on the other hand, refers to historical figures and actual events, providing a realist setting into which he inserts a fictional country and its inhabitants. In inventing Costaguana, Conrad mixes the salient features of America—jungle, mountains, Indians, revolutions, seacoast, precious metals, maté—and sprinkles Spanish-sounding names and Spanish terms throughout the novel. In creating a generalized Latin American country from the particulars at hand, given his status as a British subject (albeit a Polish one) it is not surprising that Conrad includes Argentine particulars in his Latin American narrative.

These early twentieth-century conceptions of an undifferentiated Latin America easily incorporate Argentina. If Conrad evokes Latin America with a mélange of recognizable elements from all over the continent, Woolf's British resort in Latin America is much more impressionistic in its evocation of the locale. Its primary spaces of interchange are British: the ship that carries its passengers from England proper to an English resort; the path between the hotel where the majority of the characters are vacationing and the private home where the protagonist is staying. Woolf's South American physical geography is deeply literary. The picnic on the mountain is reminiscent of Jane Austen, and the trip upriver into the jungle is derived from Conrad's own *Heart of Darkness*.

In both Woolf and Conrad an undifferentiated Latin America easily encompasses Argentina, Woolf's through its very lack of precision and Conrad's because of that precision. Today, however, according to Hugo Achugar, the North excises the countries of the Río de la Plata from the imagined place that is "Latin America":

From the current standpoint of the countries of the North, "Latin America" cannot be incarnated by the Río de la Plata. Within today's ideological horizon, a cultural representation *(Darstellung)* that includes the Río de la Plata is not possible. The place of "Latin America" in the North's cultural representation has little to do with the representation of the totality or the reality of Latin America; instead, Latin America is the mirror in which the societies of the North contemplate themselves. This gaze simplifies and enables the transfer of the ideological horizon and of the site of reading that reigns in the North. Human rights violations, the phenomena of South-North migration, the problematic of multiculturalism, and the world of drug trafficking make up a scenario in which the promise of riches symbolized by the Río de la Plata has no place; and, instead, the landscape of the deforestation of the Amazon jungle, the

"backyard" threat from Cuba, or from Central American migrants, like
the natural disasters of Central America, or the oppression of the Indians,
act as reaffirmations of the role that Latin America plays in the Western
imaginary, and in particular the Western imaginary that comes from the
North. (2000, 327)[15]

Achugar, writing from the eastern bank of the Río de la Plata in
Uruguay, a country that in fact means little to the European imagination,
is perspicacious, but his analysis does not account for the persistence of
Argentina in the global imaginary despite its bad fit as a "Latin American" nation.[16] Internationally legible signs, including the tango, Eva
Perón, Che Guevara, the Mothers of the Plaza de Mayo, Patagonia, and
the pampas all continue to hold meaning and draw the gaze of Europe
and the United States. The Río de la Plata, as a metonym for Argentina, is
not the powerful symbol it once was, but it remains a living part of the
Western/Northern imaginary. It is a pentimento, its later images superimposed on its earlier ones. Although the Río de la Plata did not lead to
the mineral wealth its name so hopefully held out, in the early decades
of the twentieth century it was still part of the mythology of an America
whose streets were paved with gold. If Achugar means that the idea of
Latin America is now impoverished, that is certainly true. But Argentina
is still part of the imaginary of the West. It persists in the memory, however badly shoehorned into an oversimplified story of Latin America.

CHAPTER FOUR

Europe's Uncanny Other

Argentina, we might say, lives at the tip of the collective unconscious of the North. Its land mass stretches down almost to Antarctica, but even its temperate parts are too far away for everyday travel. It does not have the weighty history of Greece or Rome, or the centuries of exotic kingdoms of China, nor is its capital immediately familiar in the way of New York, Paris, and London. Nevertheless, Argentina is a not entirely blank screen on which European desire and fear are projected. Argentina serves as a familiar other, a foggy mirror to Europeans concerned about their own identity, or avoiding those thoughts, projecting onto Argentina their own fears and desires. Perhaps an even more apt—because more globalized and postmodern—metaphor than the mirror is the karaoke machine. Argentina provides the familiar rhythm, tune, and even lyrics, but the singer, re-creating himself as the star of the show, is free to improvise identity within their constraints.

Graciela Scheines contends that what is special about Europe's attraction to America (which, as we have seen earlier, she conflates with Argentina) is not the appeal of the wholly exotic but rather of the presence in Argentina of something that is recognizably their own:

> The avidity for exoticism in Europeans over the ages that has made Russian, Japanese, Indonesian, or Tahitian objects fashionable is not comparable to Europeans' passion for savage America. In contrast to what fascinates them about other countries and cultures that are equally faraway and different from their own, America always represented a hidden, secret, or lost aspect of themselves (of Europe); their future (America as Utopia) or their past (savage America). (1991, 48)[1]

Scheines implies here that America in general and Argentina in particular have a special meaning for Europe. It is a meaning derived from the sense that Argentina is both like Europe and deeply different from it, a paradox we can understand in light of Freud's theory of the uncanny as that which meshes the familiar with the unknown. The incommensurable two become one, and this union produces a sense of unease and fascination.

Thinking along similar lines, Néstor García Canclini, positing an imaginary contrast between the Latin American anthropologist and the North American cultural studies specialist and posing the question, "Who are our others?" (2000, 31), comes to the conclusion that it is impossible to generalize about either the anthropologist or the cultural studies specialist. Each of them is specifically located, and the differences within Latin America and North America make speaking from either as a monolith intellectually irresponsible. Beyond this recognition that the "other" is as internally fragmented as the self is the realization that the "other" as pure difference is impossible.

Dominique Bona's 1984 novel, *Argentina*, which deals with a French immigrant to Argentina in the 1920s, captures this play between the exotic and the familiar. Buenos Aires is wild and dangerous, primitive but comprehensible insofar as it can be understood with reference to Paris:

> The frenzy of nights in Buenos Aires had given the capital a shocking reputation: its voluptuousness, its parties, its mad escapades, afforded it a power of attraction in the Southern hemisphere comparable to extravagant pre-war Paris. (1986, 69)[2]

Bona's Argentina is, moreover, a profoundly feminized space, complete with woman's stereotypical inconstancy:

> Argentina is a female nation, infatuated, an explosion in a coal mine. She is fickle: *a feminine people.* (43)[3]

I have already discussed briefly how gender difference can serve as a model for other kinds of alterity, that is, how the national, ethnic, or racial other can be symbolically diminished by associating it with femininity and how the modern subject is, conversely, elevated by means of a symbolic association with virile masculinity. The othering accomplished by this process is, however, necessarily incomplete. Man takes woman to be his other precisely because she is also familiar. In her early interrogation of the analogy "woman is to nature as man is to culture," anthropologist Sherry Ortner (1974) discusses the intermediate position that "woman" holds, neither fully within culture nor fully consigned to nature. Woman is, instead, the mediator between the two for "man." She is, in other words, man's uncanny, the same/other in which he finds himself uneasily reflected.

Ortner's insistence on refining the notion of gendered otherness holds, I believe, for the production and functions of alterity more generally. In order for the other to be legible and therefore useful to the subject, it must share some point of contiguity. In each of the texts under discussion in this study, the Argentinean other is a projection, a continuation, or a variation of the self. In the most extreme case, Claudio Magris's *A Different Sea*, Argentine difference is desirable for its very blankness, as an emptiness that offers no distractions to the self-in-making. In that novel, the protagonist, Enrico Mreule, endeavors to empty out his life and finds the ideal place to do so is in what he imagines to be the nowhere of Argentina. He is committed to living the emptied life prescribed by his philosopher-friend, Carlo Michelstaedter, and he finds in Argentina the perfect space of emptiness. For Michelstaedter, the city is the space where the weak come together; the Argentine pampas would seem to afford Mreule a place to grow strong. Enrico and Carlo are trained in German philosophy, in the tradition of Hegel. It is no surprise, then, that Argentina would emerge as the site of nowhere in which to engage in this philosophical experiment of nonbeing. As narrated in *A Different Sea*, Argentina is populated only by the protagonist, a few shadowy and fleeting acquaintances, a handful of gauchos, fleetingly evoked Indians, and occasional prostitutes. Magris's protagonist is a self-involved nihilist whose experiment in utter alienation masquerades as ascetic and aesthetic perfectionism. This, the reader is led to believe, harms no one while he is in the wilds of Argentina, but it has painful consequences to his wife, his tenants, and his mistress once he returns to a Europe that demands a certain level of social conformity even of its eccentrics.

A Different Sea is based on historical characters. The Gorizian poet and philosopher Carlo Michelstaedter did indeed dramatically commit suicide in 1910 after completing his major philosophical work, *Persuasion and Rhetoric*. His friend and former classmate, and protagonist of the novel, Enrico Mreule, did emigrate to Argentina and live there for thirteen years before returning to Gorizia, and later to Umago, where he lived until his death in December 1959. In Magris's fictional account of Mreule's life, in which these and other historical data are dutifully recorded, the Argentine wilderness offers Enrico the space in which he can live out Carlo's vision of the essential life, stripped of all extraneous matter, a life that makes no mark on the landscape. Enrico therefore admires the austerity of the Indians he observes, living in Patagonia and on the pampas, but he regards them as not quite human and therefore unlikely to burden him with the demands of society. (Enrico is, however, puzzled by the behavior of Indian women with whom he has sexual relations. Unlike the criolla prostitutes who are trained to please their customers, the Indian women are interested in their own pleasure, not his. He tends, therefore, to avoid such interactions.)[4] While he is in Argentina, Enrico identifies most closely with the gauchos: like them he drives cattle and lives an austere life. He is wealthy enough to buy and sell cattle as well, but he lives with few possessions, surviving on the simple diet that in the end drives him home to recover from scurvy.

Magris, a native of Trieste and scholar of twentieth-century Central European literature and thought, sets most of his fiction in the territory of Middle Europe, the landscape he knows best. Commenting on his novel *Danubio,* he says:

> Every writer uses settings that are familiar to him. I cannot situate a story in Pescara because I do not know Pescara well; I situate it in Trieste because I am familiar with that world, with those streets, with those buildings—but not in order to describe those streets and buildings. And in the same way, I chose Mitteleuropa as a stage, as a pretext to recount the encounter between one individual and the grotesque nature of contemporary history. (Interview downloaded from Web)

For a writer who is so sensitive to place, perhaps the alternative to writing the utterly familiar landscape is to cast oneself into one that is entirely unfamiliar. Enrico, set down in the bleak Argentinean landscape imposed on Magris by the historical coordinates that provide the framework of the novel, finds an apt model in the figure of the lonely gaucho. Back home his stories of Argentina are less about his own life there than a recycling of the already-available narratives. He entertains people with after-dinner stories of Patagonia, a place he knows only through the stories told by other European writers:

He condescends to talk about Patagonia only when they really beg him. Collecting his thoughts for a moment he begins to speak, with inspired mien and furrowed brow, softly clicking his tongue. The ocean breakers boom like big guns against the isles of the coast of Desolation. Battalions of birds of prey the size of geese plunge from the craggy heights, the *guanayes* screech deafeningly. Whales beach on the rocks, their gaping maws big enough to swallow boats; throngs of scarlet-headed vultures flap into the air and obscure the sky. Patagonian hunters club to death condors gorged, till incapable of flight, on sheep carcasses left as bait. Guanaco they capture by enmeshing their legs with *boleadoras*. Araucanian Indians, with strangely gleaming eyes, are quite untamable.

The ladies listen, giggling, as he describes the Indian women. But no one is more amazed than he to hear the passion in his voice. All this has nothing to do with his cabin, his horses, or his cows. He is telling stories about things he has never seen and never experienced, just read about in novels—by Salgari and Karl May. He never even went as far south as the tip of Patagonia. But he has no choice. Words can only echo words, not life itself. And his life has been colourless, like water. Yet, just occasionally, one must try to be good company. (Magris 1993, 64–65)[5]

Enrico's appropriation of a fictional America written by Europeans in order to represent it in a comprehensible and entertaining way to other Europeans suggests not only that Enrico is a less-than-reliable narrator, but also that Argentina, as a European concept, is malleable. Moreover, part of the reason Argentina retains its usefulness to Europe and the United States as a screen on which to project both themselves and the other is that Argentina's meanings internally are flexible as well. As Nicolas Shumway argues, for example, the emblematic figure of the gaucho is not simply conscripted in Argentina to serve a single version of the national project. Shumway points out that two ideological currents, one that champions populism and the other that "parodies . . . gaucho speech and rural backwardness" (1991, 68), run through gauchesque literature. The gauchesque invents the figure of the gaucho as much as it derives from it. The gauchesque's literary and political significance as described by Shumway, as well as by Josefina Ludmer (1988), offers a clear and bounded example of a basic presupposition of this book: that literary texts create and perpetuate ideas about nations, ideas that then circulate in and beyond those nations.[6]

Whereas most Argentine thought on the gaucho is inwardly focused, regarding the gaucho either as a self-generated symbol of the best of the Argentine character or as the country bumpkin who is best kept in his place, Graciela Scheines, ever pessimistic about the capacity of the Argentine intelligentsia to think for itself, looks outside Argentina to explain the importance of the gaucho in the Argentine national mythology. She argues that the return to the true Argentineity of the gaucho and the gauchesque proposed by Argentine nationalists is a reflection of the prestige of American noble savagery in Europe (1991, 48). Certainly Magris's Mreule sees the gaucho this way, improving on the austere gaucho life only with the addition of his small library of classical literature and philosophy. The meaning of the gaucho is contested, flexible, and available for multiple purposes, but the figure always retains its connection to the land and his fierce hold on masculinity.[7]

The gaucho remains a potent symbol of Latin American masculinity and of an earthy, elemental freedom that is deployed beyond the borders of Argentina. Miriam Gárate (2000), implicitly protesting Argentine hegemony in matters gauchesque, reclaims the gaucho's Uruguayan origins. She thereby lays claim to a potent symbol of masculinity for a country whose claim to urbane political sophistication as the Switzerland of Europe dissolved in the caustic lye of a military junta in the 1980s. Others merely exploit the gaucho figure and its virile and potent masculinity for commercial purposes. A billboard advertising campaign that ran in Spain in 2001, for a Venezuelan rum called "Pampero," divides the visual image in half horizontally: the top half in black and white representing the buttoned-down urban man from the waist up, in one case carrying what look like rolled-up architectural or engineering plans, in another in a library setting, looking at a book with a woman; the bottom half, the same figures from the waist down, in yellow and red tones, in the first running on the beach in shorts, the second dancing in a discotheque. The freedom of Pampero rum, whose heraldic trademark is a gaucho on a rampant horse, promises to reconnect the civilized, intellectual man, whose intent expression suggests he spends a lot of time thinking and whose head is the focal point of the half-image, with his libidinal self, a figure we see only from below the waist. The promise of a generalized freedom for the architect or engineer in the first image becomes the prospect of sexual freedom for the bookish couple in the second. The advertising campaign's slogan, "tu Yo latino" (your Latin self), has Freudian overtones, although it is the ego rather than the libido that the text, unlike the image, addresses. The pampero, the cold southwest wind of the pampas, may seem an unlikely symbol for a Caribbean product, but the generalized Latin American claim to unfettered masculinity that the gaucho figure provides overrides the geographical imprecision of the emblem.

Argentina generates and encourages others' imagining of it, since such imagining is a central component of the nation's vision of itself. Argentina's cosmopolitan center—its analogue to New York, or Paris—Buenos Aires, also invents itself in relation to other capitals. Moreover, its elite longs for the mind of the North to know it so that it may know itself. In its desire to play with the big kids, Buenos Aires often surpasses them in what it is that marks them: sophistication, style, elegance, wit, culture. It is by no means a mere copy. Still, the unique and always-changing self that it is, is a self-in-relation: in relation to Europe, which it has emulated, in relation to the United States, in relation to the rest of Latin America, in relation to the rest of the nation. For the Porteño elite, what others have to say about their country, and the fact that others see it, is critical. This vision ratifies Argentina's existence. No longer a colony, it still requires the gaze of the former colonial or neocolonial power. Yet the desire to be acknowledged by the powerful other and thereby be made real to itself is not the only story. Argentina projects its desired version of itself outward, hoping to recoup that version when it is reflected back in the eyes—and words and images—from elsewhere. To the extent that all identity (personal, national, racial, religious, ethnic) is relational, there is nothing exceptional about Argentina. What makes it stand out is the explicit desire to be seen and acknowledged, reflected in the histori-cal obsession with national identity among Argentine thinkers, writers, and social critics.

Scheines argues that Argentina passively accepts and willingly feeds Europe's images of it, and that these images, which predate Columbus, constitute a prophetic myth of America that Argentina is only too happy to fulfill.[8] "Paradise, utopia, savagery. The three images are European visions of South America that we, the South Americans, receive, accept, and feed" (1991, 72).[9] Scheines contends that Argentina receives, accepts, and feeds Europe's version of it in a process that nourishes Europe but, for the most part, diminishes Argentina:

> [T]he man of civilization, the European, feels himself to be a stranger
> in the American paradise, intuited as the antiworld where he cannot

establish residency. As a stranger in paradise he assumes diverse attitudes: He plunders it and returns to his distant country, he walks it and travels it with his eyes, dumbfounded because everything astonishes him, he celebrates it, or he becomes annihilated in its geography. (72–73)[10]

These words resonate with the expectations and behavior of Magris's Enrico Mreule, who seeks alienation from human society that an evacuated Argentina provides. *A Different Sea* narrativizes, even as it exaggerates, the European penchant to empty out Argentina. Enrico, who lives meagerly, does not plunder the Argentine landscape in any material way. Instead, he engages in an imaginative erasure of the native (both indigenous and criollo) and usurps the now-bleak landscape for his own philosophical purposes.

In contrast to Magris, who colludes with his protagonist in the evacuating of life and self-generated meaning from Patagonia, the Argentine novelist Sylvia Iparraguirre heads even further south to affirm a presence that the Argentine metropole, no less Europe, has disregarded in its accounts. Her novel *La Tierra del Fuego* is based on the experiences of a Yamana Indian, renamed Jemmy Button by his British captors, who was brought to London in the middle of the nineteenth century as an experiment in the power of Britain's civilizing influence, and also as a money-making venture.[11] The narrator, Jack Mallory, tells us that the young Yamana man, when first confronted with a mirror, is surprised and a little afraid, but soon learns to consult it regularly. This brief anecdote resonates with the trope of the mirror and the famously Argentine penchant for self-reflection and introspection. The reflection of (and on) the self is made possible by the technology of the other, who is colonizer, kidnapper, and enemy, raising such questions as, What made Argentina turn its gaze toward its own reflection in the mirror? What does it mean that the technologies of reflection were those of the other? What is this mirror that reflects both what Argentina itself projects and what others say about Argentina?

La Tierra del Fuego illustrates the unequal quality of mutual othering, in this case as it occurs between the British and the indigenous Yamana of Patagonia, whom the former capture and take to England as part of the imperial project of staking claim to the commercially strategic Cape Horn, the southern tip of South America. Iparraguirre also rehearses the internal differences within Europe's other. The Yamana Jemmy Button is captured, dressed in English clothing, renamed, taken to England as a curiosity, taught English, and catechized. When his people are very nearly destroyed by the rapaciousness of the British settlers and he participates in an uprising against the invaders, he is tried by a British court. Although he has far more knowledge of the British than they have of him, and although he and his fellow Yamana have crafted their own narratives concerning the British, only the British have the power to act upon their stories. When the Yamana attempt to seize that power, they are treated to dreadful brutality.

Moreover, the British assume that Jack, of British and Argentine criollo parentage, who speaks English as well as Spanish, and who has learned to read from English books (England is everywhere, says the captain approvingly), will inevitably choose British loyalties.[12] Instead, Jack enters into a friendship with the indigenous other, without claiming a cultural or ethnic connection to his companion. Jack is Argentine as the Argentine elite would have him: the literate son of a British immigrant and a criolla woman. But Jack's illegitimacy places him beyond the pale of the criollo elite, and his befriending Jemmy Button would be as incomprehensible to his Buenos Aires relatives as it is to the British. The complexity of the other, when the other is multiply placed and makes claims to territory and nationality that are internally conflictive, suggests that there is no easy way to think about Europe and its others. For those others—Asia, Africa, Latin America—are not only different from each other, but are rife with differences within, as has been amply demonstrated by the ethnic, class, race, and religious fissures that have made the process of decolonization so painful.

None of the main characters is unproblematically Argentine in Iparraguirre's text. Jemmy Button, the indigenous man, is no more naturally Argentine than is Jack, who, as the son of an Englishman and an Argentinean criolla woman, chooses his Argentine nationality. Yet because Jack is illegitimate, his mother's parents would not have been happy to welcome him into the (national) family. There are no "natural" Argentines in this novel, unless they are the minor, women characters: Jack's mother and his mistress. This is not chance; women as both mothers and lovers are typically the transmitters of national and cultural belonging.[13]

The other is not only incompletely and insufficiently different from the point of view of the self; s/he is also internally fragmented. Jemmy

Button, whose ancestral ties to the land long predate European claims to it, is for that very reason not an acceptable representative of Argentineity in the eyes of the nation's elite. We might recall here the experience of visitors to the Argentine pavilion at the Paris world fair, which took place not long after the events in this novel. They, too, sought evidence of an indigenous presence in Argentina that the Argentine planners strove to deny. Argentina claims its identity both against and through Europe; a "pure" Yamana would not fit the second criterion. On the other hand, Jack is excluded from the circles of the criollo elite not because he has the wrong parentage, but because his parents were insufficiently observant of the social rules concerning reproduction.

La Tierra del Fuego is a straightforward historical novel, without much resonance in the Argentine literary canon, not only because it is so recent, but also because of its subject matter. Nevertheless, it captures and reflects upon the cultural and historical complexity of otherness within and between Argentina and Europe in ways that seem quite beyond (because of scant interest to) Conrad, Woolf, and Magris. Iparraguirre writes about the disastrous consequences of othering for the colonized in the context of the relations of domination of imperialism and colonialism. Her British characters try to construct an Englishman out of the raw material of the Yamana. They see their failure to do so as a flaw in the indigenous man rather than in their own inability to comprehend his worldview. The Englishmen who populate Iparraguirre's novel persist in their desire for the exotic Fuegian native as the other who, once he is exposed to the self-evidently superior ways of England, can be re-created as British. Button is the quintessentially uncanny figure: different enough to warrant a complete makeover, same enough to be presumed capable of standing trial in a British court. He elicits desire and fear, and in the end is contained and repressed for his refusal to accede to the norms of the powerful dominant subject. Argentina's self-placement in the role of Europe's uncanny other carries with it the danger that the powerful center will continue to attempt to engulf it, make it its diminished same. Jemmy Button refuses that destiny, but Jack Mallory might still be seduced into giving up his own illegitimacy in favor of stepchild status.[14]

Iparraguirre's Patagonia is not only populated, it is the home of a treasured culture that is endangered by European rapaciousness and ignorance. In contrast, the impression that Patagonia and, even more,

Tierra del Fuego are empty spaces ripe for filling with European fantasy is evident in more than one European text. In Eva Hoffman's *Lost in Translation*, the child Ewa and her friend Marek fantasize travel to exotic places by invoking place names as magic words to transport them out of their ordinary lives in Cracow. Ewa and Marek re-create this childhood game when they meet again as adults, having emigrated, he to Israel and she to Canada and then to the United States. Hoffman's book is about displacement, and she trolls the depths of difference between North America and her native Poland. The eastern European Jew's sense of her own otherness pervades this text, as does the strangeness she encounters in the places she comes to live. These places, however, become real to her and, in time, even (if partially) familiar and comfortable. Some places, though, are forever magically other, and Marek's invocation of "the talismanic words: Tahiti; Patagonia; Madagascar" name them as such (Hoffman 1989, 228). The islands of the South Pacific and Africa, and the end-of-the-earth Patagonia, are the absolute other, the "faraway places" that must ever remain so.

Similarly, Georges Perec's hybrid text, *W, or the Memory of Childhood*, contains the narrative of a child's imaginary voyage to an island located in Tierra del Fuego and life as he imagines it to be there. For Perec, Tierra del Fuego is no more or less than a signifier for the farthest reaches— perhaps even the end—of the world. His narrator, who in the realist chapters of this memoir/novel is trying to piece together his memories of a Jewish childhood in Nazi-occupied France, invents the Fuegian island as a correlative for the Fascist state and its death camps. In her study of *W*, Elaine Marks points out that the actual description of the deportation to and subsequent death in Auschwitz of the boy's Polish-born mother is told in a spare, straightforward manner, in a total of four pages, ending with the words. "She saw her native land before she died. She died without understanding" (Perec, cited in Marks 1996, 122).[15] The mother's native Poland is transformed into Auschwitz, a place beyond understanding. The son's detailed invention of a remote island society in the imaginary space of Tierra del Fuego, whose murderous rules slowly come to light, is an attempt to make sense of the incomprehensible.

For Perec and Hoffman, both Holocaust survivors, the far-end-of-the-world version of Argentina is related to a sense of their own marginality. In fact, neither actually names the more familiar, European space of "Argentina" in their texts. The Polish-French writer's Tierra del

Fuego is the most desolate and remote part of the earth imaginable, and the Polish-American writer's Patagonia is a talisman of the exotic.[16]

Similarly, in his short story "The Tumblers," Nathan Englander uses Argentina as an anchor to establish the reach of his narrative into the far-flung Diaspora:

> In the Fulton Street Fish Market the dockworkers laughed with Yiddish good humor upon hearing how Gronam had tried to drown a carp. At a dairy restaurant in Buenos Aires, a customer was overcome with hiccups as his waiter recounted the events of the great sour cream shortage, explaining how Gronam had declared that water was sour cream and sour cream water, single-handedly saving the Feast of Weeks from complete and total ruin. (1999, 27)

Here Buenos Aires is a recognizably Jewish location, connected by the familiar narrative of the fools of Chelm to other Jewish sites.

Argentina is the familiar exotic, associated with distance and journeys of Diaspora, and with the mysterious artist. Paul Auster's Chaplin-like Hector Mann (né Chaim Mandelbaum) in *The Book of Illusions* was, it is suggested, born while his Galician Jewish parents were on board a Dutch ship bound for Argentina. Argentina is the probable original destination of this character, who, purported to be one of the great silent-screen comedians, chose to destroy his few works—all masterpieces. Argentina is, here, the familiar exotic, a perhaps never-reached place, but one that is on the map of the Jewish Diaspora.

In contrast, for Spanish writers in the first half of the twentieth century, Argentina is more than the uncanny other, it is the former colony that represents Spain's own future. In her analysis of Latin America in the Spanish imaginary, Nuria Tabanera García argues that Argentina held a special place in the discourse of America as what she calls Spain's "compensatory myth."[17] Spanish national identity, she argues, is wrapped up in its colonial adventures: "America has always been present in Spanish thought as an extension of its own national identity or its own national project" (1997, unpaginated).[18] Despite the political loss of the colonies, devastating to Spain's sense of importance in the world, the fact of a shared language and history gave Spanish thinkers such as Miguel de Unamuno, José Ortega y Gasset, and María de Maeztu, different as they were in their political positions and approach to the world, a way of projecting Spain into the future via its link to America in general and Argentina in particular. Moreover, those whose goal it was to regenerate

Spain looked to America, and especially to Argentina, for a model of modernization. Tabanera García cites González Posada, who in 1910 visited Argentina and noted the intricate weave of Argentine/Spanish identity:

> The Spaniard who dives into and swims in Argentine waters experiences the utter sensation that it is only then that he fully and entirely sees a Spain with a future, like the Argentine who sees, from Spain, an Argentina with a marvelous history. (1997, unpaginated)[19]

The Spanish novelist Vicente Blasco Ibáñez, who drew on his travels to Argentina in some of his writing, describes that nation as a very real place, where he tried to make his fortune but failed. As Gutiérrez and Sánchez note:

> After writing "Argentina and its Greatness" in 1910, he dedicated all his effort to these projects, in which America was no longer just a symbol, an allusion, or a background, but rather a direct presence and a stage. (1995, 118)[20]

For Spain, Argentina is not only an effect of discourse. Two very different Spanish writers, Azorín and Carmen Nestares, one writing at the beginning of the twentieth century and the other at the beginning of the twenty-first, assimilate a more material Argentina to the Europe of their respective eras. In her 2001 novel, *Venus en Buenos Aires,* Nestares first links Argentina to Spain via the Internet: her twenty-three-year-old Spanish protagonist, Cristina, falls in love with an Argentine woman in a chat room that could have connected her to virtually anywhere on the globe. When Cristina and her mother, accompanied by a family friend, travel to Buenos Aires, ostensibly so that Cristina can undergo plastic surgery, the virtual connection becomes real. Argentina, as wealthy Spanish women know, is replete with excellent plastic surgeons; Cristina easily convinces her mother that they should make the trip. There are vestiges of Argentina as cliché in this novel: Cristina invokes the tango to explain the melodrama of Argentine life; but for the most part, Argentina is just a plane ride, a phone call, or an Internet connection away from Madrid. Nevertheless, Cristina experiences Buenos Aires differently from the two older women. Her Buenos Aires is familiar: at first the streets remind her of the Paseo de la Castellana and the Gran Vía, emblematic thoroughfares of the Spanish capital; later she frequents the cafés of the anodyne Puerto Madero, distinguishable from their counterparts in upscale Madrid only by their location near the Río de la Plata. Cristina's Argentina becomes ever more grounded and familiar as she deepens her relationship to her Porteña lover. In contrast, as her mother's suspicion that Cristina is involved with a lesbian grows stronger, her Buenos Aires becomes darker, more dangerous, and more the spectral other of an overwrought imagination. Argentina remains available as a site of dangerous alterity to the homophobic older generation, who displace the threat of homosexuality onto the questionable space of an unstable, corrupt nation in which familiar social boundaries are breached and unimaginable dangers lurk.

The upper-class Spanish characters in Nestares's lesbian coming-out novel experience Buenos Aires as like Madrid, only dirtier and more dangerous. Cristina, the young protagonist who discovers her desire for another woman in an Internet chat room, finds Argentina interesting only because the woman with whom she has fallen in love lives there. The nation's recent political and economic crises are simply boring, and the Dirty War is long past. For the Madrileño upper class, Argentina is a good place to go for plastic surgery—Cristina's unfortunate harelip is the excuse she gives her parents for the journey. A privileged child of the globalized age, Cristina experiences Buenos Aires as familiarly other, the place where she can express her newly discovered sexuality. Her parents, on the other hand, are horrified by the idea that she might be a lesbian, and they struggle to remove her from what they perceive as the space of danger. For them, the sexually unthinkable cannot happen in the normality of Spain, among Spaniards. For Cristina's parents, "the words Buenos Aires are not a synonym for a city or a climate, but for aberration and immorality."[21]

Almost eighty years earlier, and with a far more chaste vision, Azorín imagines an Argentina that is connected to Europe through visual representation, architecture, and a history of migration. In his 1925 novel, *Doña Inés*, the title character recovers from a broken heart by leaving behind all that is known to her to settle in Argentina. Like Nestares's Cristina, however, Inés does not go to a mysterious, blank nowhere. The school she founds for poor Spanish children is on the land where the man she loves, the son of Spanish immigrants, spent his late childhood and adolescence. It is located on a liminal site, just where the pampas meet the capital, a site of possibility and transformation. Like other liminal spaces, it is both outside of conventional temporality and the space in which the passage of time is marked.

Inés is first associated with Buenos Aires and its surroundings through an old lithograph hanging in a room in which she spends much time, and which she regularly contemplates. It is, in the way of all visual representations, an image of a particular time as well as a specific place. Azorín notes the passage of time in the yellowing of the image:

> Whenever Doña Inés goes into the room, her eyes come to rest on the print hanging on the wall. The lithograph is inseparable from her lingering moments in the house. Time passes, not a sound is heard. Nothing disturbs the calm of the room. The lady's glance falls upon the yellowed lithograph. In our day-to-day lives, our spirit, without our knowing why, fastens onto one of the many objects that surround us. Fate, even though we do not wish it, binds us to some piece of furniture or knickknack of the many that surround us; they, inert, are stronger than we are in our mobility. . . . And always, deliberately or not, as an imperative born of the eternal and past shapelessness, our glance will infallibly light on the object that holds us. Doña Inés, in the little room, contemplates the yellowed lithograph; for the hundredth time she reads the heading: *Argentine Confederation,* and below, *Bird's Eye View of Buenos Aires.* (1925, 75–76)[22]

Azorín links this visual representation, made in France, with Doña Inés's fate; and sure enough, past the end of the novel, in a long-promised epilogue, she is an old woman, surrounded by the latest generation of Spanish schoolchildren in Argentina, under the sign of the ombú tree: "Yes, *this* is the epilogue. Where is our ombú? With the eyes of desire, the ones that show us the most, we see it on the infinite horizon" (219).[23] Doña Inés ends her life in Argentina; the Spaniard sees its symbol, the ombú, through the eyes of desire.

Like Enrico Mreule in *A Different Sea,* Doña Inés strips away all that is valuable to her, all that ties her to her home and society, to find an essential self. There is a crucial and deeply gendered difference between these characters, however. The script for living that Mreule follows was written by his friend, a nihilist philosopher who, before killing himself, wrote a treatise in which he argued that man can achieve his authenticity through extreme separation and individuation. The result, as Mreule lives it out, involves a whittling away of responsibility toward others and developing an utter egocentricity. (Part of the reason Enrico leaves home, after all, is a prosaic desire to escape the draft.) In contrast, Azorín tells the story of spiritual divestiture in the feminine mode, in which the culture itself has written the script of female self-effacement. In a spirit of self-sacrifice, the protagonist rids herself of her belongings and her desires not for her own good, but for the happiness of others. Inés's beatific end, surrounded by the children she has taken in, contrasts starkly with Mreule's, which is self-gratifying and oblivious of the needs of others. Both take Argentina as the site of this process of self-discovery and self-fulfillment, but whereas Magris's protagonist goes to the pampas because they are bereft of history, Azorín's heroine goes to a landscape that is part of Spanish history and has a pan-Hispanic future.

Doña Inés ends in an Argentina that takes over after Europe has run its course. If Inés has given up one traditional happy ending in the Western repertoire of women's stories by renouncing love and family, she attains an alternative one via a self-sacrifice that unites the usually irreconcilable ideals of virginity and maternity. She forfeits the biological reproduction of motherhood in favor of the social reproduction of nurturing and educating the children of immigrants for the new society. Inés does not come to an Argentina that is nowhere, but to one that has the heft of history as well as the weight of a future. Azorín foresees an Argentina in which the pampas and the city will inevitably collide, and his feminized version of the injunction to leave the known world for the new world recognizes not only the relationality underlying the decision to abandon all that is known for someplace new, but also the crucial role that Inés's social reproduction plays. Inés's choice of Argentina is overdetermined: the daguerreotype of her youth made its way into her consciousness even before she fell in love with a man who grew up on the pampas and became a poet there.

Both Azorín's Inés and Magris's Mreule leave home impelled by love, in Mreule's case for his philosopher friend, and in Inés's for the poet Diego, the son of Spanish emigrants to Argentina. However, Mreule chooses the timeless pampas because they are completely unconnected to European reality, whereas Inés chooses the border between the pampas and the city, a site filled with both national history and the past of her beloved Diego. To stress the connections between Spain and Argentina, and between Inés's present and her past, Azorín lingers on a description of the wall of the school built by Inés on the site of the ranch where

Diego lived as a child, and which in turn is reminiscent of a Spanish wall that has long since disappeared.

> The old ranch that rose across from the ombú tree has disappeared. Many years have passed. . . . From a distance, the sun kisses the white walls of another ranch. . . . Often have we seen this low, white wall in Spain, and these green vine tendrils alongside a window. Just as the other ranch has disappeared, so too shall this one. The material image of old and far-off Spain is breaking into pieces; a new and powerful way is laboring to be born. (1925, 219–20)[24]

This Argentina is not frozen in time; it is part of a historical process that encompasses continuity and change. Although the material promise of Argentina was a disappointment—Diego's parents died there, and Inés's students are children of other Spaniards who have failed to "make America"—the spiritual promise still may succeed. Diego became a poet, and there is hope for a new poet like him, being nurtured by the ombú.

The level of reality that Argentina represents in the texts discussed in this chapter responds largely to the extent to which Argentina, or a generalized Latin America into which it is collapsed, impinges on the material reality of the cultures to which their authors belong. At one end of the spectrum, Spain's connection with Argentina as part of its empire, and later as a destination for immigrants and political exiles, has kept Argentina grounded in material reality in the Spanish field of vision. In the past quarter century, for example, Spain has renewed its relationship with its former backwater colony as one of the most favored places for political exiles (and economic refugees), one of whom plays a key role in Laura Freixas's 2005 novel, *Amor o lo que sea* (Love, or whatever). Leonardo, an opportunistic forty-year-old Argentine exile living in France, comes to Barcelona, where he seduces an impressionable young publisher's assistant appropriately named Blanca. An easy target and a blank slate, Blanca desires in Leo all the romance and tragedy of exile:

> Leo came from the world in which fire burns, water drenches, knives cut, and bullets kill. Loving him, I loved that other world, where things were real: exile, death, the struggle to live. (Freixas 2005, 83)[25]

Blanca is smart enough to recognize that Leo's homeland is, for her, a product of a collection of cultural representations that allow her to create it in her imagination:

I didn't know Buenos Aires, but through books, records, movies, and
newspapers I imagined it: a multicolored, urgent city, filled with nooks
and crannies and surprises. Turks, Spaniards, Sicilians, Poles, Slovenians.
Rich people with estates in the Tigre Delta and poor devils who spoke
Yiddish and went hungry. A city of intense, anxious, histrionic, talkative,
cultured, entertaining, unbearable people. A great city with a noble
cemetery, English tea parlors, decrepit mansions, a Russian church with
blue domes, and a Japanese garden. (80–81)[26]

Blanca's knowledge of Buenos Aires may be indirect, the result of representations, but it is exhaustive. Moreover, it is the product of a variety
of registers: not just films and records, but books and newspapers. Her
detailed musings on Buenos Aires and its immigrant cultures serve to
situate Leo, in whom she invests her own nascent identity. As she reads
biography after biography in which literary women are overshadowed
by the men in their lives, Blanca seems unable to avoid repeating the
familiar story in her love affair with Leo, trying to invent herself in relationship to him. The Argentina that Leo represents in this novel may be
"other," but it, through him, is an other that exudes its own subjectivity.
In the cross-play of experience, gender, and identity, the still-unformed
European woman, despite being the narrative center and in possession
of the first-person voice in this novel, acquiesces to her own subservience
in relation to her powerful male Argentine lover. On the level of the
narrative, then, Freixas questions the discourse of Argentine subordination so familiar in European-authored texts. However, by skillfully conveying Leo's unprepossessing physical appearance, manipulativeness,
hypocrisy, and selfishness, Freixas reinforces the familiar negative stereotype of the egocentric Argentine.

As Spaniards, Azorín, Vicente Blasco Ibáñez, Laura Freixas, Carmen
Nestares, and Antonio Muñoz Molina (whose novel *Carlota Fainberg*
will be considered in a subsequent chapter) live in a nation whose history has long been enmeshed with Argentina's and who imagine a contemporary Argentina. Azorín, who begins his novel in the mid-nineteenth
century but ends it more or less contemporaneously, reflects the Spanish
national angst of his own era concerning the very future of Hispanicity.
In contrast, Central Europeans writing late in the twentieth century set
their narratives decades earlier in an Argentina devoid of history, as if
the distance in time reinforced the distance in space and both blurred
any local reality. Georges Perec, the son of Polish Jews living in France, for

whom memory and its distortions of time, space, and events are at the core of his writing, re-creates the horror of the concentration camps out of a remote, barren, and empty Tierra del Fuego. Eva Hoffman, also an expatriate Polish Jew, marks distance and the exotic with an emptied-out Patagonia whose purpose is to remain both distant and empty. Claudio Magris's Patagonia is also an empty space, but in his case it is the site of living-in-emptiness.

As seen through the eyes of the British writers discussed in chapter 3, Argentina emerges from the experience of England's own industrial revolution and colonial expansion as a busily occupied place. Christie, Woolf, Conrad, and Wilde, who wrote at a time when their country encouraged commerce with Argentina, comment on the extraction of Latin American mineral wealth, middle-class travel to colonized sites, the building of bridges and railroads, and the ranching of cattle, as well as on a political ineptitude and corruption that indirectly justifies perpetuating the status of their own colonies. Dominique Bona, writing in France in the 1980s, situates her novel in a geography of the past, writing nostalgically about French immigrants in search of individual advancement who encounter a pan-European society in 1920s Argentina. All these writers invent an Argentina that responds to their own desire, and all find there an uncanny other that lays bare something of the self.

CHAPTER FIVE

Victoria Ocampo and the Keyserling Effect

Tierra del Fuego was probably as exotic to Victoria Ocampo as it was to the eastern European Jews who imagined it from Poland. Her Argentina, the one she proffered to numerous foreign writers, was most decidedly the urbane world of Buenos Aires and the grand country houses of its wealthiest families. Ocampo and her literary magazine *Sur* were, for good or ill, and probably for both, critical players in the development of Argentina in the consciousness of the creators of European high modernism. Ocampo began her travels in Europe as a girl, and with each return to Europe as an adult she brought back with her more and more of its culture (to say nothing of the men who made that culture). To its critics, *Sur* stands for Argentinean subservience to European cultural norms; and Ocampo's oligarchic sense of entitlement and privilege, mixed with her feminist sense of the injustice with which the world treats women, including Ocampo herself, have made her an easy target. Nevertheless, Victoria Ocampo must be acknowledged as a pivotal figure in the construction of Argentina in the global imaginary.

The foreigners who came to visit Argentina at Ocampo's invitation also traveled, lectured, and wrote for *Sur*. They thereby influenced Argentina's own sense of its national character when they reflected back on the Argentina they came to know in part through their generous hostess. The Indian poet Rabindranath Tagore, whose heart was set on visiting the Andean nations he thought of as the authentic Latin America, instead fell ill and spent his entire 1924 stay on the continent as Ocampo's guest in a villa she outfitted according to what she knew of her guest's tastes, sensibility, and needs.[1] Despite Tagore's disappointment in not getting to see Peru and Ecuador, and his disapproval of Argentina's Europhilia, his visit was a success. Tagore's poetry gained a following in Argentina that still persists, and he and Ocampo developed a great friendship. When Tagore returned to India, Ocampo was left well disposed to offer her hospitality to other foreigners whose work she held in high regard. She thus eagerly tendered an invitation to Count Hermann Keyserling, whose writing, like Tagore's, she greatly admired.

Among the writers Ocampo introduced to Argentina, Keyserling, who inherited his Estonian title pretty much just in time for it to become a casualty of the Russian revolution, had to be one of the oddest. Proud of the fact that his ancestors had hired Kant to teach their children, engaged Bach to compose music for them, and hobnobbed with Bismarck, after the events of 1917 Keyserling himself was left with little more to live on than his ego and his sense of entitlement. He spent most of his life in Darmstadt, Germany, where in 1920 he founded his School of Wisdom. This school, still in operation, claims to promote the idea of a world culture and the belief that all spiritual traditions are equally valid, an idea that probably was the source of Keyserling's eventually running afoul of the Nazis.[2]

Hermann Keyserling's name is no longer familiar to students of philosophy; but in the decades between the two world wars he had a considerable following and was considered by many, including Carl Jung, Paul Tillich, Herman Hesse, and Ocampo's friend Rabindranath Tagore, to be a major philosophical voice. In fact, Keyserling's was one of the "great brains" of the twentieth century to be preserved in a jar in a Swiss museum, until his family thought better of it and had his brain buried with the rest of him in 1996, fifty years after the posthumous mind/body split had been perpetrated on him.

As did so many others, Keyserling first came to the attention of American intellectuals through Victoria Ocampo, who in 1927, after having read and admired several of his books, invited him to Argentina for a lecture tour.[3] She wrote to him praising his thinking; in her own estimation, her tone was that of an adoring acolyte. He responded by requesting instead that she come to Europe and suggested that he might be her guest in a posh hotel, where they could meet frequently to discuss his ideas and writings. Ocampo agreed, and in January 1929 they met outside of Paris. Ocampo acquiesced to most of Keyserling's self-indulgent demands while she hosted him in France. She arranged—and paid for—his stay in Versailles (he deemed Paris to be too noisy and dirty); fed him delicate meals of oysters, caviar, and champagne; and hosted elegant dinner parties for which Keyserling set the strictly formal dress code. What Ocampo did not do was sleep with him, despite his insistence and his expectation that she would do so.

Keyserling's exaltation of intuition over intelligence, which might well be understood as the superiority of good taste and perception over formal schooling, would certainly have appealed to Ocampo. The daughter of a traditional landed nineteenth-century family, Ocampo both lamented her lack of formal education and embraced her own haphazard, idiosyncratic informal learning with governesses and tutors and, later, in her direct experience of the avant garde in her frequent trips to Europe. Keyserling's nonprofessional attitude vis à vis the work of art and the artist is reminiscent of Virginia Woolf's common reader, who eschews formal and university-bred literary criticism in favor of a direct, careful, open, and passionate reading in which the sensibility of the reader and respect for the artist are paramount. Ocampo was, by default, one of Woolf's common readers, an autodidact who once wrote that she could only speak of her preferences, those works of literature or art or music that spoke to her directly. She explains that what drew her to Keyserling's work was his ability to express their shared enthusiasm, bordering on passion, for a wide range of writers and artists, and his ability to articulate what she felt. Keyserling's reversal of the familiar hierarchy of expertise, his interest in a spiritual life untethered to any particular religion, and the passion with which he wrote all drew Ocampo to his work. Moreover, as the incident of the gift of the blue butterflies confirms, she was accustomed to catering to the whims of those she admired. However, as Ocampo learned, Keyserling's tendency to swallow the world whole and incorporate it into his own self-referential way of fashioning reality was far from the humble attitude struck by either Woolf's common reader or her own impresario-cum-hostess role to the artists, writers, and musicians she admired.

Keyserling's belief that intuition is superior to logic probably sealed his fate among the increasingly analytical philosophers of the twentieth century. As it turns out, his own intuition, at least in the case of Argentina, was highly unreliable—but not, unfortunately, without influence. His assertions concerning the primitive nature of South America and the reptilian blind willfulness of Argentina quickly made their way into Argentineans' own discussions of their national character, including the influential Ezequiel Martínez Estrada's, and remained ensconced there for several generations.[4]

Despite the apparent humility of his declaration that his "first words on reaching the Argentine shore were: 'I have come not to teach, but to learn'" (1932, 7), Keyserling articulates his sense of superiority over all Latin America by stating quite baldly that his is a gaze downward, from a greater height (27). This perspective would be available to his ideal reader, who glances down on South America and discerns the single type of man who inhabits the continent:

> The masses of cattle of the pampa can only be understood in terms of the "Yeast of Creation." And the same holds true of the animality of Argentine Man. However much he may differ from the South American of the tropic zone—he is yet a special expression of the general type, so that from a high point of vantage one involuntarily includes in a single glance the Brazilian, the Venezuelan and the Argentine. (27)

This "Argentine man" seen from above is as much like any other South American as one steer grazing on the pampas is like another. The analogy here merely hints at Keyserling's penchant for associating Argentinean culture with the base animal instinct that he attributes as well to the indigenous peoples of the continent. In this pronouncement, he also declares to be true that which most Argentine elite writers on national identity deeply fear: that Argentina is in reality not European. Nevertheless, as Keyserling is so slippery, so disdainful of facts, and ultimately so impervious to the demands of logical thinking (he would certainly characterize my insistence on consistency as a kind of plodding North American literalism, more than a little monstrous in a woman), he also notes that "whatever is really characteristic of the present-day Argentine has, without an exception, been imported" (26).

Because Keyserling's book had such a profound effect on subsequent thinkers and writers on Argentina, it is worth looking at its representation of Argentina with some care. *South American Meditations: On Hell and Heaven in the Soul of Man* was published in 1932. It was quickly translated into English (1932), French (1932), and Spanish (1933). Keyserling himself worked on the English translation; clearly he was concerned that his work be as widely disseminated as possible. Numerous scholars and critics of Argentine social and political thought have noted the extraordinary influence that Keyserling's *South American Meditations* has had in subsequent analyses of, reflections on, and lamentations over Argentina, its purported national character, and its seemingly hopeless pessimism concerning the nation's present and future.[5] Left out of these discussions of Keyserling's pernicious influence on subsequent writing on Argentina's national malaise is any analysis of the content of Keyserling's writing on Latin America as a whole and on Argentina in particular. Much less do they address the extent to which Keyserling relied on an "intuition" that was a product of his own sense of entitlement, his hypochondria, and his wounded ego. Yet in 1951 Victoria Ocampo not only contested the content, but also made it abundantly clear that Keyserling, as his own writings indicate, was much more interested in his own perceptions and his own voice than in assessing anything like an Argentinean material reality.

Why the great minds of the nation fell for Keyserling's delirious writing in the first place, and then repeated and magnified each other's solemn agreement with his pronouncements, is a good question. It is likely that the first round of writers on Argentina were influenced by the *Meditations* when Keyserling was still well known and internationally respected, and that subsequent ones did not go back to the source, instead accepting the reliability of their immediate predecessors' judgment. Those readers who were his contemporaries were, like Keyserling himself, immersed in a culture that did not question women's inferiority to men, a hierarchy of naturally occurring races, and Europe's intrinsic superiority to America. It was this set of beliefs that made the Argentine elite bent on Europeanizing itself in the nineteenth century and on claiming its whiteness through most, if not all, of the twentieth. Keyserling's contention, that despite its refinements Argentina was not only one more nation of savages but the most deeply primitive of all, fed into the elite's most dreadful nightmare. Victoria Ocampo was a daughter of that elite, and she was not exempt from its desires; but she was not about to acquiesce to one man's assertion of the inferiority of her nation, her sex, and her own self. With the sense of entitlement and self-assurance of the oligarchy to which she belonged, Ocampo was not only affronted by her culture's assumptions about women, but sure enough of her own worth to know them to be untrue. She would not so easily consent to another's representation of her as his inferior. As a friend and sometimes patron of European writers and artists, her awe of their genius was tempered by her familiarity with them as people.

Nevertheless, Ocampo did not immediately write her rebuttal to Keyserling. Instead she waited close to thirty years, at which time, thanks to the publication of still another book, she was openly and personally implicated in Keyserling's idiosyncratic and unreliable representation of Argentina. As the individual responsible for bringing Argentina to Keyserling's attention and, eventually, Keyserling to Argentina, it is only fitting that she should have been the one to debunk his treatise. Yet she was neither given much credit for enabling the *South American Meditations* to be written in the first place, nor was her somewhat belated response to Keyserling heeded.[6] Reading Keyserling together with Ocampo allows us to get to the bottom of the count's ruminations on Argentina. To put it much less delicately than Ocampo herself did, Keyserling characterizes all of Argentina as a backward, sexually confused, primitive nation because Victoria Ocampo, who for him embodied that nation, wouldn't go to bed with him.

Keyserling's musings on Argentina and South America may have begun with Ocampo's invitation to him and his encounters with her, but his imagination, ethno- (and ego-)centrism, and even his travels beyond Argentina make it difficult to argue that his experience with Ocampo alone shaped his assessment of the nation and the continent. Still, after reading his reminiscences of Ocampo and her clarification of them, it is also impossible to deny the role Keyserling's interactions with Ocampo played in his reading of Argentina as exemplar of Latin America.

One of Keyserling's pronouncements about Latin America in general, and Argentina in particular, is that it is the land of a kind of petulant willfulness. Ocampo had told him a story of a poor child who refused to act as a golf caddy for her sister Silvina, repeatedly saying he could not do it. When pressed for the reason for his not being able to comply with the request, he said it was because he didn't feel like it ("no le dio la gana"). Ocampo's story was meant to illustrate the independent spirit of Latin Americans no matter their class, although it is even more revealing about the sense of entitlement of the upper class. Silvina Ocampo pretty much ordered the recalcitrant child to pick up her golf bags, and she was very surprised when he declined to oblige her.[7] Keyserling saw his refusal as Silvina may well have—a surprising unwillingness to acquiesce to the whims of one's superiors. When Ocampo rebuffed Keyserling's sexual importuning, he accused her of this same sort of willfulness, calling it by the Spanish term "*gana*" and imputing it to all Latin Americans, especially Argentines. Ocampo explains:

> The fact of my not being of his opinion and not bending to his desires, whatever they might be and in whatever realm, transformed me, in his eyes, from "one of the most spiritual beings he had ever known" (see *America Set Free*) into "the very incarnation of *gana*" (see *A Traveler through Time*). And he turned me into the incarnation, the slave of *gana*, precisely at the moment that I gave irrefutable proof of triumphing over it. (Ocampo 1951, 49–50)[8]

Keyserling devotes an entire chapter of his *South American Meditations* to *gana*, which he variously characterizes as "[an] unconscious elementary force which urges from within, over which consciousness has no control" (1932, 158), "neither will nor impulse nor urge nor yet an inward 'Must,' as we understand those words; it is the elementary linking together of mental image and blind organic urge" (159), "what our earlier meditations called Primordial Life and Netherworld and Blind Urge, as opposed to a life determined or co-determined by Spirit" (160), "essentially aimless and purposeless" (160), "an inarticulate anonymous power" (160) that, as soon as he "reached Buenos Aires . . . bound [him] in a mysterious manner" (160). *Gana* is "the strongest of the strong and the weakest of all that is weak. . . . It lacks all element of imagination" (160). "It acts uniformly and according to routine, as is the case with all expressions of life not ruled by the Spirit. Nevertheless, it is thoroughly unreliable" (175). "Its essence is inertia" (176).

The adjectives that Keyserling associates with *gana*—"unconscious," "elementary," "blind," "organic," "primordial," "aimless," "purposeless," "mysterious," "anonymous," "inarticulate," "unreliable"—are all negatively charged. Their meaning hinges on a fundamental binary opposition in which they are usually implicitly, but sometimes explicitly, contrasted to their positively charged opposites: conscious, complex, insightful, spiritual, advanced, meaningful, purposeful, clear, distinctive, articulate, reliable. *Gana* is "opposed to a life determined or co-determined by Spirit" and is, ultimately, selfish: "Blind Gana cannot look beyond itself. And the more a person is ruled by Gana, the smaller the part the imagination plays within him" (165). Keyserling attributes the qualities of *gana* to an other whose difference is based sometimes on gender (imagination is an essential property of spiritual Man in Keyserling's system) and other times on race, but that often combines the two. For Keyserling, *gana* is the quintessential quality of "Woman": "Primordial woman is almost purely a creature of Gana. Intrinsically passive, she must be seduced or won" (164). Later, he goes on to say, "woman is . . . entirely and completely a creature of Gana" (170). *Gana* in women might be tempered, however, by ethnic differences, where ethnicity is an effect of a greater or lesser degree of civilization. The Argentinean women who are ruled by *gana* are, Keyserling says, "pure primordial types" (165), whereas modern Western woman is "permeated by Spirit" (165)—the supreme quality in Keyserling's system—and "acquires a psychology akin to that of man" (165).

Keyserling's *Meditations* subscribes to an evolutionary model that holds that "primitive" societies such as those he found in South America give insight into the fundamental processes of human psychology and behavior: "The ancestors of all civilized races once were akin to what the South Americans are today. They all began in blindness" (186). Over and over Keyserling stresses South America's primitive nature. He delights in turning negatives into positives (beauty is connected to evil and deceit; ugliness and brutality lie at the root of truth). Correspondingly, the very primitiveness of South America may lead to the salvation of the world: "[P]recisely the lack of intellectuality and the passivity of South America, at this turning point, may have a mission for all mankind" (237).

Keyserling makes use of the science of his day, drawing on it to lend analogical credence to his ruminations:

> If now we survey all first beginnings of history we know of, we realize that all bear a resemblance to South American conditions. The first molecular order was the result of mere specific weight. There was no set purpose apart from the striving for the maintenance and increase of power as such; there was no synthetic vision. Early ages are as full of autonomous kings, as the forest is full of trees. Hence the extreme particularism of all first beginnings, such as one may witness today in the mutual hostilities and contempt of the diverse nations of South America. (200)

This neo-Darwinian thinking depends on an interlocking and mutually reinforcing system of racial, gender, and national hierarchies that Keyserling exploits. He ascribes *gana*, "primordial and essential" (165), to women, indigenous people, Argentina, and South America. "South America is the Gana continent par excellence" (174), he asserts, and being held in thrall to *gana* determines cultural characteristics he ascribes to the continent writ large. "It is on this determination by Gana that rests the notorious passivity of South Americans" (176). *Gana* makes South Americans self-indulgent, undisciplined, inconsistent, without initiative, and impetuous:

> It is a life of complete self-indulgence, lack of discipline, lack of all
> initiative and forethought, and accordingly of all consistency. All activity
> in South America is the result of yielding to inner urge. . . . This sway of
> Gana is the cause of that immense, as it were, suspended monotony of
> the psychic atmosphere of South America. (177–78)

Keyserling repeatedly makes categorical statements that rely on these deeply and stereotypically gendered characteristics in his writing on South America:

> Now in South America the essential passivity and inertia is so great, that
> one is justified in calling life there a mere "Being-lived"; it is not an active
> life. Whatever looks like activity has its roots at the surface, and this is
> why South Americans are generally held to be superficial. Fundamentally,
> they are not superficial at all; but their depths are dumb. Moreover,
> South Americans are unwilling to show their true character, they prefer
> to ape the lives of others. Woman whose life is suffering experience is as
> a type profounder than man who abreacts whatever affects him inwardly
> in outward activity. (185–86)

All South Americans are passive, inert, and dumb; the women are even more so. Presumably it is the men who "prefer to ape the lives of others." The women, deeper because of their "suffering experience," are less likely to make any sort of outward gesture at all. Gendered passivity is related to immanence, an earth-boundedness that Keyserling attributes to Iberian culture, although, distinguishing Spanish *gana* from South American *gana*, he minimizes the Spanish and Portuguese, per se, in his focus on their former colonies. South Americans, now recast as members of the "Iberian sphere of culture" and "Gana-races," take on stereotypically feminine attributes associated with embodiedness, connectedness to the earth, emotion, and reproduction:

> [T]he best proof of our thesis is provided by the nations belonging to
> the Iberian sphere of culture. They are the Gana-races proper, which
> means they are the nearest to Earth. Moreover, since they are earth-bent,

they can have no direct relationship to a Beyond: they experience the Word as Flesh. For this reason, with them the Emotional Order reigns supreme in the purest form existing today. Since they wholeheartedly consent to Earth, Flesh, and blood, all earth-born things can develop in incomparable richness. This manifests itself in the domains of vitality, of sexual potency, as also delicacy of sentiment. But its most impressive manifestations lie in the emotional sphere. Emotionally, the Iberian world is by far the deepest and richest of this age. This is so precisely because the Iberians are earth-bent. It is owing to this quality and not to metaphysical depth, that even to the most modern Iberian, things human mean more than all objective facts. (261–62)

Keyserling here simultaneously valorizes and denigrates South American culture, which he sees as unified and marked by its colonization. These are "the nations belonging to the Iberian sphere of culture." They are "earth-bent," ruled by emotion, and for this reason they can richly develop "all earth-born things," that is, "vitality," "sexual potency," "delicacy of sentiment," and most important, "the emotional sphere." This rich emotional life is not, Keyserling makes clear, a function of "metaphysical depth," which he attributes to himself, but of their "earth-bent" nature. The embedded notions of gender and race hierarchy in this passage are clarified when they are read in conjunction with other passages in which Keyserling overtly associates *gana*, earth, emotion, and sentiment to women (especially to those from South America), and vitality and sexual potency to South American men. These terms are also familiar in other racialized and gendered categorizations: the sexual potency of the men of the African Diaspora, the delicacy of sentiment of the white Victorian woman, the emotional excess of the female hysteric. One could go on. Seldom has the sexually desiring gaze of the colonizer, determined to incorporate the feminine colonized into his own self, been so baldly stated. Ocampo, whose own sense of entitlement was almost as well developed as Keyserling's, was blindsided by the conventional racialized and gendered structure through which Keyserling's Spirit perceived and understood the world.

Because his South America is limited to the countries he visited, Keyserling's South America and his Argentina regularly dissolve into one another.[9] In this he is not unlike such Argentinean theorists as Graciela Scheines, who also tend to conflate the continent and the nation. Insofar as Argentina is, for him, the quintessential South American nation, it is the one most deeply marked by *gana*:

In the Argentine the world of Gana manifests itself more impressively than anywhere on earth, because its intrinsic passivity is concomitant with outward progressiveness, intellectual alertness and great refinement of feeling. This nation lives a primordial life, and yet appears thoroughly modern. (Keyserling 1932, 185)

And because he discovered *gana* in Argentina, the whole continent is, for Keyserling, marked by it. He goes on to link *gana* with suffering and illness, one of the tropes Shumway finds in writing in Argentina on the nation's character. Keyserling writes:

[South America's] absolute surrender of consciousness to Gana [because of its fixation on and in the body] makes of life not only one single suffering experience, it also tends to turn it into a chronic disease. (189)

Keyserling claims a logical jump to a kind of South American obsession with disease, another of his grand generalizations, which he then illustrates, as is his practice in the *Meditations*, with an Argentine example:

Quite logically, disease is taken infinitely seriously in South America. In Buenos Aires, it thereby becomes a means of ascending the social ladder. Four or five influenzas duly advertised in the "Enfermos" [sick people] column of the leading newspaper which everyone reads with the greatest attention and sympathy, suffice to make a person known and to give him access to the first ranks of society. (189–90)

Although Keyserling often goes to great pains to disclaim any judgment of inferiority (his School of Wisdom maintains that all cultures' spiritual systems are of equal value), his utter disdain shimmers on the page. Given his tendency to ascribe his own illnesses to his highly evolved spirituality, the irony of Keyserling's misreading of the cause and effect of illness notices in the Buenos Aires society pages is especially acute.

In the first chapter of the *Meditations*, "The Continent of the Third Day of Creation," Keyserling lays claim to spirit as his central quality, but he is very concerned with his own body, giving much space to his bout of *puna*, or altitude sickness, in Bolivia, and noting its effects on any number of his internal organs. Characteristically, he interprets as a spiritual experience his body's reaction to oxygen deprivation (although he rejects this explanation, instead attributing his symptoms to the "emanations" of "determinate beds of ore," 8):

> During that illness I felt myself to be a part of the Cosmic Process, as
> intimately as the embryo, were it endowed with consciousness, would
> experience itself as an element of a super-individual organic evolution....
> In the melting pot of the puna, the constellation of earthly elements which
> I myself incarnate wrestled with other earthly elements with a power far
> greater than my own. (9)

One of Keyserling's physicians was none other than Carl Jung, who
deeply influenced his thinking. Thus, Keyserling duly notes that no single
individual is likely to embody the undiluted essence of the spirit/mind/
activity of masculinity or the *gana*/body/passivity of femininity. Nevertheless, Keyserling's pronouncements are replete with the hoariest, most
creaking stereotypes linking femininity to racial distinctions and national
character. These preconceived notions were familiar and accepted enough
in his own time, and hardly original with him:

> Indian impassibility is the extreme expression of Gana-life which
> entrenches itself behind nay-saying. The self-indulgence of Argentine
> woman is the original expression of her accepted susceptibility. And
> Original Fear and Original Hunger are the impulses which underlie all
> the phenomena we have considered. Original fear is the basic reason of
> that timidity typical of South America. (190)[10]

It is perhaps not surprising that many of Keyserling's Argentine contemporaries were persuaded by these assertions, since sexism and racism,
clothed in the scientific garb of Darwinian and Jungian language, were
widely embraced by deep-thinking men of the period. That such thinking condemned Argentinean males to a kind of primitive state was, perhaps, unfortunate, but it paid attention to their country even if by naming its inferiority and condemning it to malaise.

Keyserling's preoccupation with his own body, a hypochondria he
ascribes to Argentina, is one manifestation of his egocentrism. Just as he
deftly elevates the nausea and headache of altitude sickness into a spiritual moment for himself, Keyserling adeptly reduces the feminized,
racialized, colonized other to a state in which the higher consciousness
that ever accompanies him cannot find any purchase. In the South American, even the noblest qualities are rooted in the thoughtless muck: generosity is profligacy, and hospitality masks reptilian coldness.

Keyserling's bodily anxiety is intimately connected to his imperious-
ness concerning his own comfort. He expected that anyone who took on

the task of hosting him would cater to his every whim. He was famously officious with his hosts and capricious in his demands; and during the time he was her guest at the Hôtel des Réservoirs in Versailles, Ocampo put up with his behavior. When he came to Argentina, she was less tolerant, and by the time she wrote *El viajero y una de sus sombras,* she allowed her biting irony loose on him. Adrienne Rich, commenting on Virginia Woolf, said that the writer's ironic stance in *A Room of One's Own* undercut the seriousness with which her critique was received, and this may be true of Ocampo's text also.[11] Ocampo often makes us laugh at Keyserling, but the comic/ironic mode she chooses may well make her book seem lighter than its subject matter deserves. Ocampo's light touch is also evident in her autobiography, where she tells of her first encounter with Keyserling. Travelling outside of Paris to meet him at the Versailles hotel where she paid for his room and board, Ocampo tells her reader that she was much like Little Red Riding Hood, basket of goodies in hand, knocking at the door of the wolf, expecting to find grandma:

> The fact is that I showed up at the Hôtel des Réservoirs with my cake and my pot of butter (take that with or without the pun) for my grandmother, following the tradition of Little Red Riding Hood. And all of a sudden there I was before a carnivore who demanded a more substantial meal. (1983, 23)[12]

The count was nothing if not an ungrateful guest. On his account, Ocampo's generosity and hospitality, both in France and in Argentina, are nothing more than unconsidered, even unethical, foolish wastefulness. One might be willing to agree with this assessment, given what Keyserling made of Ocampo's hospitality:

> The Argentine craves the possession of inordinate wealth, but not because he has any reverence or the wish to create values, but in order to spend it foolishly, as fast as he can. To that extent even Argentine generosity, however beautiful it may be, is as a rule devoid of all ethical motives: at bottom it is squandering. (Keyserling 1932, 191)

In 1937, many years after Keyserling took advantage of Ocampo's ethics-free squandering on his behalf, he wrote to her saying that he was writing a book. Its primary subject was to be himself: "In reality, I will speak of myself in all possible aspects, but pointing in each chapter toward another spirit that was significant for me" (personal letter cited in Ocampo 1951, 11).[13] Keyserling expected to keep working on this book until he died, and indeed it was in 1950, four years after his death, that Ocampo received a letter from Keyserling's widow, Countess Goedela von Bismarck-Schoenhausen, telling her of her intention to publish the memoir. The countess offered to send her a copy of the chapter on Ocampo herself, and she hoped Ocampo would not be too distressed about its content. Ocampo became uneasy at this announcement from abroad:

> Knowing Keyserling, his overwrought imagination and his impetuous manner of massaging the "facts" (*his personal enemies*, he called them), who boasted of disdaining them just because they were facts, I began to worry. (1951, 12–13, Ocampo's emphasis)[14]

Once she read the chapter Ocampo was indeed distressed; and when Keyserling's widow published *A Traveler through Time*, Ocampo spoke out. The memoir included a chapter entitled "V.O.," which recounted Keyserling's relationship with Ocampo. She was so outraged at his representation of her that she responded in a 137-page book called *El viajero y una de sus sombras* (The traveler and one of his shadows). There she tells the story of her dealings with Keyserling and lays bare the source of many of Keyserling's pronouncements on Argentina. Ocampo, who had earlier decided not to respond to the exaggerations and distortions of *South American Meditations*, returns to that text in the response she felt compelled to write to *A Traveler through Time*. It is because of Ocampo's felt need to respond to his defamation of her that perhaps the only text contesting Keyserling's pronouncements on Argentina was written. In a letter to Gabriela Mistral, Ocampo explains why she wrote her book:

> I don't know if you've heard that [Count Hermann] Keyserling, in his [memoirs], devotes a chapter to me (which according to his wife is the most important one of the whole work). Although this chapter is full of praise, I find it unjust (even in the praise) and I've felt compelled to write a mise en point [a rejoinder]. It's a little book entitled *The Traveler and One of His Shadows*. I'm sending it to you along with the large book by Keyserling (which is very badly translated). You don't have to read the whole chapter to find out what he says about me. It's enough to begin reading on the page where my name first appears and continue to the end. It's true that in my own country no one has accorded me the importance that K. does (on a whim of his own). But there are several things in the chapter that, for reasons too long to explain, have bothered me. It's a long story. (Ocampo in Horan and Meyer 2003, 166–67)

The title Ocampo chose for her book, "The traveler and one of his shadows" *(El viajero y una de sus sombras)* makes direct reference to Keyserling's *A Traveler through Time.* Whereas Keyserling somewhat pompously refers to himself as the time traveler, and certainly centers himself in his multitome text, Ocampo self-deprecatingly, but also ironically, allows him center stage in her title. He is the traveler; she a mere shadow. Keyserling's characterization of his book is characteristic of him. He unabashedly says that he is writing about himself, but each chapter is centered on another important "spirit" whose presence in the world is a counterpoint to Keyserling's own great illuminating thoughts. Ocampo was to be one of these shadows, but this shadow talked back.

Ocampo long stayed mute on the subject of Keyserling's *South American Meditations,* even though on its publication she recognized some of her own observations, severely deformed and out of context, at the root of a number of his pronouncements. Early in *El viajero* Ocampo clarifies her earlier decision not to respond to the influential and damaging *South American Meditations:*

> In 1932 the *South American Meditations* appeared, bringing me, with its pages, another wave of indignation. . . .
> I did not want to write any more about Keyserling; I only enjoy analyzing what I can praise. And the *Meditations* did not seem to me, in its totality, worthy of praise. In this 350-page work, despite a few moments of accuracy, a frenetic generalization of capricious conclusions was repugnant. (1951, 72)[15]

Ocampo's readers will recognize this justification for her decision not to rebut Keyserling's *South American Meditations* as an example of her choosing only to write about what she calls her "preferences." But her decision not to respond to the *Meditations* also lies in the fact that although her conversations and correspondence with him gave Keyserling some of the facts he proceeded to use to his own ends, Keyserling leaves her far behind in his ruminations and pronouncements.

The combination of Ocampo's lack of interest in writing about anything she did not enjoy and her sense that the *Meditations* began with, but went far beyond, her kept her silent until Keyserling's widow published *A Traveler through Time.* Only then did Ocampo go back to the *Meditations,* since it is there that Keyserling lays out his deeply racist and sexist analysis of South America, which, as she shows, has one taproot in his own prejudices and another in his interactions, conversations, and correspondence with her. Ocampo cites specific moments in the *Meditations* in which Keyserling took incidents that really occurred and transformed them to accord with his theories; but other inaccuracies, she says, seem to have been simply the product of his prodigious imagination: "Thus analyzing the *Meditations* I discover the origin of many errors, but others seem created entirely by the unbridled fantasy of the author" (Ocampo 1951, 74).[16] Ocampo says that Keyserling often takes a single incident or impression and blows it out of proportion, or takes it out of context:

> I recognized observations and opinions that I had confided to the philosopher, but disfigured by I don't know what phenomenon of unheard-of inflation. An interpretative elephantiasis. Here and there, as usual, a bolt of genius, coming from I don't know what Magma Mater and falling back into it. (72)[17]

She also notes Keyserling's penchant for generalizing from one incident to an entire continent:

> [I]n his feverish generalizations (whose starting point may be true, doubtful, or false, depending on the case, and this time whose starting point was extremely doubtful), Keyserling doesn't mince words: "South Americans stay silent in all the cases where a European would raise his voice or break out with invectives. They would rather kill than insult." (52)[18]

Keyserling relegates Argentinean men to the same level of immanence, of being enmeshed in physicality, to which Western philosophy has traditionally assigned women:

> Sexual potency means more to the Argentines than to any other men on earth. Their life is adjusted to sensual satisfaction and procreation in a way unlike any other type of man I have ever known. (Keyserling 1932, 28)

Keyserling's characterization of South American men not only as violent, but also as sexually rapacious and indiscriminate, unable to keep a thought in their heads, and without a sense of values, contrasts with the more highly developed European man, who, unlike his *gana*-driven counterpart in South America, presumably fondly remembers and deeply treasures all the women with whom he has sex:

> The Gana-quality of this thirst for knowledge is proven by the rapidity with which things are forgotten and by the lack of a ruling sense of value; for the latter always impels man not to devour what he values,

but to treasure it. Hence the extreme don Juanism of South American men. Hence, too, the unique readiness of South American women to let their mind and soul be fecundated by Spirit. (190)

It is difficult to read that last sentence without remembering that Keyserling thinks of himself as the great embodiment of Spirit, that most noble of attributes, and of his early interactions with Ocampo, during which she was captivated by his writing. Keyserling's own desires emerge here in the sexualization of Ocampo's intellectual eagerness, generalized to all South Americans, men and women. Thus can Ocampo herself be glimpsed in the text, as Keyserling's experience of her gives shape and color to his pronouncements.

Keyserling's description of Argentinean women as deceptively sweet and acquiescent, cordial and tender but fearful of anger and passion, is surely derived from his experience with Ocampo — her early enthusiasm, her generous hospitality in France, her refusal to have sex with him, and her decision to maintain cordial but cool relations with him when he came to Argentina. He explains her attitude and behavior not as provoked by his own, but as deep and essential feminine and Argentinean characteristics that, in addition, are most flattering to him. Ocampo here is the quintessence of Keyserling's version of Argentineity:

> [T]he Argentine in particular is also the country of cordiality, impulsiveness and spontaneity. The women are of a great sweetness, and since the whole order of life is rooted in emotion, the warmest of atmospheres ought to pervade the continent. This conclusion seems so obvious, that for a long time my imagination construed the existence of this warmth. I was wrong nevertheless. Here tenderness, gentleness, sweetness and friendliness are essentially qualities appertaining to the cold-blooded creatures: chilly in himself, the man of these latitudes instinctively adjusts his whole life to being warmed through pleasing impressions. He responds to warmth like no other man, but he has none himself. . . . this is why South American women have a horror unknown elsewhere of all hardness; anger to them is vice; in warm passionateness they sense foremost the violence underlying it, and violence they cannot bear. But on the other hand in their heart of hearts they desire to be violated. (1932, 30)

And since South American women want to be raped, South American men all become rapists; hence their success with women when they come to Europe. Here Keyserling is so preposterous that Ocampo seems unable to decide whether the most appropriate response to this nonsense is indignation or ridicule:

It is difficult to ignore certain elements of contradiction and exaggeration in this interesting passage. Whoever hates violence and anger cannot want to suffer from their effects, unless it is a case of pathological masochism. This degree of masochism does not seem so widespread, as far as I know. And if South Americans, by engaging in rape as something natural (I have gone through life without observing any alarming symptoms of these customs; why would that be?) find success among European women, couldn't one deduce from this phenomenon that the women of the Old World quickly become fond of rape and adopt the habits of our Cro Magnon men? It follows, then, that it is not necessary to be a cold-blooded animal, belonging to the Third Day of Creation, to behave like one. And finally, let us generalize, since that seems to be the practice here, it can be deduced that the rape so universally, though subterraneously desired by women, can only be performed successfully by Cro Magnon (read: South American) man. Something had to be left for the poor little things. (Ocampo 1951, 61–63)[19]

If Keyserling is remembered at all today in the United States, it is for his statement that the country's greatest superstition is its belief in facts. This charming assessment of American practicality and literal-mindedness, however, is symptomatic of Keyserling's dismissal of facts in favor of their meaning—and specifically their meaning for him.[20] As its full title suggests, the *South American Meditations: On Hell and Heaven in the Soul of Man* is not primarily a meditation on South America. Instead, Keyserling uses his experience in South America as a starting point for a series of ruminations on, among other things, the origin of life, the meaning of the soul, the essence of masculinity and femininity, and only incidentally the fundamental nature of the South American character. He also expounds on Soviet Russia, North America, Spain, and to a lesser extent other European and some Asian nations. Keyserling's penchant for unmooring his thought from its grounding in material reality may allow him to get to the abstract thinking he wants to do, but it wreaks havoc on those left below in the dailiness and specificity of their embodied lives. Ocampo points out that although it is critical to get beyond the mere fact of any matter to understand what the fact means, one cannot manipulate the fact itself, lest there be nothing left from which to draw meaning:

I should like to begin by explaining that for me facts exist, to a reason-able extent, although for Keyserling they may not exist; or it is not worth the trouble to respect them. "Facts in and of themselves do not interest me; the only thing that interests me is the meaning of the things that happen." Facts are only interesting when one discovers their meaning, we are agreed. But, rightly or not, I believe that if we deform facts excessively, we end up deforming or altering meaning. (Ocampo 1951, 17–18)[21]

Ocampo was in a good position to judge Keyserling's deformation of facts. We have already seen how she acquiesced to a certain disfiguring of fact in her interactions with Virginia Woolf, allowing Woolf to maintain her whimsical image of Ocampo as an exotic Latin American and of Argentina as a land of blue butterflies and wild cows. She believed that Woolf's fancy was benign, and in any case private: it was in their exchange of letters and in their conversation that Woolf's gentle fantasy was expressed. With Keyserling it was different, and his more public distortions were pernicious in their effects. Moreover, in the Keyserling case Ocampo served as an Argentine Cassandra, unheeded in her warning about the count's misreading of America.

Ocampo is very clear about the source of Keyserling's change of attitude toward her. He took her enthusiasm for his writing as a sign that she would be sexually available, and he was hurt and angry when that turned out not to be the case:

> The unusual fervor of my enthusiasm for certain aspects of Keyserling's genius (I believed and believe that this man had sparks of genius), had led him to think that this enthusiasm was inseparable . . . from a great love that he never inspired in me. When he discovered the absence of this feeling, it made me look like a monster and a traitor in his eyes, when all I was was a woman who was pained to have misled him on this point . . . and who, in the beginning, stubbornly used endless kindness to clarify the meaning of his mistake. The chapter on Delicacy in Keyserling's *Meditations* connects this kindness to South America. "Thus, the sweetness and extreme kindness of the South Americans never signifies warmth of feeling." (Ocampo 1951, 50–51)[22]

Victoria Ocampo returns her reader to the scene where Keyserling first developed his desire-driven theory of Argentine man. Although Keyserling seems to move from the general to the particular—from the cold-bloodedness of South Americans in general to the odd mixture of sweetness and coldness in Argentinean women in particular—a reading of Ocampo's *El viajero y una de sus sombras* reveals that the move is actually from the very particular to the general. There Ocampo tells the story of a man who expected his every whim to be catered to, and when they were in France Ocampo acquiesced to most of them. Nevertheless, she disappointed him (repeatedly, it seems) in his sexual importuning. He soothes himself by attributing her rejection of him to a generalized fear among Argentine women of "the violence underlying" what he calls "warm passionateness." Ocampo's own explanation is far more prosaic, and less pleasing to Keyserling's ego: being drawn to his work did not mean she was drawn to his person. Ocampo was not interested in participating in what she characterizes as a kind of intellectual prostitution—she was not sexually interested in Keyserling and would not sleep with him just because she found his writing exciting and because he expected her to. Ironically using Keyserling's own characterizations of the Americas, Ocampo throws the notion of *gana* back at him:

> [N]either my South American delicacy nor my North American frankness found approval in Keyserling's eyes, insofar as it had to do with making him understand something he had no *gana* [desire] to understand. (Ocampo 1951, 53)[23]

Ocampo herself speaks in generalities, but in her case it is most clear she is referring to Keyserling when she contrasts George Bernard Shaw's refreshing ability to separate sexual from intellectual desire to the way "masculine nature" typically responds to women's adulation:

> I give you, oh miracle!, what [Shaw] writes about the women who were drawn to his new (or old) glory: "Not all the women who pursue me want to have sexual relations with me." I say "oh miracle!" because such a declaration from a world-famous writer is even more unusual than having kept his virginity until age 29; and the insight that such a declaration implies is as contrary to the laws of masculine nature as a miracle is to the laws of ordinary nature. (56)[24]

With a certain amount of delicacy—laced with irony, to be sure—Ocampo goes on to observe that

> The male of the species is made in such a way that he is disposed to offer a great deal to a woman who is willing to pay him with the coin of pleasure, or even with the coin of gratified self-esteem, of flattering his belief in his dominance. (56)[25]

Ocampo, however, is not about to pay in such coin, and she names Keyserling's high-sounding theories for what they are, the bleating of the wounded ego of a man with an overweening sense of entitlement:

> I think that more akin to the gods of Olympus than to the descendents of the Edenic pair, [Keyserling] was irritated simply by the fact that a

mere mortal woman dared disagree with him, and not assent to all his "poetic fantasies." (58)[26]

The count may have couched his importuning in terms of the need for great spirits to intermingle, but in the end Ocampo found his stay in the Versailles, "without ceasing to be an event of enormous interest, a daily test that was extremely hard to bear" (59).[27]

Keyserling's expectations of Ocampo are rooted in his unexamined beliefs about women and in a timeworn gender politics. His description of "woman" would seem pathological if it did not so perfectly and baldly express the Western notion of the distinction between man and woman, masculine and feminine, culture and nature, spirit and body, Madonna and whore, truth and lie. The following long passage meanders through his thinking on these interconnected binaries:

> [I]n the beginning was not Man, but woman; not Truth, but the Lie. Women who are close to the primordial depths even today and even on the highest summits of culture incarnate the modality of Being belonging to the primordial Life. Whether such women ever tell the truth with a clear conscience I cannot tell; certainly they never lie with a bad conscience, excepting when the education of children demands truthfulness as a matter of technique. But the "mother" is something widely differing from the "woman"; as a mother Woman acts from a higher plane similar to the pope who, in deciding ex cathedra, is infallible as opposed to the fallible private man. And in another dimension, the wife who grasps the meaning of marriage, or the lover who is a true partner of a man's destiny, rises above the plane of primeval woman-hood; she lives from out of a spiritual connexion. Yet nothing could be more mistaken than to draw inferences concerning the original character from these life-forms permeated by Spirit. Primordial Woman is com-pletely unchecked by spiritual or ethical motives. She is entirely rooted in the world of the Third Day of Creation. This is why beauty with woman means so much as opposed to the little it means with man: her attractive qualities are a true expression of her self; it is not, as with man, a manifestation of the genus with which the individual is connected only by what does not essentially distinguish him. This is why woman is originally devoid of moral instinct. This is why the real element of her life dwindles in every world of exclusively determinant truthfulness, such as the North American world of today; this is why man becomes enmeshed and enslaved by primeval woman, by "Carmen," by "She," and by her alone, for she catches him there where Spirit and Freedom do not reach down to.

No wonder that exclusively spiritual religions in their heroic early days stigmatized woman as intrinsically sinful. What is false, not what destroys is originally held to be wicked. Only treachery and crafty deception are thought evil by elementary consciousness, whereas killing in open fight is held to be noble and therefore good. Thus, not only the cunning tricks and artifices of woman appear wicked—all her deceptive and seductive ways of holding her own must needs impress man as being evil. But woman is "evil" only insofar as primordial Life is "evil." What is considered intrinsically feminine today belongs to the character of primordial Life: Original Impotency which expresses itself in the form of passivity, Original Fear and the Original Lie.

These characteristics of primordial Life manifest themselves most purely on the continent determined by the Spirit of the Third Day of Creation. Proceeding from the general Significance of Original Evil we can fully comprehend the true nature of the South American's reptility. (Keyserling 1932, 40–42)

Here Keyserling rehearses familiar notions of gender difference, displacing onto the feminine all those characteristics that men would just as soon be rid of in themselves: vanity, duplicity, cunning, deception, artifice. Once a woman is contained in one of her proper roles—mother, wife, lover—she leaves behind these base attributes, but only because she is infused, temporarily, with masculine spirit. Once the spirit is gone, as it inevitably will be, she will revert to type. After settling on the essential nature of woman, Keyserling proceeds to ascribe these characteristics to South America, effectively feminizing that "other." Woman is primordial life, and primordial life manifests itself not only in women, but generally in South America, the continent he associates with what he calls the Spirit of the Third Day of Creation, in a kind of case of arrested development.[28]

The claim that, by understanding the nature of Woman, one can also grasp the fundamentally reptilian nature of the South American is so jarring because of the multiple assumptions it makes, relying on a web of associations that link women to nature to underdevelopment along a negative vector of cold-bloodedness and slime. The reptilian trope becomes a leitmotif in Keyserling's ramblings on South America, especially where he conflates the continent with Argentina:

The prototype of the South American as a political animal is the *compadrito*. The concept originates in the suburbs of Buenos Aires. The *compadre*, the sponsor or godfather, played a decisive and distinctly beautiful part in the life of the gaucho, whose proud and lonely poverty found its sole support in a noble ethos of friendship. In Buenos Aires, however, the "sponsorship" which had been taken over from the cement binding together that particular underworld which is the natural train of followers and means of action belonging to the South American chieftain; and in this latter sense I shall apply the term *compadrito* to the corresponding class of men throughout the continent. (Keyserling 1932, 42–43)

In reviling these men, Keyserling once again calls on the reptilian trope:

[H]e has the grand qualities of the giant snake. But his train of followers is reptilian in the lowest sense of the word. Venal men, slanderers, black-mailers, sycophants, hypocrites, toad-eaters and willing tools of the dark machinations may be found all the world over. But never have I seen men of this kind, which thrives in all democracies, whose basic attitude was so ugly as in South America, and who, in the slimy cohesion of their "sponsorship" among themselves and other relation as clients to the chief impressed me so strongly as a netherworld. Owing to the fact that the cold substratum within them is near the surface, they display the expressions of resentment, lie, treachery and possible revenge as openly as amphibia exhibit their amphibianism. (43)

Keyserling repeatedly, almost obsessively, uses reptilian metaphors in the *Meditations.* He uses them to characterize women, and the reptile is also the key symbol of the Third Day of Creation and of Indians. Snakes and spiders writhe through his description of South American women who

furnish a perfect illustration of the truth that in the beginning was not Man, but Woman. Uncontrolled to an unparalleled degree, although for this very reason innocent and seldom dangerous, that Evil unfolds within them which is the first-born of Original Fear. Nowhere else does one find so much indiscretion, so much venomous slander among women-friends. No woman on earth makes such masterly use of all the possibilities of passivity and deceit. None has so spider-like a way of catching man in her net; none abuses the indissolubility of marriage so slyly and unscrupulously with the view of harassing him. Nowhere else does loyalty so often mean nothing but sloth; once an Argentine woman went so far as to tell me: "With us, faithfulness is a disease." And all the Argentine men present applauded the saying of a Frenchman, that a surprising number of the women of the country made him think either of tortoises or vipers. Nowhere else do the emotions of the women so easily turn into their opposite on the slightest provocation. Nowhere is the subsoil of the strongest passion so cold. Withall I do not in the least dispute the high qualities and, most of all, the possibilities of South American woman: what I have said merely goes to prove her primordial womanhood, which makes her particularly seductive. (44)

Keyserling's obsession with the reptilian nature of South America in general and with Argentina and Argentinean women in particular is intimately tied up with his feelings about Ocampo, who does not let it be lost on her readers that his nickname for her was "Anaconda." Keyserling reveals how this nickname arose out of his own fantasy:

> When, still in Europe, I had been meditating on the first South American souls I had met, I was assailed by visions of snakes: before my eyes arose mottled or tiger-spotted fragments of trunks of huge pythons, flecked by flashes of light filtering through the tree-tops; bodies welling up and rolling forth out of a bottomless opaque pond. In its native landscape this netherworld which lifted to the surface its inner correspondence within me, took its original and elementary shape and mould. (16)

He discusses the mixture of warm- and cold-bloodedness in South America, and then particularizes to Argentina:

> This cold-blood quality impresses one as something weirdly paradoxical, until one has learnt to understand; for the Argentine in particular is also the country of cordiality, impulsiveness and spontaneity. (30)[29]

The reptilian moment is a time and place of formlessness. It attaches to the primordial, to what Keyserling dubs the "Yeast of Creation":

> This spirit of the "Yeast of Creation" is dominant in the landscape of South America, wherever the earth is not "without form and void." Wherever new life comes into existence on that soil, it at once acquires the character of a primordial being. This is true of the Argentine. To its original landscape correspond only the extinct prehistoric animals; first and foremost the huge edentates. And the few ancient forms of life still extant there, all, one way or another, impress one as being antediluvian: the ombú, the sole native tree of the pampa, more sponge than wood. (26)

Argentina is a land whose "original landscape" is marked by what is so ancient that it no longer survives and by a few native life-forms so peculiar and old that they seem to defy nature itself.

When Keyserling wrote to his friend and analyst Carl Jung, sending him several chapters of the *Meditations* for his comments, Jung too noted how Keyserling dwelled on the slimy reptile world, which he merges with the continent and the woman. It is worth citing Jung's two letters to Keyserling in full:

13 August 1931

Dear Count,

First I must ask you to forgive me for not reacting earlier to your interesting MS [part of *South American Meditations*]. It is rich and significant in content. You are inaugurating a new and contemporary style of "sentimental journey," though it is considerably bloodier than its predecessors. South America has also brought you face to face, plainly and honestly, with the dark underworld, the chthonic unconscious. It is a classic case of the collective unconscious being constellated by the activation of the inferior function, which because of its contamination with the contents of the collective unconscious always drags this up with it. Simultaneously the anima emerges in exemplary fashion from the primeval slime, laden with all the pulpy and monstrous appendages of the deep. And outside, conjured up by her appearance inside, X. is forced into your magic circle—a meaningful adventure whose continuation arouses my curiosity. That was an encounter with the daemonism of the earth and it has never yet been described better.

I wish you all the luck with the continuation, but would advise you to cut down on "cultural speculation" as much as possible, otherwise you will blur what is most impressive about your work—the personal experience with its exemplary subjectivity.

I hope you are all right in health. With best regards,

Yours sincerely,
C. G. Jung (Jung 1973, 84)

Jung's response to Keyserling participates in the feminizing and othering of South America, conflating the continent with the woman, who herself is now reduced to a cipher (Victoria Ocampo as "X."). He warns Keyserling against generalizing his own psychological processes and projecting them onto an entire culture. Nevertheless, what interests Jung is Keyserling's psyche, and he easily condones that another person and indeed an entire continent full of people and history can be subordinated to that single privileged psyche. Jung is fascinated by the anima as creature from the Black Lagoon, a slimy, pulpy monster emerging from the primeval muck. The fact that the fashionably dressed, multilingual, soignée Victoria Ocampo is enlisted to play this role suggests just how powerful the idea of the primitive anima is. (This is the woman who cannot bear to be confronted by the skin that forms on the milk that is heated for her coffee. Her servant thoughtfully removes it for her every morning.) Nor is Jung above being curious about the "continuation" of Keyserling's "meaningful adventure" with Ocampo.

Jung wisely counsels Keyserling to "cut down on 'cultural specula-tion,'" advice that Keyserling did not take, much to the detriment of Argentine thinking on the subject of Argentina. Jung sees clearly that Keyserling is projecting his complex, passionate, and ultimately thwarted desire for Ocampo onto South America as a whole. Subsequent admir-ers of Keyserling would have done well to note this tendency as well. In his second letter to Keyserling, Jung explicitly states that Keyserling was deeply disturbed by his visit to South America and that he created his own South America out of Victoria Ocampo. His wise counsel this time is for Keyserling to recognize that the contents of his unconscious, trig-gered by his visit to South America and his unfulfilled attachment to Ocampo, were not in fact "located" in either the continent or the woman. He advises him not to ascribe the contents of his psyche to the external world, the material reality of South America and Victoria Ocampo. Jung advises Keyserling to think of South America as a catalyst for his own psychic processes, and to concentrate on understanding them—not on projecting his obsessions, fears, and desires onto the continent. Victoria Ocampo–cum–South America has made her way into Keyserling's psyche as his anima. Jung understands that this does not mean that they have lost their own subjectivity or ceased to have any other meaning in the world:

23 April 1931

Dear Count,

   From your description I have the impression that your South Ameri-can experience, especially the encounter with X. has constellated con-tents in your unconscious that are the source of continued disturbances. For better or worse we must (in collaboration with the South American earth) take X. as the anima, who (like South America) stands for the unconscious. The unconscious has a different rhythm from consciousness and different goals. Until now you have been accustomed, by means of intuition and literary work, to subordinate everything the psyche offered you to the aims of your conscious mind, or to create out of it a con-scious view of the world. You have made South America out of X. Now it is a question of expressing those contents which can be located neither in X. nor in S.A. (and which seem to you still completely unknown), not by moulding them into a picture of the external world or incorporating them in such a picture, but, on the contrary, by subordinating your philosophical skill and descriptive powers to those unknown contents. Then those contents will be able to mould an inner picture of the world without your guidance or intention. The initial question to be directed to the Invisible would be: "Who or what has come alive in S.A.? who or what has entered my psychic life and created disturbances and wants to be heard?" To this you should add: "Let it speak!" (Jung 1973, 82–83)

Here Jung tells Keyserling, however gently, that his experiences with Ocampo and in South America have served as fodder for his own unconscious processes, but that what he has made of them does not come from them, but from his own unconscious. Jung has little use for the complexity of a material South America or the woman Victoria Ocampo, but he understands, as Keyserling does not, that there is a difference between Keyserling's account of Ocampo/South America and their own material reality. Victoria Ocampo and South America stand for Keyserling's subconscious, but that is not their entire function in the world.

It is not only Jung, but Ocampo herself, who sees Keyserling's error in conflating her with the continent and making of both a complex symbol. She also shows that in this, Keyserling was hardly original. In a footnote to *El viajero y una de sus sombras*, Ocampo neatly psychoanalyzes Keyserling's obsession with women's primordial nature, which, she notes, he shares with "a good number of his colleagues spread around the planet" (1951, 16):[30]

> It should be enough to cite, in support of what I say, these passages from the *South American Meditations*, subsequent to the time of my Keyserlinian enthusiasm, of course. "One might, then, generalize and affirm: in the beginning was not Man but Woman, not Truth but Lie. *Woman, close to the profound original depths* [it is I who underline], incarnates still today, even at the highest levels of culture, the modality of primordial life." It is evident that this is a *projection* (in psychoanalysis, this word, as is well known, means the act of attributing to another person a desire, a character trait, or an ideal belonging to the subject himself): man associates with woman the primordial state to the extent to which she evokes it in him. (16–17, n. 1, original emphasis)[31]

Ocampo notes as well that Keyserling himself understood that South America was merely a pretext for his own projections:

> A propos of Houston Chamberlain, Keyserling writes in his *A Traveler through Time:* "Chamberlain never saw Germany as it really is. Very often he held to a chimera in which he could believe in all sincerity everything that had no true relation to German nature.... *Something analogous to what happened to Chamberlain happens most often with the predilection*

for foreign peoples and lands: they constitute the surest surface for the projection of what is one's own." [It is I who underline.] The *South American Meditations* were to be Keyserling's reaction to the Rorschach test, faced with the great inkblot of our continent. (33, n. 1)[32]

Keyserling emerges as the most egocentric of experience-gatherers, for whom the world is merely the raw material for his personal fulfillment. Not only the continent but also the people he most associated with it were fair game for his "meditations." As Ocampo notes, "If Keyserling ever used my persona in his writings it would have been for his 'self-fulfillment,' setting aside the fairness or unfairness of the thing" (77).[33] Hermann Keyserling's *South American Meditations* may well be the clearest example of the way foreigners find in Argentina a screen onto which to project their own desires, fears, and concerns. Jung was no doubt wise to advise him to avoid making cultural observations, since what Keyserling was observing more than anything else was the working of his own psyche. Because of this preoccupation with himself, and because he simply saw the whole world in relation to himself, as though it were an extension of his consciousness, to say nothing of his unconscious, it did not matter that he was there and saw the place and met the people. Ocampo alone among Argentinean writers of the day saw what Jung saw: that for Keyserling Argentina was nothing more than raw material that he would use for his own purposes, his "self-fulfillment." If at first she decided to stay mute on the subject of his text, she did eventually speak out about it. Moreover, although *El viajero y una de sus sombras* was prompted by the "V.O." chapter in *A Traveler through Time*, the argument Ocampo makes against Keyserling in her response is primarily directed toward the *Meditations*.

Keyserling's own imagined Argentina is far stronger than the facts on the ground. What is more, despite his protestations of original thought, his Argentina is the product of the racialized, gendered thinking of his age. Keyserling's Argentina, a land of his own design, is perhaps the most exaggerated example of the desire for and fear of the uncanny other that so many foreign writers have found so fruitful for their work. The screen onto which they project their desires, fears, and concerns is by no means blank. In fact the projection screen may be an inadequate metaphor for Argentina after all. This time Borges's aleph may be closer to it, although the universe that Keyserling's Argentina contains is far more limited than Borges's stunning artifact. Nevertheless, this Argentine aleph fascinates the one who contemplates it. It contains a multiplicity of images, memories, histories, and stories, out of which any single individual attaches to those that have most personal meaning. The stories of Jews in the sex trade, Italians in the labor movement, or clandestine U.S. involvement in the Dirty War respond to each contemplator's social and political history. Keyserling was interested only in the history of his own soul, which he imagined to be generalizable to the soul of the world. Argentine readers saw their name in his *Meditations* and thought he was writing about them. But then, so did he.

CHAPTER SIX

The Race for National Identity

At the tail end of the twentieth century, archeologists working with artifacts at the Ethnographic Museum in Göteborg, Sweden, began studying two masks made by indigenous people living in what is now Mendoza, in northwestern Argentina. Because they were in such good condition, the masks had been thought to have been made some two to three centuries back, but carbon dating proved that hypothesis wrong. The masks were, in fact, 2,500 years old. Other recent findings include proof of an ancient human presence in Argentine territory in various parts of the country, the oldest being 12,000-year-old remains in Patagonia, as well as the world's earliest known mummification process—older even than Egypt's. Now the fact of an ancient culture whose artifacts are still among us two and a half millennia later must, one would suppose, be incorporated into Argentina's idea of itself.[1] The old joke that goes "Mexicans come down from the Aztecs and Peruvians come down from the Incas. Argentineans come down off the boat" may no longer be so true. Like the United States, the Argentina that has conceived of itself as a purely immigrant society has been challenged in recent years by an increasingly visible transnational indigenous rights movement. The indigenous-centered revisionist histories and emancipatory anthropology that have emerged in the last decades are determined to rectify the lacunae in the enduring narrative of total conquest. Nevertheless, the narrative of absolute European conquest in hegemonic accounts of the history of America's temperate zones, North and South, continues to have the effect of masking the reality of enduring cultures.[2] The triumphalist plotline of Euro-Argentina obscures the fact that after the first brutal wave of attempted annihilation, surviving native people did not disappear but rather lived in complicated relationship with the now-dominant populations.

In both the United States and much of Latin America, the renaissance in indigenous historiography, the critical and commercial success of literary texts written by Indian peoples, and the identification with Indianness among mestizo writers and theorists are all components of the symbolic reclaiming of Indian territory.[3] Nonetheless, neither a tentative movement toward a multiculturalism that recognizes the importance of its indigenous heritage similar to the one in the United States nor the embracing of Indian culture that has been a central element of liberation movements in much of Latin America has had the purchase in Argentina that they have had in the rest of the Americas.[4] Despite the archeological findings, the history still being taught in schools in Argentina begins with cultures that produce writing.[5] Argentina holds tenaciously to its European identity.

On the other hand, popular culture provides a space for an indigenous presence. One of the most widely read comic strips in twentieth-century Argentina was *Paturuzú*, whose eponymous hero is a fabulously wealthy Patagonian Indian with a ne'er-do-well Porteño godfather named Isidoro who is always stealing Paturuzú's money.[6] Despite what a North American sensibility today would characterize as a racist depiction of the indigenous characters in the strip, Paturuzú is clearly the hero, and the reader's sympathy lies with him. The character, drawn by Dante Quinterno, first appeared in a newspaper comic strip in 1928. By 1930 the comic strip was renamed for the character, and in the 1930s it became a monthly, and finally a weekly, full-fledged humor magazine that was still going strong in the 1960s. For over three decades, it made a space for acknowledging both the indigenous presence in Argentina and the rapacious greed of urban, white Argentina in relation to its indigenous past and present. Even so, its low-culture, comic-book format makes it possible to not take the critique entirely seriously.

Isidoro's selfish commandeering of Paturuzú's wealth offers a counternarrative to the formal accounts of the Argentine nation that recall the wars against native peoples to clear the land for white settlement and exploitation as noble and heroic. Significantly, indigenous groups are rendered present in these official histories even as the plot line is about their eradication. They remain a threat to national identity, a presence that predates the European founding of the nation, a difference within that threatens to destabilize national identity. The continuing presence of an indigenous Argentina is like a flickering light in the consciousness of the urban, largely European-descended population, even among those who are most aware of the need to pay attention to the rights and needs of subaltern groups.

For example—at a benefit concert to raise money for vaccines, held in Madrid in the summer of 2004, the politically engaged and savvy Argentinean singer León Gieco spoke with real feeling of the need to make medicine available to Argentina's rural poor, the very poorest of whom are indigenous. At the same time, however, he referred over and over to Argentina as a land of immigrants, joking about the many differences among all the children and grandchildren of immigrants who comprise the country, especially those who come from Buenos Aires.[7] Even this politically astute, deeply committed, and generous performer, a man who has worked with the Mothers of the Plaza de Mayo and whose trademark song, "Sólo le pido a Dios," speaks to his desire to make common cause with the people of his country and of the world, who performs benefits for indigenous causes, thinks Argentine identity through the lens of its European past.

As I have argued elsewhere, national identity, when referring to a nation's concept of itself, is an abstraction of an abstraction.[8] A sense of identity requires consciousness; as such national identity is made manifest in people, who are capable of forming subjectivities and, therefore, identities. Nevertheless, the idea of the nation, known through the people who are part of it, and through outsiders who have some consciousness of it, requires a common language, some shared indications of what the chimera of the nation, any nation, is. To be intelligible, the language that tells of the nation need not map perfectly from one speaker's utterance to another's; it is enough that broad outlines and salient details match. It is, rather, necessary for the life of a nation's identity that it be flexible enough to grow and change, to meet new needs and new realities, to expand and contract in response to the material reality of individuals and groups that are part of, or are touched by, the nation.

A nation is not, despite what we learn from the pledge of allegiance to the flag of the United States of America, indivisible. Interconnected though its parts may be, the nation means different things to those within its borders who are distinguished from each other by the social divisors we have all come to recognize, among them gender, class, race, religion, age, place of residence, occupation, and political affiliation. Nor can one neatly sever the image a nation has of itself from the perception of that nation in the rest of the world. Moreover, any single nation will, to a great extent, be perceived differently from the outside by observers from different times in its history and different places beyond its borders. Nevertheless, this multiplicity of perceptions and representations through time and space does not preclude the mutual contamination between views from within and those from without.

To attempt to define a national character is to manifest a desire to fix categories of people much as some would fix them by categories of race and ethnicity. In traditional, now discredited, conceptions of race, character is supposed to inhere in groups by some sort of natural or divine process and find expression in individual human beings as members of those groups. The related concepts "ethnicity" and "nationality" are more likely to suppose that processes called "culture" or "socialization" do the trick. These categories originally overlapped considerably and only recently have become more or less distinct. Nations were presumed to consist of people who shared a history, culture, and language, all of which, not so long ago, also constituted what was called "race." This racialized conception of national character was common currency in the United States in the middle of the last century, short decades after the enactment of immigration policies defined national groups as races. Mid-twentieth-century writers like Luigi Barzini offered up popular books with titles like *The Italians,* and travelers' handbooks had names like *Those Perplexing Argentines.* John Gunther's television travelogue series "High Road" was watched eagerly and his "Inside" books (*Inside Africa, Inside Europe,* etc.) were consumed by avid readers. People in the United States, newly aware of themselves as citizens of a nation that played on a world stage, wanted to know about that world and what characterized national types, sometimes but not always in anticipation of foreign travel. Half a century and a cold war later, the neat parceling out of behaviors to distinct nations and calling them "national character" began to seem quaint in this country, until a newly inflamed division between Christendom and Islam spurred a new round of racialized punditry, revitalizing the barely dormant phrase "national identity." What a nation means to itself, what ideas it evokes in others, cannot be static things, yet somehow the idea of a particular place and the people that belong to it is still capable of carrying meanings that function to name and represent it both for outsiders and for those within.

Jackson and Penrose tell us that the term "nation" has three related but different meanings. The first two, articulated in the eighteenth century by the German Johann Gottfried von Herder and the French Jean-Jacques Rousseau respectively, hold that nations are "fundamental units of humanity" (Herder in Jackson and Penrose 1993, 7) and that the nation is a "political entity embodied in a state" (Rousseau in ibid., 8). In the first formulation,

> nation is a "cultural" entity defined by attributes such as language, religion, customs or traditions, and sometimes "race," harkening back to the earliest use of the term, in the thirteenth century, when nation was understood to mean "racial grouping." (7)

In the second formulation, culture, although still present, is subordinated to politics, as a democratic notion of the "people" emerges. The third use of the term "nation" is as "a casual means of denoting culturally and/or politically defined nations.... a synonym for country" (8).[9]

The earliest identification of nation with the now-discredited idea of biological race still pertains today in countries that link citizenship to ancestry. The same foundationalism that focuses on physical characteristics like "blood" and "skin" and renders them symbolic is inevitably connected to parentage. Thus, merely being born in Germany (which would only become a nation-state more than half a century after Herder's death) does not make you a citizen of that state or a member of that nation; you must have an ancestral claim to German parentage as well. In newly constructed or declared nations, like those of Africa or America, it is obvious that the racial singularity of nation is problematic. José Vasconcelos's idea of the "cosmic race" is one way to deal with this. In his 1925 treatise he asserts the emergence of a new blended race in the New World, with the best features of those that comprise it.[10] Spain's overseas colonies were from the start included in the embrace of nation, as part of an attempt to impose political, religious, and linguistic uniformity to all its territories. Yet whereas the extension of Hispaneity to those born in overseas colonies of Spanish parents was a given, the national status of indigenous peoples was another matter. In Argentina, once independence was declared, the question of citizenship, national belonging, and race became paramount.

The dispute between opposing political camps over what constitutes the "authentic" Argentina began around the time of independence. The Federalists favored a loose confederation of largely autonomous provinces. They believed in an "organic" Argentineity that naturally occurred in its gauchos, whom they considered the autochthonous men of the pampas, and in *caudillismo* (rule by local chieftains) as a natural form of government. Their political rivals, the *Unitarios* (usually translated as "Unitarians," but who are not to be confused with the religious group), wanted a strong central government and believed that the nation could only succeed as a white, European country. When they came to power, the Unitarians set about to manufacture such a reality. Both Unitarian and Federalist views have a race-based concept of nation, but of different sorts. The Federalists, with their claim of an autochthonous Argentine and a natural form of government arising from the land, come close to Herder's formulation. The Unitarians' project of whitening through education and immigration is, on the other hand, utilitarian and constructionist. Importing its whiteness from abroad, the space of Argentina was not, in this view, naturally connected to, or productive of, the race/nation. The "natural" whiteness, and therefore the natural superiority, of Europe would inhere in a populace that would *become* Argentine by virtue of its transplantation to Argentine soil.

Both Unitarians and Federalists might have made space for an indigenous presence, but they did not. The Federalists could have found in its indigenous population a more "natural" inhabitant of the land even than the gaucho. The Unitarians, building on the liberal French view of a socially contracted political entity that could represent a multiplicity of groups and interests, might well have included Indians among the represented groups. Neither did so. On the contrary, both parties were intent on removing the native population from Argentine territory and historical consciousness. The rhetoric of the Unitarians eventually carried the day, and its contemporary consequence is the national myth that holds that Argentina, unlike most of the rest of Latin America, is a white country. Ironically, because the Europeanized racism of Argentina is not entirely dependent on ideas about natural differences, it is, to a certain extent, right in step with contemporary social construction theory. The race of the nation is malleable. However, as far as the underlying belief in a natural hierarchy among naturally occurring human races is concerned, we are smack in the middle of very old, discarded ideas about race as a natural category.

Argentina has historically both cultivated its likeness to Europe and insisted upon its unique nature. Nicolas Shumway (1991) argues convincingly that the creation of the Argentine nation in the nineteenth century was characterized by a struggle over defining Argentina as either a progressive nation ruled by European enlightenment ideals or as an autonomous nation with its autochthonous, natural form of government, suited especially to it. Shumway's view supports the conclusion of other scholars and observers, who see this internal struggle as the tragic flaw in the Argentine nation, forever at odds with itself.

As destructive as this internal struggle may have been for Argentina, it is also a dynamic force that has fueled outsiders' fascination. Part of Argentina's appeal is that it may be perceived as an other; part is derived from the flattering attraction to and identification with Europe. The nineteenth-century Argentinean admirers of Europe, evangelists of globalization *avant la lettre,* projected their nation into Europe's consciousness as best they could. Domingo Faustino Sarmiento, Argentina's liberal president from 1868 to 1874, hired agents and took out advertisements in European newspapers to recruit immigrants. He cultivated an enticing image of Argentina, already white and becoming whiter. By the end of the first decade of the twentieth century, Argentina was projecting itself as racially distinct from the rest of South America.

Insofar as Europe sees itself reflected in Argentina, it is telling that the purported racial homogeneity of the place so often surfaces sooner or later in European texts. Moreover, to the extent that Argentina wants to appeal to Europe not only as its equal, but also as part of the West, it projects itself to Europe as white. The differences among nations and (therefore) among races that predominated in late nineteenth-century European thought fueled Argentina's project of racial self-construction. The most desirable Europeans were from the Protestant north, Englishmen and Germans whose work ethic would move the country forward. Less desirable were southern Europeans whose poverty, lack of occupational skills, and illiteracy were thought to be naturally determined. Jews from eastern Europe were, thanks to an imported anti-Semitism, at the bottom of the list.

The discussions about which Europeans were the most desirable, and therefore would be encouraged to resettle in Argentina, dovetailed with the desire to exclude Blacks from the national story and the discursive extermination of Indians that finished what the actual genocide began. Alberdi, who, as Shumway notes, "usually avoids the racialist caricatures found in Sarmiento" (1991, 141) resurrects the tired call to protect the national elite's daughters from the dangers of marrying into an inferior racial group, pitting race against class in a contest of disdain that race wins hands down: "Who among us would not prefer a thousand times over to see his daughter marry an English shoeman rather than an Araucanian prince?" (Alberdi 1852, 241, cited in and translated by Shumway 1991, 141). The prospective (if imaginary) son-in-law shoemaker is, in Alberdi's formulation, not only English, but also about to be assimilated into a Hispanic Argentina. Alberdi explicitly links European civilization in America to the speaking of Spanish, and to the practice of Christianity:

> In America everything that is not European is barbaric; there is no division other than this one: Indian which is synonymous with savage, and European which means those of us born in America, who speak Spanish and believe in Jesus Christ. (Alberdi 1852, 241, cited in Shumway 1991, 141)

The slippage between desirable Europeans and all Europeans becomes more and more apparent as the nineteenth century progresses and immigration to Argentina grows. Alberdi probably did not count on the relatively large numbers of non-Christians who would eventually show up at the Buenos Aires docks, among them Japanese immigrants who touted their bilingualism to prospective employers, eastern European Jews who responded to the 1881 recruitment campaign aimed at them, and many Middle Eastern immigrants who eventually made their way to the growing nation.[11] Eventually it was no longer the immigrants who would civilize the nation, but vice versa. Those who were likely to make the journey, including the English shoemaker who at least had his nationality going for him, were society's least wanted, the ones with little to leave behind. Blind Mayer, the successful "rabbi" of the Warsaw Jewish underworld in Isaac Bashevis Singer's novel *Scum,* had no reason to go to America. Max, a young petty crook with several months in a Warsaw jail behind him, had no reason not to set sail for Argentina. In *Cuando Dios bailaba el tango* (When God danced the tango) Laura Pariani depicts the desperation of Italian peasants who pinned their hopes on a future in Argentina. It was the most impoverished, those with nothing to lose, who were likely to risk the trip across the ocean.

Despite Argentina's projection of itself as a white country, there was a large, mostly nomadic, indigenous population living outside the nation's developed areas. In addition, there were a significant number of Blacks in nineteenth-century Buenos Aires, many of whom came to the city after slavery was done away with. The abolition of slavery in Argentina began as a shift from agricultural and domestic servitude to military conscription, for men at least. José de San Martín, known as Argentina's liberator, believed that Black men made the most valiant soldiers. In 1816 he required all male slaves between fourteen and forty-five years of age to present themselves for military service, thereby rounding up 710 Black men to fight in Chile and Peru (Paso et al. 1982, 142). Later, Blacks were disproportionately conscripted to fight and die in the euphemistically named "Campaign of the Desert," the war waged to take control of the frontier by eliminating its indigenous inhabitants. Federalists and Unitarians might have been ideological opposites, yet on the subject of the elimination of the indigenous population, they seemed to be very much in accord.[12] The conservatives' strategy was to subdue the Indians militarily and, apparently, to kill as many of them as they could. The liberals' was to outnumber them through immigration and assimilate them through education, but like their political rivals they also approved of the outright extermination of Indians. At the same time, however, both political parties solicited the support of enslaved and free Blacks.

Afro-Argentineans enjoyed a rise in population through much of the nineteenth century, but the death of many in the Campaign of the Desert slowed that trend. In addition, epidemics devastated the poor sections of Buenos Aires, including Black neighborhoods. The decline in the Black population was precipitous, but there have always been Afro-Argentines. They did not disappear as completely as the elite's propaganda says. There is, today, a quiet presence of Blacks in Argentina, consisting of old Afro-Argentine families, as well as of newer immigrants. Nor were the indigenous people either wiped out or fully incorporated into the dominant culture in the process the government called "pacification" and "civilization." It is a surprise to most people to learn that Argentina has a substantial indigenous population, numbering about 700,000, though estimates range from 450,000 to 1.5 million.

It is against this demographic reality that Argentina has worked hard to establish itself as European and Western through a carefully fashioned discourse of whiteness. Sarmiento's racial purification rhetoric–turned–social policy, the genocidal wars against the Patagonian Indians, the attempt to push the native peoples out of the desirable grazing lands of the pampas, the growth of Buenos Aires as a metonym for the nation, and the consequent fabrication of the idea of Argentina as a purely immigrant society all participate in the crafting of Argentine whiteness.

In the late nineteenth century, when France and England were still consolidating their empires, Argentina, as part of continental Latin America, had long since achieved independence. This is the period that is often called the Age of Empire and that Edward Said discusses in *Culture and Imperialism,* asserting that the British and the French empires were larger in scope and more profound in effect than previous empires, including the Spanish. Thus out of step with Europe (pretty much defined as the emerging imperial powers of England and France), Argentina and the rest of Latin America were breaking free of Empire during the French and British rush toward imperialism. Argentina, newly independent, was behaving as an autonomous nation seeking parity with other free and autonomous nations. European expectations of overseas subservience came up against Argentine assertion of a will of its own.

As we saw in chapter 1, the architects of Argentina's pavilion at the 1900 international exposition in Paris went to great lengths to efface any sign of indigenous presence in their national self-representation. Europeans, however, not only expected but desired evidence of Argentine racial difference. They had read about the plumed savages of the Americas in the adventure stories of Salgari and Karl May. They remembered that Darwin had brought Fuegian Indians back from his voyage of scientific exploration and paraded them before British royalty. They wanted the thrill of the exotic, a personal contact with the undifferentiated Latin America from which Argentina was trying to extricate itself. And they would create the savage and exotic Argentina themselves, if need be. Ingrid Fey notes that the French version of Argentine representations of Argentine rural life at the 1889 Paris Universal Exposition included exoticized and romanticized white-skinned, European-dressed peasants, mimicking gauchos sitting in their pampas huts looking out the window—notwithstanding the fact that in real life structures like those lacked windows (2000, 73).

The international expositions in which, according to Anthony Alan Shelton, Europe achieves "the most cogent expression" of empire (2000, 157) were the very places where Argentina was trying to insert itself into the family of nations, as civilized as the nations of Europe and on equal terms with them. Europe (understood primarily as England and France in this context, but also perhaps Belgium, Germany, and the north of Italy) was inclined to relate to the non-European world as the site of exoticism, barbarism (in the civilization/barbarism dyad that haunts Argentina to this day), the colonized or colonizable other. This tendency collides with Argentina's desire to project itself as European. Thus, when a Frenchwoman requests to see the natives or when folkloric artifacts are requested for the Paris exhibition, it is not simply in recognition of a multicultural society that the Argentine elite is too proud to admit to, but also, and more importantly, a gesture that reinforces Europe's right to make use (and meaning) of the rest of the world. It is not surprising that the Argentine elite, desiring parity with Europe, refuses to capitulate to this version of its culture but instead insists on self-representation as a forward-looking, industrializing, literate, liberal nation. Both the European insistence on extracting the exotic other from Argentina for its own consumption and the Argentinean elite's refusal to embody the exotic other are racist, colonizing gestures. They both partake in the belief of European superiority, but there is a difference. Europe is distant enough from Argentine otherness and sure enough of its own preeminence that it longs to consume the indigenous, exotic other, a tasty morsel for a jaded palate.[13] Argentina's elite suppresses the very existence of the threatening other within in order to establish itself as the rightful owner and just ruler of a precariously "European" nation.

It is only the trumped-up evidence of racial otherness that makes the fiction of racial purity viable. Hence Europe projects its own racial anxieties onto Argentina, which in turn claims that it, too, is a European country. The nations of Europe need their racialized others to satisfy their own sense of identity as racially pure. Argentina, among the many colonial sites onto which Europe deflects its racial anxiety, refuses to be so othered, choosing, rather, to engage in the same pretense of whiteness. European texts uneasily collaborate with Argentina's claim, but not before demonstrating how shaky it is, by questioning its very premises.

Argentina's racial anxiety mirrors Europe's. If Buenos Aires is the Paris of America, then Paris is the gold standard of culture and refinement.

Glory redounds to both, and the standard of racial purity needs to be upheld at both ends of the equation. Paris's own status as a city of whites, challenged by the former colonials who have moved to its suburbs, is emblematic of the familiar disquiet of postcolonial Europe even into the twenty-first century. Moreover, faced with the physical presence of its former colonial subjects pressing in on its borders, concerned with its own racial boundaries, Europe is confronted by still another challenge from an Argentina that claims that it, too, is European. Even if it does lie on a different continent, and even if its seasons are the inverse of Europe's, Argentina claims to be a European nation. Europe wants its others to be different, but Argentina insists that it is the same. Nobody is playing by the rules. As if it weren't enough that their own countries are besieged by racial difference, here is a third world nation that is refusing to be nonwhite. The boundaries are being blurred from all sides. One of the ways this anxiety plays out in literary texts is that Argentina's racial makeup surfaces as an issue to be questioned and clarified. Naive Europeans assume Argentina is racially different from Europe, sometimes Black, sometimes indigenous, and other times mestizo, but more knowledgeable characters set them straight. Over and over, European authors collude in the production of Argentina as a white nation.

It is striking how often characters in literary texts who are representing Argentina to outsiders are questioned about the racial diversity presumed of Argentina as a representative of Latin America and respond by saying that no, in fact, Argentina is quite white. The absence of Blacks in particular is an important trope in the representation of Argentina—it is a stated absence, not just something left unsaid. (There may be a dearth of South Asians in Argentina, for example, but nobody remarks on that fact.) Since Argentina is part of America and participated in the slave trade, albeit not on the level of other nations, whose need for agricultural labor far exceeded Argentina's, it is to be expected that there will be an African presence in that country. The insistence on there being no Blacks there appears to be part of Argentina's overenthusiastic adherence to its own wretched history of minimizing its nonwhite population. Argentina itself perpetrates this fiction of whiteness, and outsiders respond. In Isaac Bashevis Singer's *Scum*, for example, the protagonist, Max, who has lived for years in Buenos Aires but is now back in Poland, is asked about the Blacks in Buenos Aires:

"I hear there are Black people there."

"In America, not in Argentina."   ·

"In New York, then?"

"In New York, in Chicago, in Cleveland." (Singer 1991, 165)

Max's response, a list of U.S. cities where Black people live, is recited like a litany of distant places far from both Warsaw and Buenos Aires, which, for the racially anxious characters, are happily free of Blacks.

The trope of Argentine whiteness is a sign of unease and of racism, a concern that Argentina's Black history will assert itself. For that history exists. Some of the Africans who were brought as slaves to the Americas became property of Argentines; slavery was codified into law and eventually abolished, also by law. Marvin Lewis (1996) shows how important Blacks were in developing Argentine culture in the early nineteenth century, when one in every three residents of Buenos Aires was of African origin. But by the late 1880s less than two percent of the population was Black. A combination of a yellow fever epidemic that disproportionately struck poor neighborhoods, including those where many Black people lived, the deaths of large numbers of Afro-Argentine soldiers during the Campaign of the Desert, intermarriage with whites, and out-migration to Brazil and Uruguay greatly reduced the numbers of Blacks in Argentina at the same time that immigration from Europe boomed. Moreover, as George Reid Andrews (1980; 2004) shows, Blacks were deliberately removed from the state's census reports. This falsification not only made it seem as though there were fewer Blacks than there were in reality, but also—because as a result Blacks did not officially exist—denied them necessary social services, making them especially vulnerable. Susana Rotker, arguing that the removal of Blacks from official discourse only partly explains why Argentina is perceived as a white country, notes that "if there are no blacks in Argentina today it is because they mixed in to such a degree that *they are no longer noticed*" (2002, 22, original emphasis). Seth Meisel believes that there was a deliberate shift in the official Argentine attitude that occurred sometime between the moment of independence, when the liberation of the nation was compared to the emancipation of enslaved Blacks, and the end of the nineteenth century when the suppression of Blackness was well under way (personal correspondence).[14]

If Rotker, Andrews, and Meisel are correct, as I believe they are, Blackness is a part of Argentina's very fiber, but it has been intentionally obscured, only to emerge obliquely. Certainly, Blackness is associated with that most Argentine of urban phenomena, the tango. Urban Black culture was instrumental in the making of the tango; thus tango itself is a sign of the historical presence of Argentine Blacks in the capital. In what Marta Savigliano calls "a chain of jumpy, imprecise associations" that links tango, Blacks, sexuality, and primitivism (1995, 33), Afro-Argentines are both credited with important contributions to Argentine popular culture and framed in profoundly racist ways.

Although after emancipation the majority of Afro-Argentines resided in the city, there were also Blacks present in another prototypically Argentine sphere: the rural world of the gauchos. Some former slaves, who had worked on large estates, stayed in the countryside taking up the nomadic life of the gauchos. Others, as we have seen, were manumitted as a result of serving in the army, where eventually they were called upon to help eradicate the native population. No doubt some of them stayed in the countryside as well. But just as Blackness is invoked only to be extirpated in foreign-penned narratives of Argentina, the Black gaucho is simultaneously evoked and eradicated in a key work of Argentine literature.

In one of the most celebrated passages of what is often taken to be Argentina's national poem and the greatest exemplar of the gauchesque, José Hernández's *Martín Fierro,* the usually sympathetic and sometimes even heroic protagonist unnecessarily, and without provocation, insults a Black woman, inciting a fight with the man she is with, a Black gaucho. Fierro's slurs, later extended to the man as well, are purely racial in content, and the scene ends in a duel in which Fierro kills the gaucho he has insulted. Some critics have argued that this scene illustrates how Fierro, as a symbol of the nation, has been contaminated by the violence that has been forced upon him, both as victim and perpetrator (he was one of the many gauchos pressed into service in the war against the native peoples of the pampas). Fermín Chávez (1973) goes so far as to admonish the readers of *Martín Fierro* that race is of no significance at all in the episode and that they should not take it into account.

A handful of the poem's commentators, Shumway (1991) among them, note the racialized nature of the violence and attribute it to Fierro's own sense of marginalization, suggesting that he shores up his own masculinity by attacking someone who is even lower down on the social scale than he. Dolores Aponte-Ramos (1999) openly challenges Fermín Chávez, arguing that race is a critical element of the episode, and she links it to other nineteenth-century representations of Black characters in Argentine literature. I believe it is possible to read this startling episode as a textualization of the overwrought response to Blacks by white Argentineans. There is simply no justification for Fierro's swaggering outburst. It is nothing more or less than an expression of racial braggadocio, a claim to superiority and a provocation to fight, with the result of extirpating Blackness from the space of the quintessential Argentine, the gaucho. If *Martín Fierro* is the song of Argentine national identity, then the elimination of the Black man, also a gaucho, also making a claim to occupy the same social space as Fierro, is a fair mirror of Argentine society's rhetorical, and real, suppression of its Black population.

The unprovoked extirpation of Blackness in Argentine society expressed in this key episode has the effect of creating its own afterimage. This passage from *Martín Fierro* is one of the most often read, most frequently commented upon, most commonly anthologized sections of a poem that exalts the humanity of its protagonist. Many readers know little of the poem but this incident, arguably its protagonist's most ignoble moment. Fierro is the honorable, loyal, long-suffering true Argentine, yet in this episode he behaves unpardonably. Still, it is not clear that José Hernández approves of his behavior. Unlike other parts of the poem, where the reader sympathizes with the gaucho as he is brutally treated by the government, or with the white women who have been taken captive and brutalized by the Indians, we are given no reason to justify Martín Fierro's behavior here. Fierro recognizes that he was looking for a fight, indicating that the object of his bellicosity was not predetermined. Race is not the starting point, but it is the vehicle that he will use to provoke the fight.

> Como nunca, en la ocasión
> Por peliar me dió la tranca.
> Y la emprendí con un negro
> Que trujo una negra en ancas. (Hernández 1872, 39)

> Then, more than ever before,
> booze made me want to fight
> and I picked one with a black
> who came riding in with his woman. (Hernández 1974, 50)

This episode has been translated in a variety of ways, none totally suitable, and each translation gives different valence to race. The 1974 SUNY Press version (used here) renders "negro" as "black" and "negra" as "his woman," whereas an earlier translation published in Argentina unselfconsciously uses "nigger" and "negress."

The Black man is the object of his desire to fight, but he does not attack him directly. Instead he provokes the man to fighting by taunting the woman he is with. First he insults her directly:

Al ver llegar la morena,
Que no hacía caso de naides,
Le dije con la mamúa:
-Va . . . ca . . . yendo gente al baile. (Hernández 1872, 39)

As she came in I saw
she wasn't lookin' at nobody,
so being drunk I said,
"*Cow* . . . ming to the dance?" (Hernández 1974, 50)

This is the first of two remarks that compare the Black woman to an animal—here the wordplay, which the woman quickly understands, likens her to a cow. *Va cayendo [gente al baile]* means a lot of people are coming to the dance. The change in stress to "*vaca yendo*" changes the meaning to "a cow going." She is quick to respond, insult for insult. The woman's sharp wit does not save her from further degrading comparisons to animals: Fierro tells his audience that she has a tail bigger than a fox's, and after her partner's death she cries like a wolf. The Black woman is repeatedly degraded by the comparison to animals. On the other hand, she is quick-witted and loving. Fierro first wants to hit her to stop her crying after he has killed her partner, but he thinks better of it—out of respect for the dead:

En esto la negra vino
Con los ojos como ají
Y empezó la pobre allí
A bramar como una loba.
Yo quise darle una soba
A ver si la hací callar,
Mas pude reflesionar
Que era malo en aquel punto,
Y por respeto al dijunto
No la quise castigar. (Hernández 1872, 42–43)

At this point, up came his woman,
with eyes like hot peppers,
and the poor thing began
howling like a she-wolf.
I wanted to put my whip to her
to see if I could make her stop;
but on second thought I saw
it wasn't the right thing to do,
and out of respect for the dead
I decided not to beat her up. (Hernández 1974, 53–54)

The so-called Conquest of the Desert sets the action of *Martín Fierro* in motion: the poem documents the inhuman methods used to conscript and keep gauchos like Fierro in the army. These wars are both more overtly economic in their objectives and represent an even more extraordinary degree of racial differentiation in white attitudes toward the Indians. The Black man in *Martín Fierro* is also a gaucho; as such he is susceptible to insult, and his relationship with a woman can be understood to be chivalrous. He is a worthy opponent who fights well, and after Fierro kills him, he thinks one day he will go back and give him a decent burial. Moreover, even though the Black woman is compared to a series of animals, in an overt effort to render a human subject contemptible and ridiculous, she is still a fully human subject. The woman is quick-witted and loyal; she appropriately expresses grief when her man is killed.

Unlike the Black characters, the Indian in the poem is the absolute other. He is bestialized: represented as bereft of any moral or ethical understanding; brutal not only to his captives but to the women of his own community; incapable of understanding terms like loyalty, honor, or friendship. These thoroughly dehumanized beings might have represented, for Fierro and his friend Cruz, the hope of freedom from a constraining civilization. In *Martín Fierro,* the gaucho escapes "civilized" society, which in Argentina as in the United States is associated with cities, education, and the civilizing effects of women, by lighting out to Indian country, very like Mark Twain's Tom Sawyer and Huckleberry Finn. In Twain as in Argentine myth, Indians represent a totally unfettered life, but they are also savage and dangerous. If women are associated with civilizing behavior, the Indian offers something to be desired as well as feared. Injun Joe is the chief villain and most present danger in *Tom Sawyer;* in *Martín Fierro* the Indians kidnap white women, treat their own wives as little more than slaves, are violent, drink blood, and generally behave badly. The savagery of the Indians in *Martín Fierro* is considered self-evident once the proof of their mistreatment of both white captive and indigenous women is documented.[15]

In contrast to the antisocial behavior of the Indians, gauchos demonstrate love, friendship, and loyalty that continue on beyond death and unto the generations. (This attachment tends to be of the homosocial sort: there is little place for women in the lives of Fierro and Cruz beyond the production of sons that will allow for the perpetuation of friendship into the second generation.) Cruz and Fierro soon learn that there is no freedom in their life with the Indians—only suffering and, in Cruz's case, death. *Martín Fierro* can be taken as one instance of a discourse of othering that made it seem not only possible, but just and necessary, to destroy the Indians, in their person and in their culture. That they were in the way of privatizing land and constraining the development of property made it seem all the more reason to get rid of them. Any profit made by those members of the elite as a result of the elimination of indigenous people from the land they wanted to claim was only for the good of the nation.

Blacks and Indians are rendered absent from Argentina, both from the city, which insists on its European origins both racially and culturally, and from the countryside, where the Indian is first incorporated into the gaucho and then extirpated from him. Blacks, Indians, and gauchos are all marginal figures, alternatively criminalized, romanticized, and disappeared. Insofar as the gaucho is the quintessential Argentine, it is not surprising that Indians and Blacks, repressed in the historical consciousness of the nation, oscillate between being and not being assimilated to the gaucho. The Black gaucho who is eliminated in the foundational text *Martín Fierro* may have been historically present, even making his appearance in the poem, but the nation will have no part of him. The (putatively white) gaucho, as the national hero of the Conquest of the Desert, into which he was pressed, loses his mestizo identity. The foundational myth of the gaucho is that he is the child of a Spanish father and an Indian mother. The maternal, the indigenous, is excised by the time Martín Fierro and Cruz ride into Indian territory. They know they are going into the land of the absolute other. Theirs is a homosocial world that has little room for the feminine, whether in the form of actual women or mythic mothers. The Indian mother withers away in what the deeply conservative and patriarchal Federalists would hail as the autochthonous Argentine. Just as they balk at the suggestion that Argentina is an Indian country, they deny that it is a feminine one, or an immature one. Masculinity, whiteness, and virile adulthood are the threads that will be woven together into the fabric of Argentina.

As we have seen, the indigenous people in Argentina were discursively removed from the realm of the human and physically displaced from their land. Afro-Argentines were drastically reduced in numbers, and the remaining old families and new arrivals, mostly from Brazil and other parts of Latin America, were quietly ignored, their very existence repeatedly denied. Yet it is never self-evident that Argentina is white. On the contrary, Europe always raises the question of race. Aren't there Blacks there? Isn't the place full of Indians?

The oblique connection between the expectation of Argentine racial otherness on the part of Europeans and the suppression of that otherness among the Argentine elite emerges, the repressed returning, in unexpected ways. In European writers, for whom Argentina and Africa sometimes evoke each other, such juxtapositions generally cast Africa as even more primitive and exotic. One French writer, Raymond Roussel, details the crass and showy and spectacular wealth of the Argentine upper class in the prologue of a novel called *Impressions of Africa*. His protagonist's trip to Africa from France is preceded by a request by a young Argentine baron (one wonders where an Argentinean got a title), "an enormously rich Argentine who, for many years, has led a life of crazy spending and continuous ostentation in Paris," to create a fireworks display to celebrate his wedding.[16] This Argentine, who has a "castle" near Buenos Aires, stands in stark contrast to the Africans the narrator will soon meet, but to whom he is symbolically linked as Europe's other.

The veiled relationship between Argentina and Africa, rendered as negation, surfaces both in I. B. Singer's *Scum*, as we saw earlier, and in Dominique Bona's *Argentina*. The upper-class characters that Bona's protagonist meets crossing the Atlantic from France to Argentina go out of their way to proclaim Argentina so white a country that implausibility may be figured by the odds that one might ever see a Black person there:

> "*No!* . . . what terrible nonsense . . . all that has as much chance of happening as you or I have of running into a Black person on the streets of Buenos Aires." (Bona 1986, 38)[17]

In his reply, Jean's cabin mate, Clarance, reveals his naïveté precisely in his vision of Argentina as a mestizo country full of Indians, a supposition that provokes the exaggerated protestations of his dinner companions:

> "I have been assured on the contrary," he said, "that Argentina was the strangest and most multiple mix of peoples. Will we be met at the dock by Indians with feathers?"
>
> Campbell choked in his glass, Lady Campbell raised her delicate shoulders, the large man laughed like a barbarian, and Robert de Liniers—for that was the name of the French aristocrat—responded, sardonically, "We are a white country, sir. The only perfectly white country south of Canada." (38)[18]

The European newcomer is disciplined out of his beliefs about the racial complexity of Argentina by a whole tableful of his social superiors, whose Argentina is contained in Buenos Aires. Although this totalizing picture of Argentina as perfectly white (which itself depends on a disquieting view of a Canada equally bereft of its Native and Black populations) does not go unchallenged, that challenge is barely whispered. Marta quietly demurs. Her refutation of the myth of white Argentina is described as a "terrible and confidential" revelation, and in the end she quietly backs off, minimizing the reality of the indigenous presence by likening the name of their territory to the sound of sucking on sweets:

> "There certainly are some descendents of real Indians," murmured Marta through her painted lips, "in Salta, in Jujuy, in the North. Don Rafael," she asserted with the look of someone revealing something terrible and confidential, "Don Rafael met some Araucanians from Tierra del Fuego, who..."
>
> "Yes, yes, ..." it was the English banker this time ... "From living so long in the desert with the vicunas and guanacos, Don Rafael will end up like Robinson Crusoe, losing his grasp on reality... Dear friend, all these Araucanians, believe me, it's nothing but myth..."
>
> "By my faith, they very much exist," the large man asserted. "Their tribes occupy the whole Southern part of the River Bio-Bio, according to what I'm told."
>
> "Bio-Bio, it sounds like sucking on a candy," murmured Marta. (38–39)[19]

This discussion reflects the uneasy notions of race, as well as of the political geography of Argentina. Marta's husband behaves oddly by staying in the interior and avoiding both Buenos Aires and Europe. In the eyes of the Argentine Europhiles, it is a small step from there to madness—to believing the evidence of native people. For Campbell and

Liniers, the real Argentina is only Buenos Aires, and therefore white. The rest is the stuff of myth, to which the British lord effectively banishes the Araucanians. There they can represent a romantic notion of freedom or a demonized vision of barbaric behavior.[20] Campbell, good Englishman that he is, weighs in with data to support his position:

> "[T]hese are the numbers, the true numbers: 63 percent of Argentines are born of European decendancy, 23 percent are foreign born, that is, born in Europe . . . A residue of 350,000 people is of mixed blood. Knowing this, how can you say that the people of Argentina are mulatto?" (39)[21]

He then asserts that the true mestizos are Europeans, who intermarry across national boundaries, the Anglo-Calabrese and the London-Sevillians.

Despite his hearkening back to a Herderian concept of nation as a natural unit of humanity that can then mix with other natural units to created a blended offspring (the Anglo-Calabrese) even down to the specificity of the individual city (the London-Sevillian), Campbell bristles at the idea that Englishmen might bear race in the same way that Blacks and Jews do:

> "Hellfire and damnation," [Goldberg] bellowed. "Take a good look at the Europeans you are importing. They are no less distinctive than Blacks. The Sicilian, the Bavarian, the Turk, the Pole, the Genovese, the Corsican, there you have the picturesque sir, in the streets of Buenos Aires. . . . Along with the two most exclusive races in the world, yours, Lord Campbell and mine . . . , the English and the Jew."
> At this, the Englishman nearly choked. (40)[22]

It is one thing to tell an Englishman that southern Europeans are like Blacks. It is quite another to liken him to a Jew. Racial meaning for the imperial nations depends on naming at least one other, and allows for the racializing of a variety of them, but "race" as a category does not apply to them. For Campbell and Liniers, Argentina is not a raced country; whiteness to them is the absence of race. Even Goldberg has left the trappings of Judaism behind in Europe. Married to a Gentile woman, the father of an assimilated, Argentine-born daughter, a self-made man, he is the very sign of Argentina's capacity for whitening its inhabitants.

The idea that Argentina is a white country is belied by material reality. Goldberg, after all, continues to identify as a Jew, and the others see him that way as well (even his wealth fits the stereotype). But what remains true is that white Argentina has managed to project itself and then see itself reflected back as the most European of Latin American nations. Unlike Mexico, for example, where after the revolution the elite strove to create a mestizo culture into which its native population could be incorporated, Argentina expunges the indigenous.[23] Mexico's ideal ancestors, the Indians, would be integrated into its ideal citizenry as mestizo. In contrast, Argentina's ideal ancestor is the immigrant (he who comes down from the boat), whose descendant, assimilated by the purported Argentine melting pot is the ideal citizen—the European mestizo described by Bona's Lord Campbell.

In 2000, Néstor García Canclini, a transplanted Argentine living in Mexico, wrote that

> the study of multiculturalism and its connections to power had a different format than in the United States, and at the same time different in Mexico and Peru, where the intercultural occurs in great part because of the indigenous presence, or in the Caribbean, where the Afro-American is central, or in the Río de la Plata, where the predominance of European culture simulated a white homogeneity. (2000, 38)[24]

Whereas the rest of America in this sentence "is," the Río de la Plata "simulates." Peru and Mexico experience interculturality because of the indigenous presence that the dominant, largely mestizo society gets to see, interact with, and on a symbolic level identify with; similarly the real centrality of Afro-American culture marks the Caribbean.[25] The Río de la Plata, on the other hand, "simulates" white homogeneity. This suggests an important difference, a difference of simulated purity that also rests on a certain reality, that of the hegemony of European culture. Mexican, Peruvian, and Caribbean multiculturalism depend on indigenous and Black bodies; the Río de la Plata's racial identity depends on European culture, rather than on what in the United States would be considered white bodies.[26] In García Canclini's formulation, the discourse of whiteness simulates racial purity. The notion that Argentina's racial identity is simulated suggests that, as a nation, an entity that is "a fundamental unit of humanity" and "a political entity embodied in a state," Argentina is less real than the rest of the continent. Because Argentina projects itself as a unified people, a white nation, and because it seems to be calling on the "natural expression of a people" to justify itself as a nation, Argentina seems all the more ephemeral. Although I would argue that insofar as race (and therefore racial purity) is a cultural construct,

"simulation" is beside the point, García Canclini's use of the term suggests Argentina's constant need to shore up its story of racial purity. Its
premise of nationhood, based on melting-pot Europeanness, means it
depends on that story. "Argentina" is therefore all the more susceptible
to being made up as its inventors—both those who live inside its borders and those who narrate it from outside—go along.

CHAPTER SEVEN

The Other Within

In her study of Victoria Ocampo's autobiographical writings, María Cristina Arambel-Güiñazú creatively misreads Carlos Fuentes, who notes the Porteño need to come to self-consciousness via language. Fuentes writes:

> Buenos Aires needs to name itself to know that it exists, to invent itself a past, to imagine a future for itself: unlike Mexico City or Lima, a simple visual reference to the signs of historic prestige is not enough for it.... Could there be anything more Argentine than this necessity to verbally fill these empty spaces, to take recourse in all the world's libraries to fill the blank book of Argentina?[1]

For Fuentes, the Argentine desire to locate oneself in time and space via language is primarily about national self-definition, but Arambel-Güiñazú disregards Fuentes's insistent reflexives (to name itself, invent itself, imagine a future for itself), altering the meaning of his observation. Fuentes's reference to the universal stories that the world's libraries have in their stores, and that set the standards for Argentine selfhood, becomes, in Arambel-Güiñazú's reading, the reflection of Argentina in the eyes of others:

> Seeing itself through the eyes of the "other," of the stranger who makes the rules, from political laws to those that define good taste and culture, produces a dislocation that favors self-analysis. (1993, 123)[2]

Contrary to Arambel-Güiñazú's assertion, however, Argentina is not present in the books housed in Fuentes's very Borgesian European libraries; only its models are to be found there. Arambel-Güiñazú trans-forms what Fuentes sees as the Porteño need to speak itself via Euro-pean standards into a desire to be seen by others—the self-same visual proof that, according to Fuentes, Argentina abjures, presumably for lack of Aztecs and Incas that would bestow upon it any "historic prestige." I am not arguing that Arambel-Güiñazú is incorrect in asserting that Porteños (and by familiar extension Argentines) rely on the gaze of their European others to create a sense of national identity. On the contrary, her argument demonstrates that this narrative of Argentine dependency is so pervasive that signs of it are perceived even where they do not exist.

Eventually the European libraries invoked by Fuentes would indeed hold books that represented Argentina, thanks in part to Argentina's situation as an immigrant nation. Among the books in those libraries would be those written by the countrymen and -women of peasants, skilled laborers, victims of political and religious persecution, and entre-preneurs who had made their way to the Southern Cone and settled in Buenos Aires, Rosario, Mendoza, and other cities and towns. Insofar as the history of Argentine immigration is also the history of European emigration, with all their attendant letters, photographs, picture post-cards, and even people making their way back and forth between conti-nents, it is not surprising that more public texts would follow.

Maria Luisa Magagnoli's *Un caffe molto dolce,* for example, is an ac-count of the author's journey to Argentina to track down information on the life of Severino Di Giovanni, an Italian-born anarchist who be-came notorious in Argentina, but who for Magagnoli was a dashing, compelling figure. Executed by the Uriburu dictatorship in 1931, Di Gio-vanni was so vilified in Argentina that his biography, written by the leftist Argentine writer Osvaldo Bayer, was suppressed, censored, and burned, and projects to film his life story were repeatedly stymied. Di Giovanni's anti-Fascism and penchant for revolutionary violence fascinated the Ital-ian writer. Magagnoli's self-described obsession with Di Giovanni con-nects her to Argentina and draws her into its common history with Italy. Di Giovanni's career as an anti-Fascist began in Italy, and it was nourished by the Italian immigrant community that had set roots not only in Buenos Aires but also in the provinces. At a safe distance on the other side of the ocean, and dead for half a century, the man represented in Argentine history as a psychopathic killer is, for Magagnoli, a roman-tic figure linked to her by a common national heritage.

Also among the immigrants whose presence in Argentina would engender literary reflection were Jewish settlers, who caught the interest of both Gentile and Jewish writers. As we saw in chapter 6, Argentina has been whitewashed, its racialized others suppressed as part of its Europhilism. This identification with Europe, however, gives rise to another, more European other: the Jew. It is difficult to gauge how much the Jewish presence in Argentina enters into a sense of national identity, since the dominant Christian culture inherited from Europe shapes itself against Jewishness. On the one hand, Jewish characters turn up in many texts. Jewish filmmakers make movies, and Jewish writers write. The grand national narrative, however, keeps Argentina's Jews and the Jewish contribution to Argentine culture marginalized, either assimilated or ignored.

Sometimes assimilation is so complete as to obscure the Jewish presence altogether. Carlo Michelstaedter, the philosopher-suicide whose major work spurs his friend Enrico Mreule to undertake his Argentine adventure in Claudio Magris's *A Different Sea,* was a Jew. So, too, probably, was the historical Mreule, whose life and name find fictional representation in the novel. Michelstaedter and his group were part of a generation that was educated secularly. Their Jewishness is expressed in the alienation that results in Michelstaedter's extreme philosophy of stripping away everything that is inessential and that compromises a common humanity. Given the Jewish experience in Istria (as in the rest of Europe), being marked as Jewish was complicated. It could have been a deep part of the identity of the individual in his or her community, but it also would have marked the self as "other." For Jews entering modernity, via emancipation from the ghetto (which happened only a generation earlier) and secular education, a sense of citizenship and loyalty to the secular state or at least a sense of responsibility to that state, together with the temptation to disassociate oneself from all ties and try to find the essential humanness in oneself, must have been strong. So although Magris writes Michelstaedter and Mreule without dwelling on their Jewishness, the experience of being Jewish in the early twentieth century profoundly colors the narrative. Mreule's empty Argentina has no place for Europeanness, no less for its internal other, Judaism. At the other extreme, Jorge Luis Borges's deeply and ineluctably European Argentina is permeated with Jewishness. Thanks to Borges, Jewishness is both Argentine and laundered; actual Jews are unnecessary in the presence of Borges's literary affinity with Judaism.[3] In real life, though, the Jews are there:

were they not fictional, Emma Zunz and her factory-owning father would have found a lively Jewish community in Buenos Aires.

In the late nineteenth century, the projects of Baron Maurice de Hirsch to find a new land for beleaguered Jews intersected with the programs of Argentina's former President Domingo Faustino Sarmiento to populate Argentina with European settlers. De Hirsch was in search of safe havens for poor and embattled Jews, places where they could make a Jewish world and a Jewish life tilling the soil, free of the history of Russia and eastern Europe, the pogroms, and the Pale. A few decades earlier, Sarmiento had articulated a plan for bringing European immigrants to build a white and progressive Argentina deeply connected to another vision of Europe—Western, liberal, and rational.[4] The matchmaker who brought the baron's purposes together with the former president's objectives was a Jewish scientist, Dr. Wilhelm Lowenthal, who had been invited to Argentina in 1890 to share his technological expertise in agricultural matters. While visiting the province of Santa Fe, Lowenthal came upon a settlement of Jews who had arrived from Russia the year before, intent on establishing themselves in the rural economy, but living in such appallingly harsh conditions that many of them, children above all, had fallen ill and died of malnutrition that first year. Horrified, Lowenthal complained to the Argentine authorities; and on his return, through mutual acquaintances, he persuaded de Hirsch to fund the Jewish Colonization Association (JCA) to aid Jewish settlers in Argentina. In its years of existence, the JCA helped thousands of Jews make the journey to what was for them the "other" America and create for themselves a Jewish homeland there. These Jews from the shtetls and the cities of eastern Europe were to go to this far-distant land and, without leaving their religious culture behind, learn how to make a life on what Argentineans called "the desert." This unlikely convergence of visions, and the Jewish settlements and dispersion into the cities that followed on it, has given Argentina another distinctive characteristic that marks it in the global imaginary.[5]

With a population of more than 200,000 Jews, which is more than half of those who live in all of Latin America, Argentina is the most Jewish of Latin American countries. Jews had come to Argentina before it was a nation, centuries before Sarmiento began scouring Europe to populate Argentina or Baron de Hirsch funded the Jewish Colonization Association. Nevertheless, the liberal elite's desire to bring Europeans into Argentina, set in motion in the early days of the Republic and expanded to include the Jews of eastern Europe in 1881, and de Hirsch's project to get Jews out of Russia and eastern Europe in the 1890s were, together, a powerful force in creating both the reality and the story of the migration of Jews to Argentina.

The major work of the JCA took place between 1889 and 1905. After that, the vast majority of Jews who emigrated to Argentina, fleeing persecution without the aid of the JCA's homesteading stake, settled in the cities, particularly Buenos Aires. It is likely that both the openness of Argentina to European immigrants, including Jews, together with the already-existing Jewish settlements made Argentina a desirable goal for many impoverished and persecuted eastern European Jews. The new Jewish settlements of urban Argentina produced businessmen, physicians, writers, and artists, but also the underworld that so fascinates later Jewish writers looking in at Argentina from the outside.

The Jewish presence in Argentina has evoked different kinds of reactions from writers from elsewhere, but in the examples below, what is most clear is that Argentina is a stage on which issues of identity and meaning in the native cultures of the writers are played out. In *Carlota Fainberg,* by the Spanish novelist Antonio Muñoz Molina, the Jewishness of Argentina is central to the fascination that nation holds for Abengoa, the Spanish businessman who is the protagonist of the novel's embedded narrative.[6] The medieval Christian myth of the sexually desirable and, what is more, desiring Jewess surfaces in this late twentieth-century novel. For Abengoa, the exotic allure of Argentina resides in its Jewishness. Names like Carlota Fainberg are, for him, mysterious and thrilling. In their reflection of the abandonment of socially sanctioned marriage within religious, racial, and ethnic groups, they promise sexual pleasures unthinkable to women whose names express pure and chaste Spanish lineage, names like the ones his wife carries:

> You'll see. Argentine women have another kind of bearing, like they're more worldly, maybe it's the mix of races, or because they're all in analysis, or because of their names. You have to admit that it's not the same to be called Mariluz Padilla Soto as it is to be called Carlota Fainberg. (Muñoz Molina 1999, 115)[7]

Argentina is, for this Spaniard, a land of exotically mixed races, in which he clearly includes Jews and Christians. Moreover, the promise of a dangerous sexual pleasure resides in the register of language. It is her name that arrests Abengoa, a name that signifies hybridity: "to be called Carlota Fainberg." Taking the long historical view, and considering the mix of cultures that produced modern Spain, the idea that "Carlota Fainberg" represents a more exotic ethnic history than "Mariluz Padilla Soto" displays a splendid ignorance. Carlota became Fainberg only when she married a wealthy older man; thus "Carlota Fainberg" signifies "Jew" without necessarily being Jewish.[8]

Claudio, Abengoa's interlocutor and the novel's primary narrator, is also Spanish, but he has spent enough time as a professor in a college in the United States to have learned to be circumspect in his descriptions of the fascinating desirability of foreign women. It is always Abengoa, and never his at first reluctant but eventually spellbound listener, who characterizes Carlota as sexually exotic. Claudio is always careful to attribute any account of Carlota's deliberately seductive eroticism to Abengoa and to point out that it is Abengoa who describes Carlota as not only exotic but bestial:

> *He said* that she had long blonde hair and wore a dark jacket with wide shoulders and a tightly cinched waist, high heels that made her look taller "though she didn't need them at all," green, slanted eyes—feline *(the adjective is his)*, splendidly made up, that fixed on him immediately at the same time that her wide, fleshy mouth smiled at him frankly, the typical smile of the Porteña woman, *he declared to me*, like someone telling a traveler of the wonders of the country he is about to visit for the first time. (59–60, emphasis added)[9]

Here again Claudio is careful to distance himself from the exoticization of Carlota: "The mysterious blonde woman, *as he himself called her*, remained his top priority" (71, emphasis added).[10] Nevertheless, Claudio is also seduced by Abengoa's narrative and by the exotic Carlota, even as he professes horror at Abengoa's unreconstructed sexism and ethnocentrism. An unsuccessful academic, a literary theorist who cannot maintain the proper critical distance from the narrative he is listening to, Claudio is more troubled by his failure to keep a strict analytic distance between himself and Abengoa's story than he is by his countryman's retrograde attitude toward foreign women. Ultimately, the desire that Carlota arouses in Claudio is more narratological than sexual. He wants to know the end of the story that Abengoa terminates so abruptly and unsatisfyingly. Moreover, he wants to break the academic taboo that severs narrative from material reality.

Ironically, although Claudio refuses responsibility for the sexism and latent racism that Abengoa speaks and he transcribes, he is haunted by charges of just such racism and sexism later in the novel. Moreover, Claudio is quick to point out that his interest in Argentina, unlike Abengoa's, is not predatory: He is not motivated by the desire for either sexual or economic conquest. Instead, his interest is purely intellectual and literary. He goes to Argentina to attend a conference and to meet with a former colleague. Claudio's Buenos Aires is the Buenos Aires of Borges, not of seedy hotels and exotic women.

With a few exceptions, Muñoz Molina's erudite Claudio chief among them, Jorge Luis Borges does not represent Argentina, Jewish or otherwise. On the contrary, he is figured as the man of the universal, labyrinthine library. The Borges character in Umberto Eco's *The Name of the Rose* (1984) is the quintessential example of this ultraliterary figure, not linked to the history or specificity of any single nation, but instead rooted in Western concepts of literature, the mind, and language made material. For Eco, Borges's nation is the library.

As a writer of global significance and universal appeal, Borges's nationality is sometimes nothing more than a mere curiosity to his readers. How odd, they seem to suggest, that such sophisticated writing should come from such a faraway place; but then again Argentina is so very European, and Borges himself claims all Western civilization as his literary patrimony. Borges's importance as a figure on the international literary scene has been amply and expertly documented and studied, so I will not attempt to do that here. For many, he is a literary institution, but as such he is often seen as detached from Argentina.[11] Here, however, I am interested in how three visual artists, one Japanese, one Italian, and one American, render Borges in their own work.

Michiko Hoshino is one of the very few women working in the medium of lithography in Japan. Her *Homage to Borges* consists of a series of two-tone lithographs, with images embedded in abstraction, suggestive of but not in any way overtly translating Borges's motifs, including books and pages of manuscripts, some of which are legible and recognizable as pages of Borges's own writing. These images are sometimes of printed pages and sometimes of manuscripts with the author's corrections written in. Many of the books are illegible, representing writing, but not comprehensible as such. Some appear to have been burned around the edges. Another of Hochino's repeated motifs is an eye that might be

Borges's own. In one image the eye is embedded in a clock and set in a drizzly, abstract landscape, a dream-like abstraction. There is also one image that is reminiscent of a staircase, something suggestive of Borges's libraries.

Like the Italian artist Vija Spekke, Hoshino is fascinated by Borges and a world that seems to be disintegrating around the edges. There is a haunting quality in both artists, with touches of surrealism, of something that has just escaped. These are images of traces, or traces of images. As in many of Borges's texts, there is nothing but the trace, the commentary on an imagined text, translated by these artists into a visual image of absence. There is nothing that was there and now is gone, at least not in the material sense. These graphic representations seem somehow allegorical, but the correlative of the allegory is missing; and the images that are present seem, as a result, mysterious. They are meant to evoke something, but what, precisely? Borges himself becomes a referent in Hoshino's images, but that only takes us so far. Borges, as a man, seems benign, not quite corporeal.

Spekke, born in Lithuania, raised in Italy, lived for many years in England and now again in Italy. Her book *Il Mondo di Borges* is not quite a catalogue of the artist's exhibit; it is more like a work of art itself.[12] In it, the artist puts her art at the service of Borges's texts. She illustrates his poems: "Susana Bombal" is joined to an inky page, colors running, that contains a figure out of a painting by Leonardo, or so it appears, in profile, staring at something quite outside the frame. In another image, a sinuous splotch, reminiscent of a tiger, is superimposed on a round labyrinth, juxtaposed with a partly effaced sketch of a statue in the classical style. A simple sketch of a hand moving a chess piece occupies the same page as the poem "Ajedrez" (Chess); the opposite page mixes images from the game: a small and crumbling castle wall, a horse beginning to rear, with outsize sketches of the knight and the castle. Soft splatter background behind overlapping leaves of paper: these are pages from Borges's *El libro de arena (The Book of Sand)*. Another image of books, paintbrushes, lettering, the shadow of a human figure, "Las cosas comunes" (Ordinary things) faces the text of "El amenazado" (The threatened man). Two female figures occupy one page, the words of the poem fanning out between them. On another, the poem "Yo" (I) is printed and illustrated with a skeleton, while on the facing page the same poem is handwritten and the skeleton is a blurry x-ray, the image bleeding into the words. Another image, associated wth a poem dedicated to Susana Bombal, contains the sketch of the Leonardo-type face earlier associated with her, superimposed on a group of geometric figures. The poem's title is written, faintly, across it all: "La rosa profunda" (The profound rose). The "Milonga de Manuel Flores" (Manuela Flores's tango session) is simply illustrated with a pistol and a dagger. It is the only image that might be construed to have a specifically Argentine content.

The American artist Jules Kirschenbaum writes that he is drawn to "the possibility of imminent revelation, which is the feeling in many of Borges's stories" (1990, 244). Unlike Spekke, Kirschenbaum "[does] not try to illustrate anything, but rather to 'sustain a mood' derived from reading the same text over and over" (244). In contrast to the other artists' blurred edges and runny images, his canvas *Dream of a Golem*, inspired by "El Aleph" (The Aleph), "La escritura del Dios" (The God's script), and "Las ruinas circulares" (The circular ruins), is crisply rendered and fully detailed. Its visual ancestry includes the surrealism of Dalí, juxtaposing the meticulously drawn bones of a leg and two feet, an eggshell-like skull, an open-ended box with wires dangling from it, and a flask of liquid in the grasp of a man, whose knuckles point to the Hebrew letters that suggest the kabbalistic charm that animates inert matter, or perhaps spelling out the words meaning "the infinite." The man is, presumably, the dreamer of this "Dream of a Golem," intent on creating life. For Kirschenbaum, the artist is the golem maker who creates the powerful monster that both saves and destroys; but his Borges has nothing to do with Argentina. Not only is Kirschenbaum's Borges free of national identity, "he seems to stand above the mindless strife of the world" (235).[13]

As interpreted by these three artisits, Borges is an emblem of the cosmopolitan, as he is for Antonio Muñoz Molina. In *Carlota Fainberg*, Claudio's intellectual interest in this Borges who is not subject to the limitations of Argentina-as-other is the counterweight to Abengoa's fascination with the overdeterminedly embodied and Argentine Carlota. The scholar's professional interest signals sophistication, intellectual attainment, a connection to Argentina that refers to its international nature in contrast to its exotic allure. Abengoa relates to Argentina as prey, although it ultimately refuses to be so. The hotel he hopes to acquire spits him out as soon as he is recognized as a scout for his conglomerate, and the desired woman turns out to be the predator. Claudio's Argentina, in contrast, is the site of a literary pilgrimage. The idea that his intentions may be predatory or colonizing seems absurd to him, the traditional literary critic, a humanist whose attitude to his subject is reverence. In Borges, ironically, we come back around to Abengoa's fascination with Carlota's racial exoticism. Borges, too, was fascinated by Judaism, although not, apparently, for any erotic reason.[14]

Abengoa is the new conquistador, on the prowl for the modern exploitable resources of the non-European world, sturdy but mismanaged hotels like the Town Hall, where he encounters Carlota. As recycled and reconstituted by Abengoa's company, Argentina can be brought into the fold of globalized tourism, based in a Spain that is making use once again of the former Empire. Buenos Aires is another of the places he must travel for the business of what is, in a sense, repossessing Empire. Claudio is engaged in a similar project, although in the cultural rather than the commercial sphere. He is excoriated, he believes unfairly, for his act of colonization of the literature of the former colony, and it is true that the charge is on one level silly. On another, however, his travel to Argentina is, also, about globalization. Claudio's attitude toward Argentina is that of the humanistically trained literary scholar, whose motives are less those of the colonizer than those of the hajji who reverently travels to the land of the birth of the text. He describes his journey as a literary pilgrimage, in terms that might be comprehensible to believers on the road to Santiago de Compostela. His attitude toward the text is one of knowledgeable devotion, born of a love for the word itself, and he also reveres the author of the text. Still, the work of such a scholar, a scholar like me as well as like Claudio, is part of a larger institution of knowledge making that is conscripted to uses that may, in fact, reenact colonization and empire. Moreover, literary pilgrims love stories; and in the end Claudio is drawn into the Town Hall Hotel to write the ending to Abengoa's sexually predatory narrative.

Abengoa, echoing the discourse of Empire, speaks as if Argentina were utterly different from Spain, available as a source of commercial gain and sexual pleasure, but otherwise inscrutable. But a difference that is so absolute would be unrepresentable. It would cast a shadow so dark that nothing of it could be seen. On the contrary, it is possible to broach the difference that Argentina represents because it is not absolute. As I argue throughout this study, Argentina is compelling because its difference from the metropolitan center, be it Europe or the United States, only seems complete at the first, quick glance. In fact there are numerous handholds of similarity that make it possible for the outsider to connect, to make sense of the difference and to use it.

Abengoa's Argentina is the site of the reenactment of Spain's own racially diverse history. That history was, during the long years of the Franco dictatorship, suppressed as a matter of state policy. Franco was the heir of the Catholic monarchs Fernando and Isabel, who ejected Jews and Muslims from their united kingdoms, and who completed the seven-hundred-year-long "reconquest" of Spain by defeating the last of the Muslim rulers on the European continent. The consolidation of Spain as a militantly Catholic monarchy at the end of the fifteenth century was reinforced by the similarly militant Catholic dictatorship of the mid-twentieth, when all traces of Judaism or Islam were relegated to the long-dead-and-buried. Abengoa is old enough to have been educated under the Franco regime; for him, Jews are mythic creatures from the dimmest past. In contrast, the new Spain, set in motion by the socialist government that followed Franco's death, has embraced its Jewish and Muslim history. Impelled, in part, by the global recognition among forward-looking nations that a mix of cultures (no longer to be considered "races") is a good thing, Spain now celebrates its long multicultural past. Statues of Jewish cultural figures have been erected in Andalucía; compact disks of Ladino songs can be found in any music store. Cookbooks devoted to Sephardic cuisine share shelf space in bookstores with scholarly studies of Mozarabic and Mudéjar art, architecture, and poetry. Popular foreign novels with titles like *La judía de Toledo* (The Jewess of Toledo) and *El último judío* (The last Jew) compete with, and perhaps whet the appetite for, more serious literary texts like Muñoz Molina's own *Sefarad* and Camilo José Cela's *Judíos, moros y cristianos* (Jews, Moors, and Christians).[15]

Yet Jewishness in Spain has become oddly domesticated. One scholarly discussion of the Sephardic Museum in Toledo begins with the following pair of anecdotes. When the ticket taker at the Synagogue of Santa María la Blanca in Toledo, Spain, was asked, "Are the Jews of Toledo funding the restoration of this old synagogue?" the answer was, "There are no Jews in Toledo." But when the mayor of Toledo and president of the museum's Friends Association, Juan Ignacio de Mesa Ruiz, at the reopening of the Synagogue of Samuel Ha-Levy was asked, "Why are you, a non-Jew, so committed to funding the restoration of this old synagogue?" he replied, "Because we are all Jews in Toledo" (Holo 1999, 55).

Spain is currently engaged in and by this double vision of the same reality—that the Jews were expelled over five hundred years ago and now none remain, and that the seven hundred years of contact among Jews, Christians, and Muslims preceding that expulsion left every family a little Jewish. The hyperassimilation of the second formulation, a Jewish history that nourishes a safely secular Christian present, handily eliminates the need for living Jews (what we see expressed in the first), although current political discourse would indicate, perhaps overly optimistically, that they would be welcome should they appear.[16] Yet when Jews do turn up, as Carlota Fainberg does in the Buenos Aires hotel Abengoa is scouting for a Spanish takeover, they are, it turns out, not only exotic, maddeningly sensual, and demandingly sexual, but also phantasmagoric. The living Jewish woman doesn't have a chance in this text. She is only available to the reader as the narrativized object of desire of one Spaniard, as recalled to another who finds, ultimately, that she has always been a ghost.

For Abengoa, Carlota Fainberg's supposed Jewish blood (for he still sees race where more up-to-date Spaniards see culture), if it refers back to Spain at all, does so in a mysterious, ancient way. He certainly represents Carlota to Claudio in all her exotic difference:

> She was too much of a fantasy-woman, Abengoa thought now, extremely dangerous in her long and flattering passion, her alarming feline ecstasy, as potentially scandalous as the cries she emitted at the moment of orgasm. (Muñoz Molina 1999, 102)[17]

In *Carlota Fainberg*, Jewish Argentina can be read as the projection of Spain's own coming to terms with the exotic other within. How different from the Argentineans for whom the name Fainberg, even when attached to Carlota, is thoroughly prosaic, for whom this nomenclature only suggests the assimilation of the second or third generation of Jews, or in the case of this character, simply Fainberg-by-marriage and quite possibly not Jewish at all.

Argentina's incorporation of Jews in large enough numbers to make up recognizable neighborhoods (Once and Villa Crespo in Buenos Aires) and towns (like the legendary Moisésville of Santa Fe province) is a blurry and inexact reminder of Spain's own Jewish past. Although the Jews who arrived earliest in what would later become the Argentine Republic were Sephardic (that is, from "Sepharad," a biblical geographic designation that came to signify Spain), Argentina's Jews are mostly Ashkenazi, from eastern Europe. The Spanish language came later to them and was often Yiddish-accented even among second-generation speakers.[18] Their linguistic progress was the mirror image of the Jews expelled from Spain in 1492. The Sephardim held on to what is now to others' ears an archaic Spanish, of special interest to linguists. They retained that fifteenth-century Spanish even as they learned new languages to live in new places. It is unlikely that Abengoa knows that history; Claudio almost certainly does.

In contrast to Abengoa's exaggerated notion of Jewishness, which establishes the character as a little anachronistic yet recognizably Spanish in his worldly provincialism, Dominique Bona writes a Jewishness that is simultaneously familiar in its stereotypes and utterly diluted in its content. In Bona's 1984 novel, *Argentina,* set nostalgically in the early part of the twentieth century, the Jewish beef exporter Goldberg is recognizably Jewish in his success at business and his devotion to family.[19] An adoring father to his only child, Sarah, he is lovingly faithful to the memory of his wife. Bona's portraits of Goldberg and Sarah are sympathetic, yet they partake of stereotypes that have most often been mobilized to anti-Semitic ends: the successful Jewish businessman, the frivolous Jewish daughter. The engagement with the characters and their inner lives characteristic of Muñoz Molina's novel is absent in Bona's *Argentina.* Bona's novel is a schematic text, not well realized as a literary work. Yet even in this context, where even those characters who Bona seems to suggest would care about their identity are fairly devoid of introspection, the Jewish characters are simply bereft of any trace of connection to a lived Judaism. Goldberg has already intermarried by the time he comes to Argentina. Sarah, slightly embarrassed by her Jewish heritage, wants only to assimilate. All that is left of Goldberg's Jewish identity are his name and his stereotypical wealth (in contrast with the relative poverty of the majority of Argentine Jews of the period). In Bona, even a Jew can eventually become an Argentine like any other.

Whereas in the novels by Jewish writers Judith Katz and Isaac Bashevis Singer the Jewish characters live and move within a singularly Jewish world, Bona's Léon Goldberg desires assimilation.[20] He leaves his Judaism behind in Europe, is not a believer, and has no connection with the Jewish community. There is no struggle over Jewish identity, just a wish to become part of the larger society and, ultimately, the ability to do so. Both Katz and Singer see Argentina as a Jewish space, or as having provided a Jewish space, in which questions of Jewish ethics and identity could be rehearsed, and in which there is no interaction with the Gentile world.[21] For Abengoa in *Carlota Feinberg*, part of Carlota's sexual appeal is what he believes is an exotic and volatile racial mixture.

For Bona, "Jewish" means cosmopolitan, which includes an untroubled assimilation. Her Jewish character, Léon Goldberg, compares Buenos Aires to Vienna. For him, both cosmopolitan cities are thankfully free of petty nationalisms. Goldberg's wife was Catholic, so even before he left Europe he was distancing himself from a purely Jewish community. A self-made man, he worked his way to his wealth. His daughter Sarah, whose name is a constant reminder of her father's Jewish background, wants only to leave her Jewishness behind and enter entirely into Argentine society. Unlike her Argentine friends in that she was brought up without religious training or beliefs, nevertheless, she thinks of herself as Christian (Bona 1986, 92). Her father's Jewishness makes her suffer; her Christianity seems to have no effect on him.

In Bona's novel, assimilation, not just of Jews into Gentile society, but more importantly of the immigrant into the social fabric of Argentina, is an unmixed good. As an ambitious immigrant, Léon Goldberg is hardworking and stern; he tolerates the frivolity of his daughter's social set for her sake. Nevertheless, it is that frivolity that is the mark of her—and his—acceptance into the world of the Argentine bourgeoisie. Jean, like Goldberg a serious man, wins the older man's respect and, eventually, the love of his daughter. Assimilation, unthinkable in either Singer or Katz, is unquestioned, a presumed good in Bona. There is no Jewish space in the world of Bona's Jews, unlike Katz's and Singer's. The latters' characters, as early twentieth-century Jews, may cross the ocean and travel through many countries, but they never cross the border into a non-Jewish world. Much Jewish writing in Argentina also re-creates this tightly bound Argentine-Jewish past, and recent Jewish-Argentine filmmakers dwell on the tension between the safety and familiarity of the Jewish community and the chance for growth in the wider Argentine society.[22]

For Muñoz Molina's Abengoa, Jewishness is what makes Argentina exotic. In Bona, whose novel is interesting largely as a catalogue of commonplaces about Argentina in the early part of the twentieth century, Jewishness is not only stereotyped but precariously on the verge of disappearance via assimilation. Yet however dissimilar *Carlota Fainberg* and *Argentina* may be, they share the assumption that Argentineity incorporates Jewishness. In contrast, the novels of Isaac Bashevis Singer and Judith Katz represent Jewishness as outside the imagined community that is Argentina. In the work of these novelists, Jewish identity and culture are neither the mark of the exotic nor a deracinated stereotype, but rather the foothold of sameness that makes Argentina not totally foreign territory.

With *Carlota Fainberg,* Antonio Muñoz Molina creates a Spanish version of Argentine Jewishness that resonates with Bona's, insofar as his Porteño Jew is similarly perceived as part of what makes Buenos Aires the slightly exotic, but also familiar, place that it is. Like Bona's Goldberg, Muñoz Molina's Isaac Fainberg is a successful businessman. He is also the elderly, and presumably lecherous, husband of the sultry title character, Carlota. Fainberg's presence in the text is filtered through layers of narration, and it is, ultimately, incidental to the plot if not to the texture and ambiance of the novel. Marcelo Abengoa, the novel's provincial Spaniard, who has been fabulously seduced by Carlota, finds Buenos Aires compelling because of its fascinating racial blending, which for him means the mixture of Christians and Jews. Carlota herself may well not be Jewish, but Abengoa's obsession with her is fueled by his perception of her cultural overabundance. Not quite a sign of conventional urbanity, Carlota's presumptive Jewishness is a marker of the sexual exotic. Jewish Buenos Aires in the writing of non-Jews from the outside (here exemplified by the Spanish Muñoz Molina and the French Bona) plays on stereotypes, and Jews in these texts are written primarily in relation to the Gentile world.

For non-Jewish observers like Bona and Muñoz Molina, the Jew is a familiar other, easily transplanted onto Argentine soil, and fully assimilated into dominant European systems of signification: in Bona the stereotypically successful businessman; in Muñoz Molina the exotic object of desire. Buenos Aires's very meaning is produced through what for Abengoa is the title character's oxymoronic name: the sufficiently Hispanic "Carlota" literally, if surprisingly, married to the unmistakeably Jewish, eastern European "Fainberg." That this novel turns out to be a ghost story only adds to the magic of Buenos Aires in the Spaniard's imagination. In its familiar difference, the Jewish aspect of Buenos Aires is part and parcel of the city's core identity in these texts. In contrast, Jewish writers find an internal difference in the Jewish presence in Buenos Aires. More attuned to the uneasiness with which Buenos Aires, a city that learned its anti-Semitism from Europe, has absorbed its Jewish population, they recognize that the city itself has been resistant to the Jewish presence there. From the time of the *Semana Trágica* (tragic week) of January 1919, in which the violent repression of workers demanding their rights turned into a murderous attack on Jewish businesses, synagogues, and individuals, to the bombing of the Asociación Mutual Israelita Argentina (AMIA) building that destroyed irreplaceable documents and artefacts and took the lives of more than eighty people in 1994, Buenos Aires has always been associated with the threat of anti-Semitic violence and consequent danger to Jews.[23] Nevertheless, as we will see in chapter 8, the past of Buenos Aires also holds a place for Jews who did not shy away from violence themselves.

CHAPTER EIGHT

The Outlaw Jews of Buenos Aires

For Sholem Aleichem, Judith Katz, and Isaac Bashevis Singer, Argentina is not the place of untroubled Jewish assimilation that it is in the fictions of Dominique Bona and Antonio Muñoz Molina.[1] Rather, the nation as they write it emblematizes the Jew as outsider. Moreover, this is an outsiderness exacerbated by its outlaw nature. Unlike Argentine Jewish writers, who have historically wrestled with the issue of assimilation and identity, in part to demonstrate their suitability as Argentine citizens and in part as a symptom of their concern over the prospect of losing their own cultural identity, Jewish writers from outside Argentina have often been drawn to the edgy question of the Argentine Jewish underworld. With different objectives, and no need to prove themselves worthy to Argentine society, Sholem Aleichem, Judith Katz, and I. B. Singer have drawn their stories from the shady side of Argentine Jewish history.[2]

Although most Argentine Jews have been loathe to advertise Jewish participation in Buenos Aires organized crime, by 1909 the Jewish underworld of Buenos Aires had already entered the global Jewish imaginary.[3] There was enough generalized knowledge of the operations of the Zvi Migdal so that the Yiddish writer Sholem Aleichem could count on his readers' awareness of them in a short story called "The Man from Buenos Aires." In this narrative, two Jewish men traveling in eastern Europe share a train compartment, and in the intimacy that the anonymity of travel can provide, the man from Buenos Aires recounts not only his current quest to find a bride, but also his rise from poverty as a purveyor of a lucrative, if unnamed, commodity. Sholem Aleichem's tale is surprisingly faithful to the classic picaresque: the now-rich man was propelled by hunger to leave his mother's home; his first master was a blind man who mistreated him but taught him the basic skills of living on the margins of society, and particularly to lie. He is, therefore, as in the classic picaresque, an unreliable narrator. Echoing the picaresque prototype, the storyteller's travels to find a wife are connected to his life as a procurer, albeit a much more successful one than his literary ancestor, Lazarillo de Tormes.

The man from Buenos Aires never reveals exactly what his valuable merchandise is, only that he came from humble beginnings and is now wealthy beyond belief. For the reader of Sholem Aleichem's tale, the name of the city in the title of the story is already a sign of shady dealings, the traffic in women, and success for Jewish gangsters. The signifier "Buenos Aires" held enough meaning for Sholem Aleichem's Yiddish-speaking readers in the early part of the twentieth century to make the title itself the best clue to the directly posed but never fully answered question, what does he sell? The only reply the traveller gives, a wry "not prayerbooks," elides the real answer, which is contained in his refercnccs to police payoffs, threats of exposing his bosses in order to become a partner in the business, his rough background, and of course the place, the city that signifies Jewish trade in women's bodies. This is not to say that there weren't Jewish prostitution rings elsewhere, or that Jews were alone among immigrant groups in trafficking in sex in Argentina. There was a thriving sex trade in New York and Havana, where, as in Argentina, Jews and non-Jews alike were among the traffickers. But neither New York nor Havana achieved the almost mythic status of the Argentine *trata de blancas*—the so-called white slave trade.[4]

Later in the century, Isaac Bashevis Singer, who wrote in Yiddish of a people in exile, and Judith Katz, whose lesbian feminist sensibility is unmistakably of the United States, share little but a strong sense of Jewish identity that in their narratives translates into an exploration of Jewishness. Each is drawn to Buenos Aires because of the presence of the same outlaw Jews that fascinated Sholem Aleichem: the gangsters, pimps, madams, and whores who made up a significant percentage of the trafficking in women in the Buenos Aires of the early 1900s.

The Jews in the Buenos Aires written by Sholem Aleichem, I. B. Singer, and Judith Katz are both familiar and far away. Like Maria Luisa Magagnoli, distant in time and space from the reviled (and perhaps scapegoated)

Severino Di Giovanni, these Jewish writers find in Buenos Aires a site of stories about roughneck and therefore doubly marginalized Jews. These were immigrants who flourished at the turn of the century, a time when Jewish immigration to Buenos Aires was at its peak and when Jews in Europe were in crisis due to pogroms, secularization, and political upheaval.

If Argentina is a screen onto which Europeans recognize both themselves and their others, projecting both desire and fear, the Jewish version of this projection and recognition is no less compromised with its own history and mythology. In the case of Singer and Katz, the setting of Argentina is more than just backdrop; it affords these writers a way to think about Jewish experience that is both far away and close to home. Here the same/other is the Jew of Argentina who is and is not the Jew of Poland.

Although both Singer and Katz are novelists who always come back to variations on the theme of Jewish identity and experience, they are very different from each other indeed. Isaac Bashevis Singer was perhaps the last great exponent of Yiddish as a living, literary language, whereas Yiddish survives in Judith Katz's writing as the sign of a past historical moment. Singer's *Scum* was written in Yiddish; it is rendered into an equally modern English. Katz's *The Escape Artist* uses Yiddish (and to a lesser extent, Spanish) as a stylistic reminder that these are Jews from another time and another place. Singer wrote of a world that was unquestionably patriarchal. His stories revive the old world, raising questions of God, free will, and fatalism; and although many of his women characters are smart and lively, they are inevitably secondary to the male protagonists whose stories he tells. In contrast, Katz comes out of a new Jewish lesbian-feminist generation of writers, thinkers, and activists, whose exuberant coming to voice is a challenge to traditional masculinist literary arrogation of Jewish life, a prime representative of which might well be Singer himself. Katz's world view reflects an understanding of history that both recognizes the collective identity and history of a people and believes in self-determination and agency. Her stance is characteristic of not only a North American faith in individual action and self-invention, but also of a feminist conviction that on the one hand traditional norms of gender and sexuality have hurt women, and on the other that women can claim the subjectivity necessary to tell their own stories and can be agents who effect change in their own lives. Katz and Singer, drawn to stories of Jewish identity and ethics, found in the demimonde of turn-of-the-century Jewish Argentina a fertile history and geography for their fiction. The Argentina of both Katz and Singer rests on a historical reality. In the early part of the twentieth century, at a time when prostitution flourished in the port city of Buenos Aires, approximately one half of all the brothels in Buenos Aires were operated by Jews. This breathtaking disproportion must have seemed even larger, as the presence of a minority in any visible number in whatever context is always magnified in the perception of the majority.

In both Singer's *Scum* and Katz's *The Escape Artist*, Argentina is necessarily linked and implicitly compared to the vibrant and endangered Jewish life of Poland. Warsaw functions as the fundamental reality in relation to which Argentina is to be comprehended. In these novels the Jews of Poland are the standard of Jewish authenticity.[5] Katz's novel of a young Polish girl who is deceived, drugged, cajoled, and threatened, and winds up in a Buenos Aires brothel, begins with the grounding of her "real" life in Warsaw; and Singer's novel of a shady Polish character who returns to Warsaw after his son's death in Argentina is set entirely there. In *Scum*, Argentina is a site of memory: as Max recounts his life there, the reader learns that he had been involved in schemes that skirted the law, but that he has since become an almost entirely legitimate businessman. Max's almost legitimate status, signaled by his acceptance into the burial society of expatriate Polish Jews in Buenos Aires, is meaningless in the "real" world of Poland, where he reverts to type. Once Singer's characters move from this center of gravity, they begin to lose some of their most fundamental characteristics. This is true of Katz's as well, but her women characters are able to develop parts of themselves that never would have emerged in Poland. In *Scum* the unworldly assistant rabbi asks Singer's protagonist, Max, "What's going on in the world? Jews are Jews, eh?" Max answers,

> "Yes, Rabbi, Jews are Jews. But not like here. In Whitechapel there are synagogues and ritual baths and all of that, but the younger generation speaks English. You talk with one of them and suddenly he will say, 'I am a Jew.' If he hadn't said so, you wouldn't know. In Paris, they speak French. In Argentina, the younger generation has begun to speak Spanish." (1991, 35)

Katz's narrator in *The Escape Artist* tries to hold on to her identity in the Argentine brothel to which she is taken by reciting her Polish reality:

Each night before sleeping I recited my life out loud: Sofia Teitelbaum,
sixteen years old, born in Warsaw, Grzybowski Street 42. Daughter of
Bayla and Yakov, best friend of Tamar. Kidnapped by Tutsik Goldenberg
in May 1913. (1997, 63)

After a time of living in the brothel, the details of that old life elude
Sofia, yet she says that to have remembered them would have destroyed
her. (For her part, Sofia's rescuer Hankus does not recover her memory
of the pogrom in which her village was massacred until she comes to
wholeness in her relationship with Sofia.) But even before losing the
memory of the small details of her Polish-Jewish world, Sofia is deprived of the precious accoutrements of a woman's Jewish identity, her
grandmother's candlesticks, given to her by her mother in anticipation
of her beginning a domestic life. This loss signals an end to any hope
for respectable domesticity and is the sign of Sofia's entrapment in Perle
Goldenberg's sexual enterprise:

> Perle looked at me sadly. "I'm afraid the candlesticks are nowhere to be
> found, my dear. But don't despair. The Sabbath is strictly observed in
> this house, and you may say blessings over our candles every Friday
> night if you like. As to your other luggage, it's all right here in this room."
> She snapped her fingers and Sara put the wedding dress box in my lap.
>   "There," pronounced Madam Perle brightly, "just like Chanukah."
>   That is the moment my heart broke in Buenos Aires, once and for
> all. Was it the loss of the candlesticks, or the fact of my practical joke of
> a wedding dress? To this day I can't tell you. In spite of myself, I burst
> into tears. (53)

In traditional Judaism the woman's religious domain is the home. Sofia,
installed in Perle's brothel, is deprived of that domain. Moreover, Perle
creates a parody of Jewish piety in the kosher bordello, one in which she
fully believes, but which Sofia sees as a travesty that nevertheless is all
that connects her to her former life.

As I have discussed at length elsewhere and have begun to suggest
here, men who are forced to leave home and settle in a new country often find that uprooting more painful and difficult than do women, who
may find freedom in a new place that would have been unavailable to
them at home. In Katz's novel, Perle Goldenberg, the prodigious
madam, has worked very hard to get out of Poland and finds the upside-
down world of Argentina appealing, where "summer was winter and
winter wasn't nearly as dreadful as it was at home" (66). Her younger
brother Tutsik, however, hates Argentina:

Unlike his sister, Tutsik Goldenberg detested that winter was summer and summer winter. He loathed that when it was winter it never snowed, only rained in a way so huge and horrifying it made even soggy Warsaw seem a desert. More than anything, the young Tutsik Goldenberg could not abide in the least that when a person went out the door in this upside-down city, left became right and right left. It was impossible for him to find his way even to the neighborhood candy store, or the *confitería*, without becoming completely at sea, and this made him feel a fool, which, for Tutsik Goldenberg, was the most loathsome thing of all. (67)

Perle, in contrast, is anything but a fool. She quickly learns the political terrain of the Argentine underworld and earns the respect of the people around her:

> Among people who knew her, both here and in Europe, Perle Goldenberg was considered to be the most learned of madams. Unlike her interpretations of the Bible, her reputation as a courtesan with remarkable intelligence and scholarly leanings was not a thing she invented. Her monumental library, which, Hankus, you saw with your own eyes, was a well-established fact and bragging point in Varsovia Society mythology, as were Madam Perle's mental and physical prowess. Visiting rabbis and the men of their flocks regularly found their way with pleasure and great determination to the doors of Talcuahano Street 154. (65)

Perle Goldenberg

> was enthusiastic at the prospect of becoming a part of the Buenos Aires *zoineh* frontier. For if ever there was a place where a woman could make a respectable living doing reprehensible things, this indeed was it. (66)

Similarly, though more ethically, Hankus makes a fulfilling life for herself in Buenos Aires. Poland was the site of the destruction of her village, whose carnage she escaped but witnessed. She was able to pass as a boy for a short time in Poland, but as her mentors there knew, she needed to be in a wholly new world to be truly safe. Even Sofia, after enduring the terrible trial of being taken from her parents' home and prostituted, makes a new and happy life on the pampas.

In Singer, this gendered response to the new geography takes shape in the aftermath of family tragedy. After their son's death, Max is inexorably drawn home to Warsaw. Without Arturo, Argentina has no meaning for him. His wife, Rochelle, on the other hand, can have no home other than the place where her son is buried. A shadowy and ultimately defeated version of Perle, Rochelle has remade herself in Argentina. She was a prostitute who married, became respectable, and used her business sense and her clear-sighted, hardheaded understanding of the world to help her husband prosper.

Whether in Singer's version of Argentina as a somewhat unreal place where a Jew is not quite an authentic Jew, and respectability, although ephemeral, is available as it is not in Poland, or in Katz's, where a whole new life can be mapped out after a period of trauma and suffering, turn-of-the-century Argentina provides a compelling setting for a Jewish tale. It evokes fascinating characters and the possibility of galvanizing action for writers like Katz and Singer, for whom story is paramount, but who also have an ethical social vision.[6]

In both *Scum* and *The Escape Artist* the travel between Warsaw and Buenos Aires is a part of the weave: a difficult and long voyage, unimaginable for some characters in both novels, but undertaken multiple times by others. In these texts, Buenos Aires and Warsaw are part of a particularly Jewish map of the world. Each city is understood in light of the other. The characters displaced from the Polish city and installed in the Argentine capital long for the familiar sounds, smells, and tastes of home, but gender makes a difference in their longing. Street names and even house numbers trigger the return of memories. The men who make the return trip (Max in *Scum*, Tutsik in *The Escape Artist*, and Sholem Aleichem's train traveler) rhapsodize over the food, the Jewish feel of the place. On the other hand, Sarah, who accompanies Tutsik on his shopping trip for a new woman to install in Madam Perle's bordello, can get pleasure nowhere but from the drugs to which she is addicted. And Perle has no desire to make that return trip, at least not until she can return for good, with her respectability intact. Perle, rather, re-creates Poland in Argentina, running her brothel by familiar, if somewhat revised, Jewish law and commentary. The Sabbath is honored: none of the women works Friday evening or Saturday. All the holidays are observed, and Perle has taught her cook (Marianna—fancifully, a Jew from Toledo) to prepare the kosher dishes familiar to and loved by eastern European Jews.

In *Scum* and *The Escape Artist* Jews may live in Argentina, but they are never of it. Neither Katz's characters nor Singer's aspire to assimilation into the greater Argentine society. Both Katz's Madam Perle and Singer's Max Baramber long for respectability and legitimacy within the Jewish community, which in turn has re-created the familiar institutions of eastern Europe in Argentina: synagogues, burial societies, theaters. The *mestizaje* taken for granted by Muñoz Molina's Abengoa, whose Porteña woman is by definition an exotic racial mixture, is not even considered by Singer's characters or Katz's.

Nevertheless, I am deliberately minimizing here the historically important fact of Jewish assimilation in Argentina. By the time Muñoz Molina's novel takes place, there has indeed been much intermarriage and cultural assimilation that had not yet occurred in the time period about which Katz and Singer write. The distinct temporal settings of *Carlota Fainberg* on the one hand, and *Scum* and *The Escape Artist* on the other, will determine the way Jewishness and Argentineity interact. But what seems most important to me is the choice that Katz and Singer make in setting their novels in a particular moment in Argentine and Jewish history that makes possible the story of as yet unassimilated Jews. They are interested in Argentina as a site of Jewish life at a time of upheaval. Change is inevitable in this uncertain time, but much of that change lies ahead. In contrast, Muñoz Molina's Argentina is not emergent but decadent, and it is thoroughly permeated by the trace of Jewish presence, not for the Jews themselves, but for the Spaniards who project their own problematic onto that same/other nation.

In Abengoa's mind, Argentine "otherness" is not only palpable, it is Jewish. In *Scum* the characters Max encounters in Warsaw perform the mirror-image of this othering, mixing Argentina up with Spain. On learning from Max that he lives in Argentina, the rabbi responds, "'There is a ban on Jews living in Spain'" (Singer 1991, 35). Max tries to explain that these are two different places:

> "Argentina is not Spain. The Spaniards came there and conquered the land. They drove out the Indians and killed them." (35)

Yet even Max, who explains how Argentina is distinct from Spain, collapses Argentina into Spain when he refers to Argentinean women as "Spanish."

To Abengoa, Spain and Argentina are utterly unalike; to the rabbi they are indistinguishable. Abengoa's Argentina is a land permeated by Jewishness. For Max being Jewish and, moreover, a barely reformed criminal means inhabiting a precarious margin in Argentina. Similarly, the prostitutes of *The Escape Artist,* no less than the gender outlaw Hankus, live on the margin of respectable Jewish society, itself a marginal status in overwhelmingly Catholic Argentina. One of Katz's most unsavory characters, Marek Fishbein, reminds Perle and her partner Red Ruthie of this, albeit to terrorize them into paying protection money:

> "You ladies might think we're all better off and safe here, thousands of miles away from the Tsar and the Tsarina, far away from all those *goyisher* peasants, but mark my words: no matter where he lives, the Jew is never safe." Fishbein hit the table again. Perle and Red Ruthie jumped just a bit. He leaned toward them as if to let them in on a monumental secret. "And we, the Jews who provide life's secret pleasures, we are the least safe of all." (Katz 1997, 72)

In both *Scum* and *The Escape Artist*, as well as in *Carlota Fainberg*, otherness is linked to the danger and pleasure of what Fishbein calls "life's secret pleasures." Carlota Fainberg's preternatural sexuality finds its counterpart in Max's observation that "the Spanish [meaning Christian Argentinean] woman is not exactly virtuous" (Singer 1991, 19). It is not coincidental that in all the novels under discussion here, sexuality and sexual desire play a critical role. In *Carlota Fainberg* they are unfailingly heterosexual and manifested as a desire to possess the exotic other.[7] In the Jewish writers they are a key to exploring the unsavory self. The covert self-scrutiny displaced onto Argentina in European authors becomes much more blatant in the case of the Jewish authors, who are looking at Jews in this other, familiar/strange space.

"Jew" and "sex" blend into a painfully longed-for and unfulfillable erotic desire in *Carlota Fainberg*. The title character's own sexual desire astounds Abengoa, whom she entices with her look, her smell, and the music she plays. All his senses are enlisted in her all-out onslaught to entrap him. He is, he admits, a willing victim, but it is clear from the outset that he is her prey. Her desire and capacity for sex overwhelm Abengoa: he admits to fearing that she is too much for him. Even after Abengoa leaves Argentina, Carlota continues to possess him emotionally: he sees glimpses of her in women everywhere. In this she is a kind of essentialized everywoman in the aspect of seductress. Carlota's desire is a desire beyond death, so strong that it survives the physical body that, in most accounts, gives such desire meaning. Here sexual desire and the will to seduce are virtually autonomous, facts of the exotic woman's very nature, even after her body has been destroyed in a nasty elevator accident.

In Singer and Katz, where all the characters are Jews and many trade in sex, the exotic other dissipates into the sordid world of pimps, prostitutes, and madams. The element of the exotic is thus absent from the line of symmetry connecting Jewish women and sexuality. Singer and Katz plant the axis Jew/sex/desire in Argentina, such that the whole universe of madam, procurer, pimp, prostitute, and client is Jewish. Or rather this axis casts its shadow on the side streets of Buenos Aires, where the unforgiving cement allows for little planting or transplanting, and the characters do not expect ever to become Argentinean. Their marginality as Jews is exacerbated by their marginality as criminals. This is a radical departure from Muñoz Molina's *Carlota Fainberg,* where the exotic charge of Argentina resides in its Jewish element, assumed to be fully integrated and even determining of Argentineity. It is, rather, Jewish marginality, and therefore specificity, that gives Katz and Singer some purchase on the most distant land that is Argentina.

The universe of these two novels is familiarly Jewish, unfamiliarly the underworld. Sex (at least of the heterosexual variety) is stripped of its charge of mystery and is reconstituted as a commercial transaction. Its power is no longer the power of women to unleash masculine desire: Max is trying to recover his desire for sex and Tutsik learns to look women up and down but gets little pleasure from it. Thus, the sexual predator is no longer the woman, out after a likely Gentile prospect. It is now a man, first the procurer who gets young women to go with him from eastern Europe to Argentina, then the enforcer who makes sure she does not escape, and finally the client. The madam, who has managed to work her way up from the feminized role of sex worker to the masculinized status of owner, represents not so much an exception to the rule of gender as an instance of mobility realizable in a new landscape. In Warsaw, even Singer's redoubtable Reyzl is incapable of going into business on her own. She says she wishes she were a man, so she could make her mark on the world. Yet Singer can imagine Reyzl's sister in Argentina flourishing as the owner of a brothel, willing to exploit other women and even to rationalize that exploitation, even if still in need of a male partner to help her recruit new women.[8] Katz's Madam Perle does not go into business for herself until she reaches Argentina, but once she is there she takes sexual and economic control. Her male helpers are clearly her subordinates. Moreover, by donning skull cap and prayer shawl and reading Torah, she assumes religious privileges reserved for men in the old country.

Singer and Katz focus on sexuality and prostitution but do not tell tales of unbridled, magical heterosexual passion. They tell, instead, of troubled sex, prosaic and commercialized, between men and women. In *The Escape Artist,* Sofia's story of degradation and salvation is the central story. Sofia enjoys sex not with men, but with other women; still, in the context of Perle's bordello even lesbian sex is compromised. Not only is it a voyeuristic variation available to the customers, it is also the method of training new recruits. Worse, Sofia finally realizes, it is a trap that looks like love and makes survival possible, but that is really the exercise of power and ownership. Sofia desires Perle and Sarah, but she desires escape more than anything else.

In Judith Katz's novel, lesbianism is a simple reality of women's lives— as a young girl, her protagonist is in love with her best friend. Sophia is torn from Tamar, as well as from her family, by the false promise of marriage, wealth, and respectability. For Katz, the Jewish and the gay are inextricable. Hankus is taken in and nursed by a gay couple who teach her their tricks. She passes as a man and later becomes Sofia's lover. The women in the brothel all have sex with each other, as well as with their clients. The sex with each other is both training ground and the place where they find some comfort, love, companionship. Compare this to Sholem Asch's 1907 play, *Got fun Nekome* (God of vengeance), where the lesbianism of the daughter is divine punishment for a Jewish brothel owner. In that play, the father tries to protect his daughter from his sordid business, but she enters into a relationship with one of the prostitutes in his brothel.

The instability of gender norms that ultimately frees Katz's Sofia haunts Singer's Max. In dreams Max encodes the danger of a transgression, a shift from one state to another, that takes the form of transoceanic voyages and gender instability. In both dreams the female who behaves like a male is dangerous to others and is punished for her transgression:

> Once again he began to dream. This time he found himself in a city that was both Buenos Aires and New York. His ship, after riding out a storm, had arrived at port and the passengers were being taken to Ellis Island. Rochelle had disguised herself as a man, but from under her jacket a pair of women's bloomers protruded. Even a blind man could see what she had done. Max screamed at her to hide the lace, but she didn't listen to

him. He struck her with his fist and awoke covered with sweat, his heart palpitating. (Singer 1991, 38–39)

In the dreams Max is "his old vigorous self" (39), perhaps because the transgressive women were put back in their place, perhaps because those figures also represented the instability of his own masculinity, set right first by Tsirele and then by himself. Male heterosexuality is a central concern in *Scum*, and prostitution is the primary site of women's sexual activity. Max's wife had been a prostitute, Reyzl proposes trafficking in women, Basha is seduced with the intent of turning her out, and Theresa feels as if her lover, for whom she acts as a medium, is prostituting her to a rich client. Conventional gender behavior does most of these women no good, but there is no alternative in Singer's heteronormative world. In Katz's novel, sex and gender normativity result only in the sexual enslavement of women, but transgression is an alternative and it provides the means for escape.

Despite the fact that I. B. Singer and Judith Katz tell quite different stories about Jewish prostitution and male sexuality, both examine the characterization of women as men's prey within the Jewish community. Katz's procurers and enforcers are open about their practices, at least with each other. Singer's are more evasive. When asked about the white slave trade, Max maintains that nowadays women go to Argentina and prostitute themselves willingly and fully conscious of what they are doing.[9] The traffic in Jewish women, largely perpetrated by Jewish men, Max asserts, is a fiction. It is a common and current story that gets told among the Jews of Poland, he says, but he himself will not acknowledge its veracity.

> On the ship he had heard all kinds of stories about South American pimps who kidnapped girls, dragging them off in carriages, selling respectable women into prostitution and forcing them to lead lives of shame. But Max had laughed at these farfetched stories; *they may have done this sixty years ago, but nowadays it was impossible.* Anyway, you could always get girls to make the journey willingly. (Singer 1991, 7, emphasis added)

But the story is persistent, and Max is required to repeat his denials:

> "Is it true that they snatch girls off the streets and carry them away to Argentina?" [asks Schmuel.]
> "They go there by themselves," [Max answers.] (17)

Max is self-deceptive enough to convince himself of a gentler version of the story, a sweet seduction in which women find him irresistible and willingly prostitute themselves for his sake. This slippage between force and seduction allows Max to claim that the women act freely and in something like full knowledge of what they are letting themselves in for. In the scene where Max talks Basha into going to America with him, he tells her nothing of the work she will be required to do—just that women can be modern and respected but, contradictorily, that she will need to obey him and not tell anyone what she is doing. From Max's point of view, any girl must understand what this is all about. At most, she is not "abducted," but sweet-talked off the street. Reyzl makes the same slippery arguments, like Max acknowledging abduction only as a thing of the past:

> "They always talk about girls being abducted. Nonsense! It's no longer a matter of abduction. Girls are walking around here who want to see the world, but they have no money to foot the bill. They can't even get decent jobs as servants. And as to getting married, not a chance," Reyzl said. (84)

Katz, in contrast, writes the entrapment and seduction from the point of view of the woman who is transported from Poland to Argentina.[10] In *The Escape Artist* there is nothing like Max's prodigious promise of masculinity that dazzles Tsirele, Basha, Reyzl, and Esther. On the contrary, Tutsik ignores Sofia and instead sets about seducing her father with displays of wealth and piety. In a parallel scene to Max's arrival at Tsirele's home, Tutsik, who has already scouted out the daughter he wants to seduce and learned which father is attached to her, comes with signs of wealth and generosity. Sofia is dressed up and trotted out, and she feels cheapened and frightened. Unlike Tsirele, who is slowly drawn to Max, Sofia is repulsed by Tutsik. Katz describes in brutal detail the kidnapping in carriages and ocean vessels that Singer's Max dismisses. The realization that the promises Tutsik made of marriage were lies designed to get her parents to allow her to be taken away are at the core of Sofia's despair. The loss of her grandmother's precious Sabbath candlesticks and the mockery of the wedding gown her mother sewed for her add to her misery. Katz's readers are disabused of the notion that an innocent and sheltered young woman would know that those promises were a charade, but they will also see how those already inside the world of prostitution find such innocence hard to credit.

In *Scum,* acknowledgment of the harm done to women always threatens to boil up and break the simmering surface of denial. The procedure Reyzl describes is very like the one enacted in *The Escape Artist*, however much Reyzl tries to minimize its violence:

> Naturally, with each respectable girl you have to talk differently. While you can show your hand to some, others want to be sweet-talked. You almost have to pretend to be in love with them. A real man knows which women to kiss and which to slap. As soon as a girl finds herself in a foreign country, without a passport, without a penny, rendered dumb, she will do whatever you want. The police could be bribed. The main thing was to get the woman over the border and booked on a ship. The rest was easy. (Singer 1991, 85)

Like Perle Teitelbaum in *The Escape Artist*, Reyzl acknowledges that there is at least a measure of force involved in recruiting new prostitutes. But she also projects her own somewhat commercialized view of sex onto the young women she convinces—that in the long run this is a wise decision, the best way to make a decent life for a smart and attractive Jewish woman. Katz's fabulous creation, Madam Perle, bears Reyzl out. Perle is a sexual prodigy, parlaying her role as mistress to wealthy Europeans into a stake that she gambles and increases and takes to Argentina to make her fortune. She has, it is rumored, been the lover of Rasputin, Georges Sand, a Rothschild, and Baron de Hirsch, who gave her the idea that she should emigrate to Argentina. Perle protects her investments: she feeds them well on familiar Jewish food, and she makes sure that they are not beaten either by her customers or by the men, including her brother, whom she keeps around both to protect them and to keep them from running away. She breaks them in sexually, teaching them the techniques they will need to know to pleasure their clients, and she teaches them an idiosyncratic form of Judaism in which she holds that their job is a good deed, a *mitzvah*, that brings pleasure to others.

The deception and self-deception around the freedom of choice among the women who leave Poland for the brothels of Buenos Aires is realized in Max's dreams, where this master self-deceiver and deceiver of others is brought face to face with the truth his unconscious, or his God, will not let him evade. In one, Max dreams of traveling with Tsirele, the rabbi's daughter, on a ship, and

> he had also taken other women with him, penned up like chickens in coops. As he brought food to them he said, "Doesn't the captain know what's going on, or is he just pretending to be ignorant?" (Singer 1991, 38)

In the unguarded dream state, where Max is both the captain and the observer, he knows that the traffic is ongoing and that the women are treated like livestock.

Max's evasive answers concerning the ensnaring of women for the sex trade in Argentina is a symptom of his more general refusal to acknowledge reality. He lies to Tsirele and her family, saying that he is a widower, and tries to convince himself that he can easily divorce his wife anyway; he makes promises he cannot fulfill to Reyzl, Basha, and Theresa. Ultimately Max gets caught in his own dream machine, the nightmare of prison in Poland. The sweet fantasies of easy wealth attainable by bringing new prostitutes to Argentina and of a new and young wife are overtaken by the fearsome dream of prison, and the deceptions Max practices to attain the first are instrumental in his being entrapped by the second.

If young, inexperienced women's sexuality is commercialized in *Scum* and *The Escape Artist,* male heterosexuality is also uneasy. For Katz's Sofia, satisfying the pedestrian desires of men is nothing more than a job.[11] Tutsik and his buddies are latent homosexuals, too homophobic to face their own desire. On the whole, the subject of male heterosexuality is not of much concern to Katz. Singer, on the other hand, sets his novel in motion around the protagonist's sexual problems. Max is driven to travel back to Poland by the deadening of his sexual desire. Once a powerful lover, he has become impotent. His potency is connected with fathering a child; the child is dead and so is Max's sex life. Max's quest is to reconnect with his masculinity, which is also linked to his youth as a criminal. He feels manlier when he is fantasizing about trafficking in women again, when he is seducing and lying, when his senses are awakened by the smells and sights of his old haunts. He becomes potent again with Reyzl, who proposes the exporting of women scheme. She may even be the image of his wife Rochelle, also a great businesswoman, once a prostitute, who was full of life and was the only woman who could keep Max in line sexually but who, with Arturo's death, has withdrawn from him. Max's sense of authenticity, masculinity, and sexual potency is now all tied up with Poland.

In both *Scum* and *The Escape Artist,* criminality, associated with the traffic in women, is a central issue, but so is the way Argentina, as far away as it is, holds the hope of cleansing and purification. Just as he is on the brink of becoming respectable, Max is pulled back to Warsaw to fulfill his nightmare of ending in prison. The death of Arturo is the catalyst, but it is his own rotting soul that is drawn over and over to deception and his preoccupation with his sexual inadequacy.

Max's impotence is a manifestation of a loss of interest in life that takes the form of self-destructive behavior, making impossible promises that can only bring disaster down upon him. He thinks he may have recovered his desire to live when he is able, finally, to perform sexually; but he overrides the moment of sexual performance by inadvertently shooting and killing Reyzl. Ironically, then, his return to sexual activity ends with making his fear of imprisonment come true. Sexual pleasure first eludes and then undoes Max. Sofia, in contrast, enjoys a sexual trajectory that begins with her desire for her friend Tamar, is awakened in the company of Sarah, continues with her training by Perle, and finally binds pleasure to freedom with her lover, Hankus.

Fantasy plays an important role in *Scum* on the level of the story itself, where Singer's bleak view of Max's irredeemability is bound up in the character's insistence upon living in a fantasy of his own creation, in full knowledge that reality is different, and with the result that he behaves unethically throughout the novel, reverting to type. Argentinean wealth and respectability have no purchase in the real world of Warsaw, the true identity that Max was born with and carried through his life. Max plays with fantasy—he tells an outright lie, saying that his wife has died, in order to inveigle his way into being the suitor of a rabbi's daughter and to imagine a life for himself with the beautiful young woman. Perhaps most telling is Max's own fantasy of continuing his underworld life, a fantasy that ends in fear of what might happen should his child be a daughter, and therefore prey to men like himself:

> He had fantasies about great robberies, counterfeiting rings, and get-rich-quick schemes. After he had broken with his disreputable friends and become a member of the Burial Society, which admitted only the most respectable community members, he still couldn't stop dreaming of shady deals. Nor could he rid himself of the desire to corrupt innocent women, to entice a wife away from her husband, a fiancée away from her betrothed. In his fantasies he still carried girls off on ships to Buenos Aires and other South American countries. When Rochelle was pregnant, Max trembled for fear that she might give birth to a girl. (Singer 1991, 60–61)

Argentinean wealth itself is a kind of fantasy. In both Katz and Singer the Jews who return to Poland from Argentina seem fabulously wealthy, but it is a precarious wealth, connected to a precarious respectability. Argentina may be the place where Max became rich, but it is an evanescent wealth. He may be flush with money, but Max weaves the narrative of his own destruction when he returns to Warsaw. Tutsik's flashy clothes and diamond pinky ring dazzle Sofia's mother, and both Max and Tutsik come to the impoverished Jewish households of the women they plan to seduce, laden with delicacies for the Sabbath dinner, or with money for the family to buy sweets and lessons for their children. Their apparent wealth, the treacherous wealth of Argentina, allows them to lie their way into the homes of the families they will despoil. Max's inescapable dream of prison is not only the dream of a woman and a murder (which comes true in the end), but also about counterfeit money, that is, fantasy wealth that in the end cannot purchase him his masculinity, his respectability, or his freedom (Singer 1991, 113).

Max, obsessed with his loss—of Arturo, of his masculinity—seems to have the ability to move freely in the world, an ability allowed him by his now-legitimate wealth. The structure of the novel, the telling of the dream of return and prison, inexorably unfolding as the novel progresses, belies the apparent freedom afforded by Argentine wealth. *The Escape Artist,* which begins with entrapment and imprisonment, is also about freedom, but it has little to do with wealth. In Katz's universe, where suffering is real, the possibility of overcoming suffering is also real. In Katz, the promise of freedom is genuine. Hankus escapes from Poland and its pogroms, as well as from gender norms, and she engineers Sofia's escape from sexual slavery. Sofia is not passive in this either. She, too, plots to get Hankus to help her. Even opium-besotted Sarah masterminds her own escape.

Both Katz and Singer incorporate a kind of flamboyance or superabundance in their writing. *Scum* is written as though the last line has determined the whole structure of the novel; *The Escape Artist* is written beyond its ending. Its story must go on past escape, but once *The Escape Artist* performs that great feat, the rest is epilogue. In *Scum,* return is inevitable because it is a return to reality. In *The Escape Artist,* the two main characters disappear into the mythology of the Jewish gauchos: the magical Hankus, now transformed back into Hannah, and the newly adept horsewoman Sofia living as lovers in the Jewish pampas. Katz sends

Perle back to Poland, married, pious, wealthy, learned, and respectable, but she takes her two main characters not back but forward, into fantasy, deeper into the Jewish mythology of Argentina.

Argentina in *Scum* is the most faraway place a Jew might go and still be among Jews. Motke and Max, Hankus's benefactors in Cracow, think of Argentina as an ideal place. Not only is it so far away that Hankus is likely to keep the fact that she is a girl secret, it is a place that actually welcomes Jews:

> It was decided then and there that [Hankus] should book passage on the next boat in Baron de Hirsch's fleet and sail away to Argentina. "It's a wonderful place," Motke said, as he unfolded the leaflet Pipke had given him. "JEWS!" it read, "BECOME A PART OF HISTORY! SETTLE THE NEW ZION OF THE PAMPAS. SAIL WITH BARON DE HIRSCH AND BECOME A CITIZEN OF THE JEWISH COLONY OF MOISESVILLE!" (Katz 1997, 93)

Katz's Hankus can perpetuate her gender transformation in distant Argentina, and Singer's Max tries to remake himself there and nearly succeeds. In the end, though, there is no remaking in Singer. The dream of Warsaw, persistent in Buenos Aires, the return to the prison of eastern Europe, is inevitable in this novel. It is written in the beginning and in the end. As in Claudio Magris's *A Different Sea*, Argentina is imaginary space. Even the real life that transpired there is ephemeral, the stuff of memory, over with. His wife, Rochelle, is no longer alive to Max. He kills her off in his retelling of his life to Tsirele; since his life revolved around his son, his business, and his sexuality, once Arturo dies, there is little that remains of his connection to Rochelle. She has withdrawn sexually; she has stopped being his astute business partner. He leaves her behind to go back to his past that is future, the one place that is real in the novel—Warsaw.

In *Scum* Argentina is the site of memory, and of intermediate memory at that. The most important memories are the ones Max evokes by being in Poland again. Argentina is also a point of reference in the novel. It is the America that is not New York, the very new world that is unreal for the vast majority of the novel's other characters. That may be why Max can so easily fabricate a story about his wife's death there. Only Reyzl, whose sister runs a brothel in Buenos Aires, knows anything about Argentina and, since the Polish-Jewish world there is small, about Max.

Argentina remains an idea in this novel, not a space of action, a place that is undifferentiated from the rest of America:

"Where are you from?" he asked.

Straightaway Max began to choke up. "From Buenos Aires in Argentina."

"What kind of country is that?"

"It's in America."

"New York?"

"No, from Buenos Aires to New York is as far as from Buenos Aires to Warsaw."

The men shrugged their shoulders. (Singer 1991, 126–27)

Buenos Aires merges into New York, not only for the Jews of Warsaw, but, in his dream, for Max himself. In Katz, Buenos Aires achieves the same level of reality as Warsaw does in Singer, knowable by its street names and house numbers. It is the space within which the characters move, from brothel to synagogue, to its plazas, its river, and its avenues. Still, like Muñoz Molina's Abengoa, Singer's Max will never return to Argentina. The first half of *Carlota Fainberg*, like all of *Scum*, takes place in another country, and Argentina is an elsewhere that has great meaning for the character who is telling about it, but who is not there at the moment of telling and, moreover, will never return. For *Scum*'s Max, storytelling turns into fantasizing, which in turn becomes lying. His own narrative, and the desire he expresses in it, is a web he cannot escape. Argentina becomes real in the act of telling, but it is also falsified, fictionalized, and forever estranged from the teller, who will not return. In *The Escape Artist*, Argentina is the site of the redemptive fantasy. Sofia suffers, but she is redeemed by a woman who has broken all the rules of appropriate gendered behavior. Hankus's own ability to re-create herself was born of terrible violence as well. She and Sofia disappear into a mythic terrain, more fable than realist novel, as they escape the narrow, gritty Argentina of the Buenos Aires underworld. The magical and ephemeral Argentina at the end of *The Escape Artist* is as unreal as anything in *Scum*, where it is only memory. *Scum* ends with the fulfillment of a nightmare, *The Escape Artist* in the middle of a safe and happy dreamlike landscape.

In the end, both Singer and Katz leave Argentina behind. Their stake there consists of the piece of the Jewish world it holds; their Argentina is a Jewish Argentina. I would venture to say that the fact that Jews outside the nation reflect on Argentina, and reflect a Jewish Argentina back to their readers, has had little impact on Argentina's dominant representations of itself. White, Catholic Argentineans (under which rubric I include nonbelievers who are nevertheless part of the dominant social order by virtue of ancestry and cultural, if not religious, practice) are certainly aware that Jews live among them, but they do not for the most part consider Argentine identity to be marked by Jewishness. The dominant culture is privileged to ignore the others among them, and although there is no active repression of the knowledge of the presence of Jews (as there has been of Blacks and indigenous people), that presence does not seem to have had an impact on the creation of a national identity. Despite their considerable contributions as writers and thinkers, and the important scholarly work of intellectuals like Edna Aizenburg, Nora Glickman, Saúl Sosnowski, and others who specifically address Jewish contributions to Argentine literature notwithstanding, there has not been much acknowledgment in the dominant culture of Jews *as* Jews in Argentina's intellectual, literary, and cultural life. Neither the Jewish exoticism that entices Muñoz Molina's Spanish businessman nor the attraction of dangerous Jews in Singer and Katz have much purchase there, but the fact of its large Jewish community explains why some outsiders have turned their gaze toward Argentina.

CHAPTER NINE

Dirty War Stories

To many casual U.S. and European observers, the military dictatorship that controlled Argentina in the 1970s and 1980s was just another in a series of calamitous governments that have plagued the continent since independence. These dictatorships have been represented as vaguely comic: Woody Allen's *Bananas* parodies the cliché of revolution in what have disdainfully been referred to as banana republics, confusing Central America with South America and one nation with another; and Paul Mazursky's *Moon over Parador* does the same. Kirk Anderson's political comic strip lampoons George W. Bush by portraying him as an especially inept, violent, and petulant South American dictator.[1] Nevertheless, the decade-long period of state violence initiated under Isabel Perón's incompetent and ruinous government that escalated into the so-called Dirty War by the military junta that ousted her in 1976 slowly captured the horrified attention first of the world's journalists and then of writers and filmmakers, and it wasn't funny.

Given the spectacular nature of what was euphemistically called the "Process of National Reorganization," or the "Proceso," in which the junta relentlessly staged its idea of nation, it is not surprising that the Dirty War eventually elicited textual performances of resistance in the form of fiction and film, as well as such public displays as those of the Mothers of the Plaza de Mayo.[2] Even so, both inside and outside of Argentina, knowledge of the Dirty War was attenuated, interrupted, and censored. First, most obviously, the junta itself denied that it was conducting raids, abductions, torture, and murder. Police officials told distraught family members that they had no knowledge of the whereabouts of the disappeared, and they cynically suggested that parents should keep better tabs on their children. This sort of official denial coexisted contradictorily with the suggestion that anyone who was arrested had done something to deserve it. People witnessed disappearances and then, under these conditions of doublespeak and implied threat, wondered if they had actually seen anything at all. State terror induced a willful not-knowing among much of the populace. It was far safer to acquiesce to the illogic of official discourse than to question internal contradictions, less dangerous to not see what passed before one's eyes.[3] The majority of texts examined in this chapter all reflect, in one way or another, this tension between knowing and not-knowing. Some address the desire to know and the fear of what knowledge might bring; others dramatize ways of knowing things that are kept hidden; still others express the frustration of not being able to communicate what one knows.

The tension between knowing and a not-knowing that is more or less willed comes from the actual fear of reprisals, but also from the struggle to convince oneself that one is living in, and is part of, a sane, civilized world. The monopolizing narrative crafted and propagated by the state to the exclusion of all others creates the conditions for not-knowing and at the same time reinforces them. The voices of dissidents from within the nation are not only suppressed, they are vilified and ridiculed. As I argue elsewhere, it was not only difficult to express dissent from within Argentina under dictatorship, it was even difficult to see what was going on in all its fullness.[4]

The Dirty War, waged by the Argentine military junta against dissidents and possible dissidents, including students, trade unionists, psychiatrists, writers, and artists, as well as against an underground guerrilla movement, suppressed just about every shred of dissent Argentina's civil society could muster, usually by violence or the threat of violence. It chose ridicule, however, as its primary weapon against the women who gathered every Thursday in a square bordered by the nation's symbols of political, religious, financial, and cultural/historical power. This was to underestimate the power of the image of white-kerchiefed mothers bearing photographs of their missing sons and daughters quietly circling the Plaza de Mayo in the shadow of the presidential palace, the Metropolitan Cathedral, the National Bank, and the museum housed in the colonial-era Cabildo. In their weekly silent demand that the government return their children to them alive, they eventually came to the world's outraged attention, inspiring similar mothers' movements in other parts of Latin America and elsewhere.[5]

The external accounts that contest the official, state-authored narrative of the Proceso enter into a struggle that on one level is less about Argentine identity than it is about the fact of events and practices. In the pivotal instance of the mothers of the disappeared, the struggle over such meaning is paramount. When foreign reporters covering a soccer tournament came upon a group of these women demonstrating quietly in the Plaza de Mayo, they simultaneously brought them to the attention of an international readership and contested the junta's characterization of them as madwomen. They reinterpreted the demonstrators through the lens of a familiar and powerful maternalist discourse as aggrieved and outraged mothers who were risking their own safety for the sake of their disappeared children. They were brave, not insane, and the act of taking them seriously gave them recognition and standing.

In this rewriting of meaning attached to Argentina, the attribution of national identity gives way to the attribution of individual identity. When the women marching in the plaza were reconstituted in public discourse as mothers whose purpose was justified, their self-identity was not altered. They knew quite well they were not mad. Being perceived and confirmed as not only sane but courageous was no doubt gratifying, and getting the support of outsiders helpful, but it probably did not change their sense of their core identity. It did, eventually, help them see themselves as a political force and empower them to broaden their demands and act on an international stage.

The actions of the mothers both intensified international scrutiny of the behavior of the state and provided another image of Argentina for the world. Moreover, they provided a visible and appealing alternative to the junta in the struggle over the meaning of proper Argentineity. Thanks in large part to them and to the universal familiarity of the discourse of maternalism to which they appealed, Argentina could be characterized as a brutal dictatorship and a dysfunctional nation, rather than as a nation of order, morality, and stability, which the junta proposed it was establishing in its Process of National Reorganization. The international image of Argentina during the Proceso is not the face of a dictator (as it is in Pinochet's Chile or Somoza's Nicaragua), but rather the face of resistance, the image of the Mothers of the Plaza de Mayo in their dogged and dignified persistence.

Like the images of aggrieved motherhood and kidnapped children, the terrible tales of torture that slowly leaked out of the clandestine prisons, and even the peculiar sights of soccer-as-usual and the Malvinas/Falklands fiasco, all played in the international press. Later, these spectacles, together with the devastating revelations of an oddly unrepentant but guilt-ridden navy captain, Adolfo Francisco Scilingo, his sense of honor wounded, telling the left-wing journalist Horacio Verbitsky of the regular death flights in which drugged clandestine prisoners were stripped naked and dumped out of naval airplanes, stimulated the fascination and repugnance of novelists, short story writers, and filmmakers. Captivated by its compelling force, they exploited the Dirty War's drama to bring the world's attention to the crimes committed by the Argentine government against its own citizens. The first to write about these horrors were Argentineans and their closest neighbors, Chileans and Uruguayans, who lived through similar military-political horror stories in the 1970s. Luisa Valenzuela, Alicia Partnoy, Ricardo Piglia, and Nora Strejilevich are among the Argentineans who wrote about the disappearances, torture, and executions in more or less direct ways.[6] Writing between Uruguay and Spain, Mario Benedetti, in his book of short stories *Buzón de tiempo* (Mailbox of time), includes stories about the aftermath of dictatorship—a message on the answering machine of a former torturer from one of the prisoners he murdered, a devastatingly sad letter written to a lover killed by the military, another letter from a daughter to her "adoptive" mother saying she knows quite well that her real mother was tossed from an airplane.

The writing of Argentineans, Chileans, and Uruguayans about the years of state terror in their countries has a special urgency about it. The texts written as testimony during the time of the Dirty War in Argentina, together with the documentary films exposing the government's actions, were designed to jolt the world into awareness. Written testimony becomes *testimonio*, a genre of its own, whose primary task is to broadcast events, galvanize world opinion, and create political pressure.[7] This production and distribution of knowledge is all the more necessary in the face of active silencing and the apparatus of state-controlled discourse. As it turned out, the testimonial texts produced in Argentina and its nearest neighbors also had the effect of precipitating representations from outside the Southern Cone. These works, written in solidarity with the political opposition, also spread knowledge, even when the final products were somehow belated and flawed.

The first U.S. novel to take the Argentine Dirty War as its subject matter was Lawrence Thornton's *Imagining Argentina*. Published in 1987, it was nominated for the 1988 PEN-Faulkner Award for fiction and subsequently made into a film. The novel enjoyed considerable critical and commercial success in the United States, although it was angrily dismissed by some readers, who argued that it traded in titillation, turning torture into entertainment.[8] The movie, directed by Christopher Hampton and starring Antonio Banderas and Emma Thompson, like the book, was aimed at a broad audience. Thornton's interest in telling the story began in the immediate aftermath of the Dirty War, but it has persisted in the form of the film, which was not made until after the millennium and was released in 2004. The film is overtly concerned with remembering the abuses of the junta, and in the end with generalizing the Argentine experience. Written text, a postscript to the film, lists country after country in which people have been disappeared, together with the number of the missing.

Hampton's film begins with a prologue under the titles, a montage that intercuts images of the dictatorship—people being beaten by police and forced into cars, video footage of the generals, the marching Mothers of the Plaza de Mayo—with a brief fictional scene of children rehearsing a version of the Orpheus legend. This montage, designed to remind us that the story is based in historical fact, is accompanied by a voice-over that tells the story of Orpheus looking back and losing Eurydice, and informs the viewer that looking back is nevertheless necessary. The voice of Antonio Banderas, in the role of the protagonist, overtly situates the narrative in recent Argentine history and links it to the Orpheus story—"When the military dictatorship fell in 1983 here in Argentina we were told that we should not look back." The next voice we hear is that of one of the Mothers of the Plaza de Mayo, pleading with an unseen interlocutor to "help us." The body of the film, marked by text that places the narrative in 1976, tells a story of the dictatorship that centers on the disappearances perpetrated by the state, and it ends with another Banderas voice-over again exhorting the viewer to remember so that history will not repeat itself. Yet as we will see, memory is the end-piece in a chain of knowledge whose other links are vulnerable.

Imagining Argentina's protagonist, Carlos Rueda, is a musician and the director of a theater company for children, an artist who discovers he has the power to see what has happened to the disappeared. The novel's narrator, Martín Benn, who is not present in the film, is a friend of Rueda's who works on the same newspaper as Rueda's wife, Cecilia. Benn's position in the narrative is that of an interested observer, not quite an actor, but not an absolute outsider, either. One of his primary functions is to absorb the disbelief of the reader. He is a hard-nosed newspaperman, a man who insists on the facts and who has little patience for magic or the supernatural. When his artist-friend Carlos starts telling the stories of the disappeared, stories that come to him in a kind of clairvoyant vision, Martín is the first to register the reader's skepticism of what is at bottom a historical novel with a political message. Carlos's inexplicable visions of the horrors of the repression would elicit utter disbelief if it were not for this mediating character who expresses that disbelief but nevertheless witnesses the veracity of the stories. In the film, another character, the cynical and apolitical Silvio, performs this function.

Carlos makes literal the somewhat romantic and idealistic notion that the unfettered imagination will in the end triumph over the narrow-minded stupidity of repression. The logic of the novel tells us that the cramped vision of those responsible for the kidnapping, torture, and murder in the name of the nation is self-defeating because it cannot comprehend the free mind. What is more, the pinched and limited reality that the junta propounds is based on lies. The regime's procrustean idea of the nation, which excludes and destroys so many, passes for truth only because the military government has the brute force to impose and enforce its version of reality. Carlos's imagining is more real than the routinized daily life of the city that obscures the practices of the junta; his visions reveal a truth that this insistence on quotidian normality is at pains to deny. Still, even though the central conceit of the novel, the political premise on which it is founded, is that the free imagination of those who love liberty will triumph over the constricted vision of the forces of repression, in fact Carlos's imagining is controlled by their actions. He sees what they perpetrate.

Carlos, nevertheless, is a visionary—first in the prosaic if metaphoric sense of being the director of a children's theater company, and then literally, if fancifully, as a man who sometimes has visions of what has happened to the disappeared. Within the logic of the text, Carlos is capable of keeping his disappeared wife Cecilia alive as long as he can conjure up a story for her. When he loses the thread of his daughter Teresa's story he assumes she is dead.

Thornton's novel is a kind of testimonial fantasy. He describes with accurate historical detail the procedures of the clandestine kidnappings, torture, and murder. His fictional characters move in a world populated by real people, among them the generals who ran the government and its Dirty War from 1976 through 1983; the Mothers of the Plaza de Mayo; the Argentine journalist Jacobo Timerman, whose prison memoir, *Prisoner without a Name, Cell without a Number,* was widely translated and read in Europe and the United States; and some of the junta's foreign victims, including the French nuns Alice Domon and Léonie Duquet and Dagmar Hagelin, the Swedish teenager who was gunned down in the street and murdered in the clandestine prison housed in the Naval Mechanics School. Thornton's success in making his readers aware of the dire happenings in Argentina during the Dirty War is in part due to his use of an old and familiar literary device. The frame story of which Carlos is the protagonist provides the scaffolding and the justification for telling the individual accounts of children, husbands, lovers, friends, and wives who have been kidnapped by government and paramilitary forces during the Dirty War. Each story has its protagonist, each has its key interlocutor, usually the mother or father of the disappeared, who tells the beginning of the story to Carlos, who in turn narrates the rest of the tale. As a result of this layering of narrator upon narrator and story upon story, there is a kind of receding presence in the protagonizing of this novel. The storyteller, Carlos, the one who sees and knows, is the main character, and his own story of the kidnapping of first his wife and then his daughter is the emotional center of the narrative. Nevertheless, each person who comes to his weekly gatherings in the hope of hearing the fate of his or her own family member experiences that individual's story as its principal one. As Carlos's interlocutors they are present in the novel in a way that their missing relatives are not. They come to his garden, each hoping to hear the one story that means the most to them, but the disappeared protagonists of those narratives are by definition absent. Carlos's continuations of their stories serve as Ariadne's threads that can lead his listeners to those protagonists, whose presence is made most palpable as an absence.

Several commentators have noted, some with disdain, that Thornton has dipped his pen into the well of magic realism in writing *Imagining Argentina,* yet I do not think that is quite correct.[9] One characteristic of magic realism is that it decontextualizes real events in such a way that it makes them seem strange, and makes strange events seem utterly commonplace. In *Imagining Argentina,* even details taken from reality, such as the kidnapping of people in broad daylight before witnesses and torture in such normally benign sites as car repair shops, that could easily be reimagined as beyond the realm of what is possible are described realistically. On the other hand, what is fancy, that is, Carlos's ability to envision the stories of the disappeared, is repeatedly received with skepticism among the better educated of the novel's characters. Carlos's clairvoyance is by no means naturalized, and it is far from commonplace. With the character of Martín to absorb the reader's reluctance to accept Carlos's suddenly acquired powers, Thornton breaks down the reader's resistance and seduces his reader into accepting the novel's fantasy premise.

Nevertheless, Carlos's visions, which are not only fictional but even at the level of the fiction itself strain credulity, might well make the excesses of the dictatorship seem less real to the reader. Those who attend the theater director's weekly sessions long to take his words seriously, but even some of them are skeptical of what, on the surface, appears to be just another theatrical performance. Deracinated and declawed, the terrible details of rape, torture, and murder have been conscripted for the purposes of the novel, and Carlos's clairvoyance might be read as mere entertainment, whatever Thornton's intention.

The second novel in Thornton's Dirty War trilogy, *Naming the Spirits,* is more thoroughly magical-realist than its predecessor. Whereas Carlos's clairvoyance can be read as a symbol of the power of the imagination over the brutish single-minded fanaticism of the generals, the second novel of the trilogy is lush with the pleasures of the magical. Narrated by the communal voice of the bones and spirits of eleven of the disappeared (something like Elena Garro's narrator in *Recollections of Things to Come,* or the dead who populate Juan Rulfo's *Pedro Páramo), Naming the Spirits* is told with the authority of the unjustly killed. At the center of the novel is a young nameless woman who, having survived the killing field, is reminiscent of García Márquez's more ethereal female characters. As might be expected of someone who has undergone the trauma of torture and witnessed a mass murder that she has barely escaped, she bears the mark of a bullet that should have killed her, suffers from amnesia, and only slowly recalls snatches of stories of the people who died around her. But this character is somehow magical as well. She turns up, as prophesied by the storyteller Carlos Rueda, at the door of a couple who have lost their own daughter. The impression of her body remains mysteriously imprinted on a bed of leaves where she was left for dead, and she, like her father, is often guided by birds. Her own paper cranes fly great and small distances to land precisely at the doorstep of those characters who are crucial to the trilogy. Her story concerns the demands of memory under conditions of forgetfulness, and although she does eventually recall the stories of her fellow prisoners, it is, in fact, their spirits themselves that communally tell the tale of the girl and individually tell their own.

Like *Imagining Argentina* before it, the driving force of *Naming the Spirits* is the need to tell the stories of the disappeared. Storytelling in Thornton is not just about the production of knowledge, but also about the creation of reality. Rueda keeps his wife alive by telling her story, that is, by giving her a narrative reality in which to live. This is the strongest, if most fanciful, claim the novel makes for the power of storytelling. Less implausibly, the account Cecilia herself ultimately gives of her experiences of abduction and imprisonment makes that history exist for her readers. To be unknown or forgotten is to cease to exist or never to have existed in the first place.

For that reason, the dead of the second novel in Thornton's trilogy want nothing more than to be named and to have their stories told. Silent and fearful throughout the time of their imprisonment, when they realize they are facing death, they tell each other about their lives. They are interrupted by their executioners before the last of them, whom they only refer to as "the girl," can tell hers. Her survival should mean that their stories will be remembered and passed on, but for a long time the girl can remember nothing. Later she will remember the time before the mass execution, when she was held fast and secure by the web of narrative that her father wove for her. In the fictional world Thornton creates, storytelling is deeply powerful.

Although Thornton himself rewrites the bloody history of the dictatorship as fantasy, he is committed to the notion that the telling of the
story is the best monument to the victims of the junta. The character
of Cecilia Rueda, Carlos's wife, who in the first novel of the trilogy was
abducted by the regime and underwent torture, including the torture of
seeing her own daughter raped, survives to write the story of her experience. In Thornton's telling, this *testimonio* is an instantaneous best-
seller, and Cecilia becomes a celebrity for having written it. Soon after it
is published, she attends the theater to see a play denouncing the church's
complicity with the junta, and she becomes the object of a standing
ovation led by one of the actresses in the play she is about to see. The
play, however, never does become the spectacle it was meant to be. As
Diana Taylor has eloquently argued, the main show during the time of
the dictatorship was the political spectacle staged by the military government, and resistance was publicly staged as well. True to this observation,
the play-within-the-novel is not performed. Instead, a more dramatic
spectacle is staged, first by the insistence of the actors that Cecilia be acknowledged and celebrated, and then by the competing demand for
attention by a disruption in the theater. Members of Opus Dei, a conservative lay organization active in the church, shout and hiss to keep this
play about their church's responsibility for condoning the Dirty War from
being shown. Their disruptive performance makes the performance of
the play impossible, but the spectacle of the ovation for Cecilia, in which
the audience participates and is thereby empowered, undercuts the force
of their disruption. Moreover, the behavior of the church's supporters
amply demonstrates the play's own message.[10]

Cecilia's act, the writing of the best-selling *testimonio*, refers back to
Thornton's own successful first novel. Nevertheless, apart from the publication of the Argentine Commission on the Disappeared's *Nunca Más
(Never Again)*, which did sell in record numbers, the only testimonial
writer whose work came close to having the impact that Thornton's
fictional Cecilia's does is Jacobo Timerman, to whom Cecilia is compared in the novel. It is impossible to read Thornton's trilogy without
coming to the conclusion that these novels, too, are a form of testimony,
that Thornton is claiming solidarity with those who insist that Argentina
should neither forgive nor forget the horrors of the Dirty War. Diana Taylor names this practice "witnessing," and she characterizes it as both interactive and performative (1997, 261). But whereas Thornton sometimes

teeters on the edge of turning Argentina into what Taylor calls "a spectacle of excess" (260), with an appealing prose style that makes reading about torture almost bearable, two other testimonial novelists, Douglas Unger and Erich Hackl, write in a straightforward manner, loading their texts with facts that display those barbarities unvarnished.

In 1995, the year Thornton published *Naming the Spirits,* both Unger's *Voices from Silence* and Hackl's *Sara und Simon* appeared.[11] Like Thornton, Unger and Hackl write as outsiders. Witnesses to state terror from, respectively, the United States and Austria, they have a stake in social justice and in being part of the testimonial edifice put in place by the opposition. The counternarrative they write emerges from a need to gainsay the official story, invented and reiterated by a regime that had not only silenced thousands of individuals through censorship, abduction, torture, murder, and exile, but that had endeavored to place its own triumphal rhetoric in the center of national and international consciousness.

As I have noted many times in this study, one motive for writing about Argentina is the sense that one's own cultural history is tied up with that nation's. Argentina's trajectory in the imaginary of the West faithfully registers what the nineteenth and twentieth centuries have come to mean for Europe and the United States. Captivated by the lure of the positivist promise of progress of the late nineteenth century, Argentina cast its longing gaze toward Europe for affirmation and for new blood. The metaphor of blood, suggesting health and the life force, meant energy circulating from Europe to the Argentine; and Argentina offered the young, wide corridors through which that blood might travel, picking up oxygen, delivering it where needed. It was envisioned as a symbiotic relationship: Argentina was poised to be developed, turned into a modern nation, with the capital and labor available from a Europe exploding with both population and wealth; two classes inexorably separated in the Old World would come together in the New. It is a vision of progress, if not order. It is the Argentina that calls on its own vision of civilization triumphing over barbarism, European enlightenment vanquishing native, rural backwardness.

Then in the late twentieth century Argentina, having defaulted on its promise, becomes a symbol of barbarity, but a barbarity that is, ironically, the heritage of Europe. It is the barbarity of a dictatorial government, of concentration camps and torture. The image of Argentina in a

Europe that not so many years ago repented of that sort of brutality, and in a United States whose government sanctions and supports it on the one hand and whose tender populace decries it on the other, is that of a prototypical land of state terror.[12] For many writers, Argentina's Dirty War resonates with the Nazi Holocaust. Erich Hackl's reference to his protagonist's neighbors, who continued in their daily routines, oblivious to what was going on as she was being kidnapped and tortured, brings to mind the complacency of Germans and Austrians who chose not to be aware of Auschwitz and Buchenwald. At the level of language, former prisoners in the junta's torture centers refer to their clandestine prisons as concentration camps; and when those prisoners were Jews, their torture was frequently accompanied by anti-Semitic slurs and threats relating to the Nazi death camps.[13] In *Imagining Argentina* Thornton makes the connection between the Dirty War and the Shoah overt by including a Holocaust subplot, in which Carlos's vision reunites a grandfather and grandson separated by the Nazis, and by creating a family of survivors who play an important role in Cecilia's story.

Given the Dirty War's evocation of the Holocaust, especially in light of the presence of former Nazis in Argentina at the time of the Proceso and the suggestion that some of them were called upon to share their expertise in torture techniques, the Dirty War has particular significance in the context of Jewish history and with reference to the Jewish community in Argentina. Marguerite Feitlowitz writes that one of the most troubling parts of *A Lexicon of Terror,* a book that must have exacted a profound emotional price to research and write in toto, was the chapter on the behavior of Jews and of the DAIA, the primary institution of organized Jewry in the country:

> Within the Jewish community, the dynamics of the Terror were extremely complicated and divisive. I am a Jew, and this is one of the most vexing chapters in a book that is full of vexation. It is but a facet of the prism, albeit a crucial one, for certain themes—identity, memory, collective trauma, contamination of history—come into startling focus.
> (1998, 90)

The regime's rhetoric, as Feitlowitz describes it, resonated with Nazi echoes that were far from lost on the Jews of Argentina. Feitlowitz remarks as well on the disproportionate number of Jews who were taken by the regime. She is quick to point out that this was not a matter of targeting Jews *as* Jews, but rather was an effect of the concentration of Jews in

urban areas, in the universities, and in professions such as psychoanalysis, the arts, and journalism that were particularly suspect. On the
other hand, she also notes the anti-Semitic content of the torture techniques used on the Jewish prisoners:

> Since late 1976 it has been documented that once in the camps, Jews were
> subjected to special torments. Verbal abuse and other degradations came
> straight from the Nazis; pictures of Hitler embellished numerous blood-
> stained walls. (106)

Feitlowitz's study goes far to explain the complicity of the DAIA, who
tried to placate the regime, as well as the fury of Jewish parents of disappeared who were refused help from that organization. Most observers
outside Argentina, however, do not get beyond the broad stroke similarity between the generals and the Nazis and the presence of Jews among
the disappeared, missing the complexity of the Argentine Jewish response
during the time of the Proceso.

Canadian Sylvia Maultash Warsh shifts this relationship between
figure (the Dirty War) and ground (the Holocaust) in a murder mystery
that begins with the recurrent flashbacks to the abduction and torture
of an elderly Jewish woman during the Argentine Proceso in order to
focus on the Holocaust itself. Goldie Kochinsky's abduction and torture
follows the familiar pattern—taken at night, beaten, tortured with elec-
trodes placed in her mouth, asked questions about the whereabouts of
her son. The details are convincing, knowing. Yet the central trauma of
the novel is not the Dirty War, but rather the Holocaust, of which the
Dirty War appears as an aftershock. Goldie immigrates before the Holocaust; former victims and perpetrators wind up in Argentina; the content of the Dirty War in the novel is almost entirely a Jewish content, in
which the Nazis and former Nazis, as well as their victims and their descendants, take center stage. For Goldie, the torture she undergoes in
Argentina is simply the torture she escaped in Poland catching up with
her. The Argentine dictatorship is another chapter in Nazi-Jewish history,
not its own story.[14]

The Jewish ambience of the novel is convincing, and the details per-
taining to the behavior of the regime during the Dirty War are precise:
the targeting of psychiatrists, the details of torture, even a few key names
and dates. However, other references to Argentina are utterly unconvincing. Apart from its dreadful military dictatorship and its consider-

able number of Jews, Argentina in this text is undifferentiated from the rest of the Spanish-speaking world. The tango club in Toronto, run by Argentines, is improbably decorated with bulls' horns and other accoutrements of the bullfight. The tango singer even more improbably uses castanets, and the tango orchestra plays the wrong instruments. In other words, the Argentine content of this text is shallow; Argentina here holds meaning only insofar as it plays a part in the Jewish history that interests the author.

Georges Perec's *W, or The Memory of Childhood* also links an imagined Argentina to the Holocaust, but in a different way, locating a dystopian society in Tierra del Fuego. *W* intertwines the struggle to remember the past with the child's creation of an imaginary society that, as the narrative progresses, looks more and more like Nazi Germany's concentration camps. Sure knowledge of real places and historical events is thwarted by the grown man's imperfect memory of his childhood in France during the Second World War, but the nowhere that Tierra del Fuego represented in his childhood takes on the reality he created for it during the time of the dictatorships in the Southern Cone, specifically Chile rather than Argentina. The last line of Perec's narrative, dated 1970–74, before the Argentine generals came to power, but presaging their arrival, reads:

> I have forgotten what reasons I had at the age of twelve for choosing Tierra del Fuego as the site of *W.* Pinochet's Fascists have provided my fantasy with a final echo: several of the islands in that area are today deportation camps. (1988, 164)[15]

Perhaps paradoxically, Argentina was a haven both for Jews during the Second World War and for Nazis escaping justice in its aftermath. The populist/nationalist government, headed by a charismatic, powerful leader in Juan Domingo Perón, was hardly unsympathetic to the defeated Nazis and allowed them to enter Argentina and hide quietly there. In Dacia Maraini's 1999 short story, "A Number on Her Arm," a concentration camp survivor visiting from Italy confronts "the most brutal member of the camp's SS" (105), now an old man living under an assumed name in Buenos Aires. There is a felt need, half a century after the Holocaust, to document and remember that history while the last of its victims and perpetrators are still alive. Maraini's story is one of many cultural manifestations of that felt need, and insofar as Argentina was part of that history in its harboring of fleeing Nazis, it remains present in the cultural imagination of Europe and the United States, and certainly in the imagination of the Jews of those places. In Maraini's story, Buenos Aires is, at the beginning, a relatively benign place, the city that is part of a transnational economy where the protagonist's daughter is now living because her husband works for Alitalia and he is sent to the company's Argentine office. It is a place of wide shopping streets, where the protagonist can spend a pleasant morning:

> The sky is a crystalline blue, almost a sparkling glass through which a placid, mild sun filters. Maria Grado takes a deep breath: it has been a long time since she has felt so free and calm; professional difficulties become small and insignificant on the other side of a million waves, alone in an unknown city among people who speak such a lyrical and modulated language. (104)

Maraini goes to some pains to depict Buenos Aires as untroubled, a distant place that allows a European woman to forget the pressing worries of home, whose fine weather and lilting language lull her into a state of calm. The contrast between this Buenos Aires and the one that harbors old Nazis is striking. The shopkeeper's jarring German accent transforms the pleasant space of the small shop into a space of perceived danger. The protagonist fears that if she identifies this man as her former tormentor, he will simply kill her.

The practices of the Holocaust and the arrival of both camp survivors and former Nazis creates one link between Europe and Argentina's Dirty War. For Spain, the questions of historical memory raised in Argentina in the aftermath of the Dirty War find resonance in its own struggle to come to terms with the long dictatorship it suffered under Franco. The narrator of Carme Riera's *La mitad del alma* (Half the soul) is a woman striving to learn the truth about her background, a truth that is grounded in the identity and behavior of her parents in the years following the Spanish Civil War.[16] Riera's protagonist, however, does not get to the truth—far from it. Memory in this novel is treacherous, historical evidence is unreliable, and truth is impossible to determine. As the novel progresses, the protagonist grows increasingly frustrated in her efforts to make the bits of information she accumulates cohere, and the reader grows ever more uneasy as this character slowly reveals just how unstable and obsessed she is. The novel includes an Argentinean character, the protagonist's sister-in-law, who counsels her to forget her quest and just get on with her life. The sister-in-law dismissively compares the narrator to the grandmothers of the Plaza de Mayo, who are also trying to determine paternity within a context of family tragedy and national crisis. She thus draws a parallel between Argentina's Dirty War and Franco's dictatorship; recent Argentine history functions as a correlative of the Spanish past. Moreover, Riera presents the Argentine character as atypical in her urging her sister-in-law not to remember. Certainly, the dominant attitude among Argentine exiles and intellectuals was that remembering was essential if the country were to heal. The equally loud voices in Argentina advocating amnesty and forgetting were a low murmur across the Atlantic.

For the United States, Argentina's Dirty War meant being implicated in the establishment of the dictatorship and the practice of torture. The CIA and the School of the Americas provided training, and the Reagan administration recognized and backed the Argentine military government. Like other progressives, Douglas Unger and Lawrence Thornton had little use for the United States' support of the dictatorship. They position themselves, properly, I would argue, in solidarity with the victims. Paradoxically, however, this stance can only be maintained from outside; and it depends on a gap between self and other that undermines the traditional power of the novel as a genre to draw the reader into another's consciousness. In Unger's narrative, the Argentine protagonists of history are on the other side of a divide that separates them from the protagonist of the novel. Thornton, on the other hand, attempts to make the imaginative leap to create an Argentine protagonist. This maneuver was considered suspect by some, as though Thornton were usurping the experience of the "other," or presuming to speak for him. Unger, in contrast, maintains a respectful distance between his North American protagonist, Diego, and his Argentine characters. Diego is the conduit through which the story will be told, as in *testimonio*. But as commentators of *testimonio* have argued persuasively, the relationship between the testimonial subject and the writer who serves as the channel for the testimonial narrative is complicated and contested.

Moreover, the novel as a genre lies in uneasy relation to *testimonio*. Despite the problems attendant upon any narrative claims of transparency, *testimonio*'s endeavor to be unvarnished witnessing distinguishes it from the aesthetic and, more to the point, fictional domain to which even the most realist of novels belongs. John Beverley, whose thinking on *testimonio* is particularly helpful in making this distinction, makes room for a novel like Unger's *Voices from Silence,*

> in which an "author" in the conventional sense has either invented a *testimonio*-like story or . . . extensively reworked, with explicitly literary goals . . . a testimonial account that is no longer present except in its simulacrum. (Beverley 1989, 43)

Unger's own experience in a study-abroad program in Argentina gives him a personal connection to Argentina and to a family there. Still, his novel takes a U.S. perspective, not because the author is from this country, but because his protagonist, Diego, is. As an exchange student in Buenos Aires before the generals came to power, Diego lived with the Benevento family. Now married and working as a freelance reporter, he returns in the aftermath of the Dirty War to a family that has been shattered by its events. Two sons were abducted and killed, their parents were impoverished in their futile attempt to locate and save them, and a third son went into exile. As an American who deeply sympathizes with the family—after all these young men were his friends—Diego also stands apart from them.

In an emblematic interaction with a former schoolmate who verbally attacks him because as an American he represents U.S. imperialism, Diego, not the Beneventos, is the center of attention. Although the novel's theme is the Dirty War, that event is the great lacuna in the life of the protagonist, who was back in the United States during that time, unable to communicate with his Argentine host family. The memory of the Dirty War is not his; rather it is mediated through him, and Diego's own centrality as both narrator and main character deflects the reader's attention from the central concern of the novel. In contrast to Thornton, who in *Imagining Argentina* also uses the device of the journalist-observer to narrate the story, Unger's Diego is not only American, but the author's fictional double as well. And whereas in *Imagining Argentina,* the narrator is present just enough to witness the action, entering into it only rarely, Diego always occupies center stage.

With Diego as mediator, Unger puts long speeches into the mouths of each of the differently positioned characters, miming the relationship between the speaker and collector/editor of *testimonio.* Mama and Papa Benevento tell related stories, but each tells something the other does not know, something they have kept secret, trying to protect one another. Their one surviving son tells a story of exile. A close family friend who loved the dead boys, but who had a cousin killed in a guerrilla raid on the government building in which he was working, expresses the experience of the Argentines caught in the middle who say that they did not know that there was widespread kidnapping, torture, and murder sponsored by the government. Diego's anti-American friend, ruined financially and destroyed psychologically, rants against Yanqui colonialism but leeches off the other characters, especially the protagonist. A general tries to exonerate himself by saying he disapproved of the excesses of his comrades-in-arms, but he also reveals that the military engineered the opposition so as to have an excuse to step in. Some of these voices are given moral priority, but the overall effect is of set pieces designed to provide an equal-time global view of the period.

Voices from Silence springs from the desire to make the story of state violence known, to do something to bring the perpetrators to justice, or at least to expose them to the opprobrium of decent people. It is intolerable that they are free to walk the streets of Buenos Aires, enjoy their wealth, and avoid any state-imposed punishment for their crimes. Unger's anger and his sense of impotence at this state of affairs fairly ring from the page. Painstakingly documenting the minutiae of the Dirty War, he is, however, unsuccessful in translating the emotional impact of the family's experience to the reader.[17] In the end, Unger's Diego is left with the feeling that he can do nothing to help, nothing to change the situation. His attempt has failed: memory is impossible, and forgetting begets just another round of bloodshed. In a poetic passage that stands in stark contrast to the determinedly sere prose of the rest of the novel, Diego meditates on the futility of memory:

> So, the river was constant in its forgetting, like the country it flowed past. Tradition and reality would clash heads like two pampas bulls. The cycles of power and cruelty would come around again. The recent memories would be erased, the tens of thousands gone, my own brothers among them. I saw it then, clearly, captured in liquid hands. The newest soldiers of the *conquista* would march once more into the past. Everything would happen again. The River Plate was red, not silver, a sickly, rusted, decaying red, a wash of red as from pre-Columbian human sacrifice, a dark, sad red like the mood of a tango of abandoned love. The river was as red as in the beginning and always. As red as the last light of the southern sun on a land of vanquished and forgotten graves. (Unger 1995, 285–86)

As if awash with blood, the river is witness to endless cycles of violence and repression, enmeshed in the natural order of things: pampas bulls, the river itself, the setting sun. Forgetting frames the passage: the river's forgetting, the forgotten graves of the vanquished.

Still, the giving of testimony, which is, fittingly, the climactic event in this testimonial novel, allows for some small bits of information to enter the record that might make a difference in the future. In his formal testimony before the Commission on the Disappeared, concerning the kidnapping and murder of his youngest son, Miguel, Papa Benevento inserts the name of another disappeared son, Alvaro, into the record. Like Thornton's storytellers, he rescues a second son from oblivion and plants the seed for a future investigation, one that the courts are not yet willing to make. Similarly, this novel, packed as it is with the details of the Dirty War—names, dates, practices—is a site of archived knowledge, a reference for the future. Like Unger, whose desire to write the testimony of solidarity in *Voices from Silence* is admirable, Papa Benevento is to some extent successful in making this truth known. The novel insists on its roots in material reality, and Unger writes what is ultimately a pedagogical novel: he grabs his reader by the collar as if to say, "you need to know about this."

Although *Voices from Silence* details much of the history of Argentina in the last quarter of the twentieth century, and although it avoids the literary flourishes that burst forth in its final passage, much in the novel goes beyond the reportorial. The figure of Betty Ann, Diego's monolingual American wife, functions as a kind of substitute reader. Diego tries to translate for her, but again and again he is unable to. Events and stories move too quickly; he can barely keep up himself. Moreover, translation is an impossible task because so much of what has gone on is simply unutterable. Betty Ann, the character who did not know the Beneventos or, by extension, the country before the coup cannot understand, at least on an intellectual level, the details of what is happening around her. Her first interaction with Mama Benevento, nevertheless, is an immediate emotional connection. They weep in each other's arms. By the end of the novel, no change has taken place in that relationship; Betty Ann's interactions with Diego's Argentine family remain preverbal. She has been followed by the secret police; she has been harassed and frightened. But Betty Ann remains unable to communicate with the Argentines except on the most basic emotional level. As women, Unger suggests, teetering on the verge of a dangerously stereotypical construction of the feminine, Mama Benevento and Betty Ann share an emotional connection that transcends words.

Unger writes with urgency, packing the novel full of all the information about the years of state violence that his character also tries to make available to readers in the United States. Diego is a journalist and novelist who, like Unger himself, spent time in Argentina as a student and returned after the dictatorship to visit his Argentine host family, once prosperous and whole, and now devastated by the years of violence. Not only is news from Argentina censored by the generals, Diego's attempt to get the story of the trials of the generals to the United States is thwarted by a lack of interest on the part of the public television network for whom he was trying to write as a freelancer and by the fire that destroys his computer and his notes, a fire set in retribution for Papa Benevento's testifying. To the extent that the novel is autobiographical, neither Unger nor his character could make the American public take notice of what was going on. The novel makes repeated reference to the dearth of U.S. news correspondents at the Argentine Commission on the Disappeared hearings and the general lack of interest on the part of the U.S. media. The stories of torture and of the nation's unprecedented decision to call itself to task by staging the trials barely make it to the back pages of U.S. newspapers.

Voices from Silence ends in a paroxysm of despair. Diego is thwarted over and over in the telling of the story: he cannot even communicate it to his wife. The sad irony is that Unger's novel did not find an audience either. *Voices from Silence* was a commercial and critical failure, as presaged by the novelist's fictional counterpart. Lawrence Thornton, in contrast, set aside the fact that *Naming the Spirits* did not enjoy the success of *Imagining Argentina* and went on to write a third book on Argentina's recent past. *Tales from the Blue Archives,* published in 1997, continues Thornton's fascination with Argentine politics and the personal dramas it generates. *Tales from the Blue Archives,* grounded in events and practices of the postdictatorship period, immerses the reader in the world of the grandmothers of the Plaza de Mayo, who availed themselves of sophisticated DNA tests, performed by forensic anthropologists, to establish consanguinity and thus reclaim their stolen grandchildren.

As in the real-life sequel to the Dirty War, the primary roles in the fictional sequel to *Imagining Argentina* and *Naming the Spirits* are played by the parents and children of the disappeared. One of the novel's main characters is Dolores Masson, the grandmother of two little boys who were among those children distributed to right-wing families after their parents had been killed by the regime. Dolores discovers that her two missing grandsons have been given to a childless couple, Eduardo and Beatriz Ponce, as a reward for Eduardo's services as an aide to the fictional General Rodolfo Guzman. The Ponce family has been on the run ever since, fearing that they will lose the boys if they are found out.

Tales from the Blue Archives begins with the conceit that is at the center of *Imagining Argentina*. As in the earlier novel, in which Carlos Rueda visualizes the whereabouts of victims of the junta, the same character, this time aided by his daughter, Teresa, tells the stories of Dolores's disappeared grandchildren. Teresa mixes conventional knowledge—she has seen Ponce and knows what he looks like—with her envisioning him driving south with Dolores's grandchildren. Similarly, Dolores is armed not only with the Ruedas' quasi-mystical visions, but also with documentation showing that Guzman had given the boys to his aide.

Tales from the Blue Archives is a novel of emotional trauma, not only of the grandmother, who has lost her son and daughter-in-law to the junta and her grandchildren to those responsible for their parents' kidnapping, torture, and murder. The children themselves are isolated from the rest of society because the Ponces repeatedly uproot them. Their entire emotional lives center around Eduardo and Beatriz, whom they know as their parents. Even the Ponces, desperate to hold on to these beloved children, evoke the reader's sympathy. Eduardo and Beatriz are deeply concerned that the effect of the revelations of the junta's abuses will eventually redound to them and cause them to lose the children. Very present in their minds is the confession of a navy captain, closely associated to General Guzman, Eduardo's former boss. Guzman is a fictional character, but the navy captain is not. He is Adolfo Francisco Scilingo, and in the wake of the trials of lower-level military involved in torture, he told the story of the flights in which drugged clandestine prisoners were thrown to their deaths by members of the armed forces. Horacio Verbitsky, the left-wing journalist to whom he recounted his story, published Scilingo's confession-as-complaint in 1995 as *El vuelo (The Flight)*. *Tales from the Blue Archives*, published two years after the Scilingo revelations came to light, grounds itself historically in that report.

Whereas Cecilia Rueda's devastating prison memoir in *Naming the Spirits* is one woman's story, told from the point of view of a victim of the junta, the story revealed by Captain Scilingo is shattering in another way, since it comes from one of the perpetrators. The prolongation of the trauma of the Dirty War many years after the dictatorship ended is exacerbated by revelations (for some) and confirmation (for others) of what the junta did to its illegally held prisoners. Scilingo, who was largely unrepentant, was distressed that the men who obeyed the orders of their superiors were being abandoned by the officials and institutions in whom they had trusted. The story was picked up by the international press and made sensational news in both Europe and the United States. Not unlike the Argentine elite in the nineteenth and twentieth centuries, Scilingo sought out another who he hoped would tell his story, only to find that the story as received and retold took on a different valence.

Lawrence Thornton's fictional Guzman learns about the Scilingo affair as did most real Argentineans, by reading about it in the newspaper. In his account to Verbitsky, Scilingo recalled the words of an anonymous priest who assuaged the consciences of the military men conscripted to throw drugged, naked, shackled detainees out of airplanes over the Río de la Plata and the Atlantic Ocean. Thornton gives the priest a tellingly Germanic name, Von Claussen, links him to Ponce's boss, General Guzman, and heightens the effect of his words by rendering them in the first person:

> "He came to see me the day after his first flight. His conscience was uneasy and he told me why, what they did with the people. He needed comfort and I provided it. I provided a Christian explanation."
>
> Father Von Claussen glanced angrily out the window, the muscles of his jaw working beneath the slack skin.
>
> "I told him they had died a Christian death because they were unconscious from the drugs and had not suffered. I reminded him that war was war, that they were enemies of the state, and because they were Communists, enemies of the Church as well. I reminded him of a passage in the Scriptures where we are told to eliminate weeds from our wheat fields." (Thornton 1997, 26)

If Scilingo's confession implicates Guzman, the Ponces may be found out as false parents. The conjunction of the question of the legitimacy of parenthood and the behavior of powerful men in powerful institutions is actualized in the novel's opening scene of the baptism of

Guzman's granddaughter, at which Von Claussen officiates. This child, unlike Dolores's grandchildren, will remain safely ensconced in her family, buttressed as it is by the church, the military, and the state.

The Scilingo confession haunts this novel, as it does Hans Koning's short story "Naval Aviation." Koning's story is neatly framed, presented as something like a dream, albeit one that came to the narrator as a letter. It tells the story of a man named Bocarte, a newly graduated naval officer who is ordered to help throw people out of an airplane during the Dirty War. This found narrative is followed by a double postscript, the first sketching the details of Bocarte's suicide and the second giving the history of the relationship between the narrator and the protagonist, creating an authenticating frame. Yet the story is unconvincing. Its emotional center seems meant to be Bocarte himself; yet it is hard to sympathize with this character who appears, implausibly enough, to have been entirely ignorant of the practices of the military during the time he was in the naval academy.[18] Although the story misfires, what underlies it is real—the fascination and horror produced by the terrible practice of murder perpetrated in this fashion by trained military working with and for the state.

Another post-Proceso narrative, by Catalan writer Manuel Vázquez Montalbán, is one of the writer's popular detective novels featuring private eye Pepe Carvalho. In *Quinteto de Buenos Aires,* Carvalho's uncle hires him to find his son, the detective's cousin Raúl. Raúl is both a former scientist and a former militant who has returned to Argentina from his exile in Spain. He is on the run, trying to find his daughter, stolen by the military years earlier, when a small group of militants led by his wife was found and either arrested or killed. He also wants to impede the exploitation of a scientific discovery he made years earlier and that is now about to be marketed by an unlikely consortium consisting of his erstwhile laboratory assistant, his old comrade in arms who is now a government minister, and his former torturer. The latter, as it turns out, is also the man who stole and raised his daughter. The cultural context of Vázquez Montalbán's detective novel is notably different from that of the novels written in English, with points of contact explicitly drawn between Spain's own history of Fascism and the familial connections between Spain and Argentina. For Carvalho, the Dirty War recalls the Franco era; his family was part of the Republican opposition. Moreover, Raúl is not the only relative involved in Carvalho's adventure. One of the policemen assigned to find Raúl, and who both interferes with and helps Carvalho, is a distant cousin. The policeman's father, like Carvalho's, was himself an active anti-Fascist. Vázquez Montalbán is far more familiar with the Argentine milieu than are the English-language authors. He plays with Argentine literary history, revealing an acquaintance not only with Borges, but also with Macedonio Fernández, Bioy Casares, Victoria Ocampo, and a raft of others.

Pepe Carvalho's Argentina is, literally, familiar, but Vázquez Montalbán reflects an unself-conscious, quotidian anti-Semitism that is more Spanish than Argentine, exoticizing and (at least at first) caricaturing the novel's single Jewish character. Silverstein was part of the old band of militants and now works as a playwright and director whose plays are rarely performed, earning a meager living as the master of ceremonies at a tango club. He is literally caught with his pants down in the novel, close to impotent and physically repulsive.[19] Whereas he makes immediate connections to other Argentine characters, Carvalho has to learn to appreciate Silverstein's friendship. Even so, Silverstein is merely a little ridiculous; Vázquez Montalbán paints true evil in the form of the sinister Captain and his minions, who continue to kidnap, murder, torture, and humiliate their victims, as if the Dirty War had never ended.

Not all the representations of the Dirty War side so cleanly with the opposition. V. S. Naipaul, in his troubling and cold-blooded essay "The Return of Eva Perón," can find little to recommend either side. Written during the time of the dictatorship and based on his visits to Argentina in the early 1970s, when Perón returned to the country and was elected president, "The Return of Eva Perón" is an updated version of the sort of European disdain for Argentina/Latin America that Scheines and Biagini comment on and that Conrad represents.[20] For Naipaul, Argentina is utterly hopeless. It has no sense of history, no intellectuals, no art, no literature (beyond Borges, who Naipaul thinks is overrated anyway). Naipaul writes the Argentine elite's clutching to its European identity as a pathetic, anachronistic gesture; he is even less generous to the political left, whom he represents as a mélange of middle-class guerrillas, luxury-prone trade unionists, predictably unimaginative Marxists, unregenerate *machistas* all. In his account Argentine women are uneducated, trained only for marriage or the brothel. It is a bleak caricature, which at the end, predictably, uses Sarmiento's own language of civilization and barbarism. Only there is no hope for civilizing the place.

My own indignation at Naipaul's haughty reading of Argentina, of his ignorance of its intellectual tradition and rich literary culture, is probably in part a reaction to my own wounded dignity. Why in the world would I be spending my time on so barren a terrain? What made me think that Argentinean writers were worthy of serious analysis? I had been duped, and here was Naipaul saying that Argentina was really not worth my time or energy. Mine is a pale shadow of Graciela Scheines's distress, realizing that the attitudes of Keyserling and Hegel, Ortega and Benavente are not dead.

Naipaul's baneful view cannot be entirely dismissed, however. He is a compelling writer, and much of what he condemns in Argentina fully deserves condemnation: its history of genocide against its native population, state violence against its opposition, the self-satisfied attitudes of the elite, the history of political corruption, and the inability of a nation with such promise—of natural resources, of wealth—to fulfill that promise with a functioning, stable government. But Naipaul repeatedly misrepresents Argentina's intellectual tradition, a tradition that makes its failures even more poignant. He avers that Argentina may well have annals of great men, but that it has no sense of history. Against all evidence, he asserts that Argentina is incapable of self-reflexivity, when it seems to many that Argentina is capable of little else.

CHAPTER TEN

Violent Exclusions

V. S. Naipaul is not the only outsider whose view of Argentina and its generals is more jaundiced than outraged. Actor and filmmaker Robert Duvall takes a similar stance in his film *Assassination Tango*. They differ in that Naipaul's conservatism is considered and deliberate, while Duvall's is an effect of ignoring the political implications of the story he is telling. Although it posits and depicts residual violence in the aftermath of the Dirty War, *Assassination Tango* is much less about the first word of its title than the second. The Dirty War is simply a hook on which Duvall, as producer, director, writer, and star, hangs the plot that justifies filming his real interest, the tango itself.[1] The character Duvall plays, John J. Anderson, is an aging hired killer whose redeeming characteristics are his love of dancing and his devotion to his girlfriend and especially to her preadolescent daughter. He is somewhat inexplicably hired to kill an Argentine general who was not brought to justice for the abuses he either perpetrated or condoned during the Proceso. The general is conveniently delayed in his return from his country estate to Buenos Aires, which gives the Duvall character time to learn, and learn about, the tango as it is danced in Argentina. This is, at bottom, a tango film, a genre with a long history in Argentina but that has no purchase in the United States. To appeal to audiences in this country, Duvall offers them a stock character, the professional killer, and a familiar theme, the murder gone wrong.[2] Duvall sketches in a background, as if answering the question of how to organize a film about a man from the United States who goes to Buenos Aires and discovers the authentic tango. Why not send him down as a hired killer? To kill whom? Well, the recent political history must have left some people angry at the lack of justice meted out to the military responsible for disappearances; mightn't they contract a Brooklyn murderer to do the job? The film does not give enough details about the general's past actions, the fact that someone has tipped off the police about the assassination plot, the reason that an aging Brooklyn thug would get this assignment, or why John J. is being double-crossed and set up to be killed; its heart is elsewhere. The assassination story is sketchy, but the tango atmosphere is densely portrayed with tango lessons, extended scenes of the dance, and long conversations about the meaning of tango. Duvall indulges in multiple tango fantasies, scenes in which he himself is dancing, shot as if through gauze, hazy and dreamlike.

Like its protagonist, who stops cold the explanation his Argentine employers try to give him for their desire for justice by saying that his politics can be summed up in the phrase "put the money on the table," *Assassination Tango* purports to have no political brief. Yet the film's opportunistic use of the Dirty War as mere backdrop and its cavalier and muddled treatment of its victims suggest an unexamined right-wing bias masquerading as objectivity. His Argentinean characters remain undeveloped, and their story is unclear. On the one hand they seem to be innocent victims of the Proceso; on the other they are apparently in league with corrupt officials. Moreover, John J. asserts that there are always two sides to every story—even, presumably, the story of a government that abducted, tortured, and murdered between ten and thirty thousand of its citizens.[3] In one scene, John J. is told that his hostess, the morose mother of a disappeared teenager, both knows and does not know why John J. has been called to Argentina. This twist on the vexed moral epistemology of the great majority of Argentines, who both did and did not know what the government was perpetrating in their name, impossibly places the parents of the disappeared into the same category. Nor is it a romanticization of those who lost family members to note that the response to the *punto final* that indemnified numerous kidnappers and torturers has been varied, but not violent. A revenge plot that included the assassination of the former generals was never a part of their plan.

The innocents in this film are not the junta's victims, who appear to be engaged in double-dealing and corruption, but rather John J. and his American family. This hired killer may have a very bad temper but he really loves his girlfriend's daughter. Once we realize that John J. is being set up, he becomes something like a descendant of the in-over-their-heads neocolonialist Englishmen we saw in chapter 3, whose efforts to make some honest money in Argentina are thwarted by the ruthless Argentines themselves. Sent down to Argentina to do a simple job, to murder a bad man, he winds up caught in an intrigue he does not understand. The assassination is far more complicated than John J. was led to believe, and he never figures out exactly what is going on. Nevertheless, as the hero of the film, the audience cheers him on as he completes the job he was sent to do and manages to get out of Argentina on survivor's instinct, gumption, and American know-how.

In contrast to his confusion about his professional responsibilities as a hired killer, as a dancer John J. masters the intricacies of the tango. The step that most appeals to him is the *gancho*—the hook, in which one dancer quickly bends a leg up and around her partner's knee and thigh, then quickly and gracefully swings it back down and away. The assassination may look like a kind of tango, but its hooks catch many of the participants, and the protagonist barely makes it out alive. The dancers, on the other hand, control their *ganchos*, and every one of them makes it home fine, as though those Argentines dedicated to the tango were never touched by the Dirty War.

The United States' fascination both with the failures of Latin America to consolidate democracy and with the abuse of power of military dictatorship is closely tied to U.S. exceptionalism, the notion that somehow the United States is exempt from the terrible things that happen elsewhere in the world: state violence, war on its own territory, natural disasters, and economic chaos.[4] This trust that we are an exception among the nations of the world also allows the United States to evade knowledge of its own responsibility in creating the conditions for the kind of state terror that held sway in Argentina during the Proceso. *Assassination Tango* simultaneously acknowledges and denies U.S. participation in the Argentine Dirty War. By sending an American assassin to kill one of the generals responsible for human rights abuses, the film casts a light, however murky, on the channel of violence connecting the United States to Argentina. Because the sort of state-perpetrated violence alluded to in the film is unthinkable for Americans (unthinkable on our own soil, that is), it is possible for us to watch it, abet it, and give ourselves credit for cleaning up after it. In *Assassination Tango* the U.S. support of the junta is mystified. John J. is a murderer, but he is neutral, uninformed about, and uninterested in, the details of the political situation in which he is conscripted to operate. As the film progresses it becomes less and less clear which side his clients are on, and we never really learn who they are. The film is muddled because it does not acknowledge its own complicity with willful not-knowing. *Assassination Tango* may mask U.S. involvement in setting up dictatorships, teaching torture techniques, and underwriting state violence, but the presence of the mask is evidence of the face beneath.

There is a provocative resonance between Julie Taylor's scholarly, intro-spective *Paper Tangos* and Robert Duvall's utterly personal *Assassination Tango*. At first glance it may appear that Taylor's autobiographically in-flected study of the tango shares with Duvall's autobiographically driven film the subordination of the political context to the pleasure of the tango. For in both, the violence of the junta seems to be overshadowed by individual desire, a desire that takes the shape of a virtual obsession with the dance. Tango takes center stage in Taylor's text as it does in *Assassination Tango*, even as the political drama of the Argentine dictator-ship and its aftermath, including the fictional violence of assassination in the Duvall film and the real violence of the junta, the bombings of the Israeli embassy and the Asociación Mutual Israelita Argentina in Taylor's study, lurk in the background. Yet Taylor's study is profoundly about the interconnection between tango, her own history as a dancer and anthropologist, and the disruption caused by a pervasive violence that is sometimes sexual, sometimes familial, sometimes political, and sometimes coded into the dance. The very real dread that was experi-enced by Taylor and her friends during the years of the junta is trans-formed by Duvall into the manufactured and pleasurable tension and release of the Hollywood thriller.

Taylor begins by informing her reader that she has lived more than thirty years in Argentina, a portion of which time coincided with the regime of the military junta. In the autobiographical account that weaves through her meditation on tango, Taylor notes that she "returned to Buenos Aires on the night of a military coup" (1998, 16). She remembers that she and her Argentine friends at the university "turned [their] atten-tion and professional talents to attempts at understanding the processes that swept us up for two decades—and have yet to let us go" (16). She makes specific reference to the junta, and her echo of Sarmiento in her characterization of the generals leaves no uncertainty as to where her sympathies lay: "One of those decades witnessed the savage 1976–1983 *Proceso,* the dictatorship of the Junta that added the word *desaparecido* to the world's vocabulary" (16). Taylor acknowledges the terror of living through those times; it becomes part of the fabric of daily life. In subsequent chapters, Taylor makes oblique reference to violence and danger, often displacing it onto other times and places. In her brief and allusive discussion of the African roots of tango, in which she stages Argentina's racial history as a set of unanswered questions outside the realm of scholarly discourse, Taylor invokes the word "disappeared" in the contemporary sense:

> Where did the Argentine Africans go, people ask sometimes. Were they, these conversations go, quite independent of scholarly literature, sent off to the wars where they were promised freedom but met death instead? How is it that Argentines today do not see them, hear them in the tango? They were disappeared. (66)

The chapter "Tangos and Violence," in which this allusion to Argentine Black history is indirectly linked to contemporary state violence, opens with a series of quotations on pentimento, suggesting that a layer of violence lurks beneath the surface of daily life. It then goes on to explore one woman's response to the political violence, not in Argentina, but in Colombia in the 1990s. Furthermore, that Colombian violence first evokes the tango, and only subsequently the similar state violence in Argentina. The violence of the junta is inseparable in Taylor's account from a complex and labile history of violence, not only in Argentina, but in the rest of Latin America as well, and it is all mediated through the tango:

> I was reading the comments of Doris Salcedo, concentrating on her allusions to indirect "revelations," not evocations, of terror through art, knowing she was working them out in the midst of the accelerating violence of Colombia. As I read of the absences and the sorrow underlying Salcedo's work, the tango bled through with its absences and its sorrows. I saw the only too familiar traces of the disappeared and the dead. (61)

Taylor gathers the accounts of violence in Colombia into her knowledge of violence in Argentina, a knowledge mediated by art, by dance.

In her "Afterword" Taylor explains that her approach to violence in the book has been to try not to essentialize or universalize it. The violence of the period is pervasive, impinging on everything else, but it is a specific violence. Taylor's task has been to maintain the specificity of forms and moments of violence even as she recognizes what all those forms and moments share:

> In a world where the experience of violence permeates further and further, to write in a mode that performs lived contradictions has spoken to specific forms of violence in the lives and art of specific actors. It has also helped avoid the danger of a naturalization or essentialization of the experiences of terror that share an unspeakable dimension but that also differ deeply from one another. (120–21)

The violence of the junta is not the stylized violence of the tango or even the real violence of child beating, both of which appear in Taylor's text. But violence and fear permeate *Paper Tangos.* Taylor notes the mutual interconnectedness entailed in coming to an understanding of the violences, which she defines as "exclusions," in Argentine culture and in her own life (121). This opening up of the one to the other is what makes her book so powerful. In a similar way, Colm Tóibín, in his novel *The Story of the Night,* and Martin Donovan, in his film *Apartment Zero,* compellingly explore the violent exclusions attendant upon homoerotic desire in the context of those of Argentina's Dirty War, refracting the Dirty War and its aftermath through queer desire and the dangers of abandoning secrecy.

A third tale of homoerotic desire, also set in the postjunta period and also erupting into violence, makes no reference to Argentina's historical situation. That narrative, Wong Kar Wai's film *Chun gwong cha sit (Happy Together),* finds in Argentina an empty and faraway space, devoid of any particular historical meaning of its own, in which to stage the deterioration of the relationship between two Chinese lovers. Wong was intrigued by the title of Manuel Puig's *Buenos Aires Affair* and used it as a working title for the film, but significantly only the novel's name, not its content, held his attention.[5] The director, whose own country was not implicated in the events of recent Argentine history, reduces Argentina to a few iconic signs: a tango bar, the music of Astor Piazzola, the desolate pampas, and the falls at Iguazú. Its nocturnal scenes in a rainy Buenos Aires, its bleak shots of the pampas, and its squalid interiors, bereft of any sign of domesticity or cultural meaning, provide the sites for an exploration of the emptying out of a relationship. As Charles Taylor points out, for Wong, Argentina is another empty site, made equal to all others in the process of globalization.[6] Audrey Yue, on the other hand, argues that Argentina and Taiwan line up in the film to "reinscribe" Hong Kong, as "diegetic tropes of the spaces of 'south'" (2000, 254), and that setting the film in Argentina functions to "abject" and "displace" its gay story, distancing it from the normal, that is, heteronormative, reality of Hong Kong. On Yue's reading, Argentina is Hong Kong's uncanny other, "located on the flipside of Hong Kong [mapped] as its heterotopia" (261). For Yue, as for Wong, Argentina is only a site of projection, devoid of its own history and with no political or historical resonance for Hong Kong.

Apartment Zero and *The Story of the Night*, in contrast, are haunted by recent British and American links to Argentina. Although neither of them is an overtly partisan or politically engaged work of denunciation, they are, like Taylor's *Paper Tangos*, enmeshed in the violence and dread perpetrated by the junta. All three of these texts are about pervasive violence, alienation, and disorientation. *The Story of the Night* and *Apartment Zero* explore the inextricable relationship between desire, danger, and keeping secrets. Pleasure and danger are entangled, so that the secrets of the closet mesh with the secrets of violence and corruption.

In *The Story of the Night*, the American characters are both appealing and appalling, but in a less chaotic way than is the Robert Duvall character in *Assassination Tango*. Ostensibly working on opening up trade relations with Argentina after the dictatorship, Susan Ford and her husband Donald are U.S. intelligence agents charged with making sure the right politicians get into office after the dictatorship is over. Susan acknowledges that the United States made mistakes in Chile, which she and Donald abetted when they were just beginning their work for the U.S. government; but she claims they are in Argentina only to promote democracy and economic development, overseeing a smooth privatization of the Argentine oil industry. Susan is attractive, efficient, overbearing, utterly sure of herself, and in many ways charming. Both those who are trying to get political power and those who are trying to make money off the economic shifts precipitated by the change in government and fostered by U.S. interests and the International Monetary Fund (IMF) know that Susan has the power to make things happen. No one is fooled by the Fords' cover story, but everyone agrees to acquiesce to their pretense of being economic advisors. The reader is given more than enough information to figure out that they are CIA agents.

Like the Fords, Jack Carney, the charming psychopathic killer in *Apart-ment Zero,* came to Argentina originally with the at least tacit endorse-ment of the U.S. government. As a participant in the Dirty War, his homi-cidal tendencies were channeled into the torture and murder authorized by the state. By slowly revealing Jack's participation in the Special Forces, an international brigade in league with the junta, Donovan uncovers the secret of U.S. involvement in the Argentine terror. In addition, the voice of authority, in the form of news broadcasts, overtly links the mur-ders carried out by the paramilitary to those Jack is still committing now, even after the dictatorship is over.

Jack's career as a murderer is perhaps the most transparent of the secrets of the film. Part of what makes *Apartment Zero* intriguing is the displacement of that secret onto the secret of homoeroticism, which itself is multiply repressed and displaced. *Apartment Zero*'s protagonist, Adrian LeDuc, seems to be a prim Englishman living in Buenos Aires. Forced by penury to take a roommate, Adrian eagerly settles on the seductive, movie-star handsome American Jack Carney, played by the appropriately handsome American actor Hart Bochner. The camera is relentless and often wry in establishing Adrian's queerness via his sur-roundings. In one exemplary case, it lingers on the walls of his apartment, densely decorated with photographs of film stars, many of whom— James Dean and Montgomery Clift among them—are gay icons. In an establishing shot, Bochner shares the frame with Adrian's James Dean photograph, presaging both the moment when Adrian tells his mother that Jack has a sort of "James Dean *je ne sais quoi*" and Adrian's own final James Dean moment, when he trades his uptight suit and tie for jeans and a leather jacket. Adrian's desire for Jack is palpable, but never spoken. He prepares elaborate breakfasts for Jack and offers to do his laundry, creating a domestic space for the two of them to share. In each of these scenes, Jack takes Adrian's measure, determining just how much Adrian is willing to give.

Adrian lives in and through film, barely eking out a living with the revival house movie theater he owns. His movie theater runs classic American films (of the sort the junta in fact allowed during their regime), but no one comes. A kind of opening to the rest of the world is available in his theater, but no one takes advantage of it. *Apartment Zero* itself parodies the classic film noir he sometimes shows to his ever-decreasing audiences. The mysterious, attractive American who seems so open and charming is cast in the role of the femme fatale, who is not at all what she (here, he) seems. The final scenes of the film owe much to Hitchcock's *Psycho* (but also to Faulkner's "A Rose for Emily"). Adrian not only kills Jack to keep him from leaving, propping him up at the dining room table and talking to him cajolingly, as if he were alive, he also takes on Jack's persona. A dead Jack is a compliant one, at worst a recalcitrant eater, and it is now Adrian who has the upper hand. Dressed in the James Dean–style clothes associated with Jack throughout the film, he has transformed his failing film club into a successful porno theater, whose patrons come pouring out at the end of the film under his controlling and watchful eye.

The double displacement, first of Adrian's closeted queer sexuality onto the furtiveness of daily life during the Dirty War and the violence and danger of that time and its aftermath, and then of Jack's covert life under the junta back onto sexuality, gives a depth and richness to *Apartment Zero* (and, as we shall see, *The Story of the Night*) that most foreign narratives about the Dirty War have not been able to achieve. *Apartment Zero* is far cooler and more detached than the novels by Lawrence Thornton and Douglas Unger discussed in the previous chapter. Insofar as the film is insistently self-reflexive and seductive in inviting the viewer to share in the in-jokes about the movies, *Apartment Zero* dabbles in the pleasure as well as the danger of violence as genre. (Among the films Adrian shows in his movie theater is *Compulsion,* a homoerotic murder story, but the conversation he and Jack have about the film is not about either the murder or the characters' sexuality. Instead, it is displaced onto a discussion of the director's choice to shoot *Compulsion* in black and white.)

Adrian knows the movies, but Jack is the actor. Playing the role of whomever his interlocutor most desires, Jack uses the weaknesses of others to achieve his ends. He draws Adrian to him, manipulating the other man's emotional dependence and longing for some kind of joy in his life. Jack enjoys breaking down the wall Adrian has built between himself and his neighbors. Playing to their fantasies, he takes on the persona of a closeted gay neighbor's first crush, the role of incestuous father with a woman who longs for both her absent husband and her dead father, the part of the charming gallant to two dotty old English ladies, and the character of the romantic hero to a melodramatic transsexual. When Adrian asks him who he really is, Jack replies seductively,

"Anyone you want me to be." Jack's sexuality is just another tool in his arsenal of charm and death; toward the end of the film he picks up a strange man whom he then murders, just in order to steal his passport.

Adrian, so very unlike Jack, remains utterly blind to his own desire. When Jack suggests that Adrian may not be sexually interested in women, Adrian says he's too much of a gentleman to think of women merely as objects. His palpable attraction to Jack, his lack of interest in women, his clichéd fastidiousness, his love of old movies, and the distance he maintains from his neighbors, all of whom are in some way queer themselves, all suggest that Adrian is gay, although he is so deeply closeted that he himself appears unaware of the fact.

In yet another displacement, *Apartment Zero* transfers Adrian's closeted sexual identity to his national identity: the secret Adrian knows he is keeping, unlike the secret he keeps from himself, is that he's really Argentinean. Adrian passes as English because he wants to be English, to distance himself from the chaos that he perceives as Argentine. He will be civilized, in contrast to the country's barbarism. Adrian, whose family is not British but merely spent many years in England, hopes that taking on Britishness will save him. Similarly, Richard Garay's British-born mother in Colm Tóibín's novel *The Story of the Night* becomes increasingly hostile to Argentina and more and more insistent on her English identity. As she grows older, she takes on more and more of the attitudes and postures of the refined Englishwoman she always wished to be. Argentina is the site of her failure: she is reduced to poverty there, to pretending to be well born, and to begging for help from her sister, whom she now finds unintelligible. The sister has been turned into a kind of *cautiva* character, the white woman who should want to escape the brutal and primitive life of the countryside, but who has made a life for herself with her gaucho-like husband and silent children. In the eyes of Richard's mother, her sister's husband is a brute, but in fact he is the one who tells her to stop exploiting his wife. Having abandoned any illusions of national, racial, or ethnic superiority, this sister is the one who survives. Moreover, her Argentine family ejects the self-deluded, hyper-British mother from its midst. Yet as far as Richard's mother is concerned, her sister has succumbed to barbarism.

To some extent, the radical self/other divide between Anglo and Argentine that *The Story of the Night* and *Apartment Zero* exploit is more salient from the Anglo than from the Argentine side. A significant num-

ber of the Argentine elite are the descendants of British and Irish immigrants who came to Argentina during the nineteenth century. Like some
of them, the fictional family in *The Story of the Night* has kept English as
a domestic language and affected British tastes. Richard's mother goes
them one better, assuming a class position that she never enjoyed, either
in Britain or in Argentina. Never having succeeded in Argentina she
feels especially alienated, needing to play-act a Britishness that would
confer superiority in the face of failure. The prophesies of Oscar Wilde
and Agatha Christie are fulfilled in *The Story of the Night:* this Englishwoman has been destroyed by Argentina.

Yet it is not only the Irish/British/American outsider who projects a
British difference, a split that makes it impossible to be both Anglo and
Argentine. The character of Adrian LeDuc in *Apartment Zero* was created by a filmmaker born in Argentina who himself has taken on, in his
name at least, an Anglo persona. We cannot know what moved Martin
Donovan to change his own name, but his character Adrian assumes
Britishness as a form of protection.[7] It keeps him from having to act in
and take responsibility for a society that otherwise would make too
many demands on him. On one level, Adrian's secret is absurd; when he
comes out to Jack as Argentine, the latter's amusement is shared by the
audience. On the surface, Adrian's fear seems only to be that he will be
annoyed and pestered by his nosy neighbors, but the sense of menace in
the film goes deeper. The secret *as* secret has great resonance in the film;
soon Adrian is trailing Jack to discover *his* secrets.

In *Apartment Zero,* Adrian's British persona is part of what allows
him to refuse to enter into political debates, that is, to willfully ignore
what is going on around him. Claudia, the political activist who works
for Adrian as a ticket-taker and who appears to be his only friend, tells
Adrian that his hostility to politics would be offensive in anyone but
him. She thus suggests that his being British, and Britishly eccentric,
gives Adrian leave to keep himself apart from Argentine society. Such
willed ignorance, however, is not innocent—especially since Adrian is
as Argentine as she. By the time Jack's identity as a member of the paramilitary is revealed in a clandestinely shot film, Adrian has been utterly
enraptured by him. Jack mouths the line of the mercenary soldier, saying he initially came to Argentina to help solve the country's problems.
But Jack is a psychopathic killer, and he charmingly acknowledges that
he really loves to kill. Adrian keeps silent about what he has learned

about Jack's past, as if that were a way to maintain neutrality. Claudia, on the other hand, confronts Jack. When Jack then murders Claudia, Adrian's fear of losing him is no less than his fear of the other man's potential for violence. He helps Jack dispose of Claudia's body, becoming complicit in the crime. What is more, the murder takes place offscreen and part of it is darkly comic; as viewers we laugh and thereby become complicit in Claudia's death as well. Adrian would appear to stand for the many Argentines without any political moorings. Like them, he has no way to deal with the knowledge of murder when he is confronted with it in his own living room. In a final twist, Adrian's desire for Jack turns him first into an accomplice in Claudia's murder and then into a murderer himself. By that time, the viewer is inclined to agree with Adrian and Jack's alcoholic neighbor that Adrian is likely afflicted with the same madness that claimed the mother to whom he was so devoted.

The attachment to the mother, who is sick, demented, dying, or dead, threatens to asphyxiate the sons in both *Apartment Zero* and *The Story of the Night*. In *Apartment Zero* this mother corresponds to the violent, amnesiac nation who does not know her own identity, but who nevertheless retains shreds of that identity in her vanity and sense of superiority.[8] Adrian tells Jack that his mother believes she speaks perfect English, although she has a thick accent that betrays who she really is. This aging, increasingly insane woman is repelled by her own identity. She is distraught at her own visage in the mirror, and she does not recognize her own loving son. Yet there is something regal about Adrian's mother, even in her madness. She reminds the viewer of a deluded and haughty Argentina, spiraling into chaos. Both poverty and delusion, in different doses, govern the mothers' lives in *Apartment Zero* and *The Story of the Night*. The darkness of their lives is represented in these texts in the gloomy maternal space of the apartments where the mad, dying, and ultimately dead mothers have lived. The claustrophobic maternal space that the mother defines in both texts is compelling. Neither son can easily extricate himself from it, and only in part because they lack the money to move. Both sons live in the mother's apartment, which is heavy with her presence even when she is no longer there. The mother's death midway in both narratives leaves the son both bereft and free. Adrian takes on his mother's madness, not withdrawing from the world as she does, but creating an alternate reality. Withdrawn into the apartment he had always shared with her, Adrian becomes a version of his mother.

Tóibín's Richard Garay, on the other hand, manages to escape. Significantly, when Richard does leave his mother's dark apartment in the city, it is for an extravagant, light-flooded, ultramodern space on the water.

The palette of *Apartment Zero* is dark and murky, with many nocturnal settings, as well as scenes in the gloomy apartment and Adrian's darkened movie theater. The nighttime, with its suggestion of the covert and the dangerous that is the central conceit of Colm Tóibín's novel, is a familiar trope in the other Dirty War texts as well. The face of General Guzman, the character Lawrence Thornton creates as the chief architect of the disappearances and torture in his trilogy, is "the face of the night," where night is the metaphor for state terror, generalized out from Argentina to include the Nazi death camps, the Soviet Gulag, and South African apartheid:

> [H]e had come away with Guzman's face—harsh, practiced, unforgiving, but in the end a human face, flawed by singleness of mind, zealotry, conviction. *It was the face of the night,* the one which had appeared to everyone who had been taken, a face no better or worse than those which had looked out from beneath the skull and crossbones of the SS, the faces of judges looking down upon some poor bastard on his way to Siberia, the faces of Afrikaners pushing out the infidels, making room for the chosen people. (Thornton 1987, 108, emphasis added)

The metaphor Unger briefly relies on here is most completely exploited by Colm Tóibín in *The Story of the Night.*

The Story of the Night is a story of desire, of anonymous, thrilling sex but also of the awful isolation of being closeted that makes sharing a sure death from AIDS a poignantly happy ending. Unlike Donovan's Adrian LeDuc, Tóibín's Richard Garay knows and acts on his sexuality, but it puts him in danger. Like Adrian, Richard has tried to keep himself innocent of politics, taking the stance of those who hid knowledge from themselves, a stance that is hardly innocent in its willful ignorance. With no real understanding of the political stakes he is dealing with in the period of Argentina's transition to democracy, Richard is equally willing to represent his friend's father and his Peronist cronies, and later a group of American oil entrepreneurs and the IMF. Richard's CIA is charming; its agents help him emerge from both penury and the closet. They help Richard quickly rise above the uncouth corruption of his Argentine friend's politically ambitious father. The economic corruption of his new acquaintances from the United States is far more sophisticated and genteel. Richard's political ignorance is echoed in his ignorance of dangerous sexual behavior in the era of HIV/AIDS. His lover's North American friends are astonished, and delighted, to find that the saunas and bath houses that have long been closed down in San Francisco are still functioning in Buenos Aires.

There is a happy ending to *The Story of the Night*. Richard and his lover find a beautiful, light-suffused space just outside the suffocatingly heteronormative world of Buenos Aires where they can live together and nurse each other. Yet although the political center of the novel shifts from state terror and corruption to AIDS, and the solution the novel proposes is hardly radical (by which I mean that it aims at the poisoned fruits of the AIDS epidemic, and not at the social and economic roots of the disease, or at the sociology of its treatment), this remains the most successful of the literary texts to confront the aftermath of the Dirty War.[9] Perhaps in part *because* the gaze is deflected from the brutality of the junta, the novelist finds a way to evoke the intimate terror and the way Argentineans survived by means of absenting themselves, seeing and not seeing, taking on a kind of mental illness—a willful entry into delusion. In order to survive one had to actively "not know." And that meant also knowing. Richard's withdrawal into himself, his nocturnal visits to the saunas, the very secretiveness of his life, become the vectors by which he contracts AIDS, just as the cramped and blindered lives that the majority of Argentines led during this period underwrote the violence that caught so many of their countrymen and -women.[10]

Like others who protected themselves by a remarkable psychological mechanism of cognitive dissonance during the Dirty War, Richard felt a pervasive sense of danger such that he withdrew from all society. Moreover, keeping his sexuality secret bleeds into the pervasive fear of being seen or found for any number of nebulous crimes, including a shady financial deal in which top government officials are also implicated in the Dirty War. Richard had sequestered himself and, he claims, never saw what was going on around him. By removing himself from one risk, he avoided another as well. But in both cases, the price was alienation and isolation, and in the end, a sure death:

> Everyone learned to ignore what was going on in public as though it had nothing to do with them. There was, I suppose, a climate of fear which everyone understood, but the fear was like an undertow: it never appeared on the surface and it was never discussed. (Tóibín 1997, 66)

The epistemological diffidence "present" in Richard's "I suppose" marks much of his narrative, especially in moments of emotional or ethical demand. Richard withdraws from his own responsibility to know, or even to know about knowing. In one emblematic scene, Richard responds to a question from a foreigner about the Mothers of the Plaza de Mayo by saying that he did not know anyone who had been disappeared. He recognizes that denying that knowledge was a way of denying that the disappearances had ever occurred:

> As I sat down I heard the Irishman say that he had been that afternoon to the Plaza de Mayo and he had seen the mothers of the disappeared in their white scarves. Was that still an issue here, he asked. What did we think about it? I hesitated and said that I really did not know. I said it seemed strange to me that after all these years I had never seen a list of the names of those who had disappeared, that I myself knew no one who had disappeared. I am not suggesting, I said, that it did not happen. But, for some reason, I realized, I was suggesting just that. (121)

An Argentine economist sitting at the table soon challenges Richard's deliberate ignorance, reminding him that they had met through a mutual friend at the university who was among the disappeared. Her case was widely reported in the newspapers; and, what is more, several other classmates of Richard's had been abducted along with her. Yet Richard really was not conscious of the fact that his fellow students had been victims of the junta. He had successfully shielded himself from the risk of knowing. What Richard did know was that knowledge itself was dangerous. The interchange with his former acquaintance reminds him of the choice he made not to know, one evening during a sexual encounter, when his lover tells him that the cars gunning their engines across the street at the police station are generating power for the cattle prods used for torture.

> I remember one such encounter not for the sex we had, but because of a sound that came into the room as we made love, the sound of car engines revving over and over. I asked my partner—I remember a dark-haired man in his thirties with white skin—what the noise was. He brought me to the window to show me the police station opposite and the cars outside, driverless, but still revving, with wires going from the engines to the basement of the building. They need power, he said, but I still did not understand. They need extra power for the cattle prods, he said. I still do not know if what he said was true, if that was one of the centers in the city to which people were taken, and if we fondled each other and

came to orgasm within moments of each other to the sound of the revving cars which gave power to the instruments of torture. It made no difference then, because I did not pay much attention to what he said, and I remember the pleasure of standing at the window with him, my hands running down his back, more than anything else.

It is only now, years later, that it seems significant, perhaps the only sign I was ever given of what was happening all around me. I cannot remember the name of my companion that evening, the man I stood with at the window, but I have often wondered how he knew or thought he knew, or if he imagined, what the revving of the cars' engines meant in our city at that time. (8–9)

Tóibín is masterful in describing the interplay of knowledge and ignorance in this passage. Richard may not understand the need for extra power for the cattle prods, but he does know that torture centers exist. The question is not whether they exist or not, but if this indeed is one of them, and if the pleasure Richard and his lover experienced was somehow affected, if not enhanced, by torture nearby. At the beginning of the passage, Richard says that what he remembers is the noise, not the sex, but during the encounter, the sex was primary. "I did not pay much attention to what he said." He concentrated, rather, on the pleasure of physical contact: his hands running down the man's back, their mutual orgasm. Richard could have known, did know that there was something to know, but chose not to know.

In *A Lexicon of Terror*, Marguerite Feitlowitz documents the fraught silence, product of the desire to believe things were normal and the fear that they were not, that the dictatorship generated. This weighted silence finds a resonance in the secret of homosexuality in *The Story of the Night*, and especially in *Apartment Zero*, where homosexual desire is so repressed that Adrian does not even begin to acknowledge it. In the same way the reality of disappearances and torture was both known and denied, and more furiously denied because to acknowledge that one knew about them increased one's own danger, making the reality of the disappearances real not only for those who were taken away, but also for those who were witnesses to it. *Por algo será* (there has to be a reason) and *algo habrán hecho* (they must have done something), then, were incantations invoked to keep danger away from oneself. They permitted a moment of recognition in a situation in which many people denied the evidence before their eyes. To be a witness would require an admission that state terror existed, and such a recognition would be a form, however attenuated, of denunciation. Thus even to acknowledge that one knew what was going on could mean entering into the circle of the targeted. Moreover, to concede that one was not living in normal times, but was performing a normal routine during a time of state terror in which others were targets, was to admit to one's own complicity, even if it was involuntary. Richard's oblique acknowledgement that his pleasure may have coincided with another's torture speaks to this ethical and psychological dilemma. His pleasure may not have been increased by another's pain, but it was not diminished, either.

In *A Lexicon of Terror*, Feitlowitz reports one incident, when a biochemist named Susana Barros was pulled off a city bus by a soldier dressed as a civilian, and, breaking the utter silence of her fellow passengers, one woman murmured "Not by the hair." That moment of empathy with the young woman who was being disappeared in broad daylight could have cost the witness dearly. As Feitlowitz tells the story, the woman's reaction was immediate, visceral, unpremeditated. It spoke to a connection she felt with Barros, who was, in front of a bus full of witnesses, being made into a nonperson by the kidnappers. That moment of Barros's conversion, from being another Argentine on the bus to losing her standing as a citizen among citizens, was marked by one woman's momentary identification with the physical pain of being brutally pulled by the hair. After that, as Feitlowitz notes, we do not know what happened on the bus. But Feitlowitz imagines the scene, a scene of willful unseeing, of avoidance and self-protection, that thereby consigned Barros to the otherness of nonpersonhood:

> We know what happened to Susana. We do not know what happened on the bus. But with my interviews with others who saw abductions, I will hazard this: No one spoke. The driver's eyes avoided the rear-view mirror. The passengers shrank away from one another, fearful and suspicious. Everyone rode to his usual stop, faithful to the stricture of routine. (1998, 150)

As Feitlowitz repeats Barros's own testimony, the young woman was beaten on the street, then taken to the torture center outfitted at the Navy Mechanics School where she was "stripped, blindfolded, tied to a bed frame, and electrically tortured" (150). Not permitting oneself to know that such terrible things are happening is a kind of self-protection, and it was brilliantly exploited by the perpetrators of state violence. The very constraints provided by routine functioned as rituals that would grant safe passage through times and spaces of terror.

Feitlowitz goes on to write of the numerous people who remembered seeing a kidnapping but who then denied or questioned what they themselves had just remembered. The moment at which such contradictions become impossible to sustain, the refrain *por algo será* allows the witness to see but not denounce, to know but to set aside the fullness of knowledge, to divert the attention from the savage brutality of kidnapping, torture, and murder to some amorphous offense that might serve to justify such punishment. *Por algo será* separates the abjected, violated other from the subject, who has not done or thought or perpetrated that *algo* (something), that vague transgression that has no name, no form, but that must be invoked as a way of marking the boundary between the nonperson and the self. In this way, the very act of abduction was disappeared; one could not risk being a witness to it.

In *Apartment Zero* Adrian lives that relationship to his own sexuality and desire. He does not acknowledge in himself the dangerous reality of desire; similarly, he is oblivious to the political situation of his country. Adrian lives a circumscribed and pinched life; he avoids contact with his neighbors, whom he disdains. Everything is ordered and controlled, from his schedule to his closets. Like the greater mass of Argentine society, who willfully or unconsciously did not let themselves see the reality they were living, who may have been seduced by the generals and by the easy, "sweet" money that was flowing into Argentina and into the pockets of the middle class, but who on some level knew as well that the price of complicity was demanded of them, Adrian is profoundly bound to the charming psychopath. And part of the power of that binding is Adrian's lack of self-awareness of the source in his own desire, the better for Jack, and all he represents, to exploit it.

Adrian's refusal to acknowledge his own reality is a symptom of madness, which by the end of the film has become full-blown. As the truth not only of his desire for Jack, but of the state-sponsored violence that Jack represents becomes more and more difficult to deny, Adrian works harder and harder to do just that. Insanity is perhaps the logical consequence of the avoidance of knowledge and repression of reality that characterized Argentine life during the Dirty War and that emerges as a central theme in the films and fiction discussed in this chapter. Leon

Festinger first described this struggle to maintain consistency between what one knows, one's attitudes, and one's behaviors in 1957, calling it cognitive dissonance. What is interesting about cognitive dissonance is that it combines conscious practices of avoidance with unconscious mechanisms of repression. During the Dirty War, such dissonance may well have been exacerbated by the nature of the consequences of reconciling new information (about disappearance, state violence), to which more and more people were witness, with the desire to believe that one was living in a rational, civilized nation, a notion insistently propagated by the regime itself. The conscious avoidance of information would have been compounded by incredulity concerning practices like kidnappings in broad daylight and torture in near-public places. Moreover, to acknowledge the violently immoral behavior of the state would mean having to make a decision about whether or not to enter the dangerous game of opposition. To do so could cost you your life; to turn a blind eye could cost you your soul. You cannot be held accountable for what you do not know. Occurring at the intersections between the psychological, the political, and the ethical, knowledge in the context of the Dirty War was fraught with danger. *The Story of the Night, Apartment Zero,* Thornton's trilogy, *Assassination Tango, Voices from Silence,* and *Paper Tangos* all in some way address the cognitive dissonance of Argentina during the Dirty War. They all, often in quite different ways, attend to the distressing struggle between knowledge and ignorance that turns knowing into a realm of ethics and danger.

The problem of memory that has been at the center of so much recent thinking, especially with reference to the Holocaust, takes on another wrinkle in the case of Argentina's Dirty War. Lawrence Thornton, Christopher Hampton, Manuel Vázquez Montalbán, and Douglas Unger exhort us to remember what happened then, and their narratives remind us of the details so that we do not forget. Yet as the texts discussed in this chapter and the previous one suggest, access to knowledge, which is the foundation of even partial, selective, and questionable memory, is itself at risk. State propaganda, secrets kept even from oneself, fear, and contradictory information all work against knowing and, therefore, remembering.

Still, knowledge and memory take myriad forms and may be arrived at by different routes. The memory of blood is stamped in the DNA of stolen children. It is inscribed on the body in dance—or by torture.

Clairvoyance or private detective work may penetrate the secrets of state violence. Memory may be repressed and displaced; the refusal or inability not only to remember, but also to see, know, and communicate finds another channel. The powerful conflation of secrecy and desire, both sexual and political, courses through the representations of the Dirty Wars of the Southern Cone. In "Lovelys," a story by Uruguayan writer Cristina Peri Rossi, a man whose impotence is in the end attributed to his having seen and repressed the scene of a family taken away by the paramilitary elegantly dramatizes the damage done not only to those targeted by dictatorship, but also to the rest of society. The bizarre sexual repression of the protagonist seems to have any number of possible etiologies; it is only in the end, when he brings the scene of the disappearance back to consciousness, that it becomes clear to the reader exactly what sort of repression was taking place. This little story, which presumably takes place in a Uruguay that between 1971 and 1984 was under the rule of a military junta much like the one in Argentina, neatly dramatizes the collapsing of sexual, political, ethical, and epistemological questions that faced Argentina and its neighbors in the last quarter of the twentieth century.

CHAPTER ELEVEN

The Persistence of Memory

Memory may be tenacious, but, as in the Salvador Dalí painting whose title inspired that of this chapter, it mutates in and into dreamscape. Clocks melt out of shape and swarm with ants, sterile but still menacing. The images are sharp-edged, but they do not affect transparency or pretend to represent quotidian reality. Similarly, as a projection and at its most desirable, Argentina provides the raw material for the manufacture of a dreamscape for the European imagination. The film version of Tim Rice and Andrew Lloyd Weber's *Evita,* starring pop icon and cultural studies heroine Madonna, handily illustrates this phenomenon. Not only the costumes, but many of the scenes themselves were painstakingly reproduced from photographs of the era. The filmmakers of the Hollywood version of Eva Perón's life went to great lengths to re-create the historical moment, even to the extent of reproducing, and then setting in motion, still photographs taken from popular magazines of the Perón era. The effect is of a hyperreal Technicolor version of scenes otherwise available primarily in black-and-white still photos. This jazzed-up realism is thrown into relief by the sung dialogue. The result of this meticulous attention to visual detail juxtaposed with the contrivedness of the sung, not spoken, word is a highly stylized narrative film, which is further denaturalized by the anachronistic insertion of Che as the chorus/narrator. (The "Guevara" was dropped for the film, but the green fatigues and even Antonio Banderas's physical aspect are constant reminders of the Argentinean revolutionary.) Moreover, Madonna never fully becomes Evita; the actress on screen competes with the historical figure. Viewers can never forget that what they are watching is an aesthetic construction. According to popular accounts, Madonna sought out the role of Evita because she identified with the self-fashioning and drive of the character. Nevertheless, much of the political content of Eva Perón's life and work is evacuated in the film. Juan Perón is little more than a prop, at most a supporting player. Distance is maintained; the historical reality of Argentina is placed at the service of style and artifice for the pleasure of European and U.S. audiences.

Ella Shohat and Robert Stam (1994) remind us that film, more immediate and more widely available than the written text, is a potent medium for establishing the idea of the nation. Of the different ways of making a narrative film set in a foreign place that Shohat and Stam elucidate—studio sets, location on site, location that resembles the site, and stock footage, all of which provide a visual representation that strives for verisimilitude—on-site location is the most convincing and potentially the most problematic. In cases where the film contradicts the state's official narrative or, in the case of more open societies, where the underlying politics of the film assaults cultural sensibilities, on-site location may be virtually impossible. The proposal to film *Evita* in Buenos Aires caused an uproar, with many Argentines disapproving of what they considered to be Madonna's trivialization of a national icon. Those who revered the historical Evita (or the myth that grew up around her) considered the choice of Madonna to play her a slap in the face; those who reviled the powerful figure they referred to as "that woman" did not want Argentina to play any part in glorifying her. Others were delighted that the wildly popular North American superstar was coming to their country. Eventually the Peronist government then in power gave its permission to the film's director to use the Casa Rosada, Argentina's presidential palace, for Evita's iconic speech from its balcony. Nevertheless, modern Argentina had changed too much for the funeral scene, which winds through blocks of city streets. That scene was shot in Budapest, where the architecture more closely resembles that of mid-century Buenos Aires. The architecture, not of Buenos Aires but of Eastern Europe, which, if one omitted the Soviet-style new construction, had preserved its prewar character, could therefore be called upon to represent the nostalgia-driven version of Argentina the film was aiming for. Only a part of Europe arrested architecturally and economically in the mid-twentieth century can still look like mid-century Buenos Aires, which not only participated in, and often set, Western architectural styles, but also became increasingly third-worlded. The multiple displacements (Evita/Madonna and Buenos Aires/Budapest), the hyperreal sets and costumes, and the extreme artificiality of the opera form all contrive to call up an Argentina that is and is not present, that recalls the material reality that it displaces. The more the imitation strives to be faithful through set design, makeup, wardrobe, and hairstyle, the more aware the viewer is of an artifice that is already necessarily present in the operatic form.

Like Borges's Pierre Menard, whose Don Quixote, the reader is told, is a greater achievement than Cervantes's for having been produced outside of its appropriate time and place, Alan Parker's *Evita* projects a hyperreal mid-century Argentina, more insistently Argentinean than the original. Eva Perón as played by Patti Lupone on Broadway and Madonna in the film emerges as a camp icon of retro-fashion style, just this side of parody. In Argentina, Evita is either the hated arriviste or the poor-girl who-made-good; her style represents either the height of fashion or the essence of vulgarity. From the point of view of outside she is always already dated, retro, the declawed stuff of a longing nostalgia for what one did not in fact experience oneself.

Not unlike *Evita,* but much more naive, the 1940 Hollywood film *Down Argentine Way* presents a glassy surface that manufactures desire, depicting a world of opulence, freedom, wealth, and pleasure. The principal characters, played by Don Ameche and Betty Grable, are young, beautiful, independent, and rich. They frequent nightclubs in which Latin American performers like the Brazilian Carmen Miranda headline, and they travel from one end of the world to the other to indulge their passion in acquiring and racing thoroughbred horses. The plot is flimsy: young lovers are kept apart by fathers who were once good friends, but who became rivals for the love of the same woman. Still angry at his former school chum, Ameche's father refuses to allow him to sell a horse to Grable. She follows him from New York to Argentina, and they fall in love and conspire to get their fathers to overcome their differences. As a film location, Argentina draws on gauchos for local color as much as it draws on sophisticated nightclub scenes in New York and Buenos Aires, parallel sites for the display of affluence and sophistication. Both cities are exotic to the average U.S. filmgoer, but such spaces are made familiar as well, from the movies themselves.[1] *Down Argentine Way,* filmed on location, provided stock footage of Argentina that the studio used in subsequent movies. The social and political meaning of the gaucho is drained away in this film; its vestiges are apparent only in the cliché of the loyal servant dressed in traditional gaucho gear.

Yet this slight film is suggestive of a complex weave of a delicate internal and external politics. Cynthia Enloe writes that the Latin American turn in films was a function of Jewish producers in Hollywood trying to get into the good graces, and past the anti-Semitism, of Washington:

> [W]hen President Franklin Roosevelt launched his Latin American "Good Neighbor" policy, the men who ran Hollywood were willing to help the government's campaign to replace a militaristic, imperial approach to US-Latin American diplomacy with a more "cooperative" strategy that included promoting US investment in, and tourism to, Latin America. (2000, 125)

Early in the twentieth century, Argentina and the United States were similarly situated as young and promising nations, the receivers of immigrants. The differences between the two grew larger as Argentina lost much of its wealth and became politically less stable, at the same time that the wealth and power of the United States increased. The growing distinction between the United States and Argentina coincided with the arrival of the Hollywood exotic location film and with the technical innovation of Technicolor.[2] According to film historian Lary May, the new interest in foreign locations in the 1930s and 1940s suggests a desire to incorporate the foreign into the domestic, to tame it and make it comprehensible in U.S. terms. May notes that in the 1940s "a very popular formula (though it had earlier roots), [was] to place Americans in an 'exotic locale' where they could have great humorous adventures" (personal communication). By that time, Argentina was poised to be an exotic locale that still had much of the familiar to it.[3] According to May, the Bing Crosby, Bob Hope "road films"

> were the most popular films of the forties. . . . In these films the foreign land becomes a playground, a little like Las Vegas, where the leads have a great time kidding the native costumes that they are attracted to. . . . The foreign culture is never taken seriously. It is simply there for play and humor. (personal communication)

Similarly, the Argentina of *Down Argentine Way* is the stuff of light-hearted travelogue: a round of nightclubs in New York and Buenos Aires, barbecues complete with singing and dancing gauchos in the Argentine countryside, and the serious business of international horse racing. In addition, the romance between the principals in *Down Argentine Way* is mimicked in a comic subplot about an Argentine gigolo and an older American woman that relies heavily, but plays lightly, on gender and ethnic stereotypes. The year after *Down Argentine Way* came out, RKO released the Rogers and Hart musical *They Met in Argentina*, whose plot also revolves around horse racing and international romance.

You Were Never Lovelier (1942) is another slight film, a Hollywood musical set in Argentina that, like *Down Argentine Way*, illustrates the way in which Argentina serves as the familiar exotic. The plot is reminiscent of classic farce, a romantic comedy that this time crosses class as well as national boundaries. Rita Hayworth plays the second of four daughters whose father, Adolphe Menjou, insists they be married in order of age. Setting the film in Argentina makes this contrivance more credible: Menjou is an old-fashioned, domineering father recognizable to U.S. audiences, but whose pronouncements on his daughters' marriages would be unacceptable in a modern American parent. Hayworth declares she is not about to marry, much to the consternation of both Menjou and her two younger sisters. Her father's somewhat kinky solution is to soften her up to the idea of marriage by inducing her to fall in love with a secret admirer. He proceeds to write her love letters and send her flowers. Intrigued, she falls for his deception. A comic mix-up makes her think that Fred Astaire is the admirer and soon they are in love. Eventually she discovers the ruse and becomes furious; and Astaire, now with the father's help, has to win her back. Boy meets girl, boy loses girl, boy gets girl, with a fair amount of singing and dancing along the way.

Like *Down Argentine Way*, *You Were Never Lovelier* takes place in the opulent world of Buenos Aires, which it links to New York via the Latin music that was popular at the time, thanks in part to the movies themselves. The film opens with a series of long shots of Buenos Aires and a subtitle that says "Buenos Aires, 1942." After these establishing shots, the rest of the film takes place in generic affluence, typically the fancy hotel and nightclub owned by Menjou and the domestic space of his family estate. Argentina is rarely referred to again, and when Astaire is set to leave, Hayworth says she won't let him leave "South America," collapsing the nation into the continent.

The film, shot in the studio, makes less of the physical presence of Argentina than does *Down Argentine Way*, and the Argentine horse-racing motif, if present, is marginal. At the beginning of the film Astaire is seen bemusedly tearing up his losing ticket at Buenos Aires's Palermo racetrack, where his horse has just comically ambled over the finish line well after the rest of the pack. The characters are all completely recognizable in the context of Hollywood movie making. American and Americanized Hollywood actors play "foreign" roles, thus creating a level of familiarity between the exotic locale and home. The already globalized world of popular entertainment does the same. Although nightclubs were available to few, nightclub scenes were common in films. Like Carmen Miranda in *Down Argentine Way,* Xavier Cugat plays himself as a performer in *You Were Never Lovelier.* As the headline act in Adolphe Menjou's hotel nightclub, he is the link between Menjou and Astaire, who plays a down-on-his-luck but charming and insouciant entertainer. (Astaire actually wears a silk tie as a belt in one scene; perhaps this is where fashion designer Paul Smith got the idea—see below.)

The Argentineity of Menjou's family is established by a few simple markers: the father's control over the daughters' sexuality, the fact that the family was originally from France, and reference to a grandfather who raised cattle. In all other ways, the family is utterly familiar to the American audience. Moreover, the detail of the cattle-baron grandfather emerges as a site of similarity. Astaire tries to convince Hayworth that they are too different from each other for their relationship to work by telling her that his grandfather raised cows. She replies that hers did too, calling attention to the difference-in-sameness between Argentina and the United States.

The Argentine family appears utterly European. The mother is of Breton heritage and even wears a Breton costume in one scene, and early in the film Menjou speaks French to the owner of an exclusive dress shop. But the female lead was, like Argentina itself, deliberately Europeanized before she could perform this role. Rita Hayworth was born Margarita Carmen Cansino, and early in her career she played racialized Latina parts. When she was first put under contract at Twentieth Century Fox and still using her own name, the studio highlighted her Spanish background. Her hair was darkened, she was costumed in a stereotypically Latin manner, and she spoke her lines with a Spanish accent. In 1935, before she lost her Fox contract and underwent her delatinization at Columbia, she was cast in a small part in another film set in Argentina, *Under the Pampas Moon.* This film has all the familiar elements of the Hollywood Argentine film narrative: foreign visitors to Argentina, gauchos, horse racing, scenes in both the pampas and in Buenos Aires, the posh urban hotel and nightclub. The romantic heroine in *Under the Pampas Moon,* however, is not the overtly raced Cansino, but rather a French singer played by Ketti Gallian. Only when Hayworth is repackaged as thoroughly white does she play a female lead, as an Argentine of French ancestry.[4]

An early publicity photo of Cansino depicts her with her hair dyed black to make her appear even more exotic, a wider nose, a fuller body, and dressed in what appears to be hand-loomed cloth reminiscent of Central America or the Andes, all racial markers that later were scrupulously erased.[5] *You Were Never Lovelier* was made after her transformation: elocution lessons, hair lightened and restyled, body thinned by dieting, nose thinned by plastic surgery, and name changed, as May points out, to evoke a Midwestern landscape. Hollywood artifice, even for this, the most frivolous of films, depends upon a complex play of racial otherness and similarity. Margarita Cansino, Latina by virtue of her father's Spanish (not Latin American) background, converted into all-American, white Rita Hayworth, nevertheless retains traces of the highly sexualized charge that is stereotypically Hispanic.

Argentina in *Down Argentine Way* and *You Were Never Lovelier* is the not entirely exotic other. The Rita Hayworth character in the latter film does not *turn out* to be white, as the love interest often does in the Hope and Crosby road movies; she *is* white, from the very beginning of the film, though problematically so.[6] Insofar as the class and ancestry of the character mark her as European while the actress and the site of the film suggest Latin otherness, her racial identity is ambivalent. Like *Down Argentine Way,* which establishes points of similarity between Argentina and the United States along the axis of upper-class interests and pleasures, *You Were Never Lovelier* depicts a world of nightclubs and Latin music through the familiar narrative of the love story. While a college friendship turns to enmity between the Argentine and American fathers only to be resolved in the next generation in their children's love story in *Down Argentine Way, You Were Never Lovelier*'s marriage plot is more along the lines of a watered-down *Taming of the Shrew.* In both stories, the romance between an Argentine and a North American is stymied—in one case in the classic Romeo and Juliet way by two feuding fathers and in the other in the fairytale mode of a suitor too poor to woo the haughty daughter of a wealthy man. These are films made during a time when, most film historians agree, the pleasure of film was largely escapist. The viewer got a taste of a life of glamour, affluence, and ease during times of hardship at the end of the Depression and the beginning of the Second World War. The fantasy of nightclub hopping is one-upped by the fantasy of international nightclub hopping, providing a vicarious experience of the good life. Like New York during the Depression, which retained vestiges of opulence available only to the most privileged, but accessible to a mass audience via film, Argentina could still be presented as a land of wealth and promise to an audience for whom Argentina's prosperity was a living memory.

Yet even now, more than half a century later, the memory of Argentina as a rich nation that invited immigrants to help build it and in turn become rich themselves, and as a country that sent its most prosperous abroad to acquire European refinement, is astonishingly persistent. The image of an urbane, well-traveled upper-class Argentina is particularly tenacious. Over a hundred years after the dashing, unspeakably affluent Argentine abroad first made his appearance as a cultural phenomenon, and a good eighty years after he began to disappear from the European scene as his family's wealth decreased along with Argentina's economy, he reappeared on the style page of the *International Herald Tribune*. In the year 2001, the year Argentina defaulted on its international debt and faced the worst economic crisis in its history, designer Paul Smith revived the figure of the rich Argentine playboy. Venerable fashion writer Suzy Menkes recognized that the narrative was both familiar and fresh enough to appeal to the media as well as to his intended clients:[7]

> Paul Smith talked a good story line: Young scion of wealthy Argentine family goes to school in England, picks up rebel ways, returns home with a cocky, casual style (think pants held up with silken necktie or leather belt that looks like string). (2001, 7)

Although the wealth of the Argentine oligarchy is hardly vestigial, the Argentineans in today's Europe are not what they once were. The fabled grand tour, complete with family retainers and a cow brought on shipboard to make sure the children had fresh milk, is not a part of current reality. The young Argentines in Europe at the end of the twentieth century were far more likely to be political exiles than carefree students, and they got their education in rebellion at home. Moreover, at the beginning of the twenty-first century, many Argentines, young and old, were searching for economic stability in Europe after their country's spectacular economic collapse in 2001 and 2002. Nevertheless, the same year that Argentina defaulted on a billion dollars worth of international loans, Smith uses the figure of the rich and charming Argentine ne'er-do-well as a touchstone to set the stage for how to think of the "scruffy but classy" clothing line he is showing. Menkes describes the scene:

> As a trio of ancestral chandeliers swung above the shiny floor of a school gymnasium, the scruffy but classy young men stepped out. Ruffled shirts in broderie anglaise or polka dots spilled from tailored jackets or easy pants in soft colors. (7)

The rich-as-an-Argentine story that has become part of the store of Europe's narrative archive is, in this case, just a hook to snag the interest of Paul Smith's potential clients. In the end the designer admits that his clothes are not rebellious (and who ever said that the Argentine playboy was, underneath it all, truly a rebel?); that basically he's trying to sell dry goods: "As Smith said, 'I'm aware that at the end of the day, people only want a shirt or sweater'" (7). The "people" who want a shirt or a sweater are not, of course, the scions of the Argentine oligarchy, who are, by now, nothing more than a trope, a sign of the exotic who came to Europe and returned home having learned European student politics. By the last third of the twentieth century, Argentina was perfectly capable of producing its own student rebels, and wealthy Argentine families today are as likely to send their children to study in the United Sates as in England. Nevertheless, the little story Smith tells is a pretty gloss on the relationship between Europe and Argentina that masks a complex and painful history.

The reference to the rich young Argentine abroad that lends cachet to the Smith clothing line is not meant to be understood by just anybody, however. The *International Herald*'s Style section cultivates a knowledgeable and sophisticated in-group by means of the plots fashioned by designers and fashion reporters. The sketchy story Paul Smith tells relies on a store of cultural knowledge to which, it is implied, only those who are wise to the history of style are privy. If you get the reference, you are smart enough to buy the clothes and be part of the set that can afford to spend vast amounts of money on your wardrobe. Even if you can't afford the price tag, as long as you understand the references you are a part of the hip cognoscenti who know fashion and style. Menkes confesses to have liked the story Smith told better than the designs he showed, suggesting that the Argentina narrative can be counted upon for its enduring appeal. Although story and designs are both predictable, the story conjures up an earlier era at the same time that it promises a combination of the exoticism of the South, the class stratification of Empire, and the wealth that unites the two, together with a touch of rebellion—and therefore danger—that is always already contained and therefore safe to contemplate and enjoy.

It is not merely coincidence that some of the fashion shows Menkes describes in the same column make reference to globalization and the demonstrations against the 1999 G-8 meeting, which, ironically, were set against the imminent collapse of Argentina's economy and occasioned protests in Argentina demanding that its foreign debt be forgiven.[8] The designers turn politics into fashion, and Menkes herself makes political commentary, however covertly, casting the antiglobalization demonstrations in the most conservative terms:

> Simons's show had the power. Staged like a bunch of eco-warriors let loose on Seattle, the Belgian designer had an edgy protest message of a generation fearful of globalization.
>   In the courtyard of a public school, he sent out his models in terrorist headgear. (2001, 7)

When present-day reality is perceived as powerful, dangerous, and unbridled (terrorists with covered faces, eco-warriors running amok in the streets of Seattle) and political protest is represented as violence born of fear instead of as a popular and overwhelmingly nonviolent response to entrenched power, the safely edgy throwback story of a wealthy Argentine going to school in England and returning home "cocky and casual" is bound to come as a relief. Especially when it brings the reader into a circle of sophisticated style-knowledge.

That an Argentinean student rebel might, fifty years down the road, pose a serious political challenge does not make it to the surface of the style pages that simply pile story upon story. The connections between Oxbridge impudence, G-8 protestors, and Argentina's history of student activism are not especially clear; Menkes simply sets Smith's Argentina story side-by-side with her description of protest-inspired fashion. It is as if her readers' knowledge of Argentina were still suspended in the 1920s and not contaminated by the decadence not only of the filthy rich, but of state terror and economic catastrophe. Only textual proximity seems to link them, yet there they are, their proximity challenging the reader to make the connection herself. Nevertheless, what seems somewhat astonishing is that in spite of the dictatorships of the 1970s and 1980s and Argentina's economic collapse in the first few years of the twenty-first century, the story of Argentina as a land of remarkably rich and sophisticated folks still resonates for the readers of the *International Herald Tribune.*

Two years later, in 2003, *The New York Times* magazine section updates the Smith-Menkes narrative only marginally in its own fashion story. At a time when Argentina was just barely beginning to come out of its economic crisis, the Sunday magazine section featured a lavish spread on young and charming Argentine polo players wearing designer clothes. This time, however, wealth is not ostentatiously displayed. The myth of Argentine wealth shifts slightly in the *Times* piece; it is now about what passes in the Americas for old money. The chic and photogenic polo players are descendants of the same well-heeled families who went on European grand tours, and who today can still afford tens of thousands of dollars for horses, their upkeep, and equipment. The prices of the clothing they model are as extravagant as their lifestyle; the subtext is that these are extraordinarily wealthy and sexually desirable men and that Argentina is still a place of luxurious living. The bred-to-the-manor style of the polo player and his world is shared by a supporting cast of stylish wives and more or less menial workers. The author gushes over the flair of one of the grooms, a man who cannot afford to wear—and because of his innate sense of style does not need—designer clothes. However, unlike the polo players themselves, the groom remains unnamed in the article. He is pulled out of the background for a full-page picture, but his anonymity, a product of his class, keeps him on a secondary plane. The world of polo, travel, expensive clothes and horses, and a retinue of stylish servants continues to be offered up as one version of Argentina.

The conservative underlay in the *Times*'s and *Herald*'s fashion columns emerges as well in a romance novel with an Argentine hero. Set, like the *Times* piece, among the international polo-playing crowd, Janet Dailey's *The Glory Game* was published just as Argentina was making its transition to democracy. Although the novel takes place in the present moment, apart from a brief reference to the Falklands/Malvinas War, you would never know that there was any trouble in the paradise of the Argentine world of modern-day polo. Dailey makes no mention at all of the junta and its Dirty War, but she does fall back on the familiar national tropes. She predictably presents Argentina as a white country and she just as predictably finds enough swarthy third-world otherness in it to make Raul, the male love interest, Argentine. He is true to type in terms both of the romance novel and of the exotic other: dark, sexy, mysterious, aloof, possibly dangerous, and of questionable origin. Raul's story is as banal as a tango lyric. Born poor on the pampas, his father abandons the family and his mother dies after Raul leaves her on her deathbed.

The novel recalls Argentina's past prosperity: one character notes that people used to, but no longer, say "rich as an Argentine," thereby bringing that chestnut into the present as a relic of the past. Similarly, Dailey has Raul point out that there are no more gauchos and that the tango is a cliché, thus maintaining these as Argentine totems without indulging in them overtly. In the process of gesturing toward and then dismissing the gauchos, old wealth, and tango of an exotically familiar Argentina, Dailey provides her readers with a guidebook knowledge of Argentina, steeped in received wisdom as well as useful tips for the traveler. She touches on the nation's problematic economy, the history of European immigration, the geography of the pampas, and the cultural practices of its denizens. Her Argentina also functions as a caution: she portrays it as a representative of a generalized and perilous Latin America, where rich foreigners run the risk of being kidnapped and held for ransom. The novel's silence concerning the massive practice of Argentine state-sponsored kidnapping is of a piece with its one overtly political statement. Raul observes that Argentines, like people in the United States, are wary of government's ability to solve problems. Dailey thus collapses Argentineans' postdictatorship suspicions about a strong-arm government that promises to protect them against chaos into the conservative ideology most associated with an ever-more-right-wing Republican Party in the United States.

The glamour of polo and the familiar exoticism of Argentina in Dailey's novel and in the fashion columns proffer a borrowed nostalgia. They evoke and then fulfill a longing for the elegance of a far-off but intelligible place. The perception of Argentina as a land of wealth was already abroad by 1825. By that time, as Nicolas Shumway (1991) writes, Europe's insatiable desire for leather and salted meat had made Argentina a rich land, a place to go to strike it rich. The economic success of Argentina, a success based on trade with Europe, coincides with the Argentinean elite's desire to participate in international culture on an equal footing with Europe. Still, Europe would be the producer of culture and Argentina would import it along with the industrious European immigrants who would provide the labor to attain the nation's progress. The Literary Society of Buenos Aires, established in 1822 and run under government auspices, published a journal, *El Argos,* that espoused European taste, European liberalism, and European ideals.[9] Buenos Aires's sense of its civilizing mission has made Porteños seem insufferably arrogant to people from the interior and to the rest of Latin America. However, its other face, a hunger for European approval and an attempt to be as European as possible, have made Argentina familiar enough to Europeans to be accessible to them. Its distance and newness make Argentina exotic enough to be interesting, but its efforts to constitute itself as European make it feel familiar and welcoming.

Spanish novelist Vicente Blasco Ibáñez crafts an Argentina in function of Europe in his 1916 novel, *Los cuatro jinetes del Apocalipsis,* which was made into a classic film, *The Four Horsemen of the Apocalypse,* starring Rudolph Valentino. Blasco Ibáñez's protagonist, Julio Desnoyers, is the spoiled grandson of a cattle baron who has emigrated to Argentina from Spain, bought vast amounts of land cheaply, and become the prototypical provincial landowner: wildly wealthy but crude, overbearing but sentimental, cruel but generous, and above all paternalistic. Julio's father, Marcelo, emigrates from France a generation later, too late to make his own Argentine fortune, but right in time to marry into it. When the now-rich family returns to France for an extended visit, they exhibit all the characteristics of the nouveau riche *rastaquouères.* Marcelo obsessively (and cheaply) accumulates the lavish accoutrements of an increasingly impoverished French aristocracy, the family's women deck themselves out in the latest and most expensive Paris fashions, and Julio becomes the darling of the smart set, teaching tango to Paris society.[10] At the time Blasco Ibáñez wrote his novel, and even five years later when it was made into a movie, these stereotypes were fresh and Argentina still held the promise of prosperity. *Los cuatro jinetes del Apocalipsis* is not primarily about Argentina, however. Rather, Argentina provides the opportunity for an exploration of the extent to which the colonial experience marks three generations of Europeans, two of which are then returned to the crucible of Europe during wartime. Blasco Ibáñez leaves Argentina behind as the novel follows its characters to France, where they are, eventually, engulfed in the chaos of the First World War.

Whereas the Spanish novelist traces the re-Europeanization of his characters and writes a devastating account of a horrendous war—Julio leaves behind the life of the Argentine dilettante to take up arms against the Germans, some of whom are his own family members, and his father Marcelo sheds his compulsion to acquire ever more wealth—Dailey is content to evoke the romance of rich Argentina and avoid mention of the larger political and ethical picture. Similarly, in 1984, the year before *The Glory Game* came out, and the same year that the junta lost power, the French journalist Dominique Bona published a nostalgic novel of Argentina, set in the early twentieth century. Although it is both unfair and shortsighted for readers to expect that novelists will write only in response to current issues, it still seems somewhat peculiar that Bona, a journalist by trade and therefore presumably aware of recent Argentine politics, especially as they affected French citizens, should at that time be recycling the old story of Argentina as a land of wealth and promise.[11] Moreover, the novel's title, *Argentina,* implies a kind of totalism, as if to say that this familiar but outdated story is what matters most about the place. Above all, Bona's novel is a map of a hackneyed European view of Argentina, ranging over prostitution, cattle ranching, and the opportunity for wealth, all frozen in time during the period just after the First World War.[12]

Bona's protagonist, Jean Flamant, is the literary descendant of Blasco Ibáñez's Marcelo Desnoyers, a poor young Frenchman who makes his way to Argentina where he assumes riches will be waiting. Jean's mother, whose own familiar image of Argentina comes complete with savages decked out in feathers ("cet au-delà des mers que ses cauchemars peuplaient de sauvages à plumes": Bona 1986, 15), recalls Marcelo's image of Argentina before he set sail—a land of wild horses, Indians in feathers, and hirsute gauchos. For his part, Jean pictures Argentina as a land of promise, "comme une terre d'espérance" (15), and the future:

> "But you, young man, what are you looking for in Argentina?" old Goldberg resumed when the "supreme of bass" was served.
>   "The future, sir," Jean said. (42)[13]

Before arriving in Argentina, Jean has already imagined what it would be like:

He had invented a loving Argentina for himself, seductive and sublime, all in the image of the Río de la Plata. Silver River... like the mother-of-pearl of the shimmering fish of the Atlantic leaping in the waves, or like the cloak of a fairy queen. Río de la Plata. From the front of the boat, where at all hours of the day he looked for a sign of their arrival, it was a star that would appear. The Argentine, a mirage of moonstone. La Plata... Jean yielded to the lure of that name. (19–20)[14]

The personification of the conquerable land as a sexually inviting woman is a familiar enough trope, and Bona is happy to use it. Jean thinks of Argentina as a lover:

La Plata.... That name had mysterious powers! Jean, filled with hope and enthusiasm, gazed at the sun entering the apartment. He surrendered to his dream. All Argentina shimmered in his little room.
He got up, took a blank piece of paper, and wrote: "I love you." (55)[15]

Not surprisingly, then, the first "real" Argentine he meets is a beautiful, seductive woman. His frame of reference for her is in part textual, the undifferentiated Hispanic Orientalism of a French writer's Andalusian heroines, and part out of the stock of raced and gendered clichés that combine images of darkness, sensuality, and beauty to achieve a picture of the desirable exotic:

He was answered by a laugh, a true, throaty laugh, sensual and gay. It emanated from the lady sitting on the other side of the handsome war amputee. Jean thought she looked like Barrès's Andalusian heroines, but healthier. She was dark. With tawny highlights in her hair, shining eyes, and the most beautiful shoulders in the world. There was something of the Madonna in the perfection of her features, and of the whore in the immodest and abundant cleavage of her breasts....
Marta was Argentine. That Jean understood from the first, as he was caught in an agreeable confusion of responses whose meaning escaped him too often. He understood nothing but their spirit. (34, 35)[16]

Marta's display of wantonness combined with the innocence implied by her Madonna-like features neatly, if unoriginally, explain and justify Europe's desire to conquer the new land. Marta's wealth (which she both embodies and displays as the young wife of a rich old man) and her healthy aspect represent the promise of a new world, in contrast to the decadence of her European counterparts, the equally exotic, but sickly, Andalusian women imagined by a French romantic. Virginly new and pristine, but at the same time scandalous in her abundance and near nudity, Marta is the emblem of the feminized land that evokes Jean's longing for both fortune and love:

> For Jean, fortune was, along with love, the sweetest word. He said it over and over to himself with emphasis, in Spanish, Fortuna, Fortuna..., with the name of a woman. The idea still abstract, but growing stronger by the minute, of his future conquests, filled him with fervor. He wanted to love. And he wanted to be rich. He did not know which of these two desires led the other, if he would become successful thanks to women, or if women would come afterwards. He hoped to appease the gods....
>
> "*Fortuna,*" he murmured. "*Amor y fortuna,*" the first words of a long prayer to the Argentine soil. (57, 58)[17]

Love and fortune are both to be conquered, if not as legitimate wife, at least as lover. For Jean this is a way not to presume too much of his possibilities:

> Jean felt neither foolish nor presumptuous before the breadth of his projects. He wanted to be wholly reasonable. Argentina was not a prospective wife. Jean desired her as a lover. A rich lover, but a lover after all. (60)[18]

Bona unself-consciously uses the hoary trope of the land as a feminine space to be conquered, but in so doing she makes a delicate distinction between wife and lover. Jean is not the lord and master colonizer of all he surveys: The Argentina to which Jean has come has already been conquered. A Jeannot-come-lately, he is in no position to rape the virgin land, nor even to marry the wealth to which he aspires, that is, to make legitimate claims based on a social equality with the rich that he does not possess. The best he can hope for, and what he wants, at least at the beginning, is the somewhat decadent and outlaw, but certainly pleasurable, role of lover among the rich.

Jean meets the Argentina of wealth and fortune on his trip across the Atlantic in the form of transplanted French aristocrats and British businessmen. Before the economic collapse of the 1930s, high rollers and too much money in the hands of a few made it possible for enterprising and not entirely respectable young men to pay for their passage to the Americas at the card table. Like Tutsik Goldenberg in Judith Katz's *The Escape Artist,* Jean's cabin mate Clarance gambles his way across the ocean, playing cards with the wealthiest of the passengers. As a result, Jean soon finds himself dining with the Argentine elite, but he is denied their company once he arrives.[19] Instead, he encounters the dull, gray climate of Buenos Aires, very like the one he left behind.

The contradiction that Bona describes between the European image of Argentina as a mixture of vast urban wealth and exotic savage wilderness, all ready to be punctured by the stark reality of the life of the needy immigrant, had already been related by Spanish writers in the 1920s. Buenos Aires was for the most part a marker for a new chance to earn a fortune in that period, when Argentina still offered that kind of lure to immigrants. Failure to make good on that promise makes for more engaging narrative, however. The parents of the poet Diego el de Gracilán in Azorín's minimalist novel *Doña Inés* (1925) "did not make their fortune in Argentina" (123). Instead, they died and left their child orphaned. In María Enriqueta's *El secreto* (1922), a sentimental novel about an impoverished middle-class family, an industrial accident in Buenos Aires maims the family breadwinner. *El secreto* is narrated by the mischievous and imaginative son who is left with his mother and sister when his father leaves Spain and goes to Argentina out of economic desperation. Nevertheless, the city does not make good on its promise: the father loses both arms when they are caught in the factory's machinery. This is the secret of the title: somewhere along the way the father stops writing his own letters, and it is only in the end that the family discovers why.

María Enriqueta's story of a family's suffering may be treacly, but she is steely-eyed about the ways in which Europe deceives itself about Argentina's easy wealth. The father's failure to become rich is exacerbated (and symbolized) by the industrial accident that mutilates him. This symbolic castration, which he hides from his family, neatly represents the underside of European immigration to Argentina—the exploitation of newly arrived and ultimately disposable laborers. The European, himself reduced from his former bourgeois status, is disabused of the myth of the *indiano*, the adventurous Spaniard who makes his fortune in the Americas and returns gloriously home. María Enriqueta also lays bare the disconnect between the reality of Buenos Aires and the imaginary construct created by the European mind. In the child narrator's imagination, Buenos Aires is a tropical jungle. His uncle writes to the family about the city, but these eye-witness descriptions do not have the same power that the imaginary Argentina holds:

> The letters from that distant uncle whom we loved very much and to whom we wrote frequently, brought us a celebration every time they arrived. We read them as a family. My uncle talked at length about the

beauties of Buenos Aires; but I, whenever I thought about my excellent and beloved uncle, pictured him making his way with great difficulty through giant vines, parrots, monkeys, and snakes.

Everyone laughed at the ridiculous image I created of Buenos Aires, and my father would go to his library to bring an enormous travel book where there were, in profusion, pretty views of that city, with its handsome and wide streets, crisscrossed in all directions by automobiles, coaches, and trolleys; with its beautiful buildings; with its lovely, luxuriously dressed women; with its River Plate, shining and bright as diamonds; Palermo Boulevard had an aristocratic look; according to my uncle the most distinguished society met there. There was no doubt: Buenos Aires was a completely European city. *But my whim was greater than all that, and my crazy imagination was just as wild;* thus, I never let myself think that Uncle Leonardo was not making his way through black dense forests, filled to bursting with parrots and snakes. To me, that was where the attraction lay.

That is why the letters from America gave me such inexplicable pleasure. (Enriqueta 1922, 91–92, emphasis added)[20]

Despite his uncle's first-hand descriptions and the corroborating photographs of his father's book, in the child's mind the imaginary Argentina predominates. Neither patriarchal authority nor the evidence of photographic reproduction disturbs the view of Buenos Aires as a jungle that so delights him. Significantly, it is the child narrator, not any of the adults, who, despite the evidence of his uncle's letters and the pictures of a modern city, persists in seeing Argentina as a subtropical jungle. This naïveté, appropriate in a child, is more surprising coming from adults. Yet the childish pleasure in projecting an exoticism onto the place of the other is precisely the mechanism in operation we saw earlier in the fashion articles, where pleasure is central and the production of desire—to consume, possess, and display—is a basic function. It is also operative in the anachronistic novels by Bona and Dailey, in which contemporary Argentina is elided in favor of a simpler, happier, and more fantastically wealthy version of that nation.

María Enriqueta's child narrator is much like Jean's mother in Bona's novel and the anonymous woman who wanted to see the painted Indians at the Paris exhibition. All hold fast to the notion of an untamed, primitive Argentina, undifferentiated from the rest of Latin America, which in turn is presumed to be similarly wild and exotic. Bona's Buenos Aires brothel, where the fantasy of Argentine/Latin American exotic savagery is performed by European women, encapsulates the Argentina of Europe's desire. The prostitutes are decked out in costumes that cater to foreigners' fantasies—a sexualized, savage Argentina that, because it is bought and paid for and acted out by women whose bodies and behavior are regulated and regimented, is totally safe. The most extravagant of these costumes is worn not by an Argentine at all, but by a Frenchwoman named Mandoline.

> She wore no robe, just a flimsy short chemise, over which she was fully harnessed in leather. Both funny and tragic. Criss-crossed thongs from her neck to her garters. Big nails studding a wide belt. A leather triangle covered her pubis. Amazon, gaucha, sadistic virgin, Mayan whore . . . one could have imagined her to be the descendant of cruel gods, or sprung from a garden of torture. Jean was not at all drawn to these hideous ornaments; they made him nauseous. (Bona 1986, 72)[21]

Here is Argentina, feminized and sexualized, collapsed into the rest of exotic Latin America, and performed by a European. The fear of the savage is dealt with by displacing it onto the body of the prostitute, enclosing it in the brothel, where Jean has already shown himself to be more than a little sadistic, taking out on the prostitutes his own frustration over not being helped in his quest to make a fortune by the prior wave of immigrants. Mandoline's costume is overly burdened with the signs of Latin American danger. In her leather regalia, the French prostitute not only signifies Amazon, gaucha, and Mayan whore, but also the sadistic virgin, inverting the mutable signs of bondage and domination.

Because the space of the brothel is contrived to represent a conquerable Argentina itself, the woman wearing this overdetermined costume need not be Argentine at all. Jean finds Mandoline's costume ridiculous and nauseating, and nobody is fooled by it. Nevertheless, a circuit of willful self-deception keeps the sexualized fantasy of Argentina in play. Jean and Mandoline know the signs of exotic savagery and how to fake them; Europe is not entirely unaware that its construction of the Latin American and Argentine other is simply a screen that allows itself to see itself as it wishes.[22]

Mandoline's body, like the bodies of the prostitutes in Judith Katz's *The Escape Artist* and Leonard Schraeder's film *Naked Tango*, also set in 1920s Buenos Aires, is meant in one sense to be undifferentiated. It is no more than the outlet for male sexual desire and energy. Nevertheless, the prostitutes in Katz and Bona provide a reminder of home to men for whom Argentina is still a foreign land. Pearl's brothel offers tea in a glass, the smells of Jewish cooking, and Jewish women; Mandoline, a native of Carcasonne, with all the historical baggage that city carries, represents home to Jean. Whether they re-create a mythical memory of home or a universalized fantasy of female availability, the brothels create their own space/time. I refrain from using Bakhtin's evocative term, chronotope, here because, whereas for Bakhtin chronotopes are narrative effects that function "as the primary means for materializing time in space" (1981, 250), the brothels are narrative spaces that perform the opposite operation: they are the places in which time is obliterated. Within their enclosure, the prostitutes are re-created as ahistorical. They are the always already sexually available bodies, not dressed to act in the world, but rather costumed to indulge the fantasy of the clients. The brothel offers a respite from history for the men who frequent them, and in so doing they enclose the women in a timeless space that precludes their participation in historical time. The prostitutes are consigned to the realm of monumental time, in which no change is possible and in which a person's being is coterminous with the role she is assigned. In the context of early twentieth-century Argentina, a nation whose motto includes notions of progress and modernity and that holds out the promise of social mobility and self-fashioning, the fantasy of the eternal feminine proffered by the brothels and imposed upon their inmates is striking.

Part of what is so ridiculous about Mandoline's primitive-exotic costume is that she is so patently a modern Frenchwoman. Moreover, what is understood in the novel to be her authentic identity gives Mandoline a means of survival. Because she is French, Jean forges a friendship with her. Once he does eventually make his fortune, he secures her financial future and gives her a way to escape the brothel and acquire respectability. Similarly, Katz's Sofia repeats to herself nightly the litany of her identity, and she, too, manages to escape. In contrast, a clear sign of the prostitute's abjection in Leonard Schraeder's 1991 film, *Naked Tango*, is the loss first of her identity and then of any cultural markers that would tie her to a people. The protagonist, Stephanie, is a bored young housewife who takes on the identity of Alba, a suicide who was destined for a Buenos Aires brothel. Once Stephanie deliberately gives up her identity, she sets in motion her own downfall.

Stephanie's abandonment of identity to the Argentine sex trade represents, and displaces onto the abject, perhaps the greatest fear of the European in his encounter with the exotic yet familiar other, namely the utter loss of self. Prostitutes are forced to play-act an identity that is not their own; Stephanie dies of it. Those who survive and escape, like Bona's Mandoline and Katz's Sofia, are the ones who manage to keep their own sense of self and have that identity reflected back to them, Mandoline by Jean and Sofia by Hankus. Stephanie, in contrast, dies naked, lost in Alba's identity and fate.[23] Her at first willing assumption of another person's identity thematizes the more benign pleasure of the reader, who is happily engulfed by the text, meshing with an other, and coming out whole on the other side. As readers, we run little risk of never recuperating the self, so we indulge in the delicious anxiety of identity loss.

Naked Tango takes advantage of the exotic, violent otherness of Argentina in its depiction of the tango bordello. The film, like the dance, is highly stylized in its representation of sadomasochistic desire that includes bondage, rape, sex on broken glass, and murder. The removal of the action to a remote time (the 1920s) and place (Buenos Aires), in tandem with the glamorous artificiality of the cinematography, permits the viewer to participate in the voyeuristic pleasure of abusive sexual behavior while distancing himself from it. (I am presupposing a heterosexual masculine gaze here, but it is one that can be embodied in a female as well as a male spectator.) Nevertheless, Europeans have so long and so frequently displaced the well-nigh universal problem of gender inequality onto the tango that the absolute alterity of the dance as a third world marker for institutionalized male dominance has been attenuated by years of familiarity and appropriation. In other words, tango is another site of the Argentine uncanny. In this case, the colonial "other" has become familiar through the operations of the metropole in its incorporation of the dance into a European system of meanings.

As Marta Savigliano points out in her original and provocative study of the tango, "the enhancement of male dominance is so crassly stated and obvious [in tango lyrics and tango culture] that any denouncing commentary sounds flat" (1995, 45).[24] Still, because of the overdetermined machismo of tango culture—located primarily in the discourse surrounding the dance and the lyrics of tango after tango—feminist critiques and rereadings of tango are not hard to find.[25] The representation of the Argentine tango as a stylized form of gender violence is on display in such films as *Naked Tango* (U.S., 1991), *The Tango Lesson* (U.K., 1997), and *Ein Blick und die Liebe Bricht Aus* (One glance and love breaks out, Germany, 1986), as well as in the tango-inspired ballet *Tango Buenos Aires 1907* (Sweden, 1985), which all depend on the stereotype of Argentina and its national dance as the epitome of machista culture. Sally Potter's *The Tango Lesson* openly questions the problematic of male dominance: the film explores the power dynamic between the masterful, Argentine tango dancer, a man, and the British novice, a woman film director. Both characters are frustrated: he is a well-known and respected dancer in Buenos Aires who, emblematically enough, wants to make his mark in a Paris that shows no interest in him; she is trying to make a film that is going nowhere. The locus of authority and power is unstable; it shifts from one to the other and back again. He holds the key to the dance, but she is in control of the movie he wants her to make of him. The film is located in the charged but neutral space of Paris, although part way through the film the Potter character subjects herself to tango lessons in Buenos Aires itself. Potter's film scrutinizes the machista culture of tango, but she is deeply attracted to the dance nonetheless. Similarly, Jutta Brückner's *Ein Blick und die Liebe Bricht Aus* (One glance and love breaks out) relies on the overdetermined machismo of tango to explore gender relations. For Brückner, however, the dance is less interesting in and of itself than as a metaphor for male dominance and female desire, or, more precisely, the female desire for male dominance. Brückner's use of mirrors as a motif in the film suggests that what is at stake is the self as it is reflected back in the other: Argentina and its tango tell a story about gender relations for a German audience. Much like Claudio Magris, who breaks with his practice of setting his novels in the familiar space of middle Europe and creates a "nowhere" in Argentina in *A Different Sea*, by filming *Ein Blick und die Liebe Bricht Aus* in Argentina, Brückner abandons her normal practice of closely examining her own culture in its own space and creates, for the first time, she says, "imaginary spaces on film" (Kosta and McCormick 1996, 362):

> JB: I shot this film in Argentina, and it is very important to me. In it, I discovered the possibility of creating imaginary spaces on film, and in doing so I learned to bring a narrative of the imaginary into play. Spaces are always concrete in classical camera work, but in order to tell stories that reflect projections or fantasies and not just the movement of bodies in a location, you need a different sort of space. In every film that I have made so far, I have also told the story of a culture. It is the other way around in this film.

> Here, in seven separate stories, *I tell the story of love as it is conveyed to us by our culture* and as it is written onto the bodies of women.... *Because I made the film in Argentina, these stories are like the beads of a rosary that glide through one's fingers.* (362, emphasis added)

The question here is just whose culture is being explored. Argentina is imaginary space; it has no materiality of its own for the filmmaker to convey. Each vignette is a smooth surface, like a rosary bead, whose primary function is mnemonic, not aesthetic. The beads themselves "glide through one's fingers," eliciting a familiar litany. Brückner's cause-and-effect statement is somewhat mysterious, but one way to understand the relationship between the site of the filmmaking and the metaphor of the frictionless effect of fingers on beads is to suggest that the specificity and complexity of Argentina are too subtle for the foreigner to comprehend and represent. Indeed, because Brückner's film is filmed almost entirely indoors, the conventional notion of filming "on location" all but loses its significance. It is precisely location, the specificity of bodies in a place, that Brückner seeks to strip away in order to get to "projection" and "fantasy." She goes on to say, "The stories are conveyed through the tango because it is associated with the longing for romance, passion, and sexuality in Western culture" (363). Brückner's phrases "our culture" and "Western culture" are ambiguous, oscillating between a broad connotation that includes Argentina, and a narrow one that refers more specifically to her own Europe and her interviewers' United States. She finds in the tango, which is deeply Argentine but which also has been absorbed as both symbol and practice into Western culture more generally, a stylized exaggeration of feminine abjection and a metaphor for women's desire for romantic love. When the tango becomes metaphor, the material reality of Argentina that underlies tango drops out as well. Arlene Teraoka (1996) notes that German writers often take advantage of the third world as a site where they can examine their own concerns. Brückner's use of the tango certainly resonates with that observation, as does Keyserling's romance of Latin America in which the entire continent is nothing but a sounding board for his fascination with the products of his own mind and body.[26] For Brückner, filming in Argentina is filming in the nowhere that is the birthplace of (the metaphor) tango.

Brückner's move away from filming concrete reality in order to get to a kind of cultural interiority is accomplished in part by her use of mirrors. In an interview with Ingeborg von Zadow, the director explains:

> I started using mirrors to improve my films. I learned that the better picture for me is also the more real picture. Making more visible what is normally regarded as an invisible inner reality. [In Argentina] I discovered that I had met the very cameraman . . . I needed, because he used mirrors in an unconventional way. He made a real room into an unreal one.
> (1998, 99)

The mirrors, then, turn a real space into an unreal one. Argentina is outside the walls of the room where Brückner films, and the Argentina that is also inside the room disappears into the mirrors, through which the camera produces the desired interiority. But as much as mirrors redirect the gaze from a realist exterior to an inner reality, they also reflect one back to oneself. Brückner's use of mirrors to deracinate the image suggests as well the ways in which the tango reflects a reality beyond Argentina. Like Virginia Woolf's metaphor for woman, as a mirror that reflects man at twice his size, Argentina is a mirror that reflects Europe back to itself. Argentina and its tango are the third world other that provides a reflection of, and site to reflect upon, the dilemmas of gender relations in Western culture more generally. Brückner tells an anecdote about one of the local actors, who chaffed against her appropriation of Argentina for her own means:

> It went fine for a while. . . . But then, after some time, they [the male actors] got a little angry with me. They didn't show it, really, but a woman on the set told me that one of the young men had said "What does she think, she just comes here and she tells stories about us. I think she needs"—and this is a very crude expression—"a good fuck." It was a very typical macho way of resisting. (Zadow 1998, 98)

It would be too easy to follow Brückner in simply dismissing the young man's predictable response to her behavior. Although his reaction is puerile and offensive, his critique is not unjustified. Brückner herself seems not to understand all of what is being resisted here. It is not just that she is a woman who is making up stories about Argentines, but that she is a European and an outsider who is converting the complexity of Argentine subjectivity into a simpler alterity, through which she is telling stories that are only superficially about them. The colonizing gesture that Brückner repeats here has long been understood through the metaphor of sexual desire, violence, and possession. As Marta Savigliano points out in focusing this gesture on tango in particular, "the colonizer dumps on the tango his own representation of the imperial erotic relationship with the colonized" (1995, 76). The young actor's remark is not merely the hackneyed machista reaction to the stereotypical image of the strong woman who refuses men and therefore needs to be put in her place. In his eyes, Brückner's transgression is worse: she inappropriately assumes the eroticized masculine position in colonial domination. Moreover, she is older than he and is superior to him in their professional relationship. By rendering her subordinate in his fantasy of sexual domination, he can restore his wounded national and masculine pride.

Whereas *Ein Blick und die Liebe Bricht Aus* is the most radical of these films in its nullification of Argentina as a real space, *Naked Tango* is the most extreme in its evocation of a sense of tango that is not only related to sexual dominance but that supercedes it.[27] Not even the lure of sex, the traditional coin of the prostitute, is a match for the tango in the Schraeder film. Stephanie/Alba's pimp is uninterested in sex; he cares only for the dance, in which he is utterly dominant.

In another medium, *Tango Buenos Aires 1907*, a contemporary narrative ballet from Sweden that is informed by tango lyrics and is based largely on old Argentine tango recordings, also indulges in a critique of gender relations. Here, however, the displacement onto the exotic other seems complete. Whereas the two women film directors, Potter and Brückner, see Argentine tango as the quintessence of a gender imbalance that is a mark of their own societies, the male choreographer and producer of *Tango Buenos Aires 1907*, like Schraeder in *Naked Tango*, present a completely exoticized machista culture, in which the choreographer, Ulf Gadd, and the production designer, Svenerik Goude, associate the dance with immigration, upper-class sexual repression and brutality, and the world of gangsters and prostitutes. Set in Buenos Aires 1907, the ballet is, above all, a family saga that, to an outsider at least, looks more like Bergman than Gardel, particularly in the sequence near the beginning that represents a silent meal, mother and father at each end of the table, children along one side, facing the audience, the only sound that of silverware against china, the only movements those of a well–brought up but dysfunctional family. The father's rage is sparked when the youngest girl spills a glass, and the scene ends in marital rape. The oligarchic family has its sexual secrets—the father frequents a brothel, the mother has an affair with her daughter's fiancé, the younger daughter and son are both in love with the fiancé as well, and the young brother also appears to desire his older sister.

Inspired by a series of newspaper articles on tango, choreographer Gadd, accompanied by production designer Goude, went to Argentina to study the history of the dance. The ballet they produced as a result presents tango as an emotional state that colored and was shaped by, and in, a particular moment in turn-of-the-century Buenos Aires. The program, written in part by Goude, is a rather startling sixteen-page presentation of tango history in the form of short journalistic articles accompanied by period photographs. This pedagogical gesture both circumscribes tango and distances the audience from it. The ballet-goer is guided by the expert, and the performance is not so much an aesthetic experience designed to connect with the viewer as it is an edifying entertainment that serves to reinforce the gulf between spectator and spectacle. An emblematic moment in the performance establishes the relationship between the Swedish audience and the Argentine other. Early in the ballet, the many characters onstage begin to differentiate themselves by stating their names. The roll call is punctuated by the long and convoluted name called out by one character in rapid Spanish, provoking the audience's laughter. The moment establishes ironic distance between the audience and the dance and confirms the relationship between spectator and spectacle as one of superior to inferior. As its foreign-language name implies, *Tango Buenos Aires 1907* takes place elsewhere and in another time, among another kind of people—different, exotic, and, for a fleeting moment, perhaps a little ridiculous. Gadd and Goude, like Potter, Schraeder, and Brückner, make use of the supposedly pure machismo of tango to deal with an issue that is culturally meaningful, but more comfortable to confront when deflected onto an other. The shattered glass of *Naked Tango* disperses the image and renders it both dangerous and painful; Gadd's absorption of the tango into ballet renders it unthreatening.

Texts of second-hand nostalgia such as Bona's *Argentina*, Dailey's *The Glory Game,* and the fashion column copy in the *New York Times* and the *International Herald Tribune* evoke and then fulfill a longing for an elegance presumed to have existed in the early twentieth century. The persistent memory of Argentina in them, as in the tango films and Gadd's choreography, is a time-stopper. Like the women locked in its brothels, whose identity is projected onto them by pimps, madams, and paying customers, these texts force Argentina into ahistoricity. They are the narratives of otherness that soothe the European imagination. Yet as we have seen, Argentina is not entirely innocent in the external perception of it as a nation. Argentina in the Western imaginary might fruitfully be thought of as a coproduction.

Just as much Argentine film nowadays is coproduced internationally, Argentina itself emerges from the interchange among texts and capital, light and sound. Argentina is not simply a string of images, not merely a series of frames, individual photographs shot from different angles that, taken together, form a picture of the nation, however complex. Joseph and Barbara Anderson (1993) have suggested that in understanding film it is fruitful to attend not only to the frame (the essential unit of film according to classic film theory), but to the spaces between frames. Similarly, we have seen how Argentina is produced not only in its images, but also in the spaces between. These sites of absence or lack are the occasion of faith that there will be a next image. In film, they are moments of exchange between images in which a kind of continuity is promised, which may or may not be fulfilled. We may be surprised instead by a jump cut, a fade, or a blackout. Similarly, Argentina is produced by the interplay of image and lapse, in visual and verbal texts and the interchanges among them, and the makers of those texts are complicit in producing themselves in the process. The cultural meanings of Argentina and those who gaze upon it emerge out of the energy produced in the interaction between Argentina and its global others.

Notes

Preface

1. Unless otherwise noted, or citation is given to a published translation, all translations in the volume are my own.

2. This shamefully abbreviated summary does not do justice to Rodó's elegant essay, and it completely elides the critiques of it made by feminist scholars pointing out the absence of the feminine (either as Prospero's translating daughter, Miranda, or Caliban's mother, Sycorax), or Retamar's influential rereading of the myth through the lens of race and class.

1. Bartered Butterflies

1. "En cuanto a Virginia Woolf, tuve la suerte que me le presentara Aldous Huxley en una exposición de fotos de Man Ray, y tuve otra suerte mayor: vio en mí algo 'exótico' que despertó su curiosidad. Aunque me sintiera impostora al explotar esta primera impresión, pues no creía merecerla, la aproveché y fui a conversar con Virginia Woolf varias veces. Estábamos en 1934. Ella no era una persona de acceso fácil. Mi procedencia de un país lejano en que abundan las mariposas (así veía a Argentina, dato que habría recogido, sospecho, en un libro de viajes de Darwin), me resultó utilísimo. Reforcé su curiosidad mandando a su casa de Tavistock Suare una colección de mariposas en caja de vidrio. La mayoría eran brasileñas y no la engañé sobre su origen. Pero América del Sur es un block para los europeos y hasta para los isleños británicos. . . . Y yo como ante un chico que sigue con los ojos un sonajero, o un trompo que gira, agitaba, para interesarla, un mundo de insectos, de pumas, de papagayos, de floripondios, de 'señoritas' (mis bisabuelas) envueltas en mantillas de finísimo encaje (como las vio Darwin), de ñandúes veloces, de indios mascando coca, de gauchos tomando mate, todos deslumbrantes de color local; en fin, la rodeé del torbellino humano, animal y vegetal de Hispanoamérica. Así pagaba el lenguado comido con los Woolf y entraba en su intimidad, coronada por la fauna y la flora de todo un continente."

2. "Las personas encargadas de llevar a Tavistock Square el paquete voluminoso fueron una prima mía y una institutriz inglesa, muy simpática. Ni una ni otra tienen un aspecto que llame la atención por misterioso o raro. Pero con Virginia era difícil prever a qué clase de persona investiría con un misterio que de ella manaba, o que sus antenas captaban.

"En esta ocasión, me escribe: '*Two veiled ladies* (subrayo porque jamás he visto a mi prima o a Miss May con velos), dos señoras misteriosas se presentaron en el hall de mi casa . . . Estas señoras me entregaron un paquete y después de murmurar unas palabras musicales pero ininteligibles desaparecieron.' (Aquí haré una acotación. Mi prima habla inglés. Miss May era tan inglesa como Virginia. ¿Ininteligible? Sigamos, después de este paréntesis, a la autora de *Orlando;* su fantasía es más seductora que nuestra visión, por demás *matter of fact.*) Puse—continúa—10 minutos en darme cuenta que se trataba de un regalo y que ese regalo era una caja llena de mariposas bajo vidrio. Nada podía ser más fantásticamente irreal. (Nada excepto usted misma, Virginia, pensé.)"

The letter as it appears in Nicolson and Trautmann's *Letters of Virginia Woolf* is slightly different:

"Dear Victoria,

"A week ago—no, I'm afraid it is more than a week ago—two mysterious for-eign ladies arrived in the hall . . . ; and they pressed into my hand a large parcel, murmured some musical but unintelligible remarks about 'giving it into your own hands' and vanished. It took me at least ten minutes to realise that this was your present of South American butterflies. What could have been more fantastically in-appropriate. It was a chilly October evening, and the road was up, and there was a row of little red lights to mark the ditch; and then these butterflies" (1979a, 438). Later in the letter she refers to "the veiled and mysterious ladies" (439).

3. Marta Savigliano reports a similar instance of the exoticizing of a member of the Argentinean elite, when Lucio V. Mansilla visited France in the 1850s, and the women at a dinner party he attended remarked that he must have been handsome indeed wearing his feathers (1995, 114).

4. In fact, there had once been wild cattle in Argentina. The Portuguese con-quistador, Juan Díaz de Solís, who first brought cows and horses over from Spain in 1515, was killed the following year by indigenous inhabitants who were not willing to submit to foreign rule. The animals lived to reproduce, so when later Europeans arrived, they found the now-wild descendents of those domesticated animals. In his *Life of Napoleon Buonaparte,* Sir Walter Scott mentions the wild cattle of the pampas, which is probably where Woolf got the idea. By the twentieth century, however, the cattle in Argentina were pretty much all accounted for by their owners.

5. Ocampo was very aware of the unequal relations of power between men and women, but she was pretty much oblivious to her class privilege. It may be that in this partial self-awareness she was representative of Argentina. In recent years Ocampo's reputation has begun to be rehabilitated. See, for example, Beatriz Sarlo (2001).

6. My information on the Argentine pavilion at the Paris Exhibition is taken from Ingrid Fey's excellent essay (2000).

7. Alejandro Solomianski's *Identidades secretas: la negritud argentina* came out in 2003.

8. A consciousness of gender as an internal divisor is not entirely new, however. There was an active feminist movement in Argentina at the end of the nineteenth and beginning of the twentieth centuries. Nor did historical and cultural gender analysis begin with the contemporary women's movement. Fryda Schultz de Mantovani published *La mujer en la vida nacional* in 1960.

9. Scheines (1991, 47) places the gauchos "at the margin of the two communities" ("al margen de las dos comunidades").

10. "En la luz y la tibieza de un *living-room*, de paneles pintados por una mujer, otras dos mujeres hablan de las mujeres. Se examinan, se interrogan. Curiosa, la una; la otra, encantada. . . . Estas dos mujeres se miran. Las dos miradas son diferentes. La una parece decir: 'He aquí un libro de imágenes exóticas que hojear.' La otra: ¿En qué página de esta mágica historia encontraré la descripción del lugar en que está oculta la llave del tesoro?' Pero de estas dos mujeres, nacidas en medios y climas distintos, anglosajona la una, la otra latina y de América, la una adosada a una formidable tradición, y la otra adosada al vacío *(au risque de tomber pendant l'éternité),* es la más rica la que saldrá enriquecida por el encuentro. La más rica habrá inmediatamente recogido su cosecha de imágenes. La más pobre no habrá encontrado la llave del tesoro."

11. Woolf was furious when Ocampo brought Gisele Freund to her home to photograph her, but Ocampo persisted. As a result, we have some of the best-known portraits of Woolf.

12. Count Hermann Keyserling, to whom we will return in a subsequent chapter, described the *rastaquouères* as follows, in his characteristically overblown way: "What was intended as perfect beauty, remains a mere co-existence of scintillant surface and abysmal Being. Hence the appearance of the *rastaquaire [sic]* so typical for this part of the world: his extravagant and false elegance, his diamond-studded turnout, his showy exhibition of a mostly non-existent and certainly highly insecure wealth are not the characteristics of the essential impostor, but of the incongruency of Being and form; the *rastaquaire* honestly longs to be what he can only make a show of. But for this very reason his descendants will one day be what he desires to be" (1932, 31–32).

13. Rita Felski (1995, 49) comments on the figure of modern woman over the gate of the Paris Exhibition of 1900; modernity, in Europe as in Argentina, was gendered.

14. Stuart Hall's "notion of identity as contradictory, as composed of more than one discourse, as composed always across the silences of the other, as written in and through ambivalence and desire" (1997, 49) is useful here, even if it is wrenched from its original context.

15. See chapter 2, "The Subject of National Identity," in Kaminsky (1999).

16. Here, as elsewhere in this study, I attribute agency to Argentina as a metonym for the liberal elite who, since independence, have largely controlled the discourse of nation.

17. Remember Todorov's claim (1987) that the discovery of Latin America allowed Europeans to develop self-knowledge through the knowledge of the other.

18. See Plotkin (2001) for a history of psychoanalytic culture in Argentina.

19. In the following discussion I am indebted to David Kaminsky's lucid unpublished analysis of Freud's uncanny as it relates to ideas of the specter of the state and of revolution.

20. I am indebted to the University of Minnesota Press's anonymous reader who reminded me of the dream of "La Gran Argentina" and encouraged me to comment on the representation of Argentina in Latin America.

21. A thorough examination of the representation of Argentina in Latin American narrative would require a full-length study of its own. Here I will give just one example. In *Waslala*, Gioconda Belli's novel of the search for utopia in a dystopic future, Maclovio is "an Argentine with a thick beard, around fifty, with a young man's bearing, given to jokes and murky business deals" (1998, 26). He is repeatedly identified by his nationality, "el argentino," and characterized as "ironic" (56, 103, 120), "sarcastic" (56), "malicious" (70, 120), "irreverent" (90), and "mocking" (119). As a drug supplier, he is the link between Latin America's Central American thugs and the United States as a market for drugs. The other characters do not trust him, but he is capable of acting heroically. The Argentinean is not, in the end, thoroughly evil. Argentina is, after all, part of the Latin American community.

2. Identity Narratives

1. I have rendered the practitioner of Orientalism not as "Orientalist," which, for all its problems, may still be used as a descriptor of someone who engages in the study of the "East," but as "Orientalizer," which, for all its awkwardness, more clearly captures the debilitating effects of Orientalism as Said (1978) analyzes it. In *Orientalism*, Said just as fiercely decries the scholarly Orientalist tradition; but as it will become clear, I do not believe that all views from the outside are necessarily hurtful.

2. This is Spivak's model in "Can the Subaltern Speak?" but it is, implicitly, also Said's in *Orientalism*. He later modifies his position, acknowledging the resistance to subalternity.

3. See Beardsell (2000), especially "The European Gaze: Eurocentric Views of Latin America," for an elegant discussion of Latin America as a European construction in the context of his analysis of the way Latin America returns the gaze.

4. Similarly, insofar as the United States asserts that it is founded on the thought of the European Enlightenment, it too essentially stakes its claim as a European country. Argentina's similar claim is not backed by the kind of power the United States commands. Instead, Argentina retains the memory of the moment of great economic promise starting at about the beginning of the Second World War, and all the European immigrants whose children remain.

5. Biagini (2000, 117) refers to the numerous "metaphysical characterizations, where the national appears as an invariable substance, with an absolute separation between masculine and feminine, European and American" ("las caracterizaciones metafísicas donde lo nacional aparece como una sustancia invariable, con una neta separación entre lo femenino y lo masculino, lo europeo y lo americano").

6. See, for example, Ortner's argument (1974) that woman is not absolute other in the binary (male) culture/(female) nature, but rather man's conduit to otherness. See also the Combahee Women's Collective (1977) for an early critique of a monolithic notion of "woman" that excludes differences of race and sexuality, a critique enunciated by many others and that has changed feminist thinking profoundly since the early 1980s.

7. The radical feminist notion put forward in the late 1960s that the distinction between masculine and feminine is the source of all social binaries, including class and race, was understood by some to suggest that the latter are simply expressions of the former. That idea and the absence of discussions of race and ethnicity in writing by white feminists (with its corollary, the ignoring of gender in theories of race) were already being criticized by the early 1980s. See, for example, Hull, Scott, and Smith (1982).

8. José María Ramos Mejía made this argument in 1899, when European immigration to Argentina was at a peak. See Dailey (1985, 444–45).

9. Pretty t-shirts that cleverly interconnect the cross, the crescent, and the star of David are sold in many shops catering to Spain's tourists. Spain used to advertise itself with the slogan "Spain is different," but it has now become clear that Spanish difference does not bring in tourists who, rather, want more of the same. Spain's earlier difference was very much a product of its religious conservatism. While much of the rest of Europe was becoming Protestant, Spain adamantly held on to its Catholicism. The Holy Office dealt not only with secret Jews and Muslims whose conversion to Catholicism was less than wholehearted, but also with the Protestant heresies.

10. In "To Serve and Protect," Foster discusses the narrativization of what he calls the Falklands conflict. He shows how both nations mobilized national myths in creating support. For Britain it was a way of reasserting traditional values of patriotism, class position and division, British superiority over "'a nation associated mainly with corned beef and . . . Grand Prix drivers'" (1977, 235)—the degradation of Argentina, and of its beef-exporting importance for England. Importantly, both sides engage in this kind of narrativizing. Both sides were right wing, and Argentina's loss of the war helped dislocate the generals in Argentina, but England's victory consolidated Thatcherite policy and power.

11. Savigliano observes the web of tango and national identity, authenticity, and *tanguedad* in her study *Tango and the Political Economy of Passion* (1995).

12. "También desde otra perspectiva, que podríamos llamar sociocultural, la América bárbara es un producto apetecible para los europeos. Si el Norte se convirtió en los últimos decenios en un mundo sin diferencias, homogeneizado por el confort, las técnicas y los medios masivos de comunicación, entonces necesita vitalmente un espacio incontaminado de civilización, ajeno al progreso, ámbito de lo maravilloso y lo monstruoso en versión bárbara, paraíso e infierno elementales, salvajes, apto para caminantes curiosos y ávidos de ver y tocar el pasado original, primigenio anterior a la historia y a las sofisticaciones del espríritu."

13. "Dije que el mito de América es más antiguo que Colón, que existe toda una literatura 'profética' del descubrimiento de América que se populariza al punto de generar durante la Edad Media la leyenda de un continente paradisíaco, virgen y esperante en el mar océano hacia occidente. Toda la conquista está guiada por la ilusión y la búsqueda de tal paraíso y una oscura obstinación impulsaba irracionalmente a esos aventureros a forzar la realidad hasta hacerla encajar en los moldes de la leyenda. ¿Qué otra cosa sino la ilusión pudo inspirar los nombres Argentina y Río de la Plata en una tierra sin minas como la nuestra?"

14. "La creencia de que Sudamérica—Argentina—era un espacio vacío y a la espera de la utopía nos ensoberbeció a tal punto de creernos los mejores reservados para un país inexistente, ciudadanos de Utopía sin contexto utópico."

15. As we see in chapter 3, Joseph Conrad and Virginia Woolf, writing early in the twentieth century, fold Argentina neatly into the rest of Latin America.

16. "La Argentina es, pues, América a secas; a lo sumo, una cruza de la cultura de Europa con el paisaje de América, cruza que no se deja unificar tan fácilmente como lo suponen aquellas tentativas de síntesis; de ahí nuestra búsqueda de la nacionalidad inexistente."

17. "Keyserling fue uno de aquellos intelectuales extranjeros (también Ortega y Gasset, Jacinto Benavente, Jiménez de Asúa, Le Corbusier, Levy-Bruhl) que visitaban asiduamente la Argentina de los años veinte para disertar sobre la idiosincrasia sudamericana o el ser de los argentinos, y que la 'intelligentzia' criolla agasajaba y escuchaba con unción, orgullosa de que la docta Europa se interese por nosotros. Fue Keyserling quien reafirmó y redondeó la idea de barbarie, fatalismo geográfico sudamericano, de consecuencias nefastas para nuestros pueblos. Y Ezequiel Martínez Estrada (1895–1964) la toma del conde y la difunde y enriquece con su talento."

18. "Más que nunca América es un espacio in-significante, un no lugar, pero en vez de cobijar el futuro amasado de sueños y esperanzas, es destierro donde sólo caben la nostalgia de la patria ausente y el odio parricida contra la Europa que nos expulsó de la casa natal. Pero también in-significante, vacío, porque es el tiempo de la espera." Although Scheines suggests that no one escaped from this pernicious influence, Laudato (1996) points out that shortly after Keyserling published his views on South America, Vicente Fatone wrote critically about Kant's dependence on preconceived notions of American sloth in his writing on geography and anthropology. This is not to say that Fatone's voice was widely heard.

19. "Hasta que no nos liberemos de las imágenes espaciales o geográficas de América (paraíso, espacio vacío o barbarie) de origen europeo, de las que derivan las nefastas teorías del Fatum, lo Informe, lo facúndico, lo telúrico que nos fijan e inmovilizan como el alfiler a la mariposa, y que hace de América una dimensión inhabitable ajena a toda medida humana, no superaremos el movimiento circular, las marchas y contramarchas, las infinitas vueltas al punto de partida para volver a arrancar y otra vez quedarnos a mitad de camino."

20. "A través de diversas épocas, procedencias y orientaciones se ha ido estructurando un discurso que insiste en la falta de orden que predomina entre nosotros, debido a nuestra índole impulsiva e infantil, en contraposición a la prudencia y al equilibrio nordatlánticos. Son semblanzas sobre la cultura y la nacionalidad, sobre el hombre y la mujer de nuestras tierras, en términos netamente dicotómicos y reduccionistas; caracterizaciones que al negarle a nuestro pueblo inteligencia y moralidad, en definitiva su talante humano, han contribuido a combatir los gobiernos mayoritarios y a fundamentar los tutelajes."

21. Keyserling and Ocampo had what one observer has called a "tempestuous relationship." See chapter 5 for a discussion of the extent to which Keyserling's characterization of Argentina might have had its genesis in a stormy relationship with an imperious Argentinean woman.

22. It is perhaps worthwhile to note that at least one contemporary observer finds Hegel prophetic in his assessment of the Americas. Lois Parkinson Zamora "overlook[s] Hegel's blindness to America's indigenous cultural past" in order to "observe instead that he correctly foresaw what would become a principal theme of literature in the Americas: the question of historical identity" (1997, 3).

23. With his conceptualization of the imagination as "an organized field of social practices, a form of work (in the sense of both labor and culturally organized practice), and a form of organization between sites of agency (individuals) and globally defined fields of possibility" (1996, 31), Arjun Appadurai undercuts the notion of an enforced passivity that inheres in the "West and the rest" model. His perceptive insistence on the individual as a "site of agency" interacting with "global fields of possibility" can be usefully extended to include the larger units of actors and make sense of Argentina's veritable obsession with itself. Appadurai is careful to historicize his reading of imagination, but I believe that its connection to agency holds for the modern as well as the postmodern era. I am not as concerned with individual agency here that is Appadurai's main concern as I am with symbolic fields that enable certain kinds of understanding of the interaction between place and nation.

24. "Me hicieron un chiste argentino que tengo que ponerme a reflexionar ahora porque me pareció buenísimo como chiste y vos lo escuchaste y creo que tiene que ver con esto de la literatura y la trascendencia y vamos a pensarlo entre las dos. El chiste es para los mexicanos, sobre los argentinos. Si algo hemos aportado a México es la posibilidad de hacer chistes geniales sobre los argentinos. El último que escuché dice: ¿por qué los argentinos no se bañan con agua caliente? Porque no quieren que se les empañe el espejo. Bueno, el espejo está empañado, el espejo de la historia argentina está empañado. Pero el espejo empañado dice muchas cosas, acuérdate del espejo ahumado mexicano, el espejo empañado habla" (Beltrán 1999, 5). ("They told me an Argentinean joke that I have to think about now because it seemed terrific as a joke and you heard it and I think it has to do with this business of literature and transcendence and we'll think about it between the two of us. The joke is for Mexicans, about Argentineans. If we've given anything to Mexico it's the chance to make great jokes about Argentineans. The last one I heard went: 'Why don't Argentines bathe in hot water? Because they don't want the mirror to get fogged up.' Well, the mirror is fogged up, the mirror of Argentine history is fogged up. But the fogged-up mirror says many things, remember the misty Mexican mirror, the foggy mirror speaks.")

25. See Angela Carlson Lombardi (2002) on the *escraches*.

26. Rabasa (1993) recognizes that it is somewhat problematic to submerge indigenous reality, and therefore points out that the indigenous people also invented a Europe. Further, he acknowledges the power differences inherent in this mutual invention. But whereas the indigenous people invented an other unlike itself, the colonials' invention of America became an attempt to name a new self.

27. See Shumway (1991) for a historical analysis of what he calls these two "guiding fictions" of Argentine identity.

28. "Buenos Aires necesita nombrarse a sí misma para saber que existe, para inventarse un pasado, para imaginarse un porvenir: no le basta, como a la Ciudad de México o a Lima, una simple referencia visual a los signos de prestigio histórico.... ¿puede haber algo más argentino que esa necesidad de llenar verbalmente los vacíos, de acudir a todas las bibliotecas del mundo para lenar el libro en blanco de la Argentina?" Fuentes 1974, 25, cited in Arambel-Güiñazú 1993, 151, n. 1.

29. "Seeing itself through the eyes of the 'other,' the stranger who makes the rules, from political laws to those that define good taste and culture, produces a dislocation that favors self-analysis" ("Verse a través de los ojos del 'otro,' del extranjero

que dicta las reglas, desde las políticas hasta las que rigen el buen gusto y la cultura, produce una dislocación que propicia el autoanálisis": Arambel-Güiñazú 1993, 123).

3. Imperial Anxieties

1. In her memoir of a five-month stay in Argentina published in 1920, Katherine Dreier repeatedly remarks on Argentina's "Musselman" heritage in reference to what she considers the retrograde attitude toward women.

2. See Candace Slater (2002) for a fine analysis of one version of this phenomenon.

3. There is a caveat here, in deference to Hugo Achugar who, as we will see later, argues that the countries of the Río de la Plata no longer figure in the metropole's idea of Latin America.

4. Christie makes similar references to Argentina in *Murder on the Links, The Big Four, The A.B.C. Murders, Dumb Witness,* and *Cards on the Table.*

5. This symbiotic relationship was so strong that for decades Argentina did not press its claims for the Malvinas, which it always had held to be illegally occupied by the British, who call the islands the Falklands.

6. Jordan (1980, 91) reports that "nostromo," uncorrupted, is the Genoese term for boatswain.

7. See Wynia (1990) for a useful discussion of the significant role the British played in the Latin American slave trade.

8. José Artigas, the author of Uruguayan independence from Argentina, began as an Argentine Federalist who opposed a strong central government in Buenos Aires. He ultimately led his country in its complete secession from an Argentina controlled from the capital.

9. It is perhaps just a coincidence that the invented name, Sulaco, resonates with the disrespectful, xenophobic, and racist term "sudaca" used in Spain to refer to South American immigrants.

10. The Italian national hero Garibaldi spent time in Uruguay and Argentina.

11. DeKoven (1991), Pitt (1978), and Wollaeger (2003) all comment on Conrad's influence on *The Voyage Out,* comparing Woolf's novel not with *Nostromo,* but rather *Heart of Darkness.* See Wollaeger (2003) for a persuasive and insightful analysis of the intertexts of *The Voyage Out.*

12. In his analysis of the effect on Woolf's British tourists of being stared at by silent Indian women, in which the object and subject of the traditional colonial gaze is inverted, Wollaeger (2001, 65–67) argues that these Indian women have their own point of view, even if Woolf does not attempt to represent it overtly.

13. See Wollaeger (2003) and Marshik (1999) for more discussion of these issues.

14. Marshik (1999) argues that, however real the fear of sexual trafficking during the period when Woolf was writing *The Voyage Out,* there is little historical evidence to support the claims of the drugging, kidnapping, and forced prostitution of Englishwomen to brown men. See Donna Guy (1992) for a history of the sex trade in Argentina at the turn of the twentieth century.

15. "Desde el horizonte actual de los países del Norte, lo latinoamericano no puede ser encarnado por el Río de la Plata. En el horizonte ideológico actual no es posible una representación cultural *(Darstellung)* de lo latinomericano que incluya

al Río de la Plata. El lugar de lo latinoamericano en la representación cultural del Norte poco tiene que ver con la representación de la totalidad o de la realidad latino-americana; por lo mismo América Latina es el espejo en el que se contemplan las sociedades del Norte. Esta mirada simplifica y hace posible la traslación del hori-zonte ideológico y de la situación de lectura que impera en el Norte. Las violaciones de los derechos humanos, los fenómenos de la migración sur-norte, la problemática del multiculturalismo y el universo del narcotráfico configuran un escenario en el que la promesa de riquezas simbolizadas por el Río de la Plata no tiene cabida y en cambio el paisaje de la deforestación salvaje de la Amazonia, la amenaza en el 'patio trasero' de Cuba o de los migrantes centroamericanos así como los desastres natu-rales de América Central o la opresión de los indios actúan como reafirmadores del papel que América Latina cumple en el imaginario occidental y en particular en el imaginario occidental del Norte."

16. It is possible that Uruguay did not enter the European imaginary in the same way Argentina did because its national hero, José Artigas, projected an image of an autochthonous country, not dependent on European values or ideas in its forma-tion as a nation. Uruguay, demographically similar to Argentina, did not impose itself onto Europe's consciousness.

4. Europe's Uncanny Other

1. "La avidez por el exoticismo en los europeos de todos los tiempos que les hace poner de moda lo ruso, lo japonés, lo indonésico o lo tahitiano, no es parang-onable con la pasión por la América bárbara. A diferencia de lo que los fascina de otros países y culturas igualmente lejanos y diferentes a la propia, es que América representó siempre un aspecto ignoto y oculto de sí misma (de Europa) o perdido: su futuro (América como espacio de la utopía) o su pasado (América bárbara)."

2. "La frénésie des nuits de Buenos Aires avait donné à la capitale de l'Argentine une réputation étonnante: ses voluptés, ses fêtes, ses folies lui valaient dans l'hémi-sphère Sud un pouvoir d'attraction acomparable à l'extravagant Paris d'avant-guerre."

3. "Argentine est une nation femelle, à toquades et à coups de grisou. C'est une inconstante: *ein weibliches Volk*."

4. The term *criollo* (feminine, *criolla*) is used to refer to the descendents of Spanish settlers.

5. We might recall here that Victoria Ocampo had her reasons for weaving simi-lar dinner-party fantasies for Virginia Woolf.

6. Shumway (1991) points out that there has been gauchesque literature written in every generation since its invention, and what began as a heroic genre whose intended audience was the gaucho—the rural poor and disenfranchised who were now to be encouraged to lay claim to the nation—turned into a form whose audi-ence became the urban literati. These readers were interested in being entertained, but their desire for entertainment did not preclude the genre's more serious pur-pose of working out Argentine identity. Even the word gaucho, he says, is the object of continuing debate among Argentineans, who want to settle on the "true mean-ing" of the term. The competing derivations are, tellingly, French (gauche = outlaw) and native (guacho = orphan). The discussion this discrepancy has generated about semantics is less important than the argument it masks, of the true derivation—

a question of essence and origin. More significant still is the fact of contestation. From the point of origin on, the meaning of gaucho is both contested and malleable. From within the country, different individuals and groups use the word to mean either the rural riffraff that no one of their own class would want to be identified with, or the rural, poor, mestizo folk that are the heart of the nation, or the essence of the nation itself. Sarmiento labels the western followers of Facundo "gauchos" even though the gaucho was understood previously as the pampas dweller. With this move, Sarmiento generalizes the term to mean the rural followers of a caudillo, politically unsophisticated and dangerous, bearing the signs of barbarism. José Hidalgo, on the other hand, sees patriotic wisdom and the values of generosity, democracy, and nativism in his gaucho.

7. The discursive feminization and urbanization of Jews, therefore, makes the idea of Jewish gauchos mildly preposterous. But the openness of the term and the reality of Argentine Jewish immigration history have made the idea of Jewish gauchos a possibility as well. The Jewish immigrants who were given land to work in the provinces were dubbed Jewish gauchos by one of their number, even though they were more likely to farm than to herd livestock and, as the joke goes, had a tendency to plant wheat and reap doctors.

8. This myth, according to Scheines (1991), undergoes partial metamorphosis, from paradise (the already perfect place from which only fall and corruption are possible), to utopia (the noplace in which a perfect society, theoretically, but not practically, be established), to the unredeemable place damned by its own geography.

9. "Paraíso, utopía, barbarie. Las tres imágenes son visiones europeas de Sudamérica que nosotros, los sudamericanos, recibimos, aceptamos y alimentamos."

10. "[E]l hombre de la civilización, el europeo, se siente un extraño en el paraíso americano intuido como antimundo donde no se puede establecer residencia. Como extraño en el paraíso asume actitudes diversas: lo saquea y regresa a patria lejana, lo camina y recorre con los ojos, alelado porque todo lo maravilla, lo celebra, o queda anonadado en su geografía."

11. I am grateful to the Press's anonymous reviewer for reminding me that Belgrano Rawson's novel *Fuegia* also deals with the relationship between the British and the indigenous people of Tierra del Fuego.

12. In this the captain reminds us of Conrad's inassimilable Goulds, especially of Mrs. Gould's ability to create a kind of English calm in her Costaguana home, and of Virginia Woolf's characters who simply take for granted that they will bring their Englishness with them wherever they go.

13. For a detailed discussion of this phenomenon, see Kaminsky (1999).

14. In a very differently placed novel, written in the United States and populated by Orthodox Jews, Nina, the Argentinean character in Allegra Goodman's *Katterskill Falls*, functions as an Argentine uncanny other as well. As an Argentine immigrant to the United States, Nina is an outsider to her family. She is much younger than her husband, whose primary familial alliances are with his two older sisters. Perhaps because of her (national) difference, Nina is, if anything, more committed to the Orthodox Jewish community into which she has married than are her husband or her sisters-in-law. She aspires to be like the other women of the community, and it seems that she tries too hard. Until Andras's sister tells him that his first loyalty must be to his wife, she remains outside the circle of his intimacy. In Goodman's

novel Argentina is a place where Jews can be from, but they are not quite fully members of the families or the communities they join in the United States.

15. Marks's translation differs from the published version in English, in which the sentences read, "She saw the country of her birth again before she died. She died without understanding" (Perec 1988, 33).

16. As Mary Louise Pratt (1992) points out, first-hand experience of a place does not necessarily afford knowledge or insight. Pratt points to Paul Theroux's *Old Patagonian Express* to exemplify the traveler from the North who declares a place boring and monotonous but who takes no trouble at all to learn anything about it. The Patagonia of the title is not just the name of the train Theroux takes; it is the marker for all that he does not see in Latin America.

17. "Podemos mencionar múltiples ejemplos de la idealización de la Argentina, como representación del progreso, de los logros políticos y, sobre todo, económicos que podía alcanzar la raza hispánica, de poder superar los obstáculos institucionales y culturales acumulados en la península durante siglos" (Tabanera García 1997, unpaginated) ("We can mention multiple examples of the idealization of Argentina, as representative of progress, of political and, above all, economic achievements that the Hispanic race can achieve, of being able to overcome institutional and cultural obstacles accumulated in the [Iberian] Peninsula over decades"), and in conclusion, "en el inicio y el fin de aquel período de la historia reciente de España [1898–1930], América seguía apareciendo como referente, como horizonte o, cómo hemos visto que conforma desde fines del siglo XIX, como mito compensatorio" ("at the beginning and end of that period of recent Spanish history (1898–1930), America continued to appear as referent, as horizon, or, as we have seen, since has been the case since the end of the nineteenth century, as compensatory myth").

18. "América siempre ha estado presente en el pensamiento español como prolongación de la propia identidad nacional o del propio proyecto de nación."

19. "el español que se sumerge y se baña en el medio argentino y desde él contempla a España, experimenta la sensación singularísima de que entonces es cuando ve en plenitud de visión entera y completa, una España con porvenir, como el argentino que ve desde España una Argentina con maravillosa historia" (cited from Pike 1971, 148; and Zuleta 1979, 11).

20. "Tras escribir 'Argentina y sus grandezas' en 1910, dedicó todos sus esfuerzos a estos proyectos, en los que América ya no era un símbolo, una alusión o un trasfondo, sino una presencia directa y un escenario" (cited by Tabanera García 1997, unpaginated).

21. These are the words of Lucia Etxebarría, in her introduction to *Venus en Buenos Aires* ("[esa chica para cuyos padres] las palabras Buenos Aires no son sinónimo de ciudad o la clima sino de aberración e inmoralidad," Nestares 2001, 10–11).

22. "Siempre que Doña Inés penetra en el cuarto, su mirada va a posarse en la estampa colgada en la pared. La litografía es inseparable de sus ratos de espera en la estancia. Transcurre el tiempo, no se percibe ningún ruido. Nada turba el sosiego del aposento. La mirada de la dama tropieza con la amarillenta litografía. En el vivir de todos los días, nuestro espíritu, sin que sepamos por qué, se aferra a un objeto cualquiera de los que nos rodean. La fatalidad nos une, sin que lo queramos, a tal mueble o cachivache; ellos son en lo inerte más fuertes que nosotros en lo vivo. . . . Y siempre, con deliberación o sin ella, como imperativo que partiera de la eterna y

pretérita informidad, nuestra mirada va a posarse indefectiblemente en el objeto que nos subyuga. Doña Inés, en el cuartito, contempla la litofgrafía amarillenta; por centísima vez lee arriba: *Confederación Argentina,* y debajo: *Buenos Aires a vista de pájaro.*"

23. "Sí, esto sí que es epílogo. ¿Dónde está nuestro ombú? Con los ojos del deseo—los más avisores de todos—lo vemos en el horizonte infinito."

24. "La vieja estancia que se levantaba frente al ombú, ha desaparecido. Han transcurrido muchos años. . . . El sol besa a lo lejos los muros blancos de otra estancia. . . . Muchas veces hemos visto en España este muro blanco y bajo, y estos pámpanos verdes junto a una ventana. Como ha desaparecido la otra estancia desaparecerá también ésta. La imagen material de la vieja y lejana España se va rompiendo a pedazos; una nueva y poderosa forma trabaja por nacer."

25. "Leo venía del mundo en el que el fuego quema, el agua moja, los cuchillos cortan y los disparos matan. Amándole, yo amaba ese otro mundo, donde las cosas eran de verdad: el exilio, la muerte, la lucha por la vida."

26. "Yo no conocía Buenos Aires, pero por los libros, por los discos, por las películas, la imaginaba: una ciudad abigarrada, urgente, llena de recovecos y sorpresas. De turcos, gallegos, sicilianos, polacos, eslovenos. De ricos con finca en el Delta del Tigre y pobres diablos que hablaban yiddish y pasaban hambre. Una ciudad de gente intensa, ansiosa, histriónica, gárrula, culta, divertida, insoportable. Una gran ciudad con un cementerio señorial, salones de té ingleses, palacetes venidos a menos, una iglesia rusa con cúpulas azules y un jardín japonés."

5. Victoria Ocampo and the Keyserling Effect

1. Tagore is virtually unknown today in the United States, but he remains revered in India. He is still beloved in Latin America, in great part because Ocampo so successfully promoted his work.

2. Until his death in 2005, Keyserling's son Arnold headed the school.

3. Ocampo first discovered Keyserling's writing in the Spanish journal directed by José Ortega y Gassett, *Revista de Occidente.* By 1927 she had read *El diario de viaje de un filósofo* (Travel diary of a philosopher), *El mundo que nace* (The world aborning), and *Figuras simbólicas* (Symbolic figures), and had given a talk on his work at the Amigos del Arte in Buenos Aires.

4. The novelist Eduardo Mallea, who was very close to Ocampo, was one of the few to reject Keyserling's interpretation of Argentina.

5. See, for example, Graciela Scheines (1991), Nicolas Shumway (1991), and Noé Jitrik (1998).

6. Emir Rodríguez Monegal is one of the few who makes reference to Ocampo's text, noting that few readers paid attention to it: "Versiones interesadas, como la del obseso don Juan y Conde de Keyserling en sus Memorias, eran más leídas que la devastadora réplica de Victoria en *El viajero y una de sus sombras,* que sólo conocimos más tarde" (1979, 45). Two others who speak eloquently to Keyserling's obsession with Ocampo as the grounding for the *Meditations* are Ocampo's biographer, Doris Meyer (1979), and her translator, Patricia Owen Steiner (1999).

7. Beatriz Sarlo also recounts this anecdote, in her essay on Victoria Ocampo in *La máquina cultural.* Sarlo's insightful reading of the interactions between Keyserling

and Ocampo characterizes them more as farce (vaudeville, to be precise) than the melodrama that I see in them. She emphasizes the comic aspects of their mutual misunderstandings and Keyserling's clumsy efforts at seduction. Her overall argument is that Keyserling was one of a string of Europeans and North Americans who misunderstood and exoticized Ocampo. I agree, but I believe that his effect on subsequent thinking in Argentina was more pernicious than Sarlo suggests.

8. "El hecho de no ser de su opinión y de no plegarme a sus deseos, fueren cuales fueren y no importa en qué plano, me transformó, a sus ojos, de uno de 'los seres más espirituales que había conocido' (v. *America set free*) en 'la encarnación misma de la gana' (v. *Viaje a través del Tiempo*). Y me convertía en la encarnación, la esclava de la gana, precisamente en el momento en que daba pruebas irrefutables de vencerla."

9. In addition to Buenos Aires, where he probably had the most social contact, given his acquaintanceship with Ocampo and her arranging for him to meet others, Keyserling traveled through Bolivia and Brazil.

10. Keyserling expounds upon Original Fear and Original Hunger earlier in the text.

11. "In rereading Virginia Woolf's *A Room of One's Own* (1929) for the first time in some years, I was astonished at the sense of effort, of pains taken, of dogged tentativeness, in the tone of that essay. And I recognized that tone. I had heard it often enough, in myself and in other women. It is the tone of a woman almost in touch with her anger, who is determined not to appear angry, who is willing herself to be calm, detached, and even charming in a roomful of men where things have been said which are attacks on her very integrity. Virginia Woolf is addressing an audience of women, but she is acutely conscious—as she always was—of being overheard by men.... Only at rare moments in that essay do you hear the passion in her voice; she was trying to sound as cool as Jane Austen, as Olympian as Shakespeare, because that is the way the men of the culture thought a writer should sound. No male writer has written primarily or even largely for women, or with the sense of women's criticism as a consideration when he chooses his materials, his theme, his language. But to a lesser or greater extent, every woman writer has written for men even when, like Virginia Woolf, she was supposed to be addressing women" (Rich 1993, 167).

12. "El hecho es que me presenté en el Hôtel des Réservoirs con mi 'torta' (tomar el término con o sin juego de palabras) y mi pote de manteca para mi abuela, siguiendo la tradición de Caperucita Roja. Y me encontré con buenas a primeras frente a un carnívero que reclamaba una comida más sustanciosa."

13. "En realidad, hablaré de mí bajo todos los aspectos posibles, pero apuntando en cada capítulo hacia otro esprítu que fué significativo para mí."

14. "Conociendo a Keyserling, su imaginación desbordante y su manera impetuosa de amasar los 'hechos' (*sus enemigos personales,* según decía), que se jactaba de despreciar en su mera faz de 'hechos,' empecé a inquietarme."

15. "En 1932 aparecieron las *Meditaciones Sudamericanas,* trayéndome con sus páginas una nueva oleada de indignación....

"Yo no quería escribir más sobre Keyserling; sólo me complace analizar lo que puedo alabar. Y las *Meditaciones* no me parecían, en su conjunto, dignas de alabanzas. En esa obra de 350 páginas, a pesar de algunos aciertos, una generalización frenética de conclusiones antojadizas repugnaba."

16. "Analizando así las *Meditaciones* descubro el punto de partida de muchos errores, pero otros parecen creados enteramente por la fantasía desbocada del autor."

17. "Reconocía observaciones y opiniones que yo había confiado al filósofo, pero desfiguradas por no sé qué fenómeno de inflación inaudita. Una elefantíasis interpretativa. Aquí y allá, como de costumbre, un relámpago de genio, partiendo de no sé qué Magma Mater y recayendo en ella."

18. "[E]n su fiebre de generalización (a partir de un punto verdadero, dudoso o falso según los casos, y esta vez el punto de partida era extremadamente dudoso), Keyserling no se queda corto: 'los sudamericanos se callan en todos los casos en que un europeo levantaría la voz o estallaría en invectivas. Prefieren matar a injuriar.'"

19. "Es difícil pasar por alto ciertos elementos de contradicción y de exageración en este interesante pasaje. Quien odia la violencia y la cólera no puede desear padecer sus efectos, a menos de ser un caso patológico de masoquismo. Este extremo de masoquismo no parece tan difundido, que yo sepa. Y si los sudamericanos por ejecer la violación como cosa natural (he atravesado mi vida sin observar síntomas alarmantes de estas costumbres; ¿por qué será?) tienen éxito entre las europeas, ¿no podría deducirse de tal fenómeno que las mujeres del viejo continente se aficionan enseguida a la violación y adoptan los hábitos de nuestros hombres Cromañón? No hace falta, por consiguiente, ser un animal de sangre fría, perteniciente al mundo del Tercer Día de la Creación, para conducirse como tal. Y finalmente, generalicemos, puesto que estamos en buena escuela para hacerlo, se deduce que la violación universalmente aunque subterráneamente apatecida por la mujer, sólo se consigue ejecerla con éxito el hombre de Cromañón (léase el sudamericano). Algo había que dejarles a los pobrecitos."

20. In a 1943 article in which he comments on foreigners' views of the United States, Arthur M. Schlesinger points out that many such writers "fail to distinguish the significant from the trivial" and remarks with no little astonishment, that "some visitors prided themselves upon learning much from seeing little" (227). Keyserling, whose *America Set Free* was, Schlesinger notes, widely read, is his prime example; and the historian expresses his disdain for the count's assessment of America's subconscious in understated irony. I am grateful to Martha Peach, research librarian extraordinaire, for this reference.

21. "Querría empezar explicando que para mí existen los hechos, en una medida razonable, aunque para Keyserling no existan; o tampoco que no vale la pena de respectarlos. 'Los hechos como tales no me interesan; lo único que me interesa es el significado de los acontecimientos.' Los hechos sólo son interesantes cuando uno descubre su sentido, estamos de acuerdo. Pero, con razón o sin ella, estimo que si deformamos con exceso los hechos, acabamos por deformar o alterar el sentido."

22. "El fervor inusitado de mi entusiasmo por ciertos aspectos del genio keyserliniano (he considerado y considero que este hombre tenía destellos geniales), lo habían inducido a creer ese entusiasmo inseparable . . . de un gran amor total que jamás me inspiró. Al comprobar la ausencia de ese sentimiento me hizo aparecer ante sus ojos como un monstruo y una traidora, cuando sólo era una mujer a quien le dolía decepcionarlo sobre este capítulo . . . y que se obstinaba al comienzo en emplear un sinfín de miramientos para aclararle el sentido de su equivocación. Estos miramientos acarrearon en parte a Sudamérica el capítulo de la Delicadeza en las Meditaciones. 'Así, la dulzura y los extremos miramientos de los sudamericanos no significan jamás calor de sentimiento.'"

23. "[N]i mi delicadeza sudamericana, ni mi franqueza norteamericana encontraron gracia a los ojos de Keyserling, en cuanto se trató de hacerle entender lo que no le daba la gana de entender."

24. "He aquí, ¡oh milagro!, lo que [Shaw] escribe de las mujeres que rondaban en torno de su joven (o vieja) gloria: 'No todas mis perseguidoras deseaban tener relaciones sexuales conmigo.' Digo: ¡oh milagro!, porque semejante declaración de parte de un escritor de fama mundial es más desusada aún que el haber guardado continencia hasta los 29 años; y la perspicacia que tal declaración implica, tan contraria a las leyes de la naturaleza masculina como el milagro a la leyes de la naturaleza a secas."

25. "El varón está hecho de tal manera que ofrece mucho a quien está dispuesta a pagarle con moneda de placer, o incluso con moneda de amor propio satisfecho, con moneda de sensación de dominio halagada."

26. "Creo que más parecido a los dioses de Olimpo que a los descendientes de la pareja paradisíaca, [Keyserling] se irritaba simplemente por el hecho de que una simple mortal se atreviera a llevarle la contra, y a no asentir a todas sus 'fantasías poéticas.'"

27. "sin dejar de ser un acontecimiento de enorme interés, una prueba diaria extremadamente dura de soportar."

28. The primordial nature of South America links it, in Keyserling's rhetoric, to Africa, also colonized and racialized by Europe: "Even today I cannot think of South America without experiencing a feeling of profoundest attachment and tiredness. It is not love, such as I knew of yore; it is rather what the ancient pictures found on African rocks are meant to express, when they represent roving man as tied to his far-away mother by the navel string" (1932, 7).

29. However reptilian they may be, Argentines can be grateful to have been admitted into the biological realm, which is more than can be said for the people of the Andes: "Andean man is actually of a mineral nature. . . . Never have I seen such souls of bronze as the souls of those mountain dwellers; never did anything human appear to me so strange, so altogether foreign to myself. This inertia, this lentor, this monstrous memory, this insensibility immediately below the surface, the sensitiveness of which is identical with the quick incalescence and effervescence of metals; this candid disregard of history, this dull melancholy which dwells on the near side of a mere idea of hope, are truly inorganic" (Keyserling 1932, 11).

30. "buen número de sus colegas esparcidos por el planeta."

31. "Baste citar, en apoyo de lo que digo, estos pasajes de las *Meditaciones Sudamericanas,* posteriores a la época de mi entusiasmo keyserliniano, desde luego. 'Se puede, pues, generalizar y afirmar: en el comienzo no fué el Hombre sino la Mujer, no la Verdad sino la Mentira. *La mujer, cercana de los bajos fondos originales* [soy yo quien subraya], encarna todavía hoy, aún en el más alto grado de la cultura, la modalidad de la vida primordial.' Es evidente que se trata aquí de una *proyección* (en psicoanálisis, esta palabra, como se sabe, significa el acto de atribuir a otra pesona un deseo, un rasgo de carácter o un ideal del propio sujecto): el hombre asocia a la mujer al estado primordial en la medida en que ella lo evoca en él."

32. "A propósito de Houston Chamberlain, Keyserling escribe in su *Viaje a través del Tiempo:* 'Chamberlain nunco vió a Alemania tal como ésta es realmente. Harto a menudo se apegó a una quimera en la que podía creer con tanto mayor sinceridad cuanto que no tenía ninguna relación verdadera con la naturaleza alemana. . . . *Una*

cosa análoga a lo que le ocurría a Chamberlain ocurre también las más veces con la predilección por pueblos y países extranjeros: constituyen la más segura superficie de proyección de lo propio.' [Soy yo quien subraya.] Las *Meditaciones Sudamericanas* iban a ser la reacción de Keyserling al test Rorshach frente a la gran mancha de tinta de nuestro Continente."

33. "si alguna vez [Keyserling] utilizaba mi persona en sus escritos sería para una 'realización personal,' prescindiendo de la justicia o injusticia de la cosa."

6. The Race for National Identity

1. Adriana Muñoz, a member of the archeological team that dated the masks says that the masks were thought to be "ethnographic," i.e., of fairly recent vintage, because of the good condition they were found in, and that it was only when the research team began carbon 14 tests that they discovered how old these artifacts were. The results of this research were presented at an archeology conference in Córdoba, Argentina, in 1999, but the findings have not been at all widely disseminated: "Empezamos a trabajar con las máscaras en 1996, primero pensamos que eran etnográficas por su buena condición, pero después hicimos varios fechados (Carbono 14) y el resultado fue 2500 antes del presente. . . .

"Parte del resultado de este trabajo se presentó en un Congreso de Arqueología en Córdoba en 1999, pero la verdad no ha habido casi nada de difusión. Había pensado escribir algo más popular sobre esto, pero no sé dónde se podría publicar" (Adriana Muñoz, personal communication). ("We began to work with the masks in 1996, at first we thought they were ethnographic because of the good condition they were in, but later we did various datings [carbon 14] and the result was 2,500 years before the present. . . . Some of the results of this work were presented in an Archeology Conference in Córdoba [Argentina] in 1999, but the truth is that there has been almost no dissemination [of the findings]. I had thought about writing something more popular about this [i.e., for a popular audience], but I don't know where it could be published.")

2. Beardsell notes, for example, that "even in Argentina . . . indigenous groups often organise their own activities to counterbalance the official state celebration [of October 12 as a national holiday]" (2000, 100).

3. Even the dubious appropriation of indigenous culture by New Age practitioners is symptomatic of the process. Although this New Age embrace of Indian spirituality justifies itself as a rejection of contemporary Western materialism, it might better be understood as the most recent in a series of acts that take over and pave over Indian territory for the benefit of non-Indians, usually at the expense of Indians themselves.

4. In Mesoamerica, where the indigenous presence has been most apparent and perhaps least enfolded into Western practice, this recovery has taken the form of a significant level of political participation and resistance. The work of Rigoberta Menchú is paradigmatic but not unique in this sense. The Zapatistas of Chiapas reclaimed indigenous rights; the fact that its public face, Subcomandante Marcos, was not Indian was the anomaly that made the movement more accessible and fascinating to Europeans and North Americans. Closer to home, in Pinochet's Chile, playing indigenous musical instruments was taken to be a sign of subversion, and

the suppression of indigenous culture went hand in hand with the dictatorship's nineteenth-century notion of European-style order and progress. Sectors in post-dictatorship Chile have attempted to bring together different indigenous groups in friendly competitions that inspire loyalty to the particular Indian nation and to a notion of pan-Indian solidarity.

5. I am indebted to archeologist Adriana Muñoz, who was a member of the team that dated the masks, for generously sharing this information with me. It was the Chinchorros, living in what is now Chilean and Argentinean territory, who developed the earliest known mummification process. "Ahora con lo que mencionas sobre la presencia indígena en Argentina hay una gran paradoja en la información, por ejemplo dentro de Arqueología se sabe y hay pruebas de la presencia humana en territorio argentino desde hace unos 12000 años (fechados de Patagonia). En la Puna hay fechados bien antiguos de casi 6000 años y si tomas como ejemplo Chinchorro (Chile, Atacama) hay fechados de casi 10000, plus a que justo lo que se conoce como Cultura Chinchorro tiene el proceso de momificación más antiguo conocido (momificaban antes que en Egipto).... En fin, la paradoja está en que "Historia" comienza (en casi todos los círculos académicos, educativos, políticos, etc) cuando se conoce la escritura. Y lo peor de todo es que eso es lo que se enseña todavía en las escuelas en Argentina" (Muñoz, personal communication). ("Now with what you mention about the indigenous presence in Argentina there's a great paradox in the information; for example, in Archeology it's known and there is evidence of human presence in Argentine territory from some 12,000 years ago [datings from Patagonia]. In the Puna there are quite old datings, almost 6,000 years, and if you take Chinchorro [Chile, Atacama] as an example, there are datings of almost 10,000 years, plus what we know about Chinchorro Culture, that it has the oldest known mummification process [mummification before Egypt].... So, the paradox is that 'History' begins [in almost all academic, educational, political, etc. circles] when writing is found. And the worst thing of all is that's what's still being taught in the schools in Argentina.")

6. I am grateful to Noni Benegas for telling me about Paturuzú and for providing me with copies of some of the Paturuzú comic magazines from the early 1960s.

7. The concert, part of a series sponsored by the City of Madrid as part of its Veranos de la Villa, 2004, took place at the Cuartel del Conde Duque on July 19, 2004. To my eye, it looked as if the concert was sold out, and to my ear, it sounded like the audience was made up entirely of Argentineans. In fact, Gieco thanked his countrymen and -women for coming out to hear him, since he said that in Spain no one knows who he is. His frequent references to Buenos Aires, the audience's intoning familiar Argentine chants, and the familiarity with which the audience received his songs all indicated that they were overwhelmingly Argentine. I believe that this counterculture, new song, leftist (and therefore in an odd way parochial) Argentina does not resonate internationally. Spain, like the rest of Europe, prefers the familiar Argentina of the tango.

8. See "The Subject of National Identity," in Kaminsky (1999).

9. They go on to point out that territoriality itself masks the precariousness of the idea that a nation *is* something: "Here, ambiguity about the precise constitution of the entity is downplayed by emphasizing the 'fact' of its existence as manifested in territorial boundaries" (Jackson and Penrose 1993, 8).

10. It is important not to romanticize this notion. In his later writings Vasconcelos expresses deeply racist attitudes.

11. See Higa (1999) for a fascinating discussion of Japanese immigrants in Argentina at the end of the nineteenth century.

12. As Daniel Balderston points out, David Viñas shows in *Indios, ejército y frontera* that by 1870 the Argentine intelligentsia, both liberal and conservative, agreed on the desirability of the removal or extermination of the pampas Indians (Balderston 1993, 87).

13. The Europe I evoke as a seamless whole here is, of course, internally fractured as well. The European fairs were put on by the elite, but they were attended by the working class as well as by the bourgeoisie.

14. At the time of this writing, Meisel was in the process of researching this shift. I am grateful to him for sharing his work in progress.

15. See Susana Rotker (2002) for an excellent analysis of the figure of the captive and the construction of the savage in Argentine culture.

16. "riquísimo argentino que, desde hacía muchos años, llevaba una vida de locos gastos y continua ostentación en París" (Roussel, cited in Ferrari 1999, 230).

17. "'No!... Terrible non-sens!... Tout cela a autant de chances de réussir que vous et moi en avons de croiser un nègre dans les rues de Buenos Aires.'"

18. "'On m'affirmait au contraire,' dit-il, 'que l'Argentine était le plus étrange et le plus multiple bouillon de peuples. Serons-nous accueillis au port par des Indiens à plumes?'

"Campbell s'étrangla dans son verre, lady Campbell haussa ses minces épaules tandis que le gros homme chauve riait comme un barbare, et que Robert de Liniers—c'était le nom de l'aristocrate francais—répondait, sardonique: 'Nous sommes un pays blanc, monsieur. Le seul pays parfaitement blanc au sud du Canada.'"

19. "'Il y a bien quelques descendants de vrais Indiens,' murmura Marta du bout de ses lèvres peintes, 'à Salta, à Jujuy, dans le Nord du pays. Don Rafaël,' ajouta-t-elle avec une moue comme si elle révélait une chose horrible et confidentielle, 'don Rafaël a connu des Araucans de la Terre de Feu, qui...'

"'Oui, oui...' fit cette fois le banquier anglais... 'A force de vivre dans ses steppes, entre vigognes et guanacos, don Rafael finira comme Robinson, sans prise sur le réel de l'univers... Chère amie, tous ces Araucans, croyez-m'en, ce n'est que de la mythologie...'

"'Par ma foi, ils existent pourtant bel et bien,' osa confier le gros homme. 'Leurs tribus occupent tout le Sud du rio Bio-Bio, à ce qu'on m'a dit...'

"'Bio-Bio, on croit sucer un bonbon,' soupira Marta."

20. This distinction is interestingly gendered in Borges: In two *cautivo* stories, one about a boy and another about a woman, the boy's world is made larger by his captivity—in the end he must escape the claustophobic little cabin to which he is returned; the woman's world, on the other hand, is constricted by her life as a captive. She has lost her ability to communicate fluently in Spanish and is unable to leave the narrow world to which she has become accustomed.

21. "'... tels sont les chiffres, les vrais chiffres: soixante-treize pour cent des Argentins sont nés de descendents européens, vingt-trois pour cent sont nés à l'étranger, autrement dit en Europe... Un résidu de trois cent cinquante mille personnes est de sang mêlé... Allez donc après cela citer le peuple argentin comme un peuple mulâtre?'"

22. "'Enfer et damnation,' rugit-il; 'regardez donc mieux les Européens que vous importez. Ils ne sont pas moins typiques que les nègres. Le Sicilien, le Bavarois, le Turc, le Polonais, le Génois, le Corse, voilà le pittoresque, monsieur, dans les rues de Buenos Aires . . . Avec les deux races les plus exclusives du monde, la vôtre, lord Campbell, et la mienne . . . l'Anglais et le Juif . . .'

"Sur le coup, l'Anglais faillit s'étouffer."

23. See María Josefina Saldaña-Portillo (2003) for a cogent analysis of this process.

24. "el estudio de la multiculturalidad y sus vínculos con el poder tenían formatos distintos que en Estados Unidos, y a la vez diferentes en México y Perú, donde lo intercultural pasa en gran parte por la presencia indígena, o en el Caribe, donde es central lo afroamericano, o en el Río de la Plata, en que el predominio de la cultura europea simuló una homogeneidad blanca."

25. Power in the Caribbean, however, is differentially distributed along national/racial lines. The French- and English-speaking Caribbean are largely governed by Afro-Caribbeans, whereas the politcal and cultural elite of the Dominican Republic, Puerto Rico, and even revolutionary Cuba are primarily of European descent.

26. U.S. culture operates under the one-drop rule, which holds that any African ancestry unwhitens the body. In contrast, Hispanic colonial heritage, operating on the notion of the greater strength of "white blood," allows for the "redemption" of whiteness in mixed-race families after several generations of "whitening." Thus, the white body is constituted differently in Argentina than in the United States, although both systems are profoundly racist.

7. The Other Within

1. "Para imaginarse un porvenir no le basta, como a la Ciudad de México o a Lima, una simple referencia visual a los signos de prestigio histórico . . . ¿puede haber algo más argentino que esa necesidad de llenar verbalmente los vacíos, de acudir a todas las bibliotecas del mundo, para llenar el libro en blanco de la Argentina?" (Fuentes 1974, 25, cited in Arambel-Güiñazú 1993, 151, n. 1).

2. "Verse a través de los ojos del 'otro,' del extranjero que dicta las reglas, desde las políticas hasta las que rigen el buen gusto y la cultura, produce una dislocación que propicia el autoanálisis."

3. Nor does Borges's fascination with Jewish mysticism have much to do with modern Judaism, even if some of his stories include modern-day Jewish characters.

4. Earlier, Rivadavia and Alberdi both prescribed European immigration as a solution to what Shumway ironically describes as "a population 'cursed' by Spanish tradition and racial inadequacy" (1991, 146). It was Sarmiento who most forcefully took up Alberdi's famous aphorism, "gobernar es poblar" (to govern is to populate), in his call for immigration at the end of *Facundo* and in his policies as president.

5. By the end of the twentieth century, the vast majority of Jews in Argentina had moved away from the original JCA-funded colonies. Weisbrot (1979) writes that some Jewish families spoke of "sowing wheat and reaping doctors."

6. Judaism as a trope in Muñoz Molina surfaces in earlier novels and blooms fully in *Sefarad*, which deals with European Jewry especially, and with the Jew as quintessential exile.

7. "Ya verás que las mujeres argentinas tienen otro garbo, como más mundo, será por la mezcla de razas, o porque se psicoanalizan todas, o por esos nombres y apellidos que les ponen. Me reconocerás que no es lo mismo llamarse Mariluz Padilla Soto que llamarse Carlota Fainberg."

8. Abengoa is apparently unaware that women in Argentina typically take their husbands' family names, unlike Spanish women, who retain their original last names when they marry.

9. "Dijo que lucía una gran melena rubia, un traje de chaqueta oscuro, ancho en los hombros y muy ceñido a las caderas, unos tacones que le hacían parecer más alta, 'aunque sin la menor necesidad,' unos ojos rasgados, verdes, felinos (el adjectivo es suyo), espléndidamente maquillados, que se fijaron enseguida en él al mismo tiempo que su boca grande y carnal le sonreía sin reserva ninguna, la típica sonrisa de la mujer porteña, me anunció, como quien le anticipa las maravillas de un país al viajero que se dispone a visitarlo por primera vez."

10. "La misteriosa mujer rubia, según él mismo la denominó, seguía siendo el centro de sus prioridades."

11. Daniel Balderston's 1993 study demonstrates how wrong this idea is.

12. I am grateful to Raymond Duvall for introducing me to Spekke's work and providing me with a copy of *Il Mondo di Borges*.

13. It is this implicitly conservative stance that, according to Gutiérrez Girardot (1990), has kept Borges from being understood by German readers. In his analysis, the left-wing German intelligentsia reductively faults Borges for his apparent conservatism; but more importantly, the German inability to read Borges stems from the long-standing expectation that Latin American literature will reinforce German notions of Latin American "authenticity" on the one hand and a penchant for confusing Spain with Latin America, both exotic and racially suspect, on the other. Borges is notoriously resistant to conscription into the folkloric, even when he writes about gauchos or Buenos Aires *compadritos*.

14. Nor is Claudio particularly interested in the Jewish Borges. He is drawn, instead, to the British Borges who writes a poem about Pew.

15. There is, however, a tendency to confuse the Jews and Muslims of Spain's past: in Granada a statue erected to commemorate a medieval Jewish physician is locally referred to as "el moro," the Moor. I am grateful to Margalit Chu and Vale Gámez for this piece of local Granadine lore.

16. *Semana Santa* (Holy Week) in the year 2001 was celebrated in the Spanish city of Murcia with its second annual Festival of Three Cultures, featuring two klezmer groups. *Semana Santa* is a holiday of fervent religiosity, marked by processions of Catholic fraternal orders wearing the robes and pointed hoods of the (often suspected of being secretly Jewish) victims of the Inquisition's autos-da-fé. An analysis of this clash of symbols is beyond the scope of this chapter. I mention it only to give the reader an idea of the fraught and conflicting meaning that Judaism holds in twenty-first-century Spain.

17. "Era una mujer demasiado fantástica, pensaba ahora [Abengoa], peligrosísima en su apasionamiento, tan potencialmente escandalosa como los gritos que daba en el momento del orgasmo, que era muy largo y tenía una cosa halagadora y alarmante de éxtasis felino."

18. Max Barabander, the protagonist of I. B. Singer's novel *Scum,* tells this linguistic story from a somewhat different point of view. Explaining the changes in

Jewish life that take place when Jews leave eastern Europe, he tells a devout Polish Jew that "In Argentina the younger generation has begun to speak Spanish" (1991, 35). Embedded in that statement is some degree of assurance that they have not stopped speaking Yiddish.

19. Goldberg is first introduced in a discussion of Argentina not devoid of a latent anti-Semitism that takes place among wealthy Gentile Argentines, on shipboard, i.e., in the space between Argentina and Europe (Bona 1986, 41).

20. See chapter 8 for a discussion of texts by Katz, Singer, and other non-Argentine Jewish writers.

21. Recent films about Jewish characters in Argentina such as *Esperando al mesías* (Waiting for the Messiah) and *Sol de otoño* (Autumn sun) trouble the question of Jewish identity. Daniel in *Esperando al mesías* wants to find a life outside the "bubble" of the Jewish world of Buenos Aires, and Clara's world is entirely Jewish until she meets a man who is not.

22. See, for example, literary texts by Alicia Steimberg and Nora Glickman. This is not to say that all writers of Jewish background deal with Jewish themes (see, for example, David Viñas and Alejandra Pizarnik, for example), but that when Jewish characters appear in the works of Jewish writers and filmmakers, for example, assimilation is rarely presented as a simple matter.

23. According to different reports, eighty-five or eighty-six people died in the bombing of the AMIA (Asociación Mutual Israelita Argentina) building in Buenos Aires. In the summer of 2002, the *New York Times* reported that the Iranian government financed the bombing, and that they paid off police officers and gave then-president Menem $10,000,000 to cover up the attack. In March 2003 the Argentine government indicted a group of Iranian nationals for the bombing. In October 2006, two Argentinean prosecutors formally accused the government of Iran of sponsoring the bombing and Hezbollah of carrying it out, charges that were denied by the accused.

8. The Outlaw Jews of Buenos Aires

1. Nor is it for Nathan Englander, whose novel *The Ministry of Special Cases* brings the history of Argentina's outlaw Jews together with the recent history of the Dirty War (see chapter 10). Englander's novel was published in 2007, after this study had been completed.

2. The appeal of the story of outlaw Jews is not limited to Jewish authors. Leonard Schraeder's 1991 film, *Naked Tango*, deals with a Jewish-owned Buenos Aires brothel in the 1920s. In that film, a Gentile woman, bored with marriage to an older man, takes on the identity of a woman who has committed suicide on board a ship bound for Argentina and finds herself sold into prostitution. The story on which the film is based was written by an Argentine, Manuel Puig.

3. Most Argentinean Jewish writers and filmmakers who narrate Jewish themes do not deal with the Jewish underworld. (One exception is Nora Glickman who in one work [2000] reclaims the life of Raquel Liberman, a Jewish prostitute. Glickman is also a scholar, whose study of Jewish prostitution in Buenos Aires includes a catalogue of literary works on the theme.) Their major theme is, rather, the place of Jews in Argentina. Early writers, whose primary exemplar is Alberto Gerchunoff,

concern themselves with establishing Jews as good Argentine citizens. Later ones narrate the challenges of maintaining both an Argentine and a Jewish identity.

4. See Donna Guy (1992) on this era, and Jewish participation. As Nora Glickman (2000) notes, Guy says that the actual proportion of Jews engaged in the traffic in women was exaggerated by a public happy to have a Jewish scapegoat onto whom the blame for moral decay and criminality could be pinned. A quick check on the Internet turns up an anti-Semetic white supremacist site that continues to perpetrate the notion of Jew as criminal.

5. Singer grew up on the Warsaw street he writes about in *Scum;* Katz knows Poland as she knows Argentina, from the outsider's knowledge that comes from brief visits and stories heard and read, and a good dose of research.

6. As Singer said in his Nobel acceptance speech (1978): "The storyteller of our time, as in any other time, must be an entertainer of the spirit in the full sense of the word, not just a preacher of social and political ideals. There is no paradise for bored readers and no excuse for tedious literature that does not intrigue the reader, uplift his spirit, give him the joy and the escape that true art always grants. Nevertheless, it is also true that the serious writer of our time must be deeply concerned about the problems of his generation."

7. In Bona's *Argentina* sexual desire in reference to Sarah is displaced onto her marriageability. Jean, the protagonist who ultimately does marry her, is attracted by her asexual coolness, as well as by her father's fortune. Jean's sexual needs are met by Mandoline, a French prostitute who offers not the excitement of difference, but rather the comfort of the familiar. Of all the people Jean meets during his Argentine adventure, Mandoline is the one whose class and national background most closely resemble his own.

8. Reyzl's sister is a character barely alluded to. She is important to the plot because she knows Max's past history and can therefore uncover his lies. At the same time, she allows him his fantasy of going back to the world of petty crime to which he feels so drawn.

9. The term "white slavery" as a synonym for the traffic in women is problematic. Certainly naming the kidnapping of women and girls and forcing them to work as prostitutes as a form of slavery is apt. The adjective "white," though, can be seen as a contrast to the trade in Black bodies (slavery unmodified, the dominant form) that implies that the trade in Black people for their labor did not include sexual exploitation. "White slavery" also implies that all the women victimized were white, which was not the case, especially given the racial coding of the era. And it can play on the also highly problematic white = good, black = bad metaphor to suggest that somehow this was a less brutalizing practice than "ordinary" slavery.

10. Sofia acknowledges that some women do choose prostitution in Argentina over a dull and pious family life in Poland, but they are hardly in the majority: "To be absolutely truthful, there were some women who knew what was up right from the start and went along with it anyway. For them, a whore's life seemed much more exciting than a thousand years stuck at their father's dull table, and a second thousand years stuck at a husband's dull table, and then an eternity as the dull husband's footstool in heaven" (Katz 1997, 76).

11. In contrast, Bona's Mandoline finds the same solace in Jean that he finds in her.

9. Dirty War Stories

1. Not surprisingly, the strip's title is "Banana Republic." It ran for about two years in the *Minneapolis Star Tribune* beginning in 2005.

2. Diana Taylor (1997) is enormously helpful in explaining how a nation under dictatorship and the resistance to it are performed.

3. For an extraordinary fictional account of such willful blindness under similar conditions in Uruguay, see Cristina Peri Rossi's "Lovelys."

4. See my discussion of Luisa Valenzuela's *Como en la guerra* (He who searches) in Kaminsky (1999).

5. For example, as García-Gorena (1999) shows, the Antinuclear Committee of Vera Cruz Mothers in Mexico modeled itself on the Mothers of the Plaza de Mayo, as did the Mothers of the New York Disappeared, a group working to repeal the Rockefeller drug laws.

6. Alicia Partnoy (1986), Nora Strejilevich (1997), Ricardo Piglia (1992), Luisa Valenzuela (1975). See Kaminsky (1999) and Mary Beth Tierney-Tello (1996) for further discussion of some of these texts.

7. See Jara (1986) and Beverley (1989) on *testimonio*.

8. Jean Franco writes that Thornton uses "torture and disappearance to add piquancy and sensation" and calls his depictions of torture "banal" (2002, 244).

9. Magic realism, associated with writers like Alejo Carpentier, Gabriel García Márquez, and Elena Garro, is a mode that has gone out of style, at least with serious literary critics, despite its continued popularity with readers. Part of the reason *Imagining Argentina* was disdained by Latin Americanists is precisely that it imitates magic realism, deploying it in an Argentine setting, where it never really had much hold. The contemporary Argentine baroque was always more about word play and mind games than about the sensuality of lush images and larger-than-life stories.

10. Two other plays are performed in the course of the novel, both by Carlos's children's theater. In them, the performance is not about denunciation, but about engendering hope and memory.

11. I thank Patricia McGurk for bringing Hackl's work to my attention. Since to my knowledge *Sara und Simon* has not been translated from the original German, my comments on it are based on Gabriele Eckart's discussion of the novel (2001).

12. In the 1980s Jeane Kirkpatrick famously differentiated between authoritarian and totalitarian states, using Argentina as a prototype, as if torture committed by right-wing states were more benign than the suffering perpetrated by regimes of the far left.

13. See, for example, Alicia Partnoy's darkly comic treatment of her torturers' use of Nazi slogans and threats in the stories she tells of her own disappearance (1986).

14. Nevertheless, the Holocaust and the Dirty War do not vie for dominance in the text. As Michael Rothberg reminds us, it is dangerous to assign primacy to a particular memory, here the memory of the Holocaust, which in fact overlaps, marks, and is marked by other traumatic histories: "Memory is not a zero-sum game. In place of memory competition I propose a concept of multidirectional memory, which recognizes the dynamic transfers that take place between diverse places and times during remembrance. Instead of proceeding from the assumption that the

presence of one history in collective memory entails the erasure or dilution of all others, [I pay] close attention to the circulation of historical memories in encounters whose meanings are complex and overdetermined" (2004, 1233–34).

15. I am grateful to Leslie Morris, Keith Cohen, and Michael Bernard Donals for bringing Perec's *W* to my attention.

16. Many thanks to Mary Ellen Bieder for introducing me to Riera's novel.

17. One reviewer faults him for jamming the novel too full of facts, leaving little room for anything else: "While Unger succeeds in conveying the horror of this time in Argentina's history and his outrage at the lack of world attention to the genocide, this potentially compelling novel is so weighed down with facts and figures that it leaves out any sense of drama or personal involvement" (Ross 2004, unpaginated).

18. Koning bungles certain details and falls back on cliché. For example, his reference to Che Guevara—whose family would not have thought of him as "Che," since that was a nickname he received once he joined forces with Fidel Castro, which in effect marked him as an Argentine and differentiated him from the rest— is facile and predictable.

19. As we have seen in chapter 7, Vázquez Montalbán's countryman, Antonio Muñoz Molina, also creates characters who are fascinated by what is for them the exotic Jewish presence in Argentina.

20. See chapters 2 and 3.

10. Violent Exclusions

1. At the other end of the spectrum is the 1991 made-for-television Spanish docudrama *El lado oscuro* (The dark side), by director Gonzalo Suárez, which dramatizes the interrogation of a torturer named Francisco Andrés Valdés. Suárez used tapes provided by the lawyer who conducted the interrogation to write the script.

2. *Two to Tango*, a low-budget U.S.-Argentinean coproduction made for U.S. audiences, also associates the Argentine assassination plot with tango, although in this case the tango is a subordinate theme. In her discussion of the rewriting of José Pablo Feinmann's script, *Últimos días de la víctima*, as *Two to Tango*, Tamara Falicov (2004) details the elements added to the U.S. version of the film that respond to cultural commonplaces concerning Argentina: the tango bar and the tango-dancing femme fatale, as well as Nazis in hiding and the collapsing of the Colombian drug trade into the Argentine setting. None of these elements is present in the Argentine version of the film.

3. The low number represents government figures; the high number comes from human rights organizations. Papa Benevento's testimony in Unger's *Voices from Silence* (1995) speaks to the difference. In that novel the truth commission was willing to hear about the loss of one son, but the other was not part of the official record.

4. George Bush appoints an attorney general who justifies torture as an instrument of war and calls the Geneva conventions quaint. Only the overweening sense of exceptionalism allows the American public to think that they are exempt from the fallout of such official pronouncements and the behavior that follows upon it.

5. "Wong has stressed that *Happy Together* was inspired by contemporary Latin American fiction, Manuel Puig's *The Buenos Aires Affair* in particular: 'I was besotted with the title and always wanted to use it for one of my pictures. Then, after the shooting in Buenos Aires, I finally realized the film is really not about the city, so my long cherished title went out of the window and I needed to come up with something new'" (Rosenbaum 1997, unpaginated).

6. "It's one of the recurring jokes in Wong's movies that no matter where the characters travel, they end up in the same crummy bars and apartments and fast-food joints. That every place looks like every place else is both Wong's comment on the way pop culture has remade the world and a comic rejoinder to 'one world, one people' platitudes" (C. Taylor 2004, unpaginated).

7. Passing as an Englishman in the midst of Argentineans, Adrian's drama is also the drama of the film. According to the International Movie Database (http://www.imdb.com/), Martin Donovan, the director of *Apartment Zero,* was born and raised in Argentina, where his name was Carlos Enrique Valero y Peralta-Ramos. Donovan studied film and drama in England, and he has made his career primarily in the United States, writing for television and writing and directing movies, none of which, with the exception of *Apartment Zero,* have any discernable Argentine content.

8. I discuss the symbolic link between mother and nation at length in Kaminsky (1999).

9. The place where the novel takes its political stand is around HIV/AIDS, and the solution is individualistic. Despite the presence of a doctor who is selflessly working in a clinic that attends to all those with the disease, the ultimate solution with reference to AIDS is intimate and born of privilege: embrace your lover, stand by your friends, take your meds.

10. Nathan Englander also successfully exploits the theme of deliberate, even active forgetting in *The Ministry of Special Cases.* The respectable Jews of Buenos Aires, children of gangsters and prostitutes, hire the novel's protagonist to efface their parents' names from the tombstones in the Jewish thieves' cemetary in order to obliterate a past that would connect them to unsavory behavior and might call attention to them and put them in danger during the time of the Proceso.

11. The Persistence of Memory

1. The nightclub scene, through which ordinary people could imagine themselves into a life of wealth and glamour, is so familiar from depression-era films that Woody Allen parodies it in *The Purple Rose of Cairo.*

2. In the early 1940s Walt Disney sent a crew to Argentina to scout for ideas, and there, according to local story, he found the color he would later use for *Bambi* on the bark of a tree native to Patagonia. The part live-action, part animated feature *Saludos Amigos* was a result of this trip.

3. May argues that the interest in making movies in exotic locales continued to play a role in U.S. foreign policy into the 1950s and 1960s. He says, "Hollywood in the postwar era wanted to preach tolerance and understanding of the wider world. So these films were seen as serving that function. [In addition], many were made

abroad because foreign countries were not letting American companies take their money out from film sales. [Filming locally was one way to recoup those earnings.] Lastly, these films were seen as an extension of the good American Way of Life that would help win the Cold War by showing Americans as tolerant, affluent and playful" (personal communication).

4. Note here how Hayworth's Spanish background (on her father's side) is coded not as (unmarked/white) European, but as (raced) Latin, reflecting the complexity of southern European immigration. The racialization of southern Europeans in the United States, the racial meaning of "Spanish" (whether from Spain or the Americas), and the Cansinos' own act, which blended different forms of Spanish and Latin American dance, all speak to the malleability of the markers of Spanishness, *latinidad,* and racial difference.

5. Lary May reproduces this photograph in his study *The Big Tomorrow* as part of his analysis of racial construction in the films of the 1940s.

6. Four years later Hayworth is back in Buenos Aires in *Gilda,* whose eponymous heroine is perhaps Hayworth's most famous role. This time, playing a North American nightclub singer in Buenos Aires, Hayworth is simply white, and not problematically so. Nevertheless, she is once again associated with the familiar-exotic locale, the Argentine nightclub world that in this film is far darker and more dangerous than it is in *You Were Never Lovelier.*

7. Menkes is an extraordinarily powerful figure in the world of fashion. Her pronouncements on designers' collections affect reputations and can have profound economic consequences.

8. Menkes's article came out in early July 2001. Later that month, there was another G-8 meeting, in which the world's eight most economically powerful nations considered international economic issues, this time in Genoa. As did the other G-8 meetings after Seattle, it sparked demonstrations locally and internationally, including in Argentina, which was faced with its economy's collapse.

9. *El Argos,* which came out first as a bimonthly and then as a biweekly, was published on government presses, and its European tastes prefigured by a century Victoria Ocampo's *Sur* (Shumway 1991, 87).

10. The figure of Julio may have been inspired in part by the noted Argentine writer Ricardo Güiraldes, an accomplished dancer and scion of a wealthy cattle-raising family, raised on an *estancia,* who, according to his biographer, introduced the tango to Parisian society in 1910 (Bordelois 1966, 32).

11. The journalist's research in the novel emerges in such details as the reporting of population statistics and the references to the presidency of Irigoyen and its effect on European investment.

12. Her protagonist's experience of Argentina is a catalogue of nineteenth- and early twentieth-century visions of that country. He encounters the Argentina of Europe, produced and circulated at a time when Argentina's cultural compass pointed toward France. The disputes between the literary groups of the neighborhoods of bourgeois Florida and working-class Boedo, between a Europeanized Argentina and a home-grown one, between the appeal of European modernism and a desire to document the lives of ordinary people, of two different kinds of textual experimentation, the modernism of Borges and Güiraldes and the expressionism of Arlt—all this was on the verge of happening in real life when the fictional Jean set foot on Argentine soil.

13. "'Mais vous, jeune homme, qu'allez-vous donc chercher en Argentine?' reprit le vieux Goldberg quand on servit le 'Suprême de Bar.'

"'L'avenir, monsieur,' prononça Jean."

14. "Il s'était inventé une Argentine amoureuse, cajoleuse et sublime, toute à l'image des eaux du rio de la Plata. Fleuve d'argent.... Comme la nacre des poissons scintillants de l'Atlantique qui sautaient les vagues, ou comme le manteau d'une fée. Rio de la Plata... De l'avant du bateau où à chaque heure du jour il cherchait à perte de vue son avenir, c'est une étoile que apparaissait. L'Argentine, un mirage aux éclats de pierre de lune. La Plata... Jean succombait à l'attrait de ce nom."

15. "La Plata... Que ce nom avait donc de mystérieux pouvoirs! Jean, plein d'espoir de d'enthousiasme, regardait le soleil envahir la pièce. Il était rendu à son rêve. Toute l'Argentine miroitait dans sa petite chambre.

"Il se leva, prit une feuille blanche et écrivit 'Je vous aime.'"

16. "Un rire lui répondit, un vrai rire de gorge, sensuel et gai. Il appartenait à la dame installée de l'autre côté du bel amputé de guerre. Jean lui trouva le type andalou des héroïnes de Barrès avec plus de santé. Elle était brune. Des reflets fauves dans les cheveux, des yeux brûlants, et les plus belle épaules du monde. Quelque chose de la madone dans la perfection des traits, et de la fille publique dans l'étalage impudique et abondant de sa poitrine....

"Marta était argentine. C'est ce que Jean comprit par la suite, tandis que se croisaient dans un agréable désordre des répliques dont le sens lui échappait trop souvent. Il en ignorait jusqu'à l'esprit."

17. "Pour Jean, la fortune était avec l'amour le mot le plus doux. Il se le répétait avec emphase, en espagnol: *Fortuna, Fortuna...*, comme un prénom de femme. L'idée encore abstraite, mais plus forte d'instant en instant, de ses futures conquêtes, le pénétrait de ferveur. Il voulait aimer. Et il voulait être riche. Il ignorait laquelle de ces deux voies menait à l'autre, s'il réussirait par les femmes ou si les femmes viendraient ensuite. Il espérait se concilier les dieux....

"'*Fortuna...*,' murmurait-il. '*Amor y fortuna...*,' les premiers mots d'une longue prière à la terre argentine."

18. "Jean ne se jugeat ni fou ni présomptueux devant l'ampleur de ses projets. Il s'en serait voulu d'être trop raisonnable. L'Argentine n'était pas une épouse à choisir. Jean la désirait comme une amante. Une amante riche, mais cependant amante."

19. When Jean tries to call on Liniers at the Jockey Club, he is snubbed (Bona 1986, 63–64).

20. "Las cartas de aquel lejano tío a quien mucho queríamos en casa y a quien escribíamos con frecuencia, nos traían una fiesta cada vez que llegaban. Se leían en familia. Mi tío nos hablaba largamente de las bellezas de Buenos Aires; pero yo, cuántas veces pensaba en mi excelente y querido tío, lo veía caminando con grandísimo trabajo entre lianas gigantescas, papagayos, monillos y serpientes.

"Todos reían de la estrafalaria pintura que yo hacía de Buenos Aires, y mi padre se dirigía hacia su biblioteca para traer un gran libro de viajes donde había, en profusión, lindas vistas de aquella ciudad, con sus hermosas y amplias calles, cruzadas en todas direcciones por automóviles, coches y tranvías; con sus edificios hermosos; con sus bellas mujeres, vestidas lujosamente; con su Río de la Plata, luciente y brillador como los diamantes; El Paseo de Palermo tenía un aspecto aristocrático; allí según decía mi tío, se daba cita lo más distinguido de la sociedad. No cabía duda alguna: Buenos Aires era una ciudad completamente a la europea. Pero mi capricho era más grande que todo y mi loca imaginación no le iba en zaga; así, nunca admitía en mi pensamiento que el tío Leonardo no anduviese traficando entre bosques negros y apretados, llenos a reventar, de loros y culebras. Para mí, en aquello estaba el atractivo.

"Por eso las cartas que llegaban de América me producían un placer inexplicable."

21. "Elle ne portait pas de peignoir, simplement une chemise courte en voile sous laquelle elle se révélait toute harnachée de cuir. A la fois risible et tragique. Des lanières s'entrecroissaient en tous sens du cou aux jarretières. De gros clous marquaient un large ceinturon. Un triangle de cuir couvrait le pubis. Amazone, 'gaucha,' vierge sadique, putain maya . . . on aurait pu l'imaginer descendante d'icônes cruelles, ou surgie d'un jardin des supplices. Jean n'éprouvait du reste aucun penchant pour de si hideux raffinements, qui lui donnaient même plutôt la nausée."

22. In contrast to Mandoline and her overdetermined costume, Thadea dresses in an explorer's outfit. Thadea is mestiza, though not an Argentinean, and, interestingly, she is Jean's passionate and true love at the end of the novel (Bona 1986, 202ff). Her mother was Mayan and her father Swedish. Thadea maintains that Argentina is a cultural wasteland because it has no great indigenous cultures, but that it is a delight for botanists. On the other hand, she says that she is considered inferior by the Argentines because she is mixed-blood.

23. Other female characters, especially those written by men, do not so much have identity as represent or reflect someone else's. Blasco Ibáñez's Elena, the rather stupid and utterly shallow "romantic" daughter of the cattle baron Madariaga in *Los cuatro jinetes del Apocalipsis,* is entranced by her prospective husband's noble German lineage. Once they marry, Elena takes on his pretensions to aristocracy and his faith in German superiority, and she is utterly uncritical about Germany's conduct in the war. Her sister Luisa, the "spiritual" one, is the acquiescent wife and mother without much in the way of a personality of her own. Whereas the men—Madariaga, his son-in-law Marcelo, and his grandson Julio—all carve out an identity that reconciles Europe and Argentina, the women merely reflect that identity back upon them. Julio discovers his moral fiber in Europe; his sister becomes conventionally trivial. The most extreme example of this is in Claudio Magris's *A Different Sea,* in which the male protagonist works out his identity in the empty space of Argentina, and the few female characters serve as outlets for his sexual desires, take care of his physical needs, or listen to his mostly falsified stories of his Argentine adventures, which he tailors to his assumptions of what will most hold their interest.

24. See Savigliano (1995) for a thorough and outstanding analysis of tango and what her book title names "the political economy of passion." While it would be impossible to undertake a study like the present one without some mention of tango, I have kept the discussion here brief because I do not pretend to approach Savigliano's expertise on the subject. Her insights into the tango as a site of (post)colonial relations are particularly noteworthy.

25. Mindy Aloff, for example, points out that the woman is not simply a passive partner in the dance, but rather she dances "with an attitude that is creative and active rather than passive or submissive" (1999, 34).

26. Still another German text, Fritz Hochwälder's *The Holy Experiment,* takes place in Buenos Aires, although its main characters are European Jesuits with a mission in Paraguay. The setting is incidental, and the incident that precipitates the

action serves primarily as the occasion for the author to deal with lofty ideas about obedience, religion, and ethics. It is assumed that the Jesuits are heroes because they offer salvation and an easier life than do the evil landowners, who simply exploit the Indians.

27. In this it might be considered the inverse of *Last Tango in Paris,* in which, as dance critic Mindy Aloff argues, the tango as dance form is "ridiculed, parodied, and smashed into smithereens" (1999, 35). The tango dancers in *Last Tango* merely mime the true passion of the lovers.

Bibliography

Achugar, Hugo. 2000. "'Nuestro norte es el Sur': A propósito de representaciones y localizaciones." In *Nuevas perspectivas desde/sobre América Latina: El desafío de los estudios culturales,* ed. Mabel Moraña, 319–34. Santiago: Editorial Cuarto Propio/ Instituto Internacional de Literatura Iberoamericana.

Alberdi, Juan Bautista. 1852. *Las "Bases" de Alberdi.* Ed. Jorge Mayer. Repr., Buenos Aires: Sudamericana, 1969.

Aleichem, Sholem (pseudonym of Shalom Rabinowitz). 1949. "The Man from Buenos Aires." In *Tevye's Daughters,* trans. Frances Butwin, 128–40. New York: Crown.

Aloff, Mindy. 1999. "Mindy Aloff on Dance: After the Last Tango." *New Republic,* August 2, 33–38.

Anderson, Benedict. 1983. *Imagined Communities: Reflections on the Origin and Spread of Nationalism.* London: Verso.

Anderson, Joseph, and Barbara Anderson. 1993. "The Myth of Persistence of Vision Revisited." *Journal of Film and Video* 45, no. 1 (Spring): 3–12.

Andrews, George Reid. 1980. *The Afro-Argentines of Buenos Aires: 1800–1900.* Madison: University of Wisconsin Press.

———. 2004. *Afro-Latin America: 1800–2000.* Oxford: Oxford University Press.

Aponte-Ramos, Dolores. 1999. "Cuando la pampa se colorea: los negros en la Argentina decimonónica." *Revista Iberoamericana* 65, nos. 188–89 (July–December): 733–39.

Appadurai, Arjun. 1996. *Modernity at Large: Cultural Dimensions of Globalization.* Minneapolis: University of Minnesota Press.

Arambel-Güiñazú, María Cristina. 1993. *La escritura de Victoria Ocampo: Memorias, seducción, "Collage."* Buenos Aires: Edicial.

Argentine Commission on the Disappeared. 1986. *Nunca Más. Never Again.* New York: Faber and Faber. (Originally published as *Nunca más: Informe de la Comisión Nacional sobre Desaparición de Personas,* Buenos Aires: EUDEBA, 1984.)

Asch, Sholem. 1907. *Got fun Nekome.* Repr., *The God of Vengeance: Drama in Three Acts.* Trans. Isaac Goldberg. Boston: Stratford, 1918.

Auster, Paul. 2002. *The Book of Illusions.* New York: Henry Holt.

Azorín (José Martínez Ruiz). 1925. *Doña Inés (Historia de amor).* Madrid: Editorial Caro Raggio. (Repr. Madrid: Clásicos Castalia, 1990.)

Bakhtin, Mikhail. 1981. "Forms of Time and of the Chronotope in the Novel: Notes Towards a Historical Poetics." In *The Dialogic Imagination: Four Essays,* ed. Michael Holquist, trans. Caryl Emerson and Michael Holquist, 84–258. Austin: University of Texas Press.

Balderston, Daniel. 1993. *Out of Context: Historical Reference and the Representation of Reality in Borges.* Durham: Duke University Press.

Bayer, Osvaldo. 1998. *Severino Di Giovanni: El idealista de la violencia.* Buenos Aires: Planeta.

Beardsell, Peter. 2000. *Europe and Latin America: Returning the Gaze.* Manchester: Manchester University Press.

Beauvoir, Simone de. 1953. *The Second Sex.* Trans. H. M Parshley. New York: Knopf. (Originally published as *La deuxieme sexe,* 2 vols., Paris: Gallimard, 1949.)

Belli, Gioconda. 1998. *Waslala.* Barcelona: Emecé.

Beltrán, Rosa. 1999. "Interview with Luisa Valenzuela." *La Jornada* (Mexico), January 31, http://www.monmouth.edu/~pgacarti/V-entrevista-Valenzuela.htm (accessed December 2, 2001).

Benedetti, Mario. 1999. *Buzón de tiempo.* Buenos Aires: Seix Barral.

Beverley, John. 1989. "The Margin at the Center: On Testimonio." Repr. in *Testimonio: On the Politics of Truth.* Minneapolis: University of Minnesota Press, 2004.

Bhabha, Homi K. 1994. "Of Mimicry and Man: The Ambivalence of Colonial Discourse." In *The Location of Culture,* 85–92. New York: Routledge.

Biagini, Hugo E. 2000. "¿Qué son los argentinos?" *Cuadernos Hispanoamericanos* 598 (April): 113–19.

Bivar, Antonio. 1999. "As if Virgina Woolf Were a Great Brazilian Writer." *Virginia Woolf Miscellany* 54 (Fall): 2.

Blasco Ibáñez, Vicente. 1916. *Los cuatro jinetes del Apocalipsis.* Repr., Madrid: Alianza, 1998.

Bona, Dominique. 1986. *Argentina.* Cher: Mercure de France (copyright 1984).

Bordelois, Ivonne. 1966. *Genio y figura de Ricardo Güiraldes.* Buenos Aires: Editorial Universitaria de Buenos Aires.

Borges, Jorge Luis. 1967a. "Story of the Warrior and the Captive." Trans. Irving Feldman. In *A Personal Anthology,* 170–74. New York: Grove Press. (Originally published as "El cautivo" in *El hacedor,* Buenos Aires: Alianza, 1960.)

———. 1967b. "The Captive." Trans. Elaine Kerrigan. In *A Personal Anthology,* 175. New York: Grove Press. (Originally published as "Historia del guerrero y de la cautiva" in *El Aleph,* Buenos Aires: Emecé, 1949.)

———. 1967c. "The Zahir." Trans. Anthony Kerrigan. In *A Personal Anthology,* 128–37. New York: Grove Press. (Originally published as "El zahir" in *El Aleph,* Buenos Aires: Emecé, 1949.)

———. 1971a. "La escritura del Dios." In *El Aleph,* 117–24. Buenos Aires: Emecé.

———. 1971b. "Las ruinas circulares." In *Ficciones,* 61–69. Buenos Aires: Emecé; Madrid: Alianza.

———. 1975. *El libro de arena.* Buenos Aires: Emecé.

Bruce, James. 1953. *Those Perplexing Argentines.* New York: Longmans, Green.

Calvino, Italo. 1983. "The Argentine Ant." In *Adam, One Afternoon and Other Stories,* trans. Archibald Colquhoun and Peggy Wright, 155–90. London: Secker and Warburg.

Carlson Lombardi, Angela. 2002. "Mapping Memory: Cultural Representations of the Proceso." PhD diss., University of Minnesota.

Chávez, Fermín. 1973. *José Hernández.* 2nd ed. Buenos Aires: Plus Ultra.

Chow, Rey. 1993. *Writing Diaspora: Tactics of Intervention in Contemporary Cultural Studies.* Bloomington: Indiana University Press.

Christie, Agatha. 1923. *Murder on the Links.* n.p.: Dodd, Mead. (Repr., New York: Bantam, 1985.)

———. 1927. *The Big Four.* n.p.: Dodd, Mead. (Repr., New York: Berkley, 1984.)

———. 1933. *Lord Edgware Dies.* n.p.: Grosset & Dunlap. (Repr., New York: Berkley, 1984.)

———. 1936a. *The A.B.C. Murders.* n.p.: Dodd, Mead. (Repr., New York: Berkely, 1991.)

———. 1936b. *Cards on the Table.* London: William Collins & Sons.

———. 1937. *Dumb Witness.* (Original title: *Poirot Loses a Client.*) Repr., New York: Bantam, 1985.

———. 1939. "The Yellow Iris" (1937 radio play adapted as short story). In *The Regatta Mystery and Other Stories.* New York: Dodd, Mead.

———. 1943. "The Soul of the Croupier," in *The Mysterious Mr. Quin.* In *Triple Threat: Exploits of Three Famous Detectives.* New York: Dodd, Mead. (Originally published, London: William Collins & Sons, 1930.)

———. 1944. *Sparkling Cyanide (Remembered Death).* Repr., New York: Harper Collins, 1985.

Combahee River Collective. 1977. "Black Feminist Statement." Repr. in *Homegirls: A Black Feminist Anthology,* ed. B. Smith et al., 272–82. New York: Kitchen Table, Women of Color Press, 1982.

Conrad, Joseph. 1902. *Heart of Darkness.* Repr., New York: Dover, 1990.

———. 1904. *Nostromo.* Ed. Ruth Nadelhaft. Repr., Ontario: Broadview Literary Texts, 1997.

———. 1969. *Joseph Conrad's Letters to R. B. Cunninghame Graham.* Ed. C. T. Watts. Cambridge: Cambridge University Press.

Dailey, Janet. 1985. *The Glory Game.* New York: Poseidon Press.

Daly, Mary. 1978. *Gyn/Ecology: The Metaethics of Radical Feminism.* Boston: Beacon Press.

Davis, Nira Yuval. 1997. *Gender and Nation.* London: Sage.

DeKoven, Marianne. 1991. *Rich and Strange: Gender, History, Modernism.* Princeton, N.J.: Princeton University Press.

Delaney, Jeane. 1998. "Making Sense of Modernity: Changing Attitudes toward the Immigrant and the Gaucho in Turn-of-the-Century Argentina." *Cultural Critique,* Spring, 434–59.

Dreier, Katherine S. 1920. *Five Months in the Argentine from a Woman's Point of View, 1918–1919.* New York: Frederic Fairchild Sherman.

Dussel, Enrique. 1995. *The Invention of the Americas: Eclipse of the "Other" and the Myth of Modernity.* New York: Continuum.

Dyson, Ketaki Kushari. 1988. *In Your Blossoming Flower Garden: Rabindranath Tagore and Victoria Ocampo.* New Delhi: Sahitya Akademi.

————. 1989. *Memories of Argentina and Other Poems*. Kidlington: Virgilio Libro.

Eckart, Gabriele. 2001. "Latin American Dictatorship in Erich Hackl's *Sara und Simon* and Miguel Angel Asturias's *El señor presidente.*" *The Comparatist* 25:69–88.

Eco, Umberto. 1984. *The Name of the Rose*. Trans. William Weaver. San Diego: Harcourt Brace Jovanovich.

Edschmid, Kasimir. 1930. "Die Beiden Feinschmecker." In *Hallo Welt! 16 Erzählungen*, 147–70. Hamburg: Paul Zsolnay Verlag.

————. 1956. *El mariscal y la dama (Los amores de Simón Bolívar)*. Trans. Victor Scholz (original title: *Der Marschall und die Gnade*). Barcelona: Editorial AHR.

Englander, Nathan. 1999. "The Tumblers." In *For the Relief of Unbearable Urges*, 25–55. New York: Alfred A. Knopf.

————. 2007. *The Ministry of Special Cases*. New York: Knopf.

Enloe, Cynthia. 2000. *Bananas, Beaches and Bases: Making Feminist Sense of International Politics*. 2nd ed. Berkeley and Los Angeles: University of California Press.

Enriqueta, María (pseudonym of María Enriqueta Camarillo de Pereyra). 1922. *El secreto*. Madrid: Editorial America.

Erdinast-Vulcan, Daphna. 1996. "*Nostromo* and the Failure of Myth." In *New Casebooks: Joseph Conrad*, ed. Elaine Jordan, 128–45. New York: St. Martin's.

Etchenique, Jorge. 2000. *Pampa libre: Anarquistas en la pampa argentina*. Santa Rosa, Argentina: Ediciones Amerindia/Universidad Nacional de Quilmes.

Falicov, Tamara L. 2004. "U.S.-Argentine Co-productions, 1982–1990: Roger Corman, Aries Productions, 'Schlockbuster' Movies, and the International Market." *Film & History: An Interdisciplinary Journal of Film and Television Studies* 34, no. 1: 31–38.

Feitlowitz, Marguerite. 1998. *A Lexicon of Terror: Argentina and the Legacies of Torture*. Oxford: Oxford University Press.

Felski, Rita. 1995. *The Gender of Modernity*. Cambridge, Mass.: Harvard University Press.

Fernández Moreno, César, and Jorge Horacio Becco. 1968. *Antología lineal de la poesía argentina*. Madrid: Gredos.

Ferrari, Roberto A. 1999. "El país motorizado: la Exposición Internacional de Ferrocarriles y Transportes Terrestres." In *Buenos Aires 1910: El imaginario para una gran capital*, ed. Margarita Gutman and Thomas Reese, 229–40. Buenos Aires: Eudeba (Centro de Estudios Avanzados, Universidad de Buenos Aires).

Festinger, Leon. 1957. *A Theory of Cognitive Dissonance*. Evanston, Ill.: Row Peterson.

Fey, Ingrid E. 2000. "Peddling the Pampas: Argentina at the Paris Universal Exposition of 1889." In *Latin American Popular Culture: An Introduction*, ed. William H. Beezley and Linda A. Curcio-Nagy, 61–85. Wilmington, Del.: SR Books.

Foster, K. 1977. "To Serve and Protect: Textualizing the Falklands Conflict." *Cultural Studies* 11, no. 2 (May): 235–52.

France, Miranda. 1998. *Bad Times in Buenos Aires: A Writer's Adventures in Argentina*. London: Weidenfeld and Nicolson.

Franco, Jean. 1975. "The Limits of the Liberal Imagination: One Hundred Years of Solitude and Nostromo." *Punto de Contacto/Point of Contact* 1, no. 1: 4–16.

————. 2002. *The Decline and Fall of the Lettered City: Latin America and the Cold War*. Cambridge, Mass.: Harvard University Press.

Freixas, Laura. 2005. *Amor o lo que sea*. Barcelona: Destino.

Freud, Sigmund. 1919. "The Uncanny" [Das Unheimliche]. From Standard Edition, vol. 17, trans. James Strachey, 217–56. London: Hogarth Press, 1955.

Frye, Marilyn. 1983. The Politics of Reality: Essays in Feminist Theory. Freedom, Calif.: Crossing Press.

Fuentes, Carlos. 1974. La nueva novela hispanoamericana. Mexico City: Editorial Joaquín Moritz.

Gárate, Miriam. 2000. "Atracción y repulsión: En torno a la gauchesca de gaúchos y de gauchos." Revista Iberoamericana 66, no. 192 (July–September): 533–44.

García Canclini, Néstor. 2000. "La épica de la globalización y el melodrama de la interculturalidad." In Nuevas perspectivas desde/sobre América Latina: El desafío de los estudios culturales, ed. Mabel Moraña, 31–41. Santiago: Editorial, Cuarto Propio/ Instituto Internacional de Literatura Iberoamericana.

García-Gorena, Velma. 1999. Mothers and the Mexican Antinuclear Power Movement. Tucson: University of Arizona Press.

Garro, Elena. 1969. Recollections of Things to Come. Trans. Ruth L. C. Simms. Repr., Austin: University of Texas Press, 1986. (Orginally published as Los recuerdos del porvenir, Mexico City: Joaquín Mortiz, 1963; repr. 1993.)

Glickman, Nora. 2000. The Jewish White Slave Trade and the Untold Story of Raquel Liberman. New York: Garland.

Goodman, Allegra. 1999. Katterskill Falls. New York: Random House.

Güiraldes, Ricardo. 1926. Don Segundo Sombra. Buenos Aires: Editoral Proa.

Gutiérrez, R., and A. Sánchez. 1995. "Vicente Blasco Ibáñez en la Argentina." In Exiliados: la emigración cultural valenciana (siglos XVI–XX), ed. M. García, 1:115–26. Valencia: Generalitat Valenciana.

Gutiérrez Girardot, Rafael. 1990. "Borges in Germany: A Difficult and Contradictory Fascination." In Borges and His Successors: The Borgesian Impact on Literature and the Arts, ed. Edna Aizenberg, 59–79. Columbia: University of Missouri Press.

Guy, Donna. 1992. Sex and Danger in Buenos Aires: Prostitution, Family and Nation in Argentina. Lincoln: University of Nebraska Press.

Hackl, Erich. 1995. Sara und Simon. Zurich: Diogenes.

Hall, Stuart. 1997. "Old and New Identities, Old and New Ethnicities." In Culture, Globalization and the World-System: Contemporary Conditions for the Representation of Identity, ed. Anthony D. King, 41–68. Minneapolis: University of Minnesota Press.

Hausman, Bernice. 1990. "Words Between Women: Victoria Ocampo and Virginia Woolf." In In the Feminine Mode: Essays on Hispanic Women Writers, ed. Noël Valis and Carol Maier, 204–26. Lewisburg: Bucknell University Press.

Hernández, José. 1872. Martín Fierro. Repr., Buenos Aires: Librería "El Ateneo" Editorial, 1973.

———. 1963. The Gaucho Martín Fierro. Trans. Walter Owen. 2nd ed. Buenos Aires: Editorial Pampa.

———. 1974. The Gaucho Martín Fierro. Trans. Frank G. Carrino et al. Albany: State University of New York Press.

Higa, Marcelo G. 1999. "Inmigrantes de otros puertos: los japoneses en Buenos Aires hacia 1910." In Buenos Aires 1910: El imaginario para una gran capital, ed. Margarita Gutman and Thomas Reese, 295–316. Buenos Aires: Eudeba (Centro de Estudios Avanzados, Universidad de Buenos Aires).

Hochwälder, Fritz. 1998. *The Holy Experiment and Other Plays*. Trans. Todd C. Hanlin and Heidi L. Hutchinson. Riverside, Calif.: Aridane Press.

Hoffman, Eva. 1989. *Lost in Translation: A Life in a New Language*. New York: E. P. Dutton.

Hollinghurst, Alan. 2004. *The Line of Beauty*. London: Picador.

Holo, Selma Reuben. 1999. *Beyond the Prado: Museums and Identity in Democratic Spain*. Washington, D.C.: Smithsonian Institution Press.

Horan, Elizabeth, and Doris Meyer, eds. 2003. *This America of Ours: The Letters of Gabriela Mistral and Victoria Ocampo*. Austin: University of Texas Press.

Hull, Gloria T., Patricia Bell Scott, and Barbara Smith, eds. 1982. *All the Women Are White, All the Blacks Are Men, but Some of Us Are Brave*. New York: Feminist Press.

Iparraguirre, Sylvia. 1998. *La Tierra del Fuego*. Buenos Aires: Alfaguara. (Repr., Madrid: Punto de Lectura.)

Jackson, Peter, and Jan Penrose. 1993. "Introduction: Placing 'Race' and Nation." In *Constructions of Race, Place, and Nation*, ed. Peter Jackson and Jan Penrose, 1–23. Minneapolis: University of Minnesota Press.

Jameson, Fredric. 1996. "Romance and Reification: Plot Construction and Ideological Closure in *Nostromo*." In *New Casebooks: Joseph Conrad*, ed. Elaine Jordan, 116–27. New York: St. Martin's.

Jara, René. 1986. "Prólogo: Testimonio y literatura." In *Testimonio y literatura*, ed. René Jara and Hernán Vidal, 1–6. Minneapolis: Institute for the Studies of Ideologies and Literature.

Jitrik, Noé. 1998. "Autobiografías, Memorias, Diarios." *Literatura argentina contemporánea*. http://www.literatura.org/Jitrik/njT2.html (accessed October 14, 2004).

Jones, Tom B. 1949. *South America Rediscovered*. Minneapolis: University of Minnesota Press.

Jordan, Elaine. 1980. "Conrad's Latin American Adventure: 'An Obscure and Questionable Spoil.'" In *America in English Literature: Proceedings of the Symposium Organized by the Roehampton Institute, London, February*, 78–101. (London Institute)

Jung, C. G. 1973. *Letters*. Ed. Gerhard Adler and Aniela Jaffe. Trans. R. F. C. Hull. Vol 1. Princeton, N.J.: Princeton University Press.

Kaminsky, Amy. 1999. *After Exile: Writing the Latin American Diaspora*. Minneapolis: University of Minnesota Press.

Katz, Judith. 1997. *The Escape Artist*. Ithaca, N.Y.: Firebrand Books.

Keyserling, Hermann. 1932. *South American Meditations: On Hell and Heaven in the Soul of Man*. Trans. Theresa Duerr, in collaboration with the author. New York: Harper and Brothers.

———. 1933. *Meditaciones suramericanas*. Trans. Luis López-Ballesteros y de Torres. Madrid: Espasa-Calpe.

———. 1948. *Reise durch die Zeit*. Innsbruck: Verl. der Palme.

Kirschenbaum, Jules. 1990. "Dream of a Golem." In *Borges and His Successors: The Borgesian Impact on Literature and the Arts*, ed. Edna Aizenberg, 244–45. Columbia: University of Missouri Press.

Koning, Hans. 1998. "Naval Aviation." *The New Yorker*, February, 72–75.

Kosta, Barbara, and Richard W. McCormick. 1996. "Interview with Jutta Brückner." *Signs* 21, no. 2 (Winter): 343–73.

Lagos, María Inés. 1989. *H.A. Murena en sus ensayos y narraciones: De líder revisionista a marginado.* Santiago: Instituto Profesional del Pacífico.

Langton, Jane. 1999. *The Thief of Venice.* New York: Viking.

Laudato, Ricardo R. 1996. "Coordenadas sutiles in Kant, profesor de geografía de Vicente Fatone." *Saber y Tiempo* 2:143–48.

Laurence, Patricia, ed. 1999. "Virginia Woolf in/on Translation." *Virginia Woolf Miscellany* 54 (Fall): 1–2.

Lewis, Marvin. 1996. *Afro-Argentine Discourse: Another Dimension of the Black Diaspora.* Columbia: University of Missouri Press.

Ludmer, Josefina. 1988. *El género gauchesco: Un tratado sobre la patria.* Buenos Aires: Sudamericana.

Magagnoli, Maria Luisa. 1996. *Un caffe molto dolce.* n.p.: Bollati Boringhieri Editori.

———. 1997. *Un café muy dulce.* Trans. Guillermo Piro. Buenos Aires: Alfaguara.

Magris, Claudio. 1991. *Un altro mare.* Milano: Garzanti.

———. 1993. *A Different Sea.* Trans. M. S. Spurr. London: Harvill (Harper Collins).

Maraini, Dacia. 1999. "A Number on Her Arm." In *Darkness,* trans. Martha King, 104–10. South Royalton, Vt.: Steerforth Italia.

Marianacci, Dante. n.d. "Between Kafka and Joyce: A Conversation with Claudio Magris." Trans. Tomás Prásek. (internet interview, no address)

Marks, Elaine. 1996. "*Cendres Juives.*" In *Marrano as Metaphor: The Jewish Presence in French Writing,* 114–26. New York: Columbia University Press.

Marshik, Celia. 1999. "Publication and 'Public Women': Prostitution and Censorship in Three Novels by Virginia Woolf." *Modern Fiction Studies* 45, no. 4: 853–86.

Martel, Julián. 1891. *La bolsa.* Repr., Buenos Aires: W. M. Jacson, 1953.

Martínez de Codes, Rosa María. n.d. *El pensamiento argentino (1853–1910): Una aplicación histórica del método generacional.* Madrid: Editorial de la Universidad Complutense.

Martínez Estrada, Ezequiel. 1957. *La cabeza de Goliat: Microscopio de Buenos Aires.* Buenos Aires: Editorial Nova. (Originally published 1940.)

Marún, Giaconda. 1998. "Darwin y la literatura argentina." *La Torre* 3, no. 9: 551–77.

Masiello, Francine. 1992. *Between Civilization & Barbarism: Women, Nation, and Literary Culture in Modern Argentina.* Lincoln: University of Nebraska Press.

May, Lary. 2000. *The Big Tomorrow: Hollywood and the Politics of the American Way.* Chicago: University of Chicago Press.

McClintock, Anne. 1995. *Imperial Leather.* New York: Routledge.

McCutchan, Philip. 1995. *Assignment Argentina.* North Yorksire: Dales. (Originally published 1969.)

Menkes, Suzy. 2001. "Dior's Fashion Warriors Amid the Luxury." *International Herald Tribune,* July 3, 7.

Meyer, Doris. 1979. *Victoria Ocampo: Against the Wind and the Tide.* New York: George Brazillier.

Moreno, José Luis. 1999. "El viaje del conde Angelo de Gubernatis: Una perspectiva italiana." In *Buenos Aires 1910: El imaginario para una gran capital,* ed. Margarita Gutman and Thomas Reese, 157–69. Buenos Aires: Eudeba (Centro de Estudios Avanzados, Universidad de Buenos Aires).

Mothers of the New York Disappeared. 2004. Web site http://www.nymom.org/main.html (accessed December 6, 2004).

Muñoz Molina, Antonio. 1999. *Carlota Fainberg*. Madrid: Alfaguara.

————. 2001. *Sefarad: Una Novela de Novelas*. Madrid: Alfaguara.

Naipaul, V. S. 1974. "The Return of Eva Peron." Repr. in *The Return of Eva Peron*. New York: Vintage.

Narayan, Uma. 1997. *Dislocating Cultures: Identities, Traditions, and Third-World Feminism*. New York: Routledge.

Nestares, Carmen. 2001. *Venus en Buenos Aires*. Madrid: Odisea.

Nicolson, Nigel, and Joanne Trautmann. 1979a. *The Letters of Virginia Woolf*. Vol. 5, *1932–1935*. New York: Harcourt Brace Jovanovich.

————. 1979b. *The Letters of Virginia Woolf*. Vol. 6, *1936–1941*. New York: Harcourt Brace Jovanovich.

Ocampo, Victoria. 1935. "Carta a Virginia Woolf." In *Testimonios primera serie, 7–17*. Madrid: Revista de Occidente.

————. 1951. *El viajero y una de sus sombras: Keyserling en mis memorias*. Buenos Aires: Editorial Sudamericana.

————. 1975a. "Amistades." In *Testimonios novena serie, (1971–1974)*, 25–75. Buenos Aires: Editorial Sur.

————. 1975b. "Sur: Ese desconocido." In *Testimonios novena serie (1971–1974)*, 203–47. Buenos Aires: Editorial Sur.

————. 1977. "Mujeres en la Academia." In *Testimonios décima serie*, 13–23. Buenos Aires: Editorial Sur.

————. 1983. *Autobiografía V: Figuras simbólicas. Medida de Francia*. Buenos Aires: Ediciones Revista Sur.

Oddone, Jacinto. 1949. *Gremialismo proletario argentino*. Buenos Aires: Ediciones Líbera.

Ortner, Sherry. 1974. "Is Female to Male as Nature is to Culture?" In *Woman, Culture, and Society*, ed. Michelle Zimbalist Rosaldo and Louise Lamphere, 67–87. Stanford: Stanford University Press.

Pariani, Laura. 2005. *Cuando Dios bailaba el tango*. Trans. Patricia Orts (original title: *Quando Dio ballava il tango*, 2002). Valencia: Editorial Pre-Textos.

Partnoy, Alicia. 1986. *The Little School: Tales of Disappearance and Survival*. San Francisco: Cleis Press.

Paso, Leonardo, Enrique Palomba, María Litter, and Pedro Calderón. 1982. *Compendio de historia argentina (desde la colonia hasta 1943)*. Buenos Aires: Ediciones Directa.

Pattinson, James. 1996. *Lady from Argentina*. Leicester: Ulverscroft.

Perec, Georges. 1975. *W, ou les souvenirs d'enfance*. Paris: Denoël.

————. 1988. *W or The Memory of Childhood*. Trans. David Bellos. Boston: David R. Godine.

Peri Rossi, Cristina. 1988. "Lovelys." In *Cosmoagonía*, 125–37. Barcelona: Editorial Laia.

Piglia, Ricardo. 1992. *La ciudad ausente*. Buenos Aires: Sudamericana.

————. 2000. *The Absent City*. Trans. Sergio Waisman. Durham: Duke University Press.

Pike, F. B. 1971. *Hispanismo: 1898–1936*. Notre Dame: University of Notre Dame Press.

Pitt, Rosemary. 1978. "The Exploration of Self in *Heart of Darkness* and Woolf's *The Voyage Out*." *Conradiana* 1:141–54.

Pizarnik, Alejandra. 2001. *Poesía completa*. Barcelona: Lumen.

Plotkin, Mariano Ben. 2001. *Freud in the Pampas: The Emergence and Development of Psychoanalytic Culture in Argentina.* Stanford: Stanford University Press.

Pons, María Cristina, and Claudia Soria, eds. 2005. *Delirios de grandeza: Los mitos argentinos: memoria, identidad, cultura.* Buenos Aires: Beatriz Viterbo Editora.

Pratt, Mary Louise. 1992. *Imperial Eyes: Travel Writing and Transculturation.* London: Routledge.

Rabasa, José. 1993. *Inventing America: Spanish Historiography and the Formation of Eurocentrism.* Norman: University of Oklahoma Press.

Ramos Mejía, José María. 1974. *Las multitudes argentinas.* Buenos Aires: Editorial Biblioteca. (Originally published 1899.)

Reynaud, Ana. 2000. "Sandra Kogut's What Do You Think People Think Brazil Is? Rephrasing Identity." In *Cultural Encounters: Representing "Otherness,"* ed. Elizabeth Hallam and Brian V. Street, 72–88. London: Routledge.

Rich, Adrienne. 1993. "When We Dead Awaken: Writing as Re-Vision." Repr. in *Adrienne Rich's Poetry and Prose,* ed. Barbara Charlesworth Gelpi and Albert Gelpi, 166–77. New York: Norton. (Originally published 1978.)

Richards, Thomas. 1990. *The Commodity Culture of Victorian England.* Stanford: Stanford University Press.

Riera, Carme. 2005. *La mitad del alma.* Madrid: Alfaguara.

Rodó, José Enrique. 1922. *Ariel.* New York: Houghton Mifflin.

Rodríguez Monegal, Emir. 1979. no title. *Vuelta* 30 (May): 44–47.

Rosenbaum, Jonathan. 1997. "Cult Confusion," *Chicago Reader.* http://www.chireader .com/movies/archives/1998/0198/01238.html (accessed December 15, 2004).

Ross, Patricia. 2004. untitled review of Douglas Unger, *Voices from Silence. Library Journal,* cited at http://www.amazon.com/Voices-Silence-Douglas-Unger/dp/ 0312132042/ref=sr_1_5?ie=UTF8&s=books&qid=1196877709&sr=1-5. (accessed December 7, 2004).

Rothberg, Michael. 2004. "The Work of Testimony in the Age of Decolonization: Chronicle of a Summer, Cinema Verité, and the Emergence of the Holocaust Survivor." *PMLA* 119, no. 5 (October): 1231–46.

Rotker, Susana. 2002. *Captive Women: Oblivion and Memory in Argentina.* Trans. Jennifer French. Minneapolis: University of Minnesota Press.

Roussel, Raymond. 1999. *Impressions of Africa.* New York: Riverrun Press. (Originally published 1910.)

Rulfo, Juan. 1973. *Pedro Páramo.* Mexico City: Fondo de Cultura Economica. (Originally published 1955.)

Said, Edward W. 1978. *Orientalism.* New York: Pantheon.

———. 1993. *Culture and Imperialism.* New York: Knopf.

———. 1996. "The Novel as Beginning Intention: *Nostromo.*" In *New Casebooks: Joseph Conrad,* ed. Elaine Jordan, 103–15. New York: St. Martin's.

Saldaña-Portillo, María Josefina. 2003. *The Revolutionary Imagination in the Americas and the Age of Development.* Durham: Duke University Press.

Sarlo, Beatriz. 2001. *La máquina cultural: Maestras, traductores y vanguardistas.* Havana: Fondo Editorial Casa de las Américas.

Savigliano, Marta. 1995. *Tango and the Political Economy of Passion.* Boulder: Westview.

Scheines, Graciela. 1991. *Las metáforas del fracaso: desencuentros y utopías en la cultura argentina.* Havana: Casa de las Américas.

Schlesinger, Arthur M. 1943. "'What Then Is the American, This New Man?'" *American Historical Review* 48, no. 2 (January): 225–44.

Schultz de Mantovani, Fryda. 1960. *La mujer en la vida nacional.* Buenos Aires: Galatea-Nueva Visión.

Scott, Sir Walter. 1827. *The Life of Napoleon Bonaparte, Emperor of the French.* Vol 1. Edinburgh: Longman, Rees. (Repr., New York: Leavitt and Allen, 1857.)

Senkman, Leonardo. 1983. *La identidad judía en la literatura argentina.* Buenos Aires: Editorial Pardes.

Shain, Yossi. 1989. *The Frontier of Loyalty: Political Exiles in the Age of the Nation-State.* Middletown, Conn.: Wesleyan University Press.

Shelton, Anthony Alan. 2000. "Museum Ethnography: An Imperial Science." In *Cultural Encounters: Representing "Otherness,"* ed. Elizabeth Hallam and Brian V. Street, 155–93. London: Routledge.

Shohat, Ella, and Robert Stam. 1994. *Unthinking Eurocentrism: Multiculturalism and the Media.* London: Routledge.

Shumway, Nicolas. 1991. *The Invention of Argentina.* Berkeley and Los Angeles: University of California Press.

Singer, Isaac Bashevis. 1978. Nobel Lecture. http://nobelprize.org/nobel_prizes/literature/laureates/1978/singer-lecture.html.

———. 1991. *Scum.* Translated by Rosaline Dukalsky Schwartz. New York: Farrar Straus Giroux.

Slater, Candace. 2002. *Entangled Edens: Visions of the Amazon.* Berkeley and Los Angeles: University of California Press.

Solomianski, Alejandro. 2003. *Identidades secretas: la negritud argentina.* Rosario, Argentina: Beatriz Viterbo Editora.

Sowell, Thomas. 1996. *Migrations and Cultures: A World View.* New York: Basic Books.

Spanos, William V. 2000. *America's Shadow: An Anatomy of Empire.* Minneapolis: University of Minnesota Press.

Spekke, Vija. 1999. *Il Mondo di Borges.* Verona: Casa Editrice Damolgraf.

Spivak, Gayatri. 1988. "Can the Subaltern Speak?" In *Marxism and the Interpretation of Culture,* ed. Cary Nelson and Lawrence Grossberg, 271–313. Chicago: University of Illinois Press.

———. 1989. "The New Historicism: Political Commitment and the Postmodern Critic." In *The New Historicism,* ed. H. Aram Veeser, 277–92. New York: Routledge.

Stabb, Martin. 1967. *In Quest of Identity: Patterns in the Spanish American Essay of Ideas, 1890–1960.* Chapel Hill: University of North Carolina Press.

Steimberg, Alicia. 1971. *Músicos y relojeros.* Buenos Aires: Centro Editor de América Latina.

Steiner, Patricia Owen, ed. and trans. 1999. *Victoria Ocampo: Writer, Feminist, Woman of the World.* Albuquerque: University of New Mexico Press.

Stenberg, Per, and Adriana Muñoz, eds. 1999. *Masked Histories: A Re-examination of the Rodolfo Schreiter Collection from North-western Argentina.* Göteborg: Etnografiska Museet i Göteborg.

Strejilevich, Nora. 1997. *Una sola muerte numerosa.* Miami: North/South Center Press.

Tabanera García, Nuria. 1997. "El horizonte americano en el imaginario español, 1898–1930." *Estudios Interdisciplinarios de América Latina y el Caribe* 8, no. 2 (July–

December) "Nacionalismo en America Latina." http://www.tau.ac.il/eial/VIII_2/
garcia.htm (accessed February 5, 2005).

Taube, Evert. 1968. *Flyg till Pampas.* Stockholm: Bonniers.

Taylor, Charles. 2004. Untitled review of *Happy Together. Salon.com.* http://www
.salon.com/ent/movies/1997/10/31happy.html?CP=SAL&DN=110 (accessed December 15, 2004).

Taylor, Diana. 1997. *Disappearing Acts: Spectacles of Gender and Nationalism in
Argentina's "Dirty War."* Durham: Duke University Press.

Taylor, Julie. 1998. *Paper Tangos.* Durham: Duke University Press.

Teraoka, Arlene A. 1996. *East, West, and Others: The Third World in Postwar German
Literature.* Lincoln: University of Nebraska Press.

Theroux, Paul. 1980. *The Old Patagonian Express: By Train Through the Americas.*
New York: Pocket Books.

Thornton, Lawrence. 1987. *Imagining Argentina.* New York: Doubleday. (Repr., New
York: Bantam, 1988 and 1991.)

———. 1995. *Naming the Spirits.* New York: Doubleday.

———. 1997. *Tales from the Blue Archives.* New York: Doubleday.

Tierney-Tello, Mary Beth. 1996. *Allegories of Transgression and Transformation: Experi-
mental Fiction by Women Writing Under Dictatorship.* Albany: State University of
New York Press.

Timerman, Jacobo. 1981. *Prisoner without a Name, Cell without a Number.* Trans.
Toby Talbot. New York: Knopf.

Todorov, Tzvetan. 1987. *The Conquest of America: The Question of the Other.* New
York: Harper and Row.

Tóibín, Colm. 1997. *The Story of the Night.* New York: Holt.

Unger, Douglas. 1995. *Voices from Silence.* New York: St. Martin's.

Valenzuela, Luisa. 1975. *Aquí pasan cosas raras.* Buenos Aires: Ediciones de la Flor.

———. 1979. *Strange Things Happen Here.* Trans. Helen Lane. New York: Harcourt,
Brace, Jovanovich.

Vasconcelos, José. 1925. *La raza cósmica.* Barcelona: Agencia Mundial de Librería.

Vázquez Montalbán, Manuel. 1997. *Quinteto de Buenos Aires.* Barcelona: Planeta.

Verbitsky, Horacio. 1995. *El vuelo.* Buenos Aires: Planeta.

———. 2005. *The Flight: Confessions of an Argentine Dirty Warrior.* Trans. Esther
Allen. New York: New Press.

Villordo, Oscar Hermes. 1993. *El grupo sur: Una biografía colectiva.* Buenos Aires:
Planeta.

Viñas, David. 1982. *Indios, ejércitos y frontera.* Mexico City: Siglo XXI.

Warsh, Sylvia Maultash. 2001. *To Die in Spring.* Chestnut Ridge, N.Y.: Avocet
Press.

Watts, C. T., ed. 1969. *Joseph Conrad's Letters to R. B. Cunninghame Graham.* Cambridge: Cambridge University Press.

Weisbrot, Robert. 1979. *The Jews of Argentina: From Inquisition to Perón.* Philadel-
phia: Jewish Publication Society of America.

Wilde, Oscar. 1895. *An Ideal Husband.* New York: Modern Library.

Wilson, Rob. 2000. "Afterword." *Cultural Studies* 14, nos. 3/4 (July/October): 593–605.

Wollaeger, Mark A. 2001. "Woolf, Postcards, and the Elision of Race: Colonizing
Women in *The Voyage Out.*" *Modernism/modernity* 8, no. 1: 43–75.

———. 2003. "The Woolfs in the Jungle: Intertextuality, Sexuality, and the Emergence of Female Modernism in *The Voyage Out, The Village in the Jungle,* and *Heart of Darkness.*" *Modern Language Quarterly* 64, no. 1 (March): 33–69.

Wood, E. R. 1954. Introduction to *Fritz Hochwalder: The Strong Are Lonely.* London: Heinemann.

Woodhull, Winifred. 1993. *Transfigurations of the Maghreb: Feminism, Decolonization, and Literatures.* Minneapolis: University of Minnesota Press.

Woolf, Virginia. 1938. *Three Guineas.* London: Hogarth Press.

———. 1948. *The Voyage Out.* New York, Harcourt Brace & World. (Originally published 1915.)

———. 1957. *A Room of One's Own.* New York: Harcourt, Brace Jovanovich. (Originally published 1929.)

———. 1991. *Cartas a mujeres.* Selección y prólogo de Nora Catelli. Barcelona: Lumen.

Wynia, Gary. 1990. *The Politics of Latin American Development.* 3rd ed. Cambridge: Cambridge University Press.

Yue, Audrey. 2000. "What's So Queer About *Happy Together?* a.k.a. Queer (N)Asian: Interface, Community, Belonging." *Inter-Asia Cultural Studies* 1, no. 2: 251–64.

Zadow, Ingeborg von. 1998. "Interview with Jutta Brückner: Feminist Filmmaking in Germany Today." In *Triangulated Visions: Women in Recent German Cinema,* ed. Ingeborg Majer O'Sickey and Ingeborg von Zadow, 95–102. Albany: State University of New York Press.

Zamora, Lois Parkinson. 1997. *The Usable Past: The Imagination of History in Recent Fiction of the Americas.* Cambridge: Cambridge University Press.

Zantop, Susanne. 1997. *Colonial Fantasies: Conquest, Family, and Nation in Precolonial Germany, 1770–1870.* Durham: Duke University Press.

Zuleta, E. 1979. *La idea de América en el pensamiento español contemporáneo.* Mendoza: U.N.C.

Filmography

Allen, Woody. 1971. *Bananas.* Woody Allen, Louise Lasser. Rollins and Joffee Productions.

———. 1985. *The Purple Rose of Cairo.* Mia Farrow, Jeff Daniels, Danny Aiello. Orion Pictures.

Aristarain, Adolfo. 1982. *Últimos días de la victíma.* Federico Luppi, Soledad Silveyra. Aries Cinematográfica Argentina.

Bertolucci, Bernardo. 1973. *Last Tango in Paris.* Marlon Brando, Maria Schneider. PEA, Les Artistes Associés.

Brückner, Jutta. 1986. *Ein Blick und die Liebe Bricht Aus.* Elda Araoz, Rosario Blefari. Von Vietinghoff Film produktions.

Burman, Daniel. 2000. *Esperando al mesías* (Waiting for the Messiah). Daniel Hendler, Enrique Piñeyro. Astrolabio Producciones and BD Cine.

Cummings, Irving. 1940. *Down Argentine Way.* Don Ameche, Betty Grable, Carmen Miranda. Twentieth Century Fox.

Donovan, Martin. 1988. *Apartment Zero.* Hart Bochner, Colin Firth. Producers Representative Organization and Summit Company.

Duvall, Robert. 2002. *Assassination Tango.* Robert Duvall, Rubén Blades. American Zoetrope and Butcher's Run Films.

Ferguson, Norman, Wilfred Jackson, Jack Kinney, Hamilton Luske, and Bill Roberts. 1943. *Saludos Amigos.* Animated and live action feature. Walt Disney Pictures.

Fregonese, Hugo. 1966. *Savage Pampas.* Robert Taylor. Bronston International, D.A.S.A., and Producciones Jaime Prades.

Godard, Jean-Luc. 1960. *À bout de souffle* (Breathless). Jean-Paul Belmondo, Jean Seberg, Liliane David. Les Productions Georges de Beauregard and Société Nouvelle de Cinématographie. Videocassette distributed by Connoisseur Video Collection, 1989.

Goodwins, Leslie, and Jack Hively. 1941. *They Met in Argentina.* Maureen O'Hara, James Ellison, Buddy Ebsen. RKO Radio Pictures.

Hampton, Christopher. 2003. *Imagining Argentina.* Antonio Banderas, Emma Thompson. Myriad Pictures.

Ingram, Rex. 1921. *The Four Horsemen of the Apocalypse.* Rudolph Valentino. Metro Pictures.

Lang, Fritz. 1927. *Metropolis.* Alfred Abel, Gustav Fröhlich, Brigitte Helm. UFA. Reconstructed and adapted videocassette distributed by Vestron Video, 1985.

Mazursky, Paul. 1988. *Moon over Parador.* Richard Dreyfus, Raul Julia, Sonia Braga. Universal Pictures.

Mignogna, Eduardo. 1996. *Sol de otoño* (Autumn sun). Norma Aleandro, Federico Luppi. V.C.C.

Olivera, Héctor. 1989. *Two to Tango.* Don Stroud, Adrienne Sachs. Concorde/New Horizon.

Parker, Alan. 1996. *Evita.* Madonna, Antonio Banderas. Cinergi Pictures Entertainment, Dirty Hands Productions, Hollywood Pictures, Summit Entertainment.

Parker, Oliver. 1999. *An Ideal Husband.* Jeremy Northam, Cate Blanchett, Julianne Moore. Arts Council of England and Icon Entertainment International.

Potter, Sally. 1997. *The Tango Lesson.* Sally Potter, Pablo Verón. Adventure Films.

Schraeder, Leonard. 1991. *Naked Tango.* Vincent D'Onofrio, Mathilda May. Gotan, Grupo Baires, et al.

Seiter, William A. 1942. *You Were Never Lovelier.* Fred Astaire, Rita Hayworth. Columbia Pictures.

Suárez, Gonzalo. 1991. *El lado oscuro* (The dark side). Héctor Alterio, Hugo Gorban. Ditirambo Films for TVE (Spanish Television).

Tinling, James. 1935. *Under the Pampas Moon.* Warner Baxter, Ketti Gallian, Rita Hayworth (Margarita Cansino). Fox Film Corporation.

Vidor, Charles. 1946. *Gilda.* Rita Hayworth, Glenn Ford. Columbia Pictures.

Welles, Orson. 1941. *Citizen Kane.* Orson Welles, Joseph Cotton. Mercury Productions, RKO Radio Pictures.

Wong Kar Wai. 1997. *Chun gwong cha sit* (Happy together). Leslie Cheung, Tony Leung Chiu Wai. Block 2 Pictures.

Index

Achugar, Hugo, 24, 25, 49–50, 238
Africa, 35
Afro-Argentineans, 5, 106, 107, 110, 111, 112
Aizenburg, Edna, 157
Alberdi, Juan Bautista, 106
Aleichem, Sholem: *The Man from Buenos Aires,* 138
Allen, Woody, 158, 255
Aloff, Minday, 258
Ameche, Don, 205
Anderson, Barbara, 229
Anderson, Benedict, 6
Anderson, Joseph, 229
Anderson, Kirk, 158
Andrews, George Rei, 111
anti-Semitism, 21, 46, 105, 137, 169–70, 181, 206
Aponte-Ramos, Dolores, 113
Appaduri, Arjun, 237
Arambel-Güiñazú, María, Cristina, 32, 33, 122
Araucanians, 118, 119. *See also* Argentina; indigenous people
Argentina: advertising (in), 56; advertising of, 105, 155; censorship, 161; census reports, 111; class, 15, 212; corruption, 38–39, 41, 45, 49, 184–85, 195, 196; dictatorship, 27, 30, 158–82, 212 *(see also* Dirty War); economic

wealth of Argentineans (perceived), xii, xiv, 4, 5, 10, 16, 37, 41, 50, 100, 154, 210, 211, 213, 217, 219–20; elites, xi, 5, 6, 10, 30, 31, 32, 109, 125; epidemics, 111; escape to, 36; fashion (Argentineans in fashion), 210–13; Federalist, 12, 104, 107, 117, 238; feminist movement, 232; fiction (in), xv *(see also individual novels);* foreign journalists, 160; gender studies, 5, 20; generational differences, 15, 210; geography, xiii, xv, 35–37, 118, 122, 238, government, 104; history, 3; horse racing, 205, 206, 207, 208, 213; independence, 31, 104, 108, 111; intellectuals, 3, 6; kidnappings, 160, 200, 201–2, 214; Latin American view of, 16; migration (out of Argentina), 111; military, 39, 115; national discourse, 47; natural resources, 4, 37, 38, 39, 69; nightclubs, 208; novels (in), xiv, 13 *(see also names of authors);* Process of National Reorganization, 158, 160, 184–85; self-image, 2, 3, 13, 58; soldiers, 4, 111, 199; theater (depictions of), xiii; Unitarios, 11, 16, 104, 107; universities, 5
Argentine Commission on the Disappeared (Nunca Más), 167, 176
Argentine Literary Academy, 3, 5

Amy K. Kaminsky is professor of gender, women, and sexuality studies at the University of Minnesota, where she also holds appointments in the Institute for Global Studies, the graduate faculty in Spanish and Portuguese, and the Jewish Studies Program. She is the author of *After Exile: Writing the Latin American Diaspora* (Minnesota, 1999) and *Reading the Body Politic: Feminist Criticism and Latin American Women Writers* (Minnesota, 1992) and editor of *Water Lilies: An Anthology of Spanish Women Writers from the Fifteenth through the Nineteenth Century* (Minnesota, 1995).

Made in the USA
Middletown, DE
10 February 2018